Financial Concepts

nalysis

ent in the American States

ail Industry

865–1920

st Planning

KOREAN
ECONOMIC
DEVELOPMENT

Edited by
JENE K. KWON

Contributions in Economics and Economic History,
Number 108

GREENWOOD PRESS
New York • Westport, Connecticut • London

Library of Congress Cataloging-in-Publication Data

Korean economic development / edited by Jene K. Kwon.
   p. cm. — (Contributions in economics and economic history,
ISSN 0084-9235 ; no. 108)
  Includes bibliographical references.
  ISBN 0-313-26343-4 (lib. bdg. : alk. paper)
  1. Korea (South)—Economic conditions—1960– 2. Korea (South)—
Economic policy—1960– 3. Korea (South)—Commerce. I. Kwon, Jene
K. II. Series.
HC467.K619865 1990
338.95195′009′045—dc20   89–25888

British Library Cataloguing in Publication Data is available.

Library of Congress Catalog Card Number: 89–25888
ISBN: 0-313-26343-4
ISSN: 0084-9235

First published in 1990

Greenwood Press, Inc.
88 Post Road West, Westport, Connecticut 06881
An imprint of Greenwood Publishing Group, Inc.

Printed in the United States of America

The paper used in this book complies with the
Permanent Paper Standard issued by the National
Information Standards Organization (Z39.48-1984).

10 9 8 7 6 5 4 3 2 1

Copyright Acknowledgment

The editor and publisher gratefully acknowledge the following source for granting permission to use
copyrighted material:

P. J. Kim, *The Evolution of Financial Institutions in Korea*, East Asia Economic Policy Studies,
no. 5 (Honolulu: East-West Population Institute, East-West Center, 1988). Courtesy of the East-West
Center.

This book is dedicated
to
the vision and spirit of
that shining moment in Korean history

Contents

Illustrations

FIGURES

TABLES

Contributors

Alice H. Amsden, *New School for Social Research and MIT, U.S.A.*

Bela Balassa, *John Hopkins University and Institute for International Economics* (Visiting Fellow), U.S.A.

Sang-Chuel Choe, *Seoul National University, Korea*

Jeong Pyo Choi, *Kon-Kuk University, Korea*

Kwang Choi, *Hankuk University of Foreign Studies, Korea, and University of York (Visiting Fellow), U.K.*

Yoon Je Cho, *The World Bank, U.S.A.*

David Dollar, *University of California, Los Angeles, U.S.A.,and the World Bank, U.S.A.*

Paul Evans, *Ohio State University, U.S.A.*

Wontack Hong, *Seoul National University, Korea*

Choongsoo Kim, *Korea Development Institute, Korea*

E. Han Kim, *University of Michigan (Fred M. Taylor Professor of Business Administration), U.S.A.*

Kwang Suk Kim, *Kyung Hee University (Dean, Graduate School of Management), Korea*

Kyung-Hwan Kim, *Sogan University, Korea*

Pyung Joo Kim, *Sogan University, Korea*

Young Chin Kim, *Northern Illinois University, U.S.A.*

Bon Ho Koo, *Korea Development Institute (President), Korea*

Taewon Kwack, *Seoul City University, Korea*

Jene K. Kwon, *Northern Illinois University, U.S.A.*

Jisoon Lee, *Seoul National University, Korea, and University of Chicago (Visiting Professor), U.S.A.*

Kyu Sik Lee, *The World Bank, U.S.A.*

Tong Hun Lee, *University of Wisconsin, Milwaukee, U.S.A.*

Young Ki Lee, *Korea Development Institute, Korea*

Edwin S. Mills, *Northwestern University, U.S.A.*

Se-Il Park, *Seoul National University, Korea*

Won Am Park, *Korea Development Institute, Korea*

Peter A. Petri, *Brandeis University, U.S.A.*

Kenneth Sokoloff, *University of California, Los Angeles, U.S.A.*

Jong Goo Yoo, *Hanyang University, Korea*

Kyhyang Yuhn, *University of Minnesota, Morris, U.S.A.*

Preface and Acknowledgments

Over the past three decades, South Korea has compiled a record economic performance bordering on a "miracle." Few economies have achieved spectacular growth of this magnitude in such a short span of time. Korea's growth experiences provide a sharp contrast to the lackluster growth experienced by many other developing economies. Moreover, its development process represents several characteristics which are unique even in comparison with its close neighbors, Japan and Taiwan. At the same time, certain aspects of its development remain minor mysteries awaiting further examination and scrutiny. Given the complexity of the development process in general, the debates on the alternative causes of this success are likely to continue for years to come. In the least, the meteoric rise of a small economy and its people to an international prominence after centuries of obscurity, disenfranchisement, and privation deserves careful investigation and worldwide attention.

Since the late 1960s, there has been a steady flow of articles and books dealing with a wide range of issues related to South Korea's economic transformation. Concurrently, demand for literature of Korean economic development has been rising as more world interest is directed toward the Korean economy. Some of these studies have been written in Korean, others in English; some are outdated while others are already out of print. On the whole, very few that are written in English have bee comprehensive in the coverage of diverse topics.

For the past few years, I have felt that there is a definite need for a book which puts together an updated version of the original contributions into a conveniently available form for students, economists, and policy makers. It is hoped that this book will satisfy that need. The project is an outgrowth of my longstanding interest in the Korean economy. I am firmly convinced that the story of the Korean economic development process will serve as a valuable guide for students and researchers, as well as policy makers all over the world.

The topics included in the book are not exhaustive by any means, nor does it strive for a uniform interpretation of the causes and effects of the development process. In organizing the book, a particular effort was made to achieve some balance between the narrowly focused technical approach vis-à-vis a broad perspective approach.

My acknowledgments go first to all the contributors to this book who have entrusted me with their fine research products. Second, I wish to thank Yoon Jae Lee, Joong Goo Park, Hoon Paik, and Seung Rok Park who read and painstakingly scrutinized manuscripts for errors and omissions. To Betty Holderness who undertook the almost impossible task of typing the manuscripts inundated with tables and mathematical equations goes special thanks and utmost praise for her tenacious sense of responsibility, and to Bookmakers for their exceptional workmanship in finalizing the manuscript. Also, to Brent MacLeod who undertook the preliminary editing of the manuscripts goes my gratitude for his conscientious and thorough workmanship. The Word-Processing Office of Northern Illinois University was also helpful in the early stage of the project.

Finally I gratefully acknowledge the College of Liberal Arts and Sciences and the Graduate School of Northern Illinois University for generous financial support.

Introduction

In defining economic development a distinction is often made between *initiating development* and *sustaining development* over the longer period of time.[1] More than a quarter century after the initiation of its economic development, Korea may have yet to pass the more difficult test of sustaining the development over the long run. However, if Korea's development record lacks maturity (or durability), this is more than compensated for by the rigor and the intensity of its development, which is matched by only a few other economies.

The remarkable performance of Korea along with the other Asian newly industrializing countries (NICs) in terms of high gross national product (GNP) growth rate is viewed by many as one of more striking features of modern economic history; all previous experience including that of the Industrial Revolution in Western Europe pales in comparison.[2] As such, the Korean experience is of great interest to all those interested in economic development, and valuable lessons can be drawn from its experience.

In 1961, on the eve of Korea's journey into uncharted water in its search for economic development, everything looked bleak and not much was certain. One thing that seemed certain was that the new political regime that came into power was desperately in need of a new cause to stake out its political fortune and a magical success that could bring a measure of legitimacy to itself. Having witnessed a series of economic stagnations and political failures throughout the post-Liberation period (1945–61), the new regime was determined to take a more active role in the management of the national economy. Suddenly economic policy was thrust to the forefront of national policy, and the policy emphasis shifted from that of dependency on U.S. aid to that of a more self-reliant economy, and from inward looking and import substituting to outward looking and export promoting.

New economic policies were put into effect through a series of five-year economic plans. The key elements in the five-year plans were (a) industrialization, (b) export promotion, and (c) investment in the social overhead capital.

Fortunately for the new regime and for Korea, after a period of shaky starts, several unexpected good results from the First Five-Year Plan began to bear fruit, thereby putting new life into the stagnant economy. Emboldened by this fortuitous success, the policy initiatives were followed up through a series of five-year plans.

Within less than three decades, the Korean economy transformed from a largely agricultural subsistence economy into a newly industrialized economy. From 1962, when the First Five-Year Plan was implemented, to 1986, the Korean gross domestic product (GDP) grew at an average annual rate of 8.6 percent. Thanks to the export promotion policy that has since become a central piece of Korea's development strategy, exports grew at a breakneck rate of 35 percent. The structure of the economy also went through a rapid transformation; mining and manufacturing, which accounted for 16.4 percent of the GNP in 1962, rose to 32.4 percent of the GNP in 1986. The structure of exports also changed. The share of machinery and equipment in total exports, which is often used as an indicator of industrialization, increased from 2.6 percent in 1962 to 33.5 percent.

One of the striking features of Korea's economic development is the dominant role played by the government in initiating this development. Another is the over-dominance of large business(*jaebuls*) in the economic sphere. The relationship between the government and business was akin to that of principal and agent. The government formulated economic plans and business was induced through a carrot-and-stick approach to carry out the plans and to meet the quantitative targets set by the government. During much of the rapid-growth period, commercial banks were nationalized and played a passive role of channeling the government-directed policy loans to the big businesses designated by the government. Real interest rates were held artificially low (often, negative) in order to contain the cost of capital and to stimulate private investment.

In this environment of massive government subsidies and frequent negative real interest rates on business loans, the wage rental ratio increased quite rapidly, and with the elasticity of substitution between labor and capital being equal to or larger than one, the capital-labor ratio also went up considerably, creating distortion in factor proportion and economic inefficiency arising from the misallocation of resources. However, on the positive side, the availability of capital-intensive technology made possible by cheap capital enabled the producers to take advantage of the economies of scale by building larger plants. For a small country like Korea whose domestic market was limited in size, it was the rapid increase in exports that made it possible for the producers to take advantage of scale economies and to absorb labor that might otherwise have been displaced by the introduction of capital-intensive technology.

Korean economy entered a new phase in the 1980s by taking a major stride toward market economy. Several internal and external factors forced the government to reorient its policies toward new goals: price stability, market liberalization, and balanced growth between the big businesses and small-medium businesses. Through an effective stabilization policy, inflation was successfully contained.

Government switched from the direct intervention in the market to market liberalization, for example, liberalization of the financial system as well as the import system among others. Also to nurture a more competitive atmosphere, preferential treatment of big businesses was deemphasized by making more credit available to small-medium industries.

At this very moment (1990) the Korean economy is faced with several rather serious difficulties, such as exchange rate appreciation, rising wages, rampant land speculation, and widespread and often violent labor unrest. Due largely to work stoppages and rising labor cost and exchange rate, the trade surplus that Korea enjoyed over the previous few years may decline drastically. Suddenly, income (wealth) distribution has emerged as the single most acute national issue while the "grow first and distribute later" policy of yesteryear is called into question. The nation is reassessing its past policies in order to plan for its future.

There are several similarities and dissimilarities in the economic development among Korea, Japan, and Taiwan. The most striking and familiar similarity is the export-led growth. Another important similarity includes the quality of human capital—"the great reverence and importance attached to learning in [these] countries and the high educational and skill levels of their populations,"[3] may have served as a precondition essential for economic growth.

As for the dissimilarities, first, in Korea the role of government was much more direct and intrusive than in Taiwan and Japan. In Japan and Taiwan, as in Korea, the government was responsible for planning various economic development programs, but in Taiwan and Japan the economic controls of the government tended to be moderate and generally made use of the market in a selective way, for example, by providing economic incentives and realistic exchange rates and interest rates. Conversely, in Korea the government more often than not directly intervened in the market by setting prices, including interest rates, and often making managerial decisions especially during the early days of economic development (1960s and 1970s). Korea's low interest rate policy juxtaposed with the high rate of time preference led to a low average saving ratio of 9 percent between 1953 and 1981, as compared with the 30 percent and 20 percent for Japan and Taiwan, respectively, during the same period. In order to satisfy the excess demand for investment funds in the face of meager domestic savings, government resorted to foreign borrowing until the early 1980s. Throughout this period, the proportion of foreign capital in the total capital formation hovered around 30 percent. Although Korea's *jaebuls* are modeled after the Japanese *zaibatsu*, the degree of market concentration is significantly higher than it is in Japan. In contrast to Korea and Japan, Taiwan's businesses are the least concentrated; Taiwan's economy is more of a grass-roots economy, which benefits the masses. Whereas in Korea large business groups constitute the backbone of Korean industry, in Taiwan a similar role is played by the small-medium enterprises. Furthermore, Korean industries are more capital intensive than the industries in the countries whose per capita GNP is considerably higher. These differences, at least in part, explain the high degree of inequality in income distribution in Korea relative to Taiwan; current labor unrest in Korea also seems to reflect the underlying problem of income (wealth) inequality in Korea. Due largely to the government's leniency toward big business in Korea, large business groups tend to be highly leveraged. Very often, government-designated banks have bailed out ailing big businesses in fear of the economic and political repercussions of the bankruptcy of a big business.

This book focuses on the evolution of economic policies and the rapid transformation of Korean economy. In seeking to trace relationships among various economic factors and to provide some insight into the process of economic development, this volume has marshaled a considerable array of statistics and institutional description as background for analysis.

The present volume consists of 24 articles of original contribution to the Korean economic development. Some of the salient features of the Korean economy that are dealt with in the volume are (1) an overview of Korea's development strategies and assessment of Korea's success and its development characteristics; (2) Korea's export policies, exchange rate policies, import liberalization, factor price distortions, and changing comparative advantage; (3) production technology in Korean manufacturing and total factor productivity; (4) macroeconomic perspectives—financial system, fiscal policies, and labor market; (5) conglomeration and business concentration and a profile of Korea's management practices; (6) income distribution and labor issues; and finally (7) urban and regional policies.

Although these topics by no means cover all elements needed to be taken into account to explain what has happened in Korea, I hope that they provide some of the major building blocks from which an overall assessment of the modernization can be constructed.

NOTES

1. Meier (1976, p. 7) suggests that an underlying upward trend over decades—at least two or three decades—is a strong indication of development.
2. See Findlay (1981, p. 30).
3. See Scitovsky (1986, p. 140).

REFERENCES

Findlay, Ronald, "Export-Led Industrial Growth Reconsidered," A Comment, in Wontack Hong and L. B. Krause, eds., *Trade and Growth of the Advanced Developing Countries in the Pacific Basin*, Seoul: Korea Development Institute, 1981.

Meier, Gerald M., *Leading Issues in Economic Development*, New York: Oxford University Press, 1976.

Scitovsky, Tibor, "Economic Development in Taiwan and South Korea, 1965–1981," in Lawrence J. Lau, ed., *Models of Development*, San Francisco: ICS Press, 1986.

Korean
Economic
Development

Part One

ASSESSMENT OF DEVELOPMENT POLICIES AND DEVELOPMENT RECORD

In the opening article of this section, Bela Balassa presents a rather comprehensive overview of Korea's economic development, which, by itself, serves as the more appropriate introduction for this book, thus requiring no further introduction.

Every nation strives for development; some make it while others do not. For the past three decades much has been theorized about the ways to accelerate the growth rate of national income, yet the truth remains that we still know very little about the forces that cause a traditional society to transform itself into a modern society or a developed economy. Our lack of knowledge, in part, reflects the enormous complexity of the process of economic change. Keeping this complexity in mind, chapters by Y. C. Kim and J. K. Kwon, though contrasting in views, represent modest attempts to provide some insight into the process of economic development and also to put the question of economic development into a proper perspective based on their own observations of the development experiences of Korea and other countries.

By examining the historical records of Korea's (and Taiwan's) economic growth in light of the Japanese (and world) standard of performance, Kim argues that Korea's economic success began much earlier (circa 1910) than is generally assumed. He further contends that, except for war-related random-shock disturbances, South Korea, Taiwan, and Japan are hardly distinguishable from one another in terms of growth rates in the respective country's modern periods. Based on his view of the historical experiences of the East Asian economies, Kim allays the widespread, well-meaning pessimism that modern economic growth may not be transmittable to societies of non-European origin.

In presenting a view somewhat different from Kim's, Kwon points out that, in what is known as the "government-led" economic development of Korea, many elements of the government policies were counter to the free market principle. With massive export subsidies, market distortions and import restrictions, a number of key elements of the outward-looking trade policies were contrary to the free trade principle, placing Korea at the opposite end of the spectrum vis-à-vis Hong Kong. During the 1960s and 1970s, the real interest rates on policy-directed bank loans were often kept negative or nearly 20 percent below the real (curb) market interest rates. Commercial banks were nationalized and were relegated to the role of channeling low-interest loans to government-designated businesses. In order to satisfy the excess demand for investment caused by the low interest rate that had discouraged domestic saving, the government resorted to massive foreign borrowing. Furthermore, the trade reflected a strategic change in comparative advantage also contrary to the classical theory. The tight nexus of government and big business gave rise to conglomeration and business concentration in Korea, to an extent unmatched in other countries. In this economic milieu of highly interventionist government policy, Korea's economy has displayed a most spectacular growth, which is truly historic by any standard.

Based on this unique Korean experience, Kwon argues that with the proper set of policies and priorities, government can play a meaningful role in economic development, and that even an outward-looking policy needs an appropriate economic environment (including select preconditions and the right set of governmental policies).

Korea's Development Strategy

Bela Balassa

INTRODUCTION

In an area of 96,000 square kilometers, Korea (the Republic of Korea or South Korea) has a population of 42.1 million. It has few mineral resources and its mountainous terrain does not favor agriculture, which nevertheless was the main-stay of its economy until independence.

After having been part of the Japanese empire between 1910 and 1945, Korea was divided into two parts after World War II. The North came under Soviet influence while the South was governed by the American military until 1948, when an independent Korean government was established on its territory.

The Korean War began in June 1950 when the North invaded the South, extending its occupation to its entire area except for the Pusan perimeter. Subse-quently, the fighting stabilized around the present dividing line between the North and the South. But much of the South's territory was devastated at the time the war ended in July 1953, with physical losses reportedly equaling Korea's annual gross domestic product (GDP).

Economic growth was slow in the 1953–60 period. Apart from reconstruction, the policies applied were oriented toward import substitution behind high pro-tection while exports were discouraged by overvalued exchange rates. At the same time, balance-of-payments deficits were financed by large inflows of U.S. military and economic aid.

In 1960, income levels in North Korea, which retained much of Korea's industrial establishment after partition, were one-half times greater than in the South. In the 1970s, however, the South surpassed the North in terms of per capita incomes, and it may now have double the incomes in the North. The transformation of the Korean economy can be indicated by a few figures.

In 1960, the export of goods and services did not exceed 3 percent of GDP. Imports were 13 percent of the GDP, so that capital inflow (mostly U.S. aid) equaled 10 percent of GDP. Notwithstanding the large inflow of foreign capital, the share of investment in Korea's GDP was 11 percent, because domestic savings were negligible.

In 1986, exports of goods and services amounted to 41 percent of GDP while imports were 35 percent of GDP, resulting in a net inflow of capital of 6 percent. In the same year, 29 percent of GDP was invested.

These changes resulted from rapid economic growth engendered by export expansion under an outward-oriented development strategy. This strategy was established in the mid 1960s following abortive attempts at exchange rate unification and liberalization in the early 1960s.

GOVERNMENT POLICIES

After the end of the Korean War, the government resumed the policy of import substitution behind high protection that was begun once World War II had ended. At the same time, exports were discouraged by the overvaluation of the exchange rate as rapid domestic inflation was not fully offset by the depreciation of the won. As a result, the real exchange rate, calculated by adjusting the official exchange rate for changes in wholesale prices at home and abroad, fell to one half of its 1948-50 value by January 1960.

Devaluations undertaken over the following year led to a depreciation of the official excahnge rate from 50 won to the dollar in January 1960 to 130 won to the dollar in February 1961. At the same time, exchange rates were unified, import controls were liberalized, and subsidies were provided to exports.

The measures reflected the liberalization philosophy of the civilian government established in April 1960. However, under the military government installed in May 1961, the real exchange rate appreciated again as rapid inflation was not compensated by further devaluations. The resulting deterioration of the balance of payments, in turn, led to the adoption of increased import restrictions and to the re-establishment of the multiple exchange rate system.

Far-reaching reforms were undertaken after the election in August 1964 of the government of Park Chung Hee, who retained power until his assassination 15 years later. The reforms involved the devaluation of the official exchange rate from 130 to 247 won to the U.S. dollar, the unification of exchange rates, import liberalization, and increased incentives to exports, representing the adoption of an outward-oriented development strategy.

In 1967 the "positive" list of admissible imports was replaced by a "negative" list of products whose importation required government authorization. This meant in practice further reduction of the scope of import restrictions.

Exporters were given the right to import their inputs duty free and without restrictions; they were also provided generous wastage allowances for the importation of raw materials. In 1965, these incentives were extended to indirect exports (the production of domestic inputs for exports) and increased credit preferences were also provided to exporters. In the following year, tariff exemptions were granted to the importers of machinery and equipment used to produce direct and indirect exports and accelerated depreciation allowances were introduced. Furthermore, inputs used in export production were free of indirect taxes and exporters received a 50 percent reduction in their income tax.

The export regime established after 1964 provided a free trade status to exporters, with some additional incentives. As a result of these changes, on the average, exports received incentives similar to import substitution, thereby eliminating the anti-export bias of the system of incentives, characteristic of countries following inward-oriented policies. Exporters also benefited from the stability of the incentive system.

Apart from price incentives, the government-sponsored Korea Trade Promotion Association (KOTRA) was founded in 1964 to promote Korean exports and to carry out market research abroad. The government further sent special trade missions to foreign countries and authorized the Korean Traders' Association (KTA) to collect 1 percent of the value of imports for use as an export promotion fund.

The government also established export targets for individual firms. The importance of these targets should not be overstated, however. The duty-free entry of imported inputs and the provision of export incentives did not depend on the fulfillment of export targets, although successful Korean exporters reportedly received advantageous treatment in pending tax cases. Thus, export targets had largely a psychological value as did the honors bestowed on large exporters.

The adoption of an outward-oriented development strategy was accompanied by the reform of the financial system. While real interest rates had been negative, with the rate of inflation exceeding nominal interest rates by a substantial margin, they turned strongly positive as deposit as well as loan rates were substantially raised. This led to considerable increases in financial savings and, while not all of this represented new savings as some of it came from the curb market, total savings also increased.

As we will discuss subsequently, the measures applied led to rapid increases of exports and GDP. The world economic environment deteriorated, however, in 1973–74, with the quadrupling of oil prices and the world recession. The initial reactions to these changes were to modify Korea's outward-oriented development strategy.

The Discussion Paper on the Developmental Strategy for the Fourth Five-Year Plan, 1977–81, argued that "it is only judicious to reduce Korea's vulnerability to the trade effects of foreign countercyclical policies and to the growing imperfections of a world market for basic commodities" (p. 24). In accordance with the proposed change in strategy, *The Guidelines for the Fourth Five-Year Economic Development Plan, 1977–81* envisaged "the increase of import substitution and conservation of resources in order to reduce the growth rate of imports to the level of the GNP growth rate" (p. 15).

In an advisory report prepared for the government of Korea, one of the authors suggested however that it would be inappropriate to change a long-term developmental strategy on the basis of essentially short-term considerations. In the end, the proponents of outward orientation won out and the continuation of this policy was decided upon in the course of preparation of the final version of the Fourth Five-Year Plan.

The measures taken involved liberalizing import restrictions and lowering tariffs. And while wastage allowances to exporters were reduced and the income tax benefits of exporters were eliminated, the subsidy equivalent of preferential export credits was increased and new medium-term and long-term export credit facilities were established. Correspondingly, on the average, exports and import substitution continued to receive similar incentives.

Policy changes occurred, however, in subsequent years. These changes favored capital-intensive industries producing intermediate goods and heavy machinery over traditional export industries.

Capital-intensive industries producing intermediate products, such as ferrous and nonferrous metals, petrochemicals and chemicals, and heavy machinery, such as electrical power generation and heavy construction and engineering equipment, were given priority in the allocation of domestic credit and in access to foreign credit. Also, the cost of credit to these industries was reduced through preferential interest rates. Fiscal incentives in the form of exemption from corporate income taxes and accelerated depreciation provisions further lowered the cost of capital to the industries in question.

The application of these measures affected the pattern of investment. In the first three years of the Fourth Five-Year Plan (1977–81), the amount of investment in basic metals was 130 percent and that in chemicals and other intermediate products 121 percent of the investment planned for the entire period, compared with an overall average of 80 percent. By contrast, only 50 percent of planned investment was undertaken in the textile industry and 42 percent in other light industries. Machinery, electronics, and shipbuilding occupied a middle position, the corresponding figures being 101 percent, with larger than planned increases in heavy machinery.

The reduced availability of funds for traditional export industries was aggravated by the increasing overvaluation of the exchange rate. Despite domestic inflation rates in excess of world market rates, the exchange rate was maintained constant at 484 won to the dollar from 1975 onward. As a result, between 1975 and 1979 the real exchange rate appreciated by 12 percent.

These policy changes could not fail to have adverse effects on exports. Export growth rates declined after 1976 and the volume of exports fell in real terms in 1979. This contrasts with the experience of Korea's major competitors as export growth rates increased in 1979 in Hong Kong and Singapore and export volume rose by 7 percent in Taiwan.

At the same time, the growth of fixed investment accelerated in Korea, financed in large part from foreign borrowing that added to Korea's external debt. The feverish construction activity, in turn, created pressures for wage increases, contributing to the acceleration of inflation.

The high import intensity of fixed investment and of industries producing intermediate goods and heavy machinery, together with the deterioration of the competitiveness of Korean industry, contributed to rapid increases in imports, with average annual increases of 21 percent in volume between 1977 and 1979, compared with 14 percent in the 1970–77 period. The acceleration of import growth was even greater excluding the import content of exports, from 11 percent in 1970–77 to 25 percent in 1977–79.

Policy changes were instituted following the assassination of President Park. The won was devalued by 20 percent in January 1980 and, following smaller adjustments in the rest of the year, the exchange rate reached 656 won to the dollar by the end of 1980. The depreciation of the exchange rate contributed to increases in exports but Korea again fell behind the other three East Asian newly industrializing countries. And GDP declined by 5 percent, although the 22 percent fall in agricultural production contributed importantly to this result.

The adverse effects of the policies applied led to a reconsideration of the policy framework. *The Preliminary Outline of the Fifth Five-Year Economic and Social Development Plan of the Republic of Korea, 1982–86*, called for a return to a full-fledged outward-oriented development strategy. It stated that "the basic strategy Korea will follow . . . will be to promote competition at home and liberalize its external economic policies" (p. 10). The document added that "there is no escape from the conclusion that during the Fifth Five-Year Plan period export expansion should continue to be the major engine of growth for Korea" (p. 13). The preliminary plan further indicates the general orientation of policies to serve these objectives:

> In order to sustain long-term growth of exports and the economy as a whole, import liberalization is essential. There is a limit to which a country can improve its industrial structure without import liberalization. Furthermore, a country cannot possibly hope to improve its price competitiveness while its cost of living rises due to import restriction. . . (P. 17)
>
> The single most important change in government industrial policy during the Fifth Five-Year Plan period will be the reduction of the government's role in promoting so-called strategic industries. Investment choices will be left to the initiative of the private sector and the government will provide only the

general framework in which such choices will be made by private entrepreneurs in cooperation with their bankers and financiers. (Pp. 22–23)

In addition, special efforts will be made to maintain the real interest rate on bank loans and deposits at a positive level and gradually reduce the scope of policy preference loans. (P. 31)

Making a greater use of the market mechanism also implies equalizing in terms of competition and policy incentives for all industries. . . . During the Fifth Five-Year Plan period the government plans to gradually phase out specific incentives and provide instead generalized uniform incentives for investment in all industries. (P. 31)

The preliminary outline for the Fifth Five-Year Plan indicates the determination of the government to reverse tendencies toward greater inward orientation and government intervention. This is based on the perception that outward orientation is not only the best guarantee for long-term economic growth, but also helps overcome the effects of external shocks.

In accordance with the plan objectives, the increases in protection undertaken in conjunction with promotion of capital-intensive industries in the second half of the 1970s were reversed during the early 1980s. According to figures published by the Ministry of Commerce and Industry, the share of liberalized import items rose from 68.6 percent in 1980 to 74.7 percent in 1982, increasing further to 87.7 percent in 1985. And while the degree of import liberalization is somewhat less in terms of import value, the same tendency is observed in this respect, too.

The Sixth Five-Year Plan (1987–91) continued the process of import liberalization. Since 91.5 percent of items were scheduled to be liberalized by 1986, and the plan called for the liberalization of 93.5 percent of the items by 1987, and 95.4 percent by 1988. However, special laws such as the Science and Technology Development Law give ministries the authority to establish and enforce local control requirements and to deny import licenses. Examples are computers, sophisticated medical equipment, and machine tools.

In turn, tariff rates were reduced in the early 1980s and, again, in the framework of the Tariff Reform Act of 1984. As a result, the simple average of tariff rates declined from 31.7 percent in 1982 to 23.7 percent in 1983 and 21.8 percent in 1984; it was set to reach 18.1 percent by 1988.

Within the overall average, the tendency has been to reduce tariffs on all major categories. Compared with average tariffs of 20 percent in raw materials, 25 percent on intermediate and capital goods, and 30 percent on final goods, the reform called for reaching tariffs of 5–10 percent, 20 percent, and 20–30–percent by 1988. At the same time, within each category, greater uniformity was targeted.

An exception to this general tendency toward liberalization is provided by agriculture. While in the 1960s industry and agriculture received similar incentives, subsequently agriculture came to be favored. Agriculture increasingly received higher than world market prices while it was sheltered from foreign competition.

Reversing earlier moves toward financial liberalization, the financial sector was strictly regulated in the second half of the 1970s. Real interest rates became negative; directed credit and extensive preferences were introduced in favor of capital-intensive industries; and the government exercised tight control over the operation of the banks.

A number of financial liberalization measures were taken during the 1980s. The monetary authorities eased restrictions on the establishment of nonbanking financial institutions, released control over the asset management of these institutions, and deregulated their interest rates. As a result, nonbank financial institutions assumed increasing importance in Korea and the ratio of the broadly defined money supply to GDP rose to a considerable extent.

Interest rate ceilings continue to operate in commercial banks. However, interest rates have been adjusted to ensure positive real interest rates for loans as well as for time deposits. Thus, real interest rates on loans reached 7–10 percent and on time deposits of over one year 4–5 percent.

The government denationalized commercial banks and reduced its control of their operations. Two new commercial banks were established, in joint ventures with foreign interests, and the local branches of foreign banks were given greater freedom in their operations. Credit ceilings for individual banks were abolished and an indirect credit control system through reserve changes was introduced while reserve requirements were simultaneously reduced. Commercial banks were permitted to enter into new areas, including the issuance of negotiable certificates of deposit, sales of public bonds with repurchase agreements and of discounted commercial bills, and trust banking. At the same time, outside the banking sector, markets for corporate bonds and commercial paper assumed importance.

Also, the scope of directed credit was reduced, credit preferences to capital-intensive industries eliminated, and the share of large conglomerates in bank credit frozen. At the same time, the government imposed an obligation on the commercial banks to provide at least 35 percent of their loans to small- and medium-size firms.

The government aimed to increase competition in the nonfinancial sector as well. In 1981 it established the Office of Fair Trade to guard against restrictive trade practices. But the unused capacity resulting from excessive investments in capital-intensive industries induced the government to undertake restructuring operations. It merged major heavy equipment producers, initiated a rationalization plan in the shipbuilding industry, and organized mergers while reducing capacity in the fertilizer industry.

At the same time, the promotional laws established during the 1970s in favor of capital-intensive industries were abolished and the industry-specific approach was replaced by a functional approach. It is of particular importance that the new industrial policy apparatus lacks a mechanism for "picking winners," who often turn out to be losers.

Among functional areas, the promotion of technology has been given pride of place. Several institutions have been established to train scientists and engineers and to conduct research. They include the Korea Advanced Institute of Science and Technology, the Korea Institute of Electronics Technology, and the Korea Electrotechnology and Telecommunications Research Institute.

Under the Fifth Five-Year Plan, spending on research and development (R&D) increased from 0.9 percent of GDP in 1980 to 2.0 percent in 1986; the Sixth Plan set out to raise this ratio to 2.5 percent by 1990. At the same time, the share of the private sector in R&D spending increased to a considerable extent. While the public sector was dominant in R&D in earlier years, by 1985 three quarters of spending was undertaken by the private sector. This reflects the effect of the tax incentives for R&D provided under the Technology Development Promotion Act of 1973 that was strengthened in 1981 as well as the establishment of the National Project for Research and Development in 1982 that funds private-public joint R&D projects in the fields of engineering and electronics.

It may be concluded that after increasing intervention in the second half of the 1970s, Korea has liberalized its economy in the 1980s. Although Korea is far from having a laissez-faire economy, it pursues an outward-oriented development strategy that provided similar incentives, on the average, to exports and to import substitution. This strategy has been supported by the government taking a favorable attitude toward exports while in inward-oriented economies exports often suffer from restrictive regulations and red tape.

An important factor contributing to Korea's ability to exploit the advantages of an outward-oriented development strategy has been education. While the 1944 census showed that 90 percent of the population had no formal education, and only 300 Korean students were enrolled at the single university at that time, rapid progress occurred after World War II. Following the introduction of compulsory public education immediately after the war, there was considerable expansion in secondary and higher education.

As shown in *World Development Report* (1987), by 1965 34 percent of children of the relevant age group were enrolled in secondary schools and this ratio reached 51 percent by 1984. The corresponding ratio was 6 percent in 1965 and 26 percent in 1984 for higher education. These ratios are considerably higher than in countries at similar levels of development, and the secondary school ratio, although not the higher education ratio, is on the same level as in industrial economies.

As noted above, Korea has also made considerable strides in R&D. In this connection, it may be added that the 1990 target for spending on R&D as a proportion of GDP is about the same as the Organization for Economic Cooperation and Development (OECD) average.

Another distinguishing characteristic of Korean industry has been the importance of conglomerates, the *jaebul*. The 55 largest firms account for more than one third of industrial output, a ratio that is considerably higher than either in Japan or in other East Asian NICs. Also, 11 out of 28 developing country firms in the *Fortune* 500 category of foreign firms are Korean.

Industrial concentration was helpful to Korea in providing economies of scale in production and in foreign sales as well as name recognition abroad. But the fewness of the large conglomerates make it easier for the government to impose its will on firms in the second half of the 1970s. Also, some of the conglomerates may be overly large and suffer losses in efficiency and in flexibility. Also, conglomerates are highly leveraged, which creates considerable risks.

The large conglomerates are domestic firms. Apart from the entrepreneurial spirit of the Koreans, this reflects the earlier policy of strictly limiting foreign direct investment, following the Japanese example. This policy has changed as high technology industries need foreign knowledge. In fact, from its inception, the electronics industry has had an important share of foreign capital, including wholly foreign-owned firms, although these have to export at least 50 percent of their output.

Furthermore, the December 1983 revision of the Foreign Capital Inducement Law greatly eased the conditions of establishment by foreign firms. The most important changes were the shift from a positive to a negative list and the introduction of an automatic approval system.

Whereas previously foreign direct investment was allowed only in specifically listed areas, it is now allowed in all areas unless specifically restricted by law. Also, as long as the foreign equity share is less than 50 percent, the investment is automatically approved while investments with a foreign share of 50 percent or higher are subject to review. The revised foreign investment law further removed restrictions on the regulation of capital and earnings.

ECONOMIC GROWTH

The policies applied led to rapid economic growth in Korea. Per capita incomes more than quadrupled between 1963 and 1986, reaching $2360 in the latter year. As a result, Korea now ranks among the higher-middle income developing countries according to the terminology used by the World Bank.

Korea's GDP increased at average annual rates of 9.3 percent in 1963–73, 8.2 percent in 1973–81, and 8.4 percent in 1981–86 (Table 1.1). This means that the problems associated with capital-intensive industries did not have a lasting effect on economic expansion in Korea.

Economic growth was concentrated in the manufacturing sector that saw its share in the gross domestic product rising from 14.7 percent in 1963 to 25.1 percent in 1973 and, again, to 29.2 percent in 1981 and to 30.0 percent in 1986. And while

Table 1.1
Economic Performance Indicators

Growth Rates	1963-73	1973-81	1981-86	1963-86
Gross Domestic Product	9.3	8.2	8.4	8.7
Population	2.3	1.6	1.4	1.8
GDP per capita	6.8	6.5	6.9	6.7
Investment	18.5	12.4	10.4	13.3
Manufacturing Production	20.3	13.9	10.4	15.8
Agricultural Production	3.3	1.0	3.7	3.0
Exports	32.9	15.6	11.1	21.5
Imports	22.8	13.8	7.4	15.5

Source: Bank of Korea, *Economic Statistics Yearbook*, various years.

manufacturing growth rates declined from 20.3 percent in 1963–73 to 13.9 percent in 1973–81 and 10.4 percent in 1981–86, the torrid pace of earlier years could not be maintained.

Agricultural growth averaged 3.0 percent over the entire 1963–86 period, with a slower increase shown for 1973–81 that includes the disastrous harvest year of 1980. As a result, agriculture's share in GDP declined from 43.4 percent in 1963 to 12.3 percent in 1986.

In turn, the share of the service sector in GDP increased from 40.2 percent in 1963 to 56.4 percent in 1986. Gas, electricity, and water; construction; transportation; banking; and public administration all experienced increases in their GDP shares, with declines occurring in wholesale and retail trade and the other services category (Table 1.2).

Economic growth was promoted by the rapid expansion of exports. Whereas the exports of goods and services amounted to only 4.8 percent of GDP in 1963, this share reached 29.7 percent in 1973, 36.6 percent in 1981, and 40.9 percent in 1986. The share of the imports of goods and services also increased but at a lower rate, from 15.9 percent in 1963 to 35.1 percent in 1986. Correspondingly, the large import surplus of 1963 gave place to an export surplus in 1986, when the outflow of savings equalled 5.8 percent of GDP (Table 1.3).

The outflow of savings was not at the expense of domestic investment. In fact, the share of investment in GDP was maintained at 29–30 percent in recent years, exceeding the ratios of 25–27 percent in the mid-1970s (except for 31.6% in 1974). Increasing investment shares and the shift from positive to negative foreign savings meant a considerable increase in domestic savings. Thus, while the share of domestic savings in GDP reached 24.1 percent only in 1976, it was above 30 percent in 1984 and 1985 and it attained 35 percent in 1986.

The shift from positive to negative foreign savings is reflected in the turnaround

Table 1.2
Industrial Composition and Trade (percent of GDP)

	1963	1973	1981	1986
Industrial Composition				
Agriculture	43.4	24.5	15.8	12.3
Mining & Quarrying	1.7	1.1	1.6	1.3
Manufacturing	14.7	25.1	29.2	30.0
Gas, Electricity & Water	1.0	1.4	2.1	3.2
Construction	2.9	4.4	7.3	7.8
Transportation	4.0	6.8	8.3	8.1
Wholesale & Retail Trade	14.3	17.8	13.1	13.1
Banking, etc.	6.1	7.2	9.5	10.6
Ownership of Dwellings	--	--	--	--
Public Administration	5.5	6.3	7.5	7.2
Other Services	6.4	4.9	5.0	5.8
Trade				
Exports of Goods & Non-Factor Services	4.8	29.7	36.6	40.9
Imports of Goods & Non-Factor Services	15.9	32.6	41.9	35.1

Source: Bank of Korea, *Economic Statistics Yearbook*, various years.

of Korea's current account balance. This turnabout was associated with the shift from a negative to a positive merchandise trade balance while the negative service balance declined relatively little.

In the capital account, an outflow is shown for both long-term and short-term capital as well as in errors and omissions that may also reflect the outflow of

Table 1.3
Savings and Investment Ratios (percent of GDP)

	1973	1974	1975	1976	1977	1978	1979
Private Savings	22.1	22.8	20.5	25.5	29.2	29.7	30.0
Government Budget Balance	-0.5	-2.2	-2.0	-1.4	-1.8	-1.2	-1.7
Domestic Savings	21.6	20.6	18.5	24.1	27.5	28.5	28.2
Foreign Savings	2.9	10.9	8.5	1.3	-0.2	3.0	7.3
Domestic Investment	24.5	31.6	27.1	25.3	27.3	31.4	35.5
	1980	1981	1982	1983	1984	1985	1986
Private Savings	25.5	27.1	28.0	28.7	31.7	31.8	35.1
Government Budget Balance	-2.2	-3.4	-3.1	-1.1	-1.2	-1.3	-0.1
Domestic Savings	23.3	23.7	24.9	27.6	30.5	30.5	35.0
Foreign Savings	7.8	5.4	2.6	1.3	0.3	-0.5	-5.8
Domestic Investment	31.1	29.1	27.4	28.9	30.8	30.0	29.2

Source: Bank of Korea, *Economic Statistics Yearbook*, various years.

short-term capital. At the same time, Korea continued to accumulate reserves. On the other side of the ledger, foreign direct investment in Korea accelerated, owing to the revision of the Foreign Capital Inducement Law, but it remained small in absolute terms.

INTERNATIONAL TRADE

The United States is Korea's principal export market. While its share declined between 1973 and 1981, it increased again afterward, reaching a peak of 38.5 percent in 1986. This result reflects the fact that Korea increased its share in the rising U.S. imports from 2.2 percent in 1981 to 2.8 percent in 1986.

In turn, Japan's share increased from 28.6 percent in 1963 to 38.5 percent in 1973 but declined afterward, hardly surpassing 15 percent in 1986. In that year, exports to Japan exceeded exports to Western Europe by only a small margin. Yet, in 1963 and 1973 exports to Japan were more than three times exports to Western Europe. These results indicate the efforts made by Korea to increase its European sales as well as the difficulties encountered in selling to Japan, which have eased only recently.

Exports to developing countries show a roller coaster ride. Their share in total exports fell from 33.9 percent in 1967 to 13.3 percent in 1973, to increase again to 33.0 percent in 1981, subsequently declining to 24.5 percent in 1986.

Within the developing country total, the share of exports to the Pacific countries declined to a considerable extent after 1963 and subsequent increases did not suffice to reach their earlier share. A similar decline occurred in exports to other developing countries, but the earlier share was surpassed in 1981 as Korea benefited from the increased import capacity of Middle Eastern countries following the rise of oil prices, with a partial reversal in subsequent years as oil prices fell again.

The U.S. import share shows a continuing decline, from 51.2 percent in 1963 to 20.2 percent in 1986. This contrasts with the rise in the share of Western Europe from 7.3 percent in 1963 to 12.7 percent in 1986. But imports from Japan alone (33.0%) exceeded the sum of imports from the United States and Western Europe in 1986, although the peak figure of 40.8 percent in 1973 was not reached.

The import share of the developing countries again showed a roller coaster ride, with 9.3 percent in 1963, 18.7 percent in 1973, 33.4 percent in 1981, and 22.3 percent in 1986. Much of this change occurred in the group of other developing countries, reflecting in part changes in oil prices and in part efforts made in Korea to economize on oil.

In turn, the share of imports from the East Asian NICs fluctuated between 2 and 3 percent without much of a trend. Finally, the share of imports from the newly exporting countries in East Asia declined from the peak reached in 1973 as the price of raw materials fell.

The commodity composition of Korea's exports underwent considerable changes over time, with the share of nonfuel primary products declining from 51.8 percent in 1963 to 6.2 percent in 1986 and that of manufactured goods rising from 45.1 percent to 91.9 percent. The share of Korea's fuel exports (coal in earlier years and petroleum products in later years) fell from 3.0 to 1.8 percent during this period.

In 1963, crude minerals (mainly tungsten ores and concentrates) and fish and fish preparations (including seaweed) dominated Korea's primary exports, followed by animals and animal products, the other agricultural products category, and natural fibers. By 1986, only fish and fish preparations had any importance.

Note that 1963 was the year before the Korean reform that led to the rapid expansion of manufactured exports. Apart from textiles, apparel, and leather products, iron and steel was an important item at the time, owing to the excess of domestic supplies. Within the textiles, apparel, and leather products category, yarn and fabrics were of importance.

Textiles, apparel, and leather products came to account for 44.0 percent of Korean exports in 1973, followed by engineering products (16.6%) and wood products and furniture (10.8%). At the same time, clothing surpassed textiles while other textile products assumed importance. Plywood and veneer, produced from logs imported mostly from the Philippines, became one of Korea's major exports, while radios and television sets dominated the exports of engineering products.

The importance of the exports of textiles, apparel, and leather products declined in subsequent years. This product category supplied 32.0 percent of exports in 1986, and it was surpassed by engineering products (40.4%). In the same year, chemicals accounted for 9.3 percent of exports and iron and steel for 6.5 percent.

Except for rising footwear exports, little change occurred in the composition of the textiles, apparel, and leather product category in recent years. In turn, radios and television sets came to account for 14.4 percent of total exports, followed by shipbuilding (5.2%) and motor vehicles (4.7%). The latter two items are of particular interest, indicating the diversification of Korean exports.

Within the chemicals category, relatively simple commodities, such as plastic products (2.2%) and rubber products (1.8%), provided nearly one half of the total, followed by a variety of miscellaneous chemicals. In turn, exports of iron and steel depend in part on domestic capacity coming on stream and in part on formal or informal restrictions imposed on Korean steel by foreign countries. Finally, with rising wages, the profitability of plywood and veneer declined greatly in Korea.

On the import side, the share of manufactured goods rose from 61.7 percent in 1967 to 75.9 percent in 1986 while that of nonfuel primary products fell from 43.1 to 20.8 percent. The increase in the share of fuels from 6.1 percent in 1967 to 15.9 percent in 1986 is largely explained by the rise in petroleum prices.

Within manufacturing, the increase was concentrated in engineering products, whose export shares rose from 22.2 percent in 1963 to 39.1 percent in 1986. This increase reflected in part the use of domestic investment in Korea's GDP and in part the importance of imported inputs for Korea's own exports of engineering products.

In turn, the decline in the share of imports of nonfuel primary products occurred largely in food and live animals, whose share in total imports fell from 21.5 percent in 1963 to 4.5 percent in 1986. These changes indicate the combined effects of the low income elasticity of demand for food, the rise in Korean food production, and the fall in food prices.

CONCLUSION

This study has considered Korea's development strategy in the postwar period. It was noted that following slow growth during the period of import substitution, growth accelerated from the early 1960s onward as Korea adopted an outward-oriented development strategy. This strategy involved providing similar incentives to exports and import substitution, adopting realistic exchange rates, and improving the operation of financial markets.

Korea maintained this strategy after the first oil shock, except at the end of the 1970s when policies adopted by President Park came to favor capital-intensive industries producing intermediate goods and heavy machinery over traditional export industries. These policies had adverse effects on exports and economic growth and were reversed in the early 1980s. In fact, Korea has increasingly liberalized its economy.

The results of the policies applied are apparent in the rapid economic growth achieved in the 1963–86 period, where Korea reached GDP growth rates of 8–9 percent a year. Economic growth was promoted by the rapid expansion of exports; whereas exports of goods and services amounted to only 5 percent of GDP in 1963, they reached 41 percent in 1986.

The commodity composition of exports also underwent considerable changes over time, with the share of manufactured goods rising from 45 percent in 1963 to 92 percent in 1986. Parallel with these changes, manufacturing activities came to account for an increasing proportion of GDP.

Rapid export expansion transformed Korea's traditional import surplus into an export surplus. It is doubtful, however, that maintaining an export surplus is in Korea's well-conceived interest. Rather, the country should aim at importing foreign capital that can earn high returns in Korean industry.

REFERENCES

Bank of Korea, *Economic Statistics Yearbook*, Seoul, various years.
Economic Planning Bureau (EPB), *The Guidelines for the Fourth Five-Year Economic Development Plan*, Seoul, 1975.

————, *The Preliminary Outline of the Fifth Five-Year Economic and Social Development Plan of the Republic of Korea 1982–86*, Seoul, 1981.

Korea Development Institute, *The Discussion Paper on the Developmental Strategy for the Fourth Five-Year Plan, 1977–81*, Seoul, 1975.

World Bank, *World Development Report*, Washington, D.C., 1987.

2

"Why Is South Korea Succeeding?"
A Heterodox Perspective

Young Chin Kim

INTRODUCTION

Fueled by modern technology and characterized by (historically) high rates of growth in per capita income as well as in population, modern economic development/growth is a relatively recent phenomenon in human history.[1] Such achievement in its origin was an offshoot of European civilization. But is its spread also confined to areas in Europe and European settlements?

Between the celestial world of the theory of society's evolution where the Karl Marxes and the Schumpeters roam and the pedestrian world where economists labor lies a free-for-all arena for socio- and psychocultural analyses of the history of economic growth. The direction of, and conclusions from, such analyses have naturally been dictated by perceived historical "facts" of economic and/or other societal achievements. From the sociocultural perspective and based on perceived historical facts, there follows a common concern voiced by Kuznets (1973, p. 254): "Emergence of a modern framework for economic growth may be especially difficult if it involves elements peculiar to European civilization for which substitutes are not easily found." Reported by, for example, Gerschenkron (1962, p. 27) are "pessimistic conclusions" from anthropological research of cultural patterns in societies of non-European origin.

The fact of Japan's economic success, however, has long been a gadfly to those seeking sociocultural explanations for what otherwise would be a uniquely European-monopolized accomplishment. The common inclination is to regard Japan's case as an "exception"—a fluke. Japan is an "honorary member," so to speak, of the Western-monopoly club.

The intent of this study is to argue that there are, at least, two other exceptions (namely, South Korea and Taiwan) and that such additional exceptions make the spread of economic growth more commonplace than is generally recognized. A single exception is perhaps ignorable but three are not. This inclusive view of historical facts of economic growth would require a significant revision in the choice of relevant sociocultural factors and in the process of deductive reasoning.

It was only in quite recent years that the economic successes of Taiwan and South Korea for the past 25 to 35 years have been widely known. What is still not well recognized is a further fact that both economies have a longer history of successful modern economic expansion. An analysis of the record further demonstrates that, except for different entry dates to modern economic growth and varying lengths of war-induced interruptions, economic performances of Japan, South Korea, and Taiwan are hardly distinguishable from one another.

RECORD OF ECONOMIC PERFORMANCE IN KOREA, TAIWAN, AND JAPAN BEFORE 1940

Though motivated by Japan's self-interest and structured only as appendages for the Japanese economy, the modern phase of Korea's and Taiwan's economies began subsequent to their colonization by Japan—in 1895 for Taiwan and in 1910 for Korea (Ho, 1978; Mason et al., 1980; Suh, 1978). Modernization of the Japanese society is usually dated from the beginning of the Meiji Restoration in 1868 (Lockwood, 1954; Ohkawa and Rosovsky, 1973). Thus, Korea's transition from a (semi-) feudal society to the modern era occurred about 42 years behind Japan's and 15 years behind Taiwan's.

Reported in Table 2.1 are available estimates of annual growth rates of total and per capita output in Korea and Taiwan during the colonial periods. In order to minimize the effects of Japanese military adventurism, the terminal periods chosen roughly correspond to the pre-World War II peaks for Korea and Taiwan in Table 2.1 (and for Japan in Table 2.2). A salient feature of Table 2.1 is the striking similarity in the growth rates of the two economies under Japanese rule.

In order to cast the historical record of Korea's and Taiwan's economies in their proper international perspective, let us first view the Japanese success vis-à-vis other nations in early industrialization and then assess how Korea's and Taiwan's performance compares with Japan's. Shown in Table 2.2 are growth rates of total and per capita output in Japan before the pre-World War II peak and estimated (unweighted) mean growth rates in Western countries between the late nineteenth century and mid-1950s.

The relative success of Japan is evident. Not only did the Japanese economy grow at above average rates (as shown in the table), but Japan's growth rates also

Table 2.1

Annual Growth Rates of Total and Per Capita Output in Korea and Taiwan Before World War II (in percent)

Sources	Periods	Total Output		Per Capita Output	
		Korea	Taiwan	Korea	Taiwan
Mizoguchi (1975)	1911-1938	3.6[a]		1.8[b]	
	1903-1938		3.8[a]		1.9[b]
Hong (1968)	1911/15-1936/40			3.5[c]	
	1902/12-1938/40				2.7[c]
Kim and Roemer (1979)	1910/12-1938/40	3.2[d] (4.6)		1.6[d] (3.0)	
Mason, et al. (1980)	1910/12-1938/41	3.8[e]		2.2[e]	
Ho (1978)	1903-1940		3.8[f]		1.8[f]
Lin (1973)	1911/15-1936/40		4.1[g]		2.0[g]

[a]Mizoguchi, p. 154.
[b]Computed from Mizoguchi, pp. 152-54.
[c]Computed from Hong (1968, p. 216).
[d]Kim and Roemer, pp. 8-10. Figures in parentheses refer to "gross commodity product." Figures in this and Mason, et al. are recomputations of data from Suh (1978).
[e]Mason et al., pp. 75-76.
[f]Computed from Ho, pp. 26-27.
[g]Lin, p. 23.

would rank either at the top or, at least, very near the top regardless of the choice of criteria (growth rates of total output, per capita output, or product per man-hour) and the choice of periods (Kuznets, 1966, pp.352–53). In fact, Kuznets takes an annual growth rate of 1.4 percent (that is, 15% growth per decade) in per capita output as a typical (though conservative) rate for the now-industrialized economies from initial phases of modern growth through the early 1960s (Kuznets, 1966, p. 67).

Even though the success of the Japanese economy has been common knowledge, scarcely noticed is the equally admirable record of Korea and Taiwan before the Sino-Japanese War (beginning in 1937) and the subsequent World War II. Even if we set aside the estimates by Hong (1968) as being exceptionally high,[2] annual growth rates in per capita income between 1.6 percent and 2.2 percent for Korea and between 1.8 percent and 2.0 percent for Taiwan during the colonial period are compatible with the Japanese performance during similar periods.[3]

Table 2.2

Annual Growth Rates of Total and Per Capita Output in Japan and Other Advanced Nations in Earlier Years (in percent)

Sources	Periods	Japan		Other Advanced Nations	
		Total Output	Per Capita Output	Total Output	Per Capita Output
Ohkawa and Rosovsky (1973, p. 28)	Between average levels				
	1897/1901-1901/17	2.2	1.0		
	1901/17-1917/31	3.3	2.0		
	1917/31-1931/37	3.7	2.2		
	Peak-to-Peak				
	1887-1917	2.7	1.5		
	1917-1937	3.7	2.3		
	Trough-to-Trough				
	1901-1931	2.9	1.6		
Yuzo Yamada in Lockwood (1954, p. 135)	1883/87-1933/37	3.4	2.2		
Maddison (1964, pp. 28 and 30)[a]	1870-1913			2.7 (1.4-4.3)	1.6 (0.7-2.3)
	1913-1950			1.9 (0.7-2.9)	1.1 (0.4-1.9)
Kuznets (1956, p. 113)[b]	From 19th century until before WW I			2.7	1.7
	From 19th century until mid-1950's			2.5	1.5

[a]Mean annual growth rates for twelve industrialized nations in Western Europe and North America. Figures in parentheses refer to the range of growth rates.
[b]Mean annual growth rates (converted from decade rates in the source) for nine industrialized nations in Western Europe and North America, and the U.S.S.R. The beginning dates in the nineteenth century vary between 1841 and 1870.

RECORD OF ECONOMIC PERFORMANCE IN SOUTH KOREA, TAIWAN, AND JAPAN AFTER WORLD WAR II

After the end of World War II, all three economies had to undergo periods of severe readjustments. Taiwan was freed from Japanese rule and then had to face a period of major dislocation resulting from political events in the mainland. Japan lost former colonies and had to recover from wartime destruction. The economic recovery to the prewar peak is usually dated 1952, 1953, or 1954 for Japan (Ohkawa and Rosovsky, 1973, p. 22; Galenson, 1979, pp. 456–57); and between 1952 and 1953 for Taiwan (Lin, 1973, p. 37; Myers, 1986, p. 14). Taking 1939 as the prewar peak, the wars cost Japan and Taiwan between 13 and 15 years.

For Korea, the problems of recovery and readjustments were much more severe. Following the decolonization in 1945 came the partition of the industrial north from the agrarian south and then the Korean War (1950–53). South Korea's recovery from the Korean War is said to have taken place by 1958 (Cole and Lyman, 1971, p. 123; Galenson, 1979, p. 455). It is probably the case that 1963 was the earliest possible date for South Korea proper to have gained the pre-World War II peak in terms of per capita income.[4] Thus, the cost to South Korea's economy of the military and political disruptions is at least 24 in terms of lost years—about 10 years longer than Japan's and Taiwan's.

The success of postrecovery economic activities in all three economies is now widely known. Having recovered to prewar peaks, all three economies once again have progressed as if in unison. Their feat can be glanced from Table 2.3, which shows growth rates of GDP and per capita GDP. If any fine distinction is to be made among the three cases, it must be that South Korea and Taiwan have been outperforming Japan in more recent years.

To summarize, the salient features in the historical record of economic growth in the three economies are as follows: (a) Japan entered the phase of modern

Table 2.3

Annual Growth Rates of GDP and Per Capita GDP in South Korea, Taiwan, and Japan During Postrecovery Periods (in percent; numbers in parentheses are growth rates of GDP)

	Early Post-Recovery Years 1953–63	1960–1970	1970–1980	1980–1986
South Korea		6.2[a] (8.6)	7.8 (9.5)	6.8 (8.2)
Taiwan	4.2[b] (7.8)	6.6 (9.2)	5.9 (8.0)	4.6 (6.3)
Japan	8.4[b] (9.4)	9.4 (10.4)	3.4 (4.5)	3.0 (3.7)

Sources: Unless otherwise noted, the World Bank, *World Development Report*, various issues; for Taiwan, unpublished data at the World Bank.

[a]Rates during 1964–1970, early post-recovery years in South Korea, were 9.9 percent for GDP and 7.5 percent for GDP per capita, as computed with additional information from OECD (1982).
[b]Computed with supplemental information from U.N., *Demographic Yearbook* (1961) and *Yearbook of National Accounts Statistics* (1966).

economic growth in 1868 (or thereabout), Taiwan in 1895, and Korea in 1910; (b) having entered the modern phase, all three economies performed equally well until they were all disrupted around 1939; and (c) after recovery (in the early 1950s for Japan and Taiwan, and the early 1960s for South Korea), all three countries have resumed their successful drive for economic expansion.

Lest one be inclined or even tempted to regard Japan's former rule as a good fortune, even only in part, for South Korea and Taiwan, it must be pointed out that "the nature of colonial relationships created tremendously great psychological barriers to behaving in ways leading to technological progress. Indeed, the *negative* correlation between colonial control and the timing and pace of economic growth is *striking*" (Hagen, 1962, p. 19, italics mine). Furthermore, as Hong (1989, pp. 2–6) has shown, the "legacy" of the Japanese rule with respect to accumulation of either human or physical capital in Korea and Taiwan was no more significant than what the Western colonial powers left behind in their own former colonies. Thus, the success (especially in postrecovery years) of South Korea and Taiwan is not because of Japan's former colonial rule, but probably in spite of it.

GROWTH RATES AND LEVELS OF PER CAPITA OUTPUT IN SOUTH KOREA, TAIWAN, AND JAPAN

To compare the *levels* of per capita income across countries is a much riskier task than to compare the *rates* of growth. The problem becomes more and more serious as we go back farther and farther in time. It may, nevertheless, be a useful check on the reported growth rates to compare the approximate levels of, say, income per capita in the three countries over the long periods under consideration. The usefulness of comparing the data on the growth rates with those on the levels arises because of the required (internal) consistency between the two measures. Because it is the case that $M_2 = M_1(1 + r)^t$ (where M_1 = initial level, M_2 = terminal level, r = annual rate of change, and t = time in years), if any two of the three unknowns (M_1, M_2 and r) are determined, the third can be readily computed between any initial and terminal periods.

What evidence there is points to the conclusion that the levels of economic growth in the three countries at the inception of the respective economy's modern era were approximately the same. According to Hong's estimation (1968, p. 216), per capita output in Korea was $42.5 (in constant 1951 prices) during 1916–20; in Taiwan, $43.4 during 1902–05; and in Japan, $42.6 during 1881–85. Moreover, per capita manufacturing product was $1.9 in Korea, $2.0 in Taiwan, and $1.9 in Japan during the same respective periods. Suh (1978, p. 35) also reported that the industrial distributions of employment and of output were very similar between Korea and Japan. These findings are as expected in light of the history of the three countries and also of the universal fact that premodern growth was negligible.[5]

In 1986, per capita GNP for Taiwan ($3,729) was 1.6 times higher than for South Korea ($2,370).[6] If it is assumed that the living standards during premodern days were approximately equal in Korea and Taiwan (as well as in Japan), Taiwan's aforementioned 15-year lead in modernization over Korea's would have placed Taiwan's per capita income at 1.35 times Korea's by 1910. (An annual rate of 2%, when compounded over 15 years, yields a multiplicative factor of 1.35.) Further, if it is accepted that South Korea's recovery to the pre–World War II peak occurred in 1963 and Taiwan's (and Japan's) by 1953, Taiwan's 10-year head start would have meant Taiwan's per capita output had grown by another factor of 1.51 (when compounded at an annual rate of 4.2%, as shown in Table 2.3). Thus the consequence of Taiwan's two head starts by themselves would be that Taiwan's per capita output is expected to be approximately twice [= (1.35)(1.51)] Korea's. That does not leave much residual difference in per capita income between South Korea and Taiwan in their respective (uninterrupted) modern periods.[7]

Similarly, Japan's 42-year lead in modernization over Korea would mean Japan's per capita income was 1.9 times (at an annual rate of 1.5%) or 2.3 times (at an annual rate of 2.0%) higher than Korea's by 1910. Further, Japan's 10-year head start in recovery after World War II would have raised Japan's income by another factor of 2.2 (at an annual rate of 8.4%, as shown in Table 2.3). The combined effect would put Japan's per capita income at as high as 5.1 times [= (2.3)(2.2)] Korea's. In the meantime, in 1986 per capita GNP for Japan ($12,840) was 5.4 times higher than for South Korea ($2,370) (World Bank, 1988, p. 223). Again, there remains not much residual difference to be accounted for by other considerations.[8]

It was shown earlier that economic performances of the three economies, as measured by their growth rates of per capita income, are hardly distinguishable from one another during their respective modern eras. It is now shown that the assertion can be further reinforced by examining the levels of income in 1986 and by reasonable conjectures about the levels of income at the start of modernization in the three countries.

WHY HAS SOUTH KOREA BEEN SUCCEEDING?

"Why Has Japan 'Succeeded'?" asks Morishima (1982) in his much-discussed book by the same title. His error is that he asks a wrong question. Considering the breakneck pace of economic expansion in South Korea for nearly a generation and in Taiwan for over a generation since the post-war recovery alone, one will need to ask the same or a similar question (Why Has South Korea/Taiwan Been Succeeding?). One will further need to add Singapore and Hong Kong to the list. Soon the list will get longer—to include, for example, Thailand and Malaysia.

One may counter by saying that one generation does not make a secular trend.

As Kuznets argued, "Given the economic cycles of modern times, . . . a cumulative increase in total or per capita product of a few percentage points even over a long period, say thirty years, can hardly be considered sustained and taken safely as a measure of secular rise" (1966, p. 26). Yet as noted earlier, the track record of the two countries goes back to 1895 for Taiwan and 1910 for Korea. Further, as Kuznets himself noted, "a substantial rise over a shorter period, say fifteen to twenty years, which even a marked cyclical contraction is not likely to reduce more than a fifth or a quarter, may be treated as evidence of a rising secular trend, i.e., of economic growth" (1966.p. 27).

Some may point out that, unlike Japan, Taiwan and South Korea have not yet attained the status of developed/industrialized/advanced countries; they are still only newly industrializing or developing economies. To so argue is to shift attention from the growth *rate* to the *level* of, say, income per capita. Any disparity in the level of income is caused by differences in the growth rate trend (exclusive of abnormal periods) of income, the beginning date of the modern era, and/or the frequency and length of random-shock interruptions. In the case of Japan, Taiwan, and South Korea, virtually all of their relative income can be "explained" by the timing of modernization and the frequency and severity of exogenous disturbances. In terms of rates of growth during disturbance-free modern periods, there is very little to choose among the three. If anything, South Korea and Taiwan have been outperforming Japan in more recent years.

Granted, it still leaves unanswered the ultimate question of why some economies "get going" sooner than others. Yet, the fundamental *causes* (and processes) of social development/change belong in the realm of grandiose, general, predictive theories of social change—a path this writer dares not tread. The precise *timing* in modernization (within, say, a generation) is left to a sub-species of historians who deal with chronological events in retrospect.[9] Albeit at the great risk of inviting criticism, it is asserted that, in the long history of mankind measured in millennia, a preoccupation with a lead-and-lag of a generation or so and with only material endeavor at that may be guilty of myopia. Within the limited interest of this chapter (and also the limits of the writer's competency), the differential timing in modernization in Japan, Taiwan, and Korea may be termed a "historical accident" (whose understanding would rank on a par in its usefulness with knowing why, for example, Germany's industrialization began after France's but before Sweden's).[10]

In short, Japan's economic advancement is ahead of Taiwan's and South Korea's not because Japan was more successful in the sense of higher growth rates, but because Japan entered the modern era before Taiwan and Korea and because South Korea had to face more severe adjustment and recovery problems than either Japan or Taiwan—both being "historical accidents." Thus, the "Japanese puzzle" is not entirely Japanese and is not even a big puzzle (not to mention a "miracle").

SOCIOCULTURAL APPROACHES—A CRITIQUE

Morishima takes great pains to differentiate Japanese Confucianism from the Confucianism of China. His need to do so is rooted in his implicit acceptance of Max Weber's assertion that Confucianism prevented the emergence of modern capitalism in China. If the original (Chinese) Confucianism is inimical to the development of capitalism and, therefore, to economic growth, the economic success of Japan (a Confucian nation) cannot be reconciled unless Confucianism is "Nipponized," to use Wan's term (1988). But, in light of the performance of South Korea and Taiwan, do we now need to hypothesize about the (South) Koreanized and Taiwanized Confucianism? If, as it seems very probable, China can sustain its recent success, then what?

Myopia has divided not only Confucianism but also the Chinese people. Characterizing the economic success of Hong Kong in the early post-World War II years as a "riddle," Szczepanik seriously contended that the major reason for the success of Hong Kong and for the failure of Taiwan (along with Singapore) was that Chinese "racial and social composition was different." The Chinese who have gone to Hong Kong, it was said, did so "prepared to work hard" while those who went to Taiwan were "ready to rule or fight but not to work" (1958, p. 5). Only if he had a slight foresight or even a little hindsight!

Analogous to such attempts at differentiation of Confucianism and the Chinese race, there also occurred differentiation of Western religion(s). Although to Max Weber, economic progress was a product of Puritanism,[11] later writers gradually expanded the growth-promoting (or growth-hospitable) religion-set, in order to accommodate new realities, to Protestantism and then to Christianity.

Attributable largely to myopia, the views expressed in these writings are innocent and downright tame in comparison with earlier times. To cite but a few earlier examples from Klineberg (1935), when Greece ruled supreme, Aristotle contended that it was the destiny of the Greeks to rule the earth because they were located geographically between the spirited-but-unintelligent northern Europeans and the intelligent-but-unspirited Asiatics. When the Romans reigned, it too was inevitable, according to Vitruvius, because the Romans were keenly intelligent while the "northern nations" possessed a "sluggish intelligence." Arthur Joseph de Gobineau, the nineteenth century father of modern racial theories, preached the superiority of the white race over other races and of the Aryans over all other whites. All civilizations, according to him, sprang from the Aryans and a civilization without the Aryans was unthinkable (pp. 1–4). In all instances, every premise, argument, and conclusion was to glorify the writer's own race—ethnocentrism in its zenith, undiluted and unself-conscious.

Nowadays, of course, racial and religious explanations are not as fashionable or overt. Nevertheless, as Hoselitz (1960) noted, essentially the same theme is still evident: Economic growth in LDCs requires their coming to resemble the Western nations in social structure (p. 55–56). In short, low-income countries will have to become "little Americas" (p. 56) if they are to succeed.

It is agreed with Wan that there exist minimum sufficient sociocultural conditions for economic progress. But it is argued that the conditions are also met by cultures other than the Protestant ethic and the Nipponized ethos. Moreover, it is further contended that, even if existing sociocultural environments are not conducive, they are adaptable enough to become either conducive or, at least, nonpreclusive, once the growth process begins (about the cause of which the author has little to contribute).[12]

CLOSING REMARKS

While the common view holds that Japan is the only non-Western society that has succeeded in the European-origin game of economic growth, it is argued that both South Korea and Taiwan now, though belatedly recognized, qualify as adept players. Japan has served to posit a troublesome question to those seeking a neat sociocultural explanation for the phenomenon of economic growth. South Korea and Taiwan (and, to a large measure, other newly industrializing countries) surely, and greatly, compound the "problem."[13]

After Japan, South Korea and Taiwan (and other NICs) have again shown by their deeds that economic progress does not belong in the exclusive province of Western culture. This demonstration should comfort those who have been concerned that economic expansion might be uniquely European in its social and cultural prerequisites, albeit at the psychic expense of ethnocentrists.

At the same time, the cases of the two economies should also serve as significant counterexamples to the "well nigh universal" anti-Westernism of the "Third World intellectuals" (Wiarda, 1988, p. 61). "Hostility" toward anything Western is the antithesis of the Western ethnocentrism. One form of ethnocentrism begets other forms of ethnocentrism and, even, xenophobia (from either of which the Koreans are not immune). South Korea and Taiwan have been successful without becoming "European" in their ethnicity, culture, religion, and political institutions; and their experiences also represent undisputable evidence that a society need not (or, even, should not) be subject to a New International Economic Order and need not (or, even, should not) become anti-Western to achieve economic progress.

In a different vein, high growth rates in the three economies have been achieved while their governments pursued policies that are quite different in specifics.[14] One must wonder how much government policies matter in terms of overall performance. Although it is readily accepted that policies clearly can do damage, claims of positive effect of any specific measure deserve to be viewed with healthy skepticism.

A conjecture is that policies do matter (in the beneficial direction and in overall performance) to the extent that the totality of policies sets a general tone (the rules of the game, so to speak) in regulating economic activities. Most important of the rules of the game, suggested especially (though not exclusively) by the experiences of the East Asian economies, is the outward-looking posture.[15] While an economy must be efficient and dynamic to be successful, the disciplinary role of the international marketplace compels its participants to be efficient just to survive and be transformation-dynamic to get ahead. An outward-oriented thrust in government policies, even only in their export-promoting dimension, force feeds efficiency and dynamism.

In closing, perhaps an important lesson from the experiences of NICs is to resist the temptation of dichotomizing economic performances of non-Western countries either as "miracles" or as (hopeless) "basket cases." Too many miracles abase divinity and time can revive dashed hopes.

NOTES

I am indebted to Wontack Hong with whom I have had running discussions on the subject over many years and Jene K. Kwon, the editor of this volume, who willingly tolerates my "biases," which greatly differ from his.

1. "Reasonable estimates for Western Europe over the long period from the early Middle Ages to the mid-nineteenth century suggest that the modern rate of growth is about ten times as high for product per capita" (Kuznets, 1973, p. 248).

2. They are "high" not only for Taiwan and Korea, but also for Japan (that is, 3.3%) during the same period (Hong, 1968, p. 216).

3. Mason et al. (1980, p. 448) even argue that an annual growth rate of nearly 4 percent for "net commodity product" in Korea was *higher* than the growth rate in Japan during the same period.

4. According to Maddison (1970), per capita output in 1950 in South Korea and Taiwan was "still about a quarter below pre-war levels" (p. 30). The period between 1959 and 1962, marked by stagnation and political unrest, produced a near-zero growth rate in per capita terms in South Korea (Cole and Lyman, 1971,p. 123).

5. See note 1, above.

6. World Bank (1988, p. 223) and unpublished data from the World Bank.

7. Any reader troubled by the disparity between the multiples of 1.6 and 2 is reminded of the imprecise nature of national income accounting, especially when making international comparisons. Also, notice that South Korea has been growing

slightly faster than Taiwan in more recent years. Moreover, Scitovsky (1986) argues that, if the shorter length of work week in Taiwan than in Korea is taken into account, "Taiwan's per capita GDP appears almost twice as high as Korea's" (p. 136).

8. The mean, annual growth rates of per capita GDP for the 1960–86 period, computed from Table 2.3, are 7.0 percent for South Korea, 5.9 percent for Taiwan and 5.6 percent for Japan—indicating marginally higher rates for South Korea. Further, it is granted that the difference in growth rates between South Korea and Japan would be somewhat larger if only the post-1963 years are considered. Nonetheless, our main contention still stands.

9. "Unlike so many of their predecessors, modern historians no longer announce to the world what inevitably will, or at least what ideally should, happen. We have grown modest. This prophetic fervor was bound to vanish together with the childlike faith in a perfectly comprehensible past" (Gerschenkron, 1962, p. 5).

10. A more interesting and potentially more fruitful question is rather why some economies (such as in Latin America) "stall" after having gotten started.

11."Puritanism," rather than the more inclusive term "Protestantism," is what is essential to Max Weber. See Hagen (1962, p. 16) and Tawney (1926, pp. 198-99).

12. "[O]nce the forces leading to economic development have been set in motion, economic and social progress tend to go hand in hand" (Adelman and Morris, 1971, pp. 184 and 188); and "the very attitudes alleged to be preconditions of industrialization could be generated on the job and 'on the way,' by certain characteristics of the industrialization process" (Hirschman, 1984, p. 99).

13. South Korea and Taiwan cannot be dismissed as Hong Kong and Singapore for which the European-origin and, albeit archaic, the entrepôt role may be invoked. Further, the pre–World War II record of Korea and Taiwan precludes any claim of their experiences being temporary and fluky.

14. See, for example, Scitovsky (1986) for a South Korea–Taiwan comparison, and Yoo (1985) for a South Korea–Japan comparison, of government policies.

15. For an analysis of export-promoting strategies in South Korea and Taiwan, see, for example, Hong (1989, pp. 11–28).

REFERENCES

Adelman, Irma, and Morris, Cynthia T., *Society, Politics, and Economic Development: A Quantitative Approach*, Baltimore: Johns Hopkins Press, 1971.

Cole, David C., and Lyman, Princeton, N., *Korean Development: The Interplay of Politics and Economics*, Cambridge: Harvard University Press, 1971.

Galenson, Walter, "The Labor Force, Wages, and Living Standards," in Walter Galenson, ed., *Economic Growth and Structural Change in Taiwan: The Postwar Experience of the Republic of China*, Ithaca: Cornell University Press, 1979, 384–447.

Gerschenkron, Alexander, "Economic Backwardness in Historical Perspective," reprinted in Alexander Gerschenkron, ed., *Economic Backwardness in Historical Perspective*, New York: Praeger, 1962, 5–30.

Hagen, Everett E., *On the Theory of Social Change: How Economic Growth Begins*, Homewood, Ill.: Dorsey Press, 1962.

Hirschman, Albert O., "A Dissenter's Confession: 'The Tragedy of Economic Development' Revisited," in Gerald M. Meier and Dudley Seers, eds., *Pioneers in Development*, New York: Oxford University Press, 1984, 87–113.

Ho, Samuel P. S., *Economic Development of Taiwan, 1860–1970*, New Haven: Yale University Press, 1978.

Hong, Wontack, "Industrialization and Trade in Manufactures: The East Asian Experience," in Peter B. Kenen and Roger Lawrence, eds., *The Open Economy: Essays on International Trade and Finance*, New York: Columbia University Press, 1968, 213–39.

———, "Comparative Study of the Industrialization Experience of Korea and Taiwan," Mimeo, Seoul, 1989.

Hoselitz, Bert F., *Sociological Aspects of Economic Growth*, Glencoe, Ill.: Free Press, 1960.

Kim, Kwang Suk, and Roemer, Michael, *Growth and Structural Transformation, Studies in the Modernization of the Republic of Korea: 1945–1975*, Cambridge: Harvard University Press, 1979.

Klineberg, Otto, *Race Differences*, New York: Harper, 1935.

Kuznets, Simon, "Quantitative Aspects of the Economic Growth of Nations, I, Levels and Variability of Rates of Growth," *Economic Development and Cultural Change*, 5, 1956, 5–94.

———, *Modern Economic Growth: Rate, Structure, and Spread*, New Haven: Yale University Press, 1966.

———, "Modern Economic Growth: Findings and Reflections," *American Economic Review*, 63, June 1973, 247–58.

Lin, Ching-yuan, *Industrialization in Taiwan, 1946–72*, New York: Praeger, 1973.

Lockwood, William W., *The Economic Development of Japan: Growth and Structural Change 1868–1938*, Princeton: Princeton University Press, 1954.

Maddison, Angus, *Economic Growth in the West; Comparative Experience in Europe and North America*, New York: Twentieth Century Fund, 1964.

Mason, Edward S., et al., *The Economic and Social Modernization of the Republic of Korea*, Cambridge: Harvard University Press, 1980.

Mizoguchi, Toshiyuki, *The Economic Growth of Taiwan and Korea* (in Japanese), Tokyo: Iwanami Shoten, 1975.

Morishima, Michio, *Why Has Japan "Succeeded"?* Cambridge: Cambridge University Press, 1982.

Myers, Ramon H., "The Economic Development of the Republic of China on Taiwan, 1965–1981," in Lawrence J. Lau, ed., *Models of Development*, San Francisco: Institute for Contemporary Studies, 1986, 13–64.

OECD, *Latest Information on National Accounts of Developing Countries*, Paris: OECD, various issues.

Ohkawa, Kazushi and Rosovsky, Henry, *Japanese Economic Growth*, Stanford: Stanford University Press, 1973.

Scitovsky, Tibor, "Economic Development in Taiwan and South Korea, 1965–1981," in Lawrence J. Lau, ed., *Models of Development*, San Francisco: Institute for Contemporary Studies, 1986, 135–95.

Suh, Sang-Chul, *Growth and Structural Changes in the Korean Economy, 1910–1940*, Cambridge: Harvard University Press, 1978.

Szczepanik, Edward, *The Economic Growth of Hong Kong*, London: Oxford University Press, 1958.

Tawney, R. H., *Religion and the Rise of Capitalism*, London: John Murray, 1926.

United Nations, *Demographic Yearbook*, 1960, New York: United Nations, 1961.

———, *Yearbook of National Accounts Statistics*, 1965, New York: United Nations, 1966.

Wan, Henry, Jr., "Nipponized Confucian Ethos or Incentive-Compatible Institutional Design: Notes on Morishima, 'Why Has Japan Succeeded?'" *International Economic Journal*, 2, Spring 1988, 101–08.

Wiarda, Howard J., "Toward a Nonethnocentric Theory of Development: Alternative Conceptions from the Third World," reprinted in Charles K. Wilber, ed., *The Political Economy of Development and Underdevelopment*, 4th ed., New York: Random House, 1988, 59–82.

World Bank, *World Development Report*, New York: Oxford University Press, various issues.

Yoo, Jang H., "Does Korea Trace Japan's Footsteps? A Macroeconomic Appraisal," *Kyklos*, 38, 1985, 578–98.

3

The Uncommon Characteristics of Korea's Economic Development

Jene K. Kwon

INTRODUCTION

One of the more unsettling issues of Korea's economic development is the role of government in this process. The issue is often clouded by emotions and sweeping generalizations. Some dismiss the government's role simply by asserting that the Korean economy has succeeded "in spite of" the government, while others faintly admit some merit in its role. And the rest simply shrug off the issue because they are not comfortable with the kinds of issues that do not lend themselves to a clear-cut calculus.

However, it is extremely important for our intellectual honesty that we confront this issue because, given the manner in which the Korean economic development was *initiated*, it is not possible to discuss its development without considering the role of the government, and also because lessons drawn from the Korean experience may have far-reaching implications for development economics in general.

As a first and modest step toward the "complete" assessment of the government's role, this study identifies several rather uncommon characteristics of Korean economy and discusses how these characteristics were shaped by government policies during the first two decades (1960s and 1970s) of Korea's economic development.[1]

THE ADVENT OF NEW POLICIES

Antecedents to the 1960s

For half a century prior to 1961, Korea was a dependent nation—politically on Japan first (1910–45), then economically on the United States thereafter. The country was partitioned into two nations—North and South—in 1945; later about two thirds of the industrial facilities in the South were destroyed by the Korean war (1950–53).

In 1961, the economy remained a poor agrarian variety with per capita income of around $80 (in current dollars) per year. Since domestic exports and savings were virtually nonexistent, over 70 percent of Korea's reconstruction projects (in the aftermath of the Korean War) and its imports were financed by U.S. economic aid. The attitude of the hapless political leaders at the time was to maximize the amount of U.S. aid for as long as possible.

The economic policy during the 1953–61 period was that of import substitution. Under the so-called "easy" import substitution, domestic production replaced imports of non-durable consumer goods, and imports of these goods were discouraged through a myriad of restrictions. Korea completed the phase of easy import substitution around 1960. This system of import restriction inevitably created a bias against exports, with overvaluation of the exchange rate deterring exports, which accounted for little more than 1 or 2 percent of the GNP.

The import substitution policy also created a scarcity in imported goods and foreign exchange. In the virtual absence of exports, the only source of foreign exchange was foreign economic aid, which tended to benefit primarily a few privileged who were favored by the government. This practice gave the owner of the scarce foreign exchange an opportunity for windfall profits through importation of scarce commodities.[2] In the end, this type of nonproductive, rent-seeking activities gave rise to rampant corruption, popular discontent, and distrust of the government. On the eve of the military coup in 1961, the national economy remained stagnant and the nation was adrift in the sea of despair and disillusionment.

The Period of Rapid Growth (1960s and 1970s)

The military regime of President Chung Hee Park came into power in 1961. With the new regime in power, policy emphasis shifted from dependency on U.S. aid to a search for a self-reliant economy. From the very beginning, the government masterminded not only the formulation of economic policy but also its implementation.

With the First Five-Year Plan, the economic policy was thrust into the forefront of national policy. The key elements in the First Five-Year Plan were the "expansion of key industrial facilities and adequate provision of social overhead capital; utilization of idle resources; some improvement in the balance of international payments, primarily through increased exports; and technological advancement" (Economic Planning Board, 1962, p. 29).

Although the First Five-Year Plan, at least in part, signals a policy shift away from import substitution toward exports, it is quite unlikely that, in the beginning, the planners had a clear notion of the outward-looking orientation. More likely, the idea crystallized as a series of export-incentive measures put into effect resulted in unexpected success. It also has been reported that the indication by the U.S. authorities that economic aid was soon to be terminated had forced the new government to turn to an alternative.[3] Whatever the initial cause may have been, the actual process of turning from the inward-looking to the outward-looking policy stance may not have been as easy as it appears at first glance. Especially for a country like Korea, which had no notable export products and had no clear notion of comparative advantage in the export of labor-intensive manufacturing goods, the decision to turn to the outward-looking policy must have been a courageous act—a bold gamble entailing a great deal of risks and uncertainty.

Under the outward-looking policy, which was to emerge as the central piece of the new economic policy, several important measures went into effect to promote exports: (a) currency was drastically devalued; (b) a multiple exchange rate system was replaced with a single, unified, floating exchange rate system; and (c) a variety of tax exemptions, direct export subsidies, and foreign exchange loans were allowed together with a tax rebate on material imported for export production as well as the import-export credits. To stimulate business investment, corporate tax incentives were increased and large government-directed loans were given to selected industries.

Equally significant was the higher incentive for productive activities assured by the new policy. Businessmen saw in the new policy, for the first time, genuine opportunities for making profits from the production and the exportation of produced goods. Economic gains from expanded international trade, government-directed bank loans, and tax credits presented themselves as viable alternatives to the rent-seeking activities, although rent-seeking still remained a factor with which to contend.

Once the Five-Year Plan was put into motion, the government made some crucial management decisions that ordinarily would be made by private entrepreneurs. It set ambitious targets for economic growth, including export growth, and used the carrot-and-iron-stick and trial-and-error approaches to push private firms into compliance. By the late 1960s uniquely distinctive characteristics of the Korean economy had begun to emerge, bearing indelible imprints of the government.

Perhaps, of all the government's policies put into effect, none was more uniquely Korean than the manner in which the government channelled its policy-directed loans to businesses through a tight nexus of government, banks, and businesses. The policy-directed government loans were a double-edged sword with which government promoted economic growth while keeping a tight leash on private entrepreneurial activities. In fact, virtually every distinctive characteristic of the Korean economy can be traced back to this unique institutional arrangement—be it changing production technology or comparative advantage, industrial organization or income distribution.

In what follows, each one of these characteristics will be discussed in some detail by highlighting their uniqueness.

SOME UNCOMMON CHARACTERISTICS

Government-Banks-Business Relationships

According to Schumpeter, in a capitalistic society, "economy could maintain its forward momentum only as long as entrepreneurs behaved like knights—or at least pioneers" and "the driving impetus for the economic change came from men of vision and courage who risked their fortunes to implement new ideas, who dared to innovate" (Heilbroner, 1961, p. 278).

Very early on, political leaders in Korea saw the potential of private business as an engine of economic growth. Likewise, business saw in government a primary source of scarce capital that it badly needed. For both the government and big business, it was a marriage of convenience.

Certainly, from its early days of economic development, Korea did not lack the entrepreneurial role, nor the "mythology" of the heroics of legendary entrepreneurs, as modern-day demigods. But what is unique is the aberrant aggrandizement of big business that has become overly dominant in the politicoeconomic sphere. The dominant role of big business, however, would not have been possible without the direct support and acquiescence of the government. In fact, government subsidies to selected big businesses were such that, in the final analysis, government took the risk out of entrepreneurship, thus creating an ideal environment for the expansion and proliferation of *jaebuls*—the business conglomerates.

Also crucial in the scheme of the government-business policy was the peculiar role of commercial banks. Under the new political regime, commercial banks were nationalized and relegated to the role of supplying policy-directed loans to government-designated large enterprises.[4]

The government instituted a low interest rate policy:[5] throughout the 1970s (the period of financial repression), the real interest rates of bank loans fluctuated around zero. In order to contain the cost and to control the allocation of capital, government refused to let the interest rates and resource allocation be determined by the market. This created a large gap between the official bank interest rates and the unregulated money market rates, which, in turn, led to a gap between domestic savings and investment demands. The government chose to satisfy the excess demand for investment by resorting to foreign borrowing. In fact, the government controlled the bank credits and foreign capital to such an extent that the survival of a firm depended on accessibility to low-cost bank loans and foreign capital.

Outward-Looking Policy and Strategic Change in Comparative Advantage

The standard Heckscher-Ohlin theory in its simplest form leads one to expect to see trade dominated by exchanges that reflect the particular strengths of a country's factor-endowment (or supply—for instance, exports of capital-intensive goods by advanced countries and exports of labor-intensive goods or raw materials by underdeveloped countries).[6] This theory was applicable to Korea only in the early 1960s, during which the economy was poorly endowed with capital relative to its labor, and not surprisingly the exports consisted primarily of labor-intensive manufactured goods.

However, the changing pattern of Korean exports, especially in the 1970s and 1980s cannot be attributed so readily to the underlying advantage of Korea. Instead, trade seems to reflect strategic change in comparative advantage created by Korean firms through the help of government policies. In other words, in Korea there was a rapid change in the structure of trade, which is somewhat contrary to the kind of exchange envisioned in classical theory.

What is remarkable is that the changing character of trade resulting from the government-led economic strategy represents a new approach in trade theory as an alternative to the classical.

The new approach envisages the possibility of an imperfect international market in which "the advantages of large-scale production, the advantages of cumulative experience, and transitory advantages resulting from innovation" (Krugman, 1987, p. 15) can explain the changing character of trade. In this sense the new approach provides a rationale for a more activist trade policy, and for "the use of subsidies to enhance the strategic position of a domestic firm engaged in competition for world markets with a foreign rival" (Brander, 1987, p. 26).

How did this occur? Again, it goes back to the government-directed low-interest loans to businesses in selected industries contributing to a drastic increase in the wage-rental ratio, thereby causing business to move toward capital-intensive technology and to export more capital-intensive goods. A more celebrated case, if not the most blatant one, involved the government's intervention to promote the "heavy and chemical industries" in the 1970s.[7]

In order to marshal funds to support the investment in these industries, the government instituted the National Investment Fund in 1974. The funds were raised by compulsory deposits from banking as well as nonbank financial institutions, among others, to the Fund, and also by mobilizing public employee pension funds.

A study by Hong (Part II, below) shows that real interest rates in the 1960s and 1970s were –5.3 percent (1962–66), 5.7 percent (1967–71), –6.2 percent (1972–76) and –3.5 percent (1977–79). By 1975, the effective rate of protection (ERP) on the relatively capital-intensive manufacturing sectors amounted to as high as 275 percent before it came down to 72.5 percent in 1978. This is in sharp contrast with the ERPs for labor-intensive and moderately capital-intensive sectors, which turned out to be –30.5 percent and –12.4 percent respectively, in 1975. Also, the annual provision of interest subsidies expanded from 3 percent of the GNP in 1962–71 to 10 percent of the GNP in 1972–79.[8]

These policies were reinforced by the second stage import substitution (for example, of intermediate materials and capital goods) in the second half of the 1970s. In order to develop the shipbuilding, automobile, steel, and petrochemical industries and products, the government resorted to a 4.7-fold increase (from $4.3 billion in 1973 to $20.3 billion in 1979) in external finance to supplement internal resources. But the interest subsidies on foreign loans averaged about 6 percent of the GNP each year in the 1970s (Hong, Part II, below).

What is learned from this experience is an understanding of how the strategic choices made by the government can determine the structure of industries and the comparative advantages. This is not to say that Korea is unique in practicing deterministic change in comparative advantage nor to say that every strategic change was an unqualified success, but that Korea was unmatched in its speed and intensity in consciously altering its comparative advantage.

The effect of the outward-looking policy has been impressive, both in terms of the immediate objective of increasing the capacity to import and of the ultimate objective of raising economic efficiency through technology imports. In Korea, with its limited domestic market, the exploitation of the scale economies mandated the development of an exports market. Otherwise, the move toward capital-intensive technology accompanied by the scale economies would have entailed a serious unemployment problem.

The indirect benefits of an outward-oriented strategy are related to productivity increases made possible by more rapid technology transfer and diffusion into the domestic economy. Direct contacts with buyers and suppliers and international competition have disciplined Korean manufacturers and exporters to be more efficient.

The changing comparative advantage in Korea is clearly discernible in the structural change in the Korean economy. From 1962 (when the First Five-Year Plan was implemented) to 1979, the share of mining and manufacturing in the GNP increased from 14.6 percent to 28.7 percent. During the same period, commodity exports grew at the average annual rate of 40 percent. Equally spectacular was the shift in the composition of exports. The share of manufacturing in total exports increased from 22 percent to 90.1 percent. Up to 1962, food and live animals (SITC #1) and crude materials (SITC #2) accounted for over three quarters of the total exports; by 1979, the export dominance was taken over by manufactured goods classified by materials (SITC #6), machinery and transport (SITC #7), and the miscellaneous goods category (SITC #8), accounting for more than 85 percent of the total exports. It is also notable that the share of machinery and transport (SITC #7), which is often used as a barometer of industrialization, increased from a mere 2.6 percent in 1962 to 20.6 percent by 1979.

Last, Korea's outward-looking policy itself was far from that of a free-trade regime. The export promotion policy, which had considerable export biases, with a myriad of subsidies and incentives, was not accompanied by a symmetrical policy of import liberalization. In fact, the imports were strictly controlled by the quantitative restrictions (QRs) and tariff barriers; and serious attempts for import liberalization were not made until 1978.[9]

According to K. S. Kim (Part II, below), the degrees of liberalization on the basis of liberalization from QRs were merely 5 percent, on the average, until 1966, as compared with around 40.5 percent during the 1967–79 period. The overall degree of liberalization was 30, 50, and 60 percent mostly in an ascending order throughout the 1960s and 1970s compared with 70 and 80 percent after 1983.

Factor Distortion, Economies of Scale, and Entrepreneurial Dynamics

That the nature of market distortion in Korea is rather unique can be deduced from the paucity of empirical analysis in the literature dealing with the similar problem in other economies. Most studies on the factor market distortion have dealt only with the theoretical aspects of distortions, and a few that dealt with the empirical aspect of the problem have touched upon rather innocuous cases (relative to Korea), such as measuring the effect of wage differentials among industrial sectors or between agriculture and manufacturing (see Floystad, 1975).

In Korea, the capital stock grew at a dizzying annual rate of 15.2 percent and 24.7 percent during the 1961–72 and 1972–80 periods, respectively. This rapid accumulation of capital stock took place concurrently with massive investment subsidies granted to business, and a rising wage-rental ratio. An estimate by Kim and Roemer (1979, p. 73) shows a 3.4-fold increase in the wage-rental ratio between 1962 and 1975.

A corollary to massive channeling of government subsidies and the low-interest policy directed to business is the problem of massive market distortion in favor of capital-intensive sectors. In this investment milieu, no consistent cost-benefit analysis was used to rank projects according to their profitability or a rational management of the firm. These policies have reduced the rental price of capital drastically below the market price, causing a distortion in factor price and, with the Allen partial elasticity of substitution between labor and capital equal to one, a major distortion in factor proportion. The obvious consequence of the distortion in the factor market generally has led to a loss of allocative efficiency resulting in the community's output below the nondistorted transformation curve (see Hong, 1976, and Part II, below).

However, these studies almost uniformly ignore the more dynamic effect of the rapid accumulation of physical capital brought about through the reduced rental price of capital, that is, economies of scale and technological change. An estimate by Kwon and Williams (1982) on seven subsectors of Korean manufacturing shows substantial scale economies.[10] Also, in a study by Kwon (1986), the technology and scale economies have accounted for 44.6 and 38.1 percent of the total factor productivity, respectively, in Korean manufacturing (1961–80).

The economies of scale and technological change are also interrelated. For example, economies of scale relate to increasing possibilities of division and specialization of labor and increasing possibilities of using advanced technological developments and/or larger machines. The possibility of lowering costs per unit of output by technological methods increases as the plant size is increased. For larger outputs and plant sizes mass production technological methods can be used to effect reductions in per unit costs. Technological possibilities represent a very important explanation of the increasing efficiency of larger plant sizes, up to a limit. As mentioned above, in Korea with its limited domestic market, the exploitation of scale economies necessitated the development of an export market. Otherwise, the capital-intensive technology accompanied by the scale economies would have caused a serious unemployment problem. Likewise, given the rate of increase in the wage-rental ratio, and the size of the elasticity of substitution between labor and capital, the increasing wage rate would have caused a severe displacement of labor. However, this was prevented by the rapid expansion of exports.

To this we must also add the entrepreneurial role and external economies of production engendered by the availability of cheap capital that in turn invigorated the economic atmosphere. An external economy occurs when an action taken by an economic unit results in uncompensated benefits to others. In this case there is a difference between private and social returns, the gains to society being greater than the gains to the firm. Indeed, in the 1960s and 1970s every aspect of these elements was played out almost to the limit in Korea.

Although it is not possible to quantify the net effect of the allocative inefficiency and the efficiency from the economies of scale and the rest, it is quite possible that the interplay of these positive and negative factors may have contributed to the relatively low growth rate of total factor productivity (that is, 1.90 percent in 1961–71 and 1.08 percent in 1971–78) (see Kwon and Yuhn, Part III, below). Nonetheless, from this, together with the records of spectacular actual growth (nearly 9 percent) of GDP, we can surmise that the inefficiency caused by the factor price distortion is unlikely to have had any significant effect on the overall efficiency of the economy or that the efficiency has more than offset the inefficiency.

Jaebul, Business Concentration, and Land Concentration

The rapid rise in big business conglomerates is another striking feature that also finds its origins in the none too delicate nexus of the government, banks, and business. Most of these conglomerates, known in Korea as *jaebuls*, were founded less than a generation ago as small businesses, have continued to expand by diversifying into a wide range of business ventures, and are engaged in the production and export of almost everything from wigs to automobiles.

In the earlier days of rapid economic development, the government explicitly or implicitly favored big businesses by placing resources in the hands of those entrepreneurs who had demonstrated their competitiveness in the international arena. The superior efficiency in terms of organizational and entrepreneurial advantages possessed by the big business groups, and/or large scale, capital-intensive production requiring modern technology were in jaebuls' favor. Especially during the period of "growth first" policy, the relationship between the government and large business groups was a principal-agency relationship in which the government acted as a principal body in designing economic plans and the businesses acted as agents for executing the plans and meeting the targets (Y. K. Lee, Part V, below). During the same period, the entrepreneurial goal was to maximize the given firm's growth to achieve a critical minimum size, at which time the government would be unable to allow insolvency or bankruptcy of large firms to occur in fear of widespread economic and political repercussion (P. J. Kim, Part IV, below). In such an environment, large firms expanded further, and quite often to the brink of bankruptcy, with certain assurance that government-designated banks would come to their rescue. More often than not, commercial banks were directed by the government to bail out large, ailing firms.

A corollary to the rapid expansion of *jaebuls* is their "excessively" high financial leverage, which constitutes another peculiarly Korean feature of financial structure among jaebuls. E. H. Kim (Part V, below) shows that during the period from 1984 through 1986, more than one third of the largest 10 percent of the firms listed with the Korean Stock Exchange had equity ratios[11] below 5 percent. The same study also shows that the average equity ratio for all nonfinancial firms (including jaebuls) listed on the stock exchange was 16 percent during the 1977–86 period, as compared with 40 percent and 50 percent for Japan and the United States, respectively. A peculiar income tax system and government's frequent bailouts of ailing large firms have been cited as key factors contributing to this extreme financial leverage.

This excessive financial leverage among large Korean firms tends to diminish the resilience of an economy in the face of adverse economic shock. Other potential dangers (the concentration of wealth and of political power that is inimical to democracy, and conflict between private efficiency and social efficiency resulting from economic concentration) are also present as discussed by others in the literature. Recent labor unrest in Korea is symptomatic of underlying problems endemic to Korean business engendered by the government policy.[12]

In Korea *jaebul* groups' control is concentrated in the hands of owner-founders. Although Korea's *jaebuls* are modeled after the Japanese *zaibatsu*, one of the basic differences between the two is that whereas Korea's *jaebuls* rely heavily on the government-controlled credit institutions, for their capital Japanese *zaibatsu* have their own banks.

The market share of the top ten *jaebuls* in terms of sales in manufacturing was 21.2 percent in 1978. Since then their share has grown rapidly and by 1982, the share rose to 30.2 percent. One of the notable aspects of the growth of the jaebuls' market share is that during the same period, their share of employment had decreased from 13.9 percent in 1978 to 12.2 percent in 1982 (Y. K. Lee, Part V, below). The leading four *jaebuls*—Samsung, Hyundai, Lucky-Goldstar, and Daewoo—are substantially larger than the next largest *jaebul*.

In 1982, 10 out of 27 private less-developed country (LDC) firms that made Fortune's list of the 500 largest non-U.S. firms were Korean. Most groups have general trading companies (GTCs) and construction companies as their major business lines (Y. K. Lee, Part V, below).

Another by-product of the government policy toward big business has been the gradual concentration of land ownership. In the fifties and early sixties when the land was redistributed to farmers under the Land Reform Act of 1949, Korea was an "egalitarian" society with even distribution of land and *poverty*. However, over the period of a quarter century since then, as the national wealth grew, land ownership shifted gradually into the hands of a selected few. Approximately 65.2 percent of the private land is now owned by the top 5 percent in income. A series of intensive speculative activities have caused the price of land to increase by 840 percent over the period between 1975 and 1988 as compared with the 290 percent increase in the wholesale price index during the same period.[13]

In the recent period when industrial activities were marred by violent labor unrest, income from land speculation had become a more lucrative channel for making money than normal business activity, so much so that as of 1987 the ratio of capital gain from land transaction to GNP was 35.7 percent. Government is currently preparing several measures to put an end to the land speculation.

KOREA VERSUS TAIWAN, HONG KONG, AND SINGAPORE

Some argue that Korea's experience is nothing unique compared with the experiences of close neighbors Japan, Taiwan, Hong Kong, and Singapore. Some go even further by arguing that since Taiwan, Hong Kong, and Singapore have done so well through market economy, Korea might have done better had it been left to the market mechanism without the government's intervention or that Korea has done so well in spite of the negative effect of governmental intervention.

These views miss some important points. First of all, one should keep in mind that the population of Taiwan, Hong Kong, and Singapore are all ethnic Chinese, who are, unlike Koreans, traditionally well versed in commerce. The second point is that even for Taiwan, the role of government in economic development was significant, although not as extensive as it was in Korea. Hong Kong's background is unique in that, "over a hundred year period, Hong Kong has served as an *entrepôt* which [has] enabled native Hong Kong business to master the art of doing business with the whole world market." Furthermore, "the extensive network of overseas Chinese merchants and massive post-war immigration of capable entrepreneurs from the mainland also enhanced Hong Kong's experience in global trading" (Hong, 1987, p. 5). A similar logic applies also to both Singapore and Taiwan if not to the same extent.

A point of significance here is that, given the commercial history of the ethnic Chinese (whether they are in Taiwan, Hong Kong, or Singapore) and their "outward" inclination in trade, government intervention may not have been as necessary as it was for Korea.

Although the abundance of economic controls exercised by the government through a succession of four-year plans makes it difficult to call Taiwan's economy a hands-off laissez-faire economy, the Taiwanese know how to let market forces take their course (Scitovsky, 1986, p. 145). Of all the differences between the two countries, perhaps none epitomizes the differences in political philosophy more sharply than the interest rate policy and the policy on business concentration. Whereas in Korea the interest rate was suppressed far below the market rate (through financial repression), in Taiwan, by and large, the interest rate was left to the market force (Cho, Part IV, below). In contrast to Korea, Taiwan's businesses are much less concentrated. It is a "grass-roots" economy that benefits the masses through a relatively even distribution of income. But one should keep in mind that the "egalitarian" system in Taiwan results from a consciousness on the part of the government stemming from a bitter lesson learned from its defeat in mainland China—neglecting the plight of the masses becomes a self-defeating prophecy.

In the final analysis, given the paucity of business experience especially in international trade, and a series of tumultuous political events that swept across Korea in the first half of the twentieth century, it is not difficult to envision a larger role for the government in Korea than in other countries.

Another notable contrast between the Koreans and the Chinese is temperament: whereas Koreans may tend to be "impetuous,"[14] "aggressive," and "adventurous," Chinese can be spoken of as being "deliberate" and "enduring." Once Koreans discovered economic development, it suddenly became a national obsession like a brush fire, a focal point that galvanized the collective yearning of the population. Economic development came to be viewed by Koreans as a vehicle for ensuring a rightful place for Korea in the modern world. In Taiwan, however, reason rather than passion prevailed, and economic development was viewed as a means of raising the standard of living.

IS THE KOREAN MODEL APPLICABLE TO OTHERS?

The first question to be asked is, "Is the Korean model of the 1960s and 1970s applicable to the Korean economy of the 1980s and thereafter?" The answer is clearly negative. By the late 1980s the economy had already outgrown the early model through its maturity toward a free market system. Korea is now at a crossroad between the "growth-first" policy and the "growth-with-equality" policy, with the latter emerging as a more likely option for the future course of development.

The second question is, "Is the Korean model applicable to other economies?" This time, the answer is "yes" provided some modification is made to suit the particular need of the country, based on its preconditions. The Korean model has worked in Korea because the particular set of policies put into practice in Korea happened to be an optimum (or fairly close to it), given the peculiar temperament of Koreans, together with its socioeconomic circumstances.

Whether or not one strictly adheres to a unidirectional view of development (in terms of stages or a specific succession of time segments) suggested by Rostow (1960), the prevailing wisdom holds that what happens now is, in a very important way, a function of how it was yesterday. In other words, economic development seldom evolves in a vacuum. If we accept this general proposition, it becomes obvious that not all the clues for Korea's economic development can be found exclusively in the sixties. Instead, some attention needs to be given to the preconditions that existed prior to the sixties.

One of the preconditions often mentioned is the legacy of Japanese colonization of Korea (1910–45). Perhaps the most important legacy of the colonial period, if there is one, may be that the Japanese-initiated industrialization in Korea's backyard, albeit an alien undertaking, might have worked as a key element in permanently altering the Koreans' view of themselves and the world, and also in changing the consciousness of the Koreans that there is an alternative to subsistence agriculture as a means of economic livelihood. When Korea regained its independence, it had a choice of rejecting the socioeconomic system established during the colonial period and reverting to its traditional system, yet there was no question in the minds of people that they would go forward with the modernization.[15]

Some may reject the validity of the colonial legacy argument by invoking the "negative correlation between colonial control and the timing and pace of economic growth" observed in some studies (Hagen, 1962, p. 19). Yet, we see today that every one of the Asian NICs—Hong Kong, Korea, Singapore, Taiwan—was a colony not too long ago.

What is evident is that even the colonial system had a silver lining in its ominous cloud, and some former colonies were able to build on the silver lining while others were not. The four Asian NICs happened to be among the few who belong to the former group.

In addition to the colonial legacy argument, the importance of education in economic development has rightfully received a great deal of attention because education tends to improve the quality of workers and to promote socioeconomic integration and modernization. One of the major accomplishments of the post-Liberation governments is the massive investment in human capital. The government (1945–60) put into effect the universal education system. The school enrollment at all levels and educational facilities expanded rapidly. Between 1945 and 1960 the illiteracy rate dropped from 78 percent to 28 percent, and the enrollment in higher education increased by the factor of 12. Moreover, a large number of students were sent overseas for advanced education. In fact, Korea's educational effort was so intense that its level of human resource development became comparable to that of countries with per capita GNPs three times the Korean level (Cole and Lyman, 1971, p. 138).

Unlike the industrialization in Western Europe, which is said to have occurred through invention and innovation, the mode of Korea's industrialization (like Japan's) has been one of learning or borrowing technology from others. Without an abundant and relatively highly trained stock of human resources, the transfer of advanced technology in Korea would have taken a much longer time.

In his schema of the stages of economic growth, Rostow (1960) suggests the "establishment of effective national government" among the preconditions. However, it is quite unlikely that the type as well as the role of government in Korea during the period of rapid growth was what Rostow had envisioned. In fact, the Korean government carried the meaning of Rostow's "effective national government" to the nth degree within the fuzzy confines of the market system in generating development in Korea. In this respect neither the Rostovian schema nor the neoclassical structural change model holds neatly for Korea. Strictly speaking, one is hard put to find a proper place for the Korean model in the conventional lexicon of development economics.

The outward-looking policy that has been adopted successfully in Korea and several other countries has proven to be an effective policy for developing an economy, but one should not hastily conclude that it is a panacea or a "free ticket" to economic growth. One is reminded of the parable of the sower: "As he sowed, some seeds fell on the edge of the path, and the birds came and ate them up, others fell on patches of rock . . ., others fell among thorns . . ., and others fell on rich soil and produced their crop" (Matthew 13:1).

In the 1960s Korea, along with several other economies, happened to be the right soil with the right set of preconditions and governmental policies, while many other countries were not.[16]

Evidence reveals that export-oriented policy cannot be successfully adopted in all countries. Krueger (1981, p. 4) suggests that a successful export promotion policy requires some initial preconditions. In reference to this, some raise the doubt that if these initial conditions are really important determinants of successful export-promotion strategies, it will be difficult to claim that export-oriented strategies, if adopted, will produce better economic performance in developing economies.

CLOSING REMARKS

This chapter has examined several uncommon characteristics of the Korean economic development that makes the Korean experience a new paradigm. Economic growth was a single overriding national concern during the period between the early 1960s and the late 1980s, and Korea was a spectacular success in this regard. Lately, however, some of the economic issues that had been neglected during the "growth-first" period have emerged as issues that can no longer be ignored. In a quick succession, the rights and the welfare of the workers on one hand and the concentration of land ownership and land speculation on the other have become the two most urgent national issues.

In the wake of these new issues, the government is forced to shift the policy emphasis from "growth-first" to more balanced growth. It appears now that Korea is about to bid a farewell to an era and grope for a new beginning in which it hopes the economic growth will be more balanced and less government-led.

NOTES

I wish to express my gratitude to Y. C. Kim for helpful and considerate comments.

1. Empirical estimations of the effect of government expenditures on output are reported in this book by Jisoon Lee and Paul Evans. See Jones and Sakong (1980) for the role of government, business, and entrepreneurship in Korea's development.

2. Jones and Sakong (1980) labelled this type of practice a "zero-sum" activity.

3. Circumstantial evidence also points to the possibility that the military leadership, many of whom had been trained in the Japanese military, must have been keenly aware of the dynamic economic change taking place in postwar Japan, and saw in Japanese success (with its outward-looking economic policy) a possible path for Korea.

4. Similar roles were also assigned to the specialized banks, that is, the Import-Export Bank of Korea, the Korea Exchange Bank, the Korea Development Bank, and so forth.

5. The interest reform of 1966–69 doubled the maximum rate from 15 to 30 percent per annum to induce domestic savings and foreign capital, but the reform was short lived. See P. J. Kim (Part IV, below) for further details.

6. A. V. Deardorff (1983) provides a comprehensive survey of empirical literature to support this.

7. The sudden shift toward the heavy and chemical industries was deemed necessary to sustain rapid growth in the face of changing domestic and external environments, for example, the importance of the heavy and chemical industries as integral elements for the self-reliant defense, growing protectionism among the industrial economies, and increasing competition for exports among the Asian NICs.

8. Interest subsidy equals the rate of return on capital minus average real interest rate on bank loans (see Hong, Part II, below).

9. A short-lived import liberalization occurred in 1967–68.

10. The dual returns to scale estimate, calculated as the reciprocal of the elasticity of cost with respect to output using the translog cost function turned out to be 1.54.

11. The equity ratios are the ratio of average equity to total value (equity plus debt). E. H. Kim used equity ratio based on market value instead of book value to avoid bias.

12. Until the mid 1980s, the labor movement was suppressed through government's authoritarian paternalism (see Se-Il Park and Choongsoo Kim, Parts IV and VI, below).

13. See Republic of Korea, *The Report of the Public-Nature-Concept of Land Study Group*, May 1989.

14. See J. H. Yoo (1984, p. 1696).

15. Institutional and attitudinal changes during this period and the period following Korea's independence are two of the six characteristics essential for the economic growth defined by Kuznets (1973).

16. Third World countries have, in the past, benefited disproportionately less from their trade with developed nations and many may have in fact even suffered absolutely from it (Todaro, 1985, pp. 392–95).

REFERENCES

Brander, James A., "Rationales for Strategic Trade and Industrial Policy," in Paul Krugman, ed., *Strategic Trade Policy and the New International Economics*, Cambridge: MIT Press, 1987.

Cole, David C., and Lyman, P. N., *Korean Development*, Cambridge: Harvard University Press, 1971.

Economic Planning Board, *Summary of the First Five-Year Economic Plan, 1962–1966*, Seoul, 1962.

Deardorff, A. V., "Testing Trade Theories," in R. W. Jones and P. B. Kenen, eds., *Handbook of International Economics*, Vol. 1, Amsterdam: North Holland, 1983.

Floystad, G., "Distortions in the Factor Market: An Empirical Investigation," *Review of Economics and Statistics*, 57, May 1975, 200–13.

Hagen, Everett E., *On the Theory of Social Change*, Homewood: Dorsey Press, 1962.

Heilbroner, Robert L., *The Worldly Philosophers*, New York: Simon and Schuster, 1961.

Hong, Wontack, *Factor Supply and Factor Intensity of Trade in Korea*, Seoul: KDI Press, 1976.

———, "Export-Oriented Growth of Korea: A Possible Path to Advanced Economy." A revised version of the seminar paper No. 382, June 1987, Institute for International Economic Studies, University of Stockholm.

Jones, Leroy, and Sakong, Il, *Government, Business and Entrepreneurship in Economic Development: The Korean Case*, Cambridge: Harvard University Press, 1980.

Kim, Kwang S., "Export-Led Industrial Growth Reconsidered," a comment in Wontack Hong and L. B. Krause, eds. *Trade and Growth of Advanced Developing Countries in the Pacific Basin*, Seoul: Korea Development Institute, 1981.

———, and Roemer, M., *Growth and Structural Transformation*, Cambridge: Harvard University Press, 1979.

Krueger, Anne O., "Export-Led Industrial Growth Reconsidered," in Wontack Hong and L. B. Krause, eds., *Trade and Growth of Advanced Developing Countries in the Pacific Basin*, Seoul: Korea Development Institute, 1981.

Krugman, Paul R., "New Thinking about Trade Policy," in Paul Krugman, ed., *Strategic Trade Policy and the New International Economics*, Cambridge: MIT Press, 1987.

Kuznets, Simon, "Modern Economic Growth: Findings and Reflections," *American Economic Review, 63*, June 1973, 247–58.

Kwon, J. K., "Capacity Utilization, Economies of Scale and Technical Change in the Growth of Total Factor Productivity: An Explanation of South Korean Manufacturing Growth," *Journal of Development Economics, 11,* November 1986, 215–26.

———, and Williams, M., "The Structure of Production in South Korea's Manufacturing Sector," *Journal of Development Economics, 11,* October 1982, 215–26.

New Testament of the Jerusalem Bible, Alexander Jones, ed., Garden City: Image Books, 1969.

Republic of Korea, *The Report of the Public-Nature-Concept of Land Study Group* (in Korean), Seoul, May 1989.

Rostow, W. W., *The Stages of Economic Growth*, Cambridge: Cambridge University Press, 1960.

Scitovsky, Tibor, "Economic Development in Taiwan and South Korea, 1965–1981," in Lawrence J. Lau, ed., *Models of Development*, San Francisco: ICS Press, 1986.

Todaro, Michael P., *Economic Development in the Third World*, New York: Longman, 1985.
Yoo, Jang H., "Korea and Japan: Some Crucial Structural Differences," in *Papers and Proceedings of the International Conference of Korean Economists*, Seoul, 1984.

Part Two

TRADE POLICIES AND DEVELOPMENT

Ever since Korea stumbled upon an outward-looking trade policy in the early 1960s, the economic fortune of the country has changed dramatically for the better. Although the trade theory provides no clear guidance as to the relative effectiveness of alternative trade policies on growth, Korea's success played a key role tipping a balance in favor of export-promotion policies over import-substitution policies as an instrument for generating economic growth.

This section starts with a rather revealing chapter by P. Petri that addresses some fundamental questions regarding the unusual success of Korea's trade. Petri identifies five specific aspects of Korea's trade performance in which Korea stands apart from averages. By analyzing each of the distinctive characteristics, Petri attempts to explain why Korean trade developed as it did and how its unique features can be traced to the policies and circumstances of the Korean experience.

Korea's trade policy consists largely of exchange rate policy, import restrictions (and more recently, import liberalization) and government subsidies of various forms. These will be addressed by the next three chapters. The chapter by B. H. Koo and W. A. Park reviews Korea's exchange rate policy in comparison with the Latin American experiences. Korea has, in general, maintained sound finance, strict capital control, and macroeconomic stability, which has prevented massive movements in the real exchange rate. Unlike Latin America, Korea focused on productivity growth as the key to maintaining export competitiveness. Upon their examination of the relationship between exchange rates, prices, and profit margins based on the estimated aggregate pass-through rates, Koo and Park conclude that

Korean firms are more concerned with maintaining their market shares abroad than with immediate profits.

Import policy (that is, import restrictions and/or import liberalization), which makes up another key element of Korea's trade policy, is taken up by K. S. Kim in the third chapter. Korea's more permanent import liberalization did not take place until 1978. The study examines the impact of liberalization (that is, loosening QRs and reducing tariff barriers) at the sectoral level, and observes that import liberalization tended to increase imports, but that the upward trends were not statistically significant. The study also shows some adverse effects of liberalization on domestic production and employment during the first period (1965-67), but no significant effects during the second period (1978-85). This may be attributable to the fact that the policy implementation was more gradual, Korea became more competitive, and the exchange rates were more realistic in the second period.

The study by W. T. Hong examines the possible effects of market distortions on the polarization of industries—between the capital-intensive sectors and the labor-intensive sectors—in Korean manufacturing. During the 1966-83 period, there was fairly rapid expansion in exports of some highly labor-intensive sectors and also in some highly capital-intensive sectors. Hong cites the "protection" of Korea's established export markets for labor-intensive commodities and the growing diversification of Korea's exports into the high-quality and skill-intensive commodities, as partial explanation for this phenomenon. The rapid expansion in the exports of the capital-intensive sector is as expected in view of the factor market distortion and massive export subsidies.

In the last chapter, D. Dollar and K. Sokoloff show that both the Heckscher-Ohlin and Ricardian models of international trade provide explanation for the changing comparative advantage in Korea's manufacturing and its exports. They also show that the rapid growth in exports in the particular industries is related to the rapid growth of total factor productivity (TFP) in the same industries, suggesting that industry-specific technological advance is also an important source of comparative advantages, as implied by the Ricardian model. They also point out that government policy, to create comparative advantages in a particular manufacturing sector, will be successful only if that particular industry has the necessary technical capability; otherwise the growth in capital-labor ratio will be offset by a relatively poor TFP performance, and it is difficult to choose the winner in advance.

Altogether, these authors offer varying viewpoints and valuable insight on Korea's trade policy.

4

Korean Trade as Outlier: An Economic Anatomy

Peter A. Petri

INTRODUCTION

The adjective "miracle" applies comfortably to Korea's trade record. In three decades, Korea transformed an internationally dependent, nonindustrial economy into the world's twelfth largest trading power—an achievement that has justifiably emerged as *the* model of outward oriented development. The question many policymakers now ask is how Korea "did it" and how its strategies might be replicated elsewhere. But what exactly did Korea do? In what respects is Korean trade exceptional? This study addresses these fundamental and yet neglected questions with quantitative and institutional detail on some particularly interesting features of Korean trade.

The study spotlights five specific dimensions of trade performance in which Korea stands far apart from world averages. The first and most obvious sense in which Korea is an outlier is in the rapidity of its export growth. Second, Korea is exceptional in the high level of its economic openness, that is, in the volume of imports and exports relative to output. Third, the composition of Korean exports has proved remarkably flexible. Fourth, Korean exports are unusually well diversified. Fifth, Korean exports have succeeded despite the fact that they are highly protection prone—that is, face higher tariffs and more frequent quantitative restrictions than the exports of other countries. These five dimensions do not encompass all that is interesting about Korean trade, but they provide a useful vehicle for contrasting Korea's experience with those of less successful countries.

One goal of this study is to put the Korean trade miracle into sharper quantitative relief. A second and more elusive goal is to explain *why* Korean trade developed as it did—how its exceptional features can be traced to the policies and circumstances of the Korean experience. The first goal is addressed by developing

Figure 4.1
World Distribution of Export Growth Rates

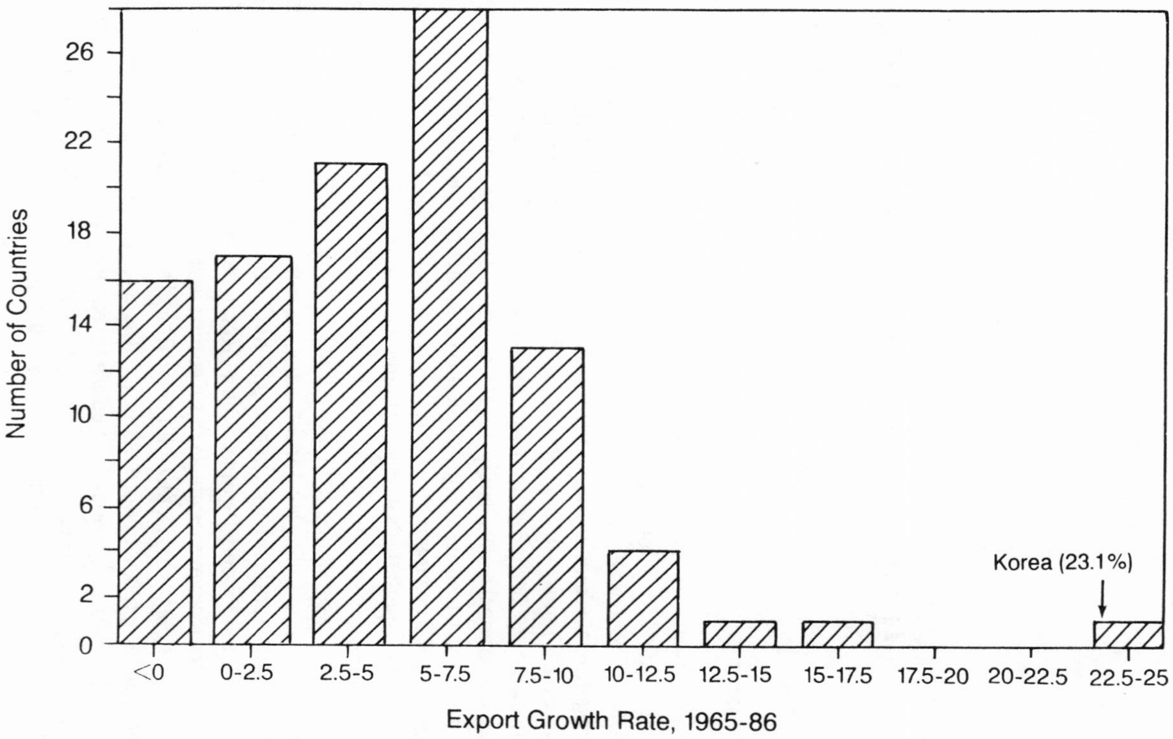

Number of Countries

Export Growth Rate, 1965-86

Korea (23.1%)

Source: World Development Report, 1988.

quantitative indicators of Korean trade performance and comparing these with corresponding global averages. The second goal is tackled by proposing several plausible explanations for each of the five unusual aspects of Korean trade. In confronting facts with alternative explanations, the chapter raises many questions for future research. Clearly, many interesting and potentially important linkages will have to be investigated in the context of the Korean experience.

In the following five sections, five distinctive features of Korea's trade performances are presented one by one along with the explanations of underlying causes. Conclusions are given in the last section.

EXCEPTIONALLY FAST GROWTH OF EXPORTS

Korea's trade takeoff began in the early 1960s with exchange rate devaluations and the introduction of comprehensive export incentives. Figure 4.1 shows the distribution of export growth rates over the 1965–86 period for all countries for which these data are available. Korean exports grew at 23.1 percent per annum, more rapidly than in any other country. Although the growth rate of Korean exports receded into the low teens in the 1980s, Korea's performance remained impressive given its now considerable market shares, and the emergence of new competitors, such as China, Thailand, and Turkey, with trade policies closely modeled on Korea's own experience.

In a sense, exceptional export growth is the key fact to be explained with regard to Korean trade. We shall begin with "narrow" explanations focusing on policies and factors that affected overall export performance. A more complete explanation, however, needs to delve more deeply into the economy's remarkable microeconomic flexibility, as manifested in the exceptional fluidity and diversity of Korea's export composition. These characteristics will be explored below.

Low Starting Rate

A trivial but often neglected reason for Korea's rapid export growth is that Korean exports started out very low. Until the early 1960s, Korean foreign exchange needs were essentially covered by U.S. military aid and procurement arising out of the war of the 1950s. Indeed, a peculiar arrangement that tied dollar payments to the official won exchange rate discouraged exports by providing a strong incentive for overvaluation (Krueger, 1979). As military revenues declined and resources were shifted into exports, Korean export growth shot into the 30–50 percent range. As will be shown in the next section, however, Korean exports became "normal" by the late 1960s, and progress since then can no longer be attributed to the special circumstances related to the Korean war.

Properly Valued Currency

Beginning with sharp devaluations in 1961 and 1963, and then following through with frequent subsequent adjustments, the Korean government generally maintained the real value of the won near the level needed for current account balance (Dervis and Petri, 1987). The main exception to this generalization occurred during an approximately five-year period in the late 1970s, when Korea aggressively sought to shift its economic structure toward heavy industry. As the government tried to control inflation by fixing the nominal exchange rate, export growth suffered. But this period represented an aberration and Korea otherwise avoided the overvaluations that have plagued economic policy in many other developing countries. Realistic exchange rate valuation and a relatively neutral incentive regime (see below) are considered the dominant factors behind Korean success in market-oriented interpretations of the Korean experience (Krueger, 1985).

Aggressive Export Promotion

In the mid-1960s Korea adopted a now famous package of innovative export promotion policies, including automatic and subsidized export credit, an extremely effective duty-drawback system, and direct subsidies to exporting activities. Exporters were also recognized in public ceremonies and received privileged access to government-controlled markets, especially including credit through the government-controlled banking system (Rhee et al., 1984; Jones and Sakong, 1980). Since interest rates on bank credit were at times 20 percent or more below interest rates in the unregulated curb market, access to bank credit offered a particularly strong financial incentive (Cho, 1986).

The important fact seems to be that in the early years after President Park gained control in 1961, government influence was used to promote exports without significant sectoral bias (Frank et al., 1975; Westphal and Kim, 1982). Export subsidies were applied essentially across the board, helping to offset the effects of import restrictions. There is even evidence that some import restrictions were trade promoting, in that they were strategically assigned to reward export-oriented firms. In this vein, Jones and Sakong (1980, p. 304) comment that the trade regime shifted from imposing zero-sum transfers designed to achieve political goals to zero-sum transfers designed to enhance the profits of successful exporters.

Entrepreneurship in the Export Sector

Regardless of which policies actually triggered the rapid growth of Korean exports, there is little doubt that the export sector was exceptionally responsive and attracted a remarkable inflow of entrepreneurial talent. The roots of Korean entrepreneurship are puzzling, since in the decades prior to World War II the Korean economy was closely controlled by Japan and few Koreans had the opportunity to own or manage enterprise. Nevertheless, Korean cultural propensities, exposure to Japanese management practices, and in a few cases Japanese university training apparently provided a solid foundation for Korean enterprise following the war. One possible explanation, based on the findings of Jones and Sakong (1980), is that many postwar entrepreneurs came from a landowning elite that was disenfranchised by the Japanese occupation and postwar land reform. These classes emphasized education (perhaps because other forms of investment were even riskier) and ultimately had few opportunities outside industry to apply their resources and skills.

Enhanced rewards in trade-oriented activities may have also helped to attract the best entrepreneurial talent into the export sector. Export success was rewarded with subsidized capital and other privileges, and sharp financial distinctions arose between profitable export businesses and other kinds of enterprise. In contrast to policies in most other countries, which more typically tax profits and subsidize losses, Korean export promotion amplified, rather than dampened, differences between successful and unsuccessful businesses. This sharply inflected reward system undoubtedly helped to select talented entrepreneurs into (and less talented entrepreneurs out of) the export sector.

Favorable External Environment

Korea's initial export takeoff occurred in the context of diminishing protection, worldwide and in the important U.S. market. By today's standards, there was little competition from other developing-country exporters of manufactured products. In addition, Korea's export drive was facilitated by the contemporaneous growth of Japan. As argued in more detail below, Japan's own progress facilitated Korean entry into a succession of important markets. To support its major industrial investments, Korea borrowed extensively in international markets, on very favorable terms. By the time world markets tightened in the late 1970s and early 1980s, Korea had established substantial market positions and a solid technological base for more advanced manufacturing. And in the 1980s, Korea's external economy received an additional favorable boost from the "three lows"—low oil prices, low interest rates, and the low dollar. In all of these important dimensions, countries attempting to duplicate Korean strategies today face a far less favorable environment.

EXCEPTIONALLY HIGH LEVEL OF ECONOMIC OPENNESS

It is not widely appreciated that by the late 1980s Korea had become the most open of the world's larger economies. Figure 4.2 shows the international distribution of a particular measure of openness, the sum of exports plus imports to GNP.

Figure 4.2
World Distribution of Openness (Larger Countries)

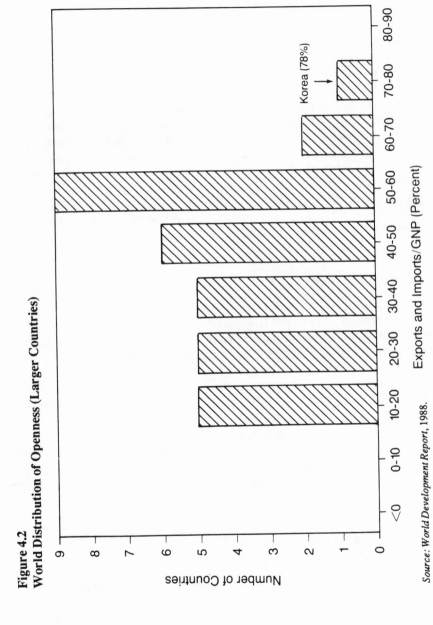

Source: World Development Report, 1988.

Figure 4.3
Exports Relative to Norm

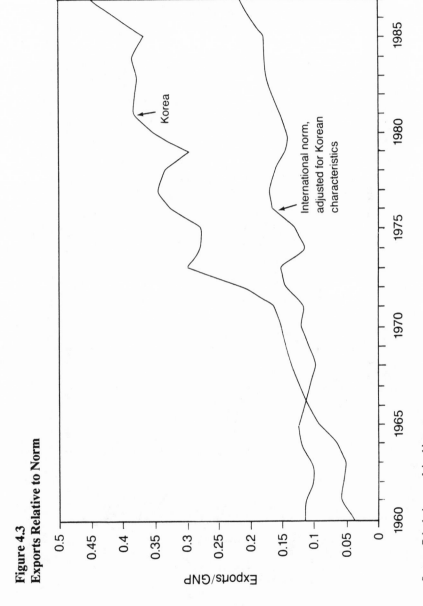

Korea

International norm,
adjusted for Korean
characteristics

Exports/GNP

Source: Calculations explained in text.

Figure 4.4
Imports Relative to Norm

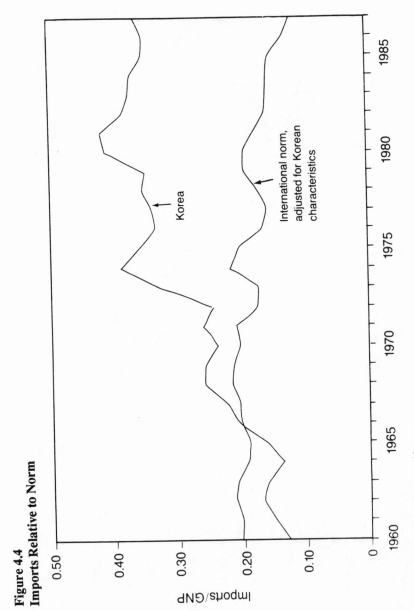

Imports/GNP

Korea

International norm,
adjusted for Korean
characteristics

1960   1965   1970   1975   1980   1985

0.50   0.40   0.30   0.20   0.10   0

Source: Calculations explained in text.

The figure is based on data for medium to large countries (here defined as having populations of 20 million or more) and indicates that Korea was the most open economy in this group. In 1986, the next most open of these larger economies, Kenya and Morocco, had trade-GNP ratios of only 64 percent compared with Korea's 78 percent.

In gauging these statistics of openness, it is useful to control four factors that are likely to lead to differences in openness across countries, including factors such as population size, income level, external resource flows, and distance from trading partners. For example, a large economy that can achieve domestic scale economies in a wide range of activities should have a lower index of openness than a smaller, necessarily more specialized economy.

On the basis of a systematic analysis of the relationship between trading propensities and country characteristics in a large sample of countries, Chenery and Syrquin (1975) have estimated regressions to predict "normal" levels of openness, given values for the factors cited, save distance from trade partners. These regressions permit us to calculate, year by year, the normal level of openness for a country with Korea's evolving demographic and economic circumstances.

The comparison of Korea's actual trade with the predicted normal level shows, to begin with, that the Korean economy was certainly *not* open in the 1950s. Figures 4.3 and 4.4[1] indicate that in 1960 Korean exports were about one-third as high, and imports about two-thirds as high, as predicted by international regressions for a country with Korea's size, income, and external aid inflows. Figures 4.3 and 4.4 also show that Korea's export and import levels passed international norms in the mid-1960s and went on to exceed them by an increasing margin in subsequent years. By the late 1980s Korean trade exceeded international norms by a factor between two and three.

These results notwithstanding, Korea is not generally viewed as an open economy. In popular discussion Korea is frequently equated with Japan as a country with unusually closed markets. These impressions are partly based on a history of interventionist industrial policy, relatively high tariffs, and strategic protection in selected manufacturing and agricultural sectors (USITC, 1985). Given protectionism, how did Korea achieve such high levels of openness?

Free Trade for the Export Sector

While general access to Korean markets has been subject to extensive tariff and non-tariff barriers (more on general liberalization below), Korean exporters enjoyed preferential access to imported components and raw materials from early on. The principal device for assuring this access was a system of "domestic letters of credit" (DLCs)—documents opened by banks to exporting companies when these companies received their export letters of credit LCs. DLCs enabled companies to receive inputs duty free and gave them automatic access to subsidized trade finance

(Rhee et al., 1984). DLCs also permitted exporters to buy imports that would have been otherwise restricted. Moreover, some of these benefits could be passed on by the exporter to its domestic suppliers, since banks were authorized to open further DLCs on the basis of a DLC.

In effect, exporters were largely exempt from trade barriers. Calculations by Westphal and Kim (1982), for example, showed that Korea collected only a fraction of its supposedly high tariffs because a large share of imports were purchased by exporters. Exporters had great freedom in sourcing components and raw materials abroad and presumably adopted import-intensive production techniques. Calculations with input-output tables show that the direct and indirect import content of Korean trade has been very high from the early 1960s on. Even in 1985, with a large and more sophisticated domestic base for exporting activities, the input-output table compiled by the Bank of Korea shows that approximately 36 percent of the value of exports consisted of imported products.

An interesting consequence of these policies, discussed in connection with the diversification of Korean exports (see below) is that many Korean export industries turned out to be rather "shallow." Intraindustry trade was high relative to inter-industry trade and many exporters concentrated on narrow segments of industries. Put another way, in this essentially free environment, Korean companies could afford to enter even those exporting activities in which their advantage was limited to small links within a lengthy production chain.

Historical Ties with Japan

In the initial years following the Japanese occupation in 1910, Korea served mainly as a source of Japanese agricultural imports. As World War II approached, Korea was increasingly integrated into the Japanese industrial effort and received invaluable exposure to advanced industrial practices. While the political context of this relationship was obviously painful, it ultimately provided tangible economic benefits. Koreans became familiar with Japanese language, culture, and enterprise, and came to rely closely on Japan for technology, machinery, and intermediate inputs.

Korea maintained an intensive trading relationship with Japan after World War II and there is considerable evidence that Korea actively "followed" Japan in its more recent industrial policies and business strategies (Petri, 1988). Korea's famous conglomerates, for example, are the result of explicit policies designed to promote heavy industry along the Japanese model, that is, through the formation of large general trading companies (GTCs). Korea has also benefited from Japan's opening of foreign markets for products that Korea would also later export. Japanese penetration established a favorable reputation for East Asian products— an externality that served Korea well as it later targeted a series of Japanese product niches.

The special relationship with Japan provides a pair of reinforcing explanations for Korea's high trading propensity. On one hand, Japan's pathbreaking trading experience made it easier for Korea to develop export markets rapidly. On the other hand, as Korea adopted a Japanese-style product mix and Japanese production technologies, it increased its demand for Japanese components and machinery and thus embarked on an implicitly trade-intensive development trajectory. Japan remains Korea's largest source of imports, accounting for about one third of imports, despite the sharp run-up in the value of the yen and policies designed to "diversify" import sources.

Historical Ties with the United States

Korea has also had a long-standing special relationship with the United States. This relationship too has witnessed ample political friction, but it also provided significant economic benefits. As a result of the U.S. military presence Korean entrepreneurs became familiar with English, U.S. business practices, market requirements, and more fundamentally, international business. For example, the early growth of such important Korean conglomerates as Hanjin and Hyundai can be traced to transportation and construction contracts awarded by the U.S. military. The Vietnam War played a particularly important role in the internationalization of these companies as they contracted international construction and transportation operations for the U.S. military in Southeast Asia (Jones and Sakong, 1980). This experience, in turn, set the stage for their enormously successful penetration of Middle Eastern markets in the mid-1970s (Woronoff, 1983). More recently, U.S. contacts have proved even more important in helping Korea penetrate lucrative U.S. consumer markets. The United States is now Korea's largest trade partner, taking 36 percent of Korean export.

General Import Liberalization

Imports destined for general domestic use were liberalized much more slowly than imports for export production. The first major steps toward liberalization were taken in the late 1960s, culminating in the "negative list" import control system that provided automatic approval for imports of all commodities except those explicitly restricted. Over the 1970s, however, some of this progress was reversed and the liberalization ratio (the proportion of all commodity categories on automatic approval) fell from around 60 percent to under 50 percent. A second important phase of liberalization began in 1978 with the gradual, preannounced delisting of restricted commodities. Temporarily suspended in the wake of the second oil shock, this program began to make an impact in the early 1980s and was accelerated with the advent of trade surpluses of the mid-1980s. By 1988 the liberalization ratio had risen to 95 percent overall and nearly 100 percent in

Table 4.1
Composition of Korean Exports

	1965	1970	1975	1980	1985
Light materials	0.454	0.292	0.271	0.238	0.130
	-----	-----	-----	-----	-----
61 Leather and products	0.000	0.000	0.002	0.002	0.002
62 Rubber products	0.010	0.006	0.022	0.032	0.017
63 Wood and products	0.171	0.146	0.056	0.026	0.002
64 Paper and products	0.001	0.000	0.008	0.009	0.004
65 Textiles, yarn	0.247	0.131	0.157	0.141	0.092
66 Non-metallic minerals	0.025	0.009	0.026	0.028	0.013
Heavy industry	0.168	0.060	0.103	0.209	0.161
	-----	-----	-----	-----	-----
51 Basic chemicals	0.002	0.002	0.010	0.014	0.010
52 Mineral tar	0.000	0.000	0.002	0.001	0.001
53 Paints and dyes	0.000	0.000	0.000	0.001	0.002
54 Pharmaceuticals	0.001	0.002	0.002	0.001	0.002
55 Soaps and fragrances	0.000	0.000	0.000	0.001	0.000
56 Fertilizer	0.000	0.010	0.000	0.022	0.008
57 Explosives	0.000	0.000	0.000	0.000	0.000
58 Plastics	0.000	0.003	0.002	0.009	0.013
59 Chemicals, nes.	0.000	0.000	0.001	0.001	0.001
67 Iron and steel	0.119	0.020	0.055	0.106	0.067
68 Non-ferrous metals	0.027	0.010	0.002	0.006	0.004
69 Metal products	0.019	0.013	0.029	0.047	0.053
Light manufacturers	0.318	0.545	0.437	0.316	0.299
	-----	-----	-----	-----	-----
81 Sanitary equipment	0.002	0.000	0.000	0.001	0.001
82 Furniture	0.000	0.003	0.003	0.002	0.003
83 Travel goods	0.000	0.004	0.019	0.017	0.017
84 Clothing	0.194	0.333	0.275	0.183	0.155
85 Fur clothing	0.039	0.027	0.046	0.056	0.056
89 Misc. manufactures	0.083	0.178	0.094	0.057	0.067
Advanced manufactures	0.056	0.098	0.187	0.240	0.411
	-----	-----	-----	-----	-----
71 Non-electrical machinery	0.024	0.012	0.019	0.024	0.041
72 Electrical machinery	0.018	0.068	0.108	0.123	0.131
73 Transport equipment	0.010	0.013	0.044	0.074	0.227
86 Precision instruments	0.004	0.005	0.016	0.019	0.012

Source: United Nations Trade Statistics.

manufacturing (Leipziger et al., 1987) and tariffs were substantially reduced (see below).

To be sure, Korea's frequently cited liberalization ratios understate the extent of protection. Special laws, enforced through industry trade associations dominated by local producers, restrict the entry of even automatic approval goods, not only for health and safety reasons as frequently claimed, but in the case of the important Telecommunications, Pharmaceuticals, and Technology Development Laws, also to protect strategic industries. Government procurement, administrative guidance, and other policies also favor strategic industries (USITC, 1985).

Overall, general liberalization did not dramatically alter Korea's trade pattern between 1965 and 1985. Nevertheless, liberalization did have a measurable impact on imports. Burton (1989) calculates that approximately 15 percent of imports in 1985 can be attributed to liberalization measures adopted since 1965. The effects of the latest round of liberalization are not included in these estimates, and indeed have not yet been fully reflected in trade results. Recent liberalization, and the steps now being implemented, are likely to be at least equally significant, and may further increase the openness of the Korean economy in the future.

REMARKABLY FLEXIBLE EXPORT COMPOSITION

The rapid growth of Korean trade is partly due to the extraordinary responsiveness of exports to market signals; Korea has been uniquely able to adapt the destination and composition of its exports to changing factor endowments and international market conditions. Flexibility in export composition and rapid general export growth facilitated each other. On one hand, the ability to develop new exports for new markets clearly contributed to the pace of export growth, and on the other hand, the phenomenal resource inflow into the export sector permitted export composition to change without cutbacks in older exporting activities.

Table 4.1 shows the evolution of the Korean export basket over the 1965–85 period. In the beginning of this period, exports were concentrated in a handful of labor-intensive manufactures. By the mid-1970s the export structure included intermediate products such as steel and ships, reflecting the construction boom in the Middle East and the rapid growth of world trade. In the 1980s the composition changed again, stressing electronics and advanced consumer durables, now mirroring the increasing technological level of the Korean economy and the general growth of import demand in the U.S. market.

Korea's ability to adjust its export basket is evident in simple quantitative measures of the compositional change in exports. One such measure is the proportion of the export commodity basket that shifted from one commodity category to another over a specified time interval.[2] This measure of compositional change was calculated at the three-digit SITC level for manufacturing (comprising 107 com-

Figure 4.5
World Distribution of the Shift to Manufactures

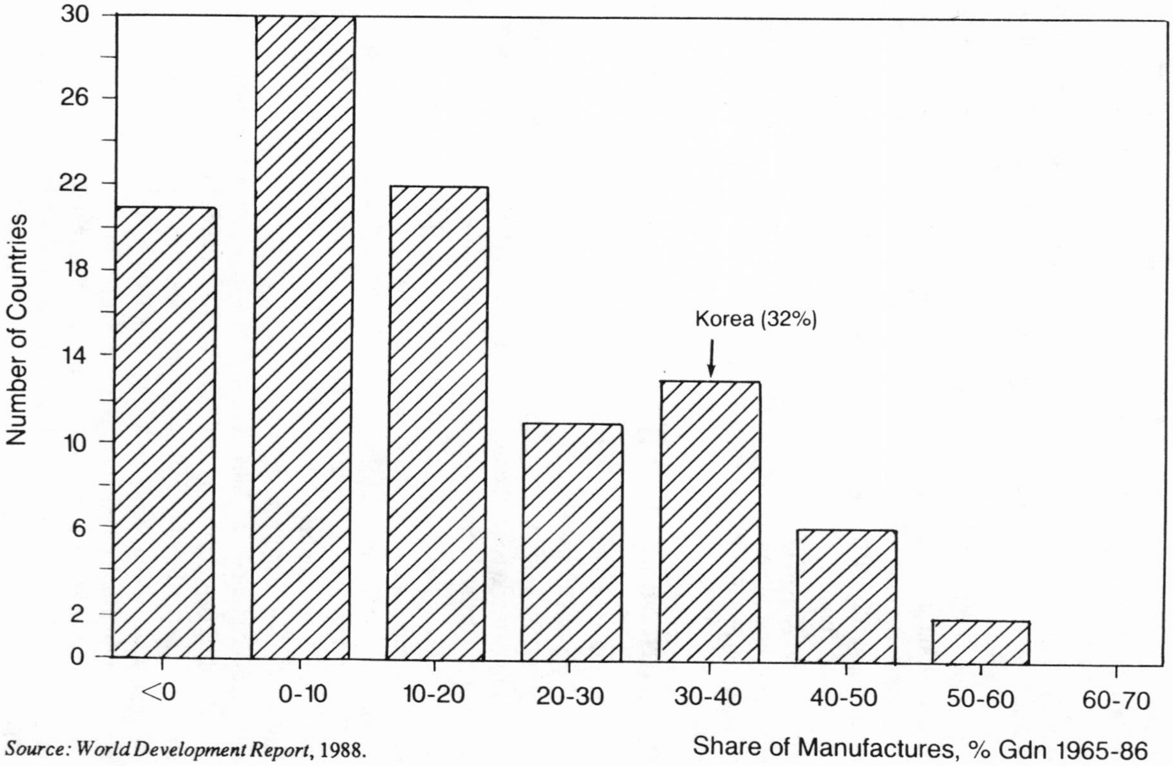

30
26
22
18
14
10
6
2
0
Number of Countries
Korea (32%)
<0
0-10
10-20
20-30
30-40
40-50
50-60
60-70
Share of Manufactures, % Gdn 1965-86

Source: World Development Report, 1988.

Figure 4.6
World Distribution of the Shift to Machinery

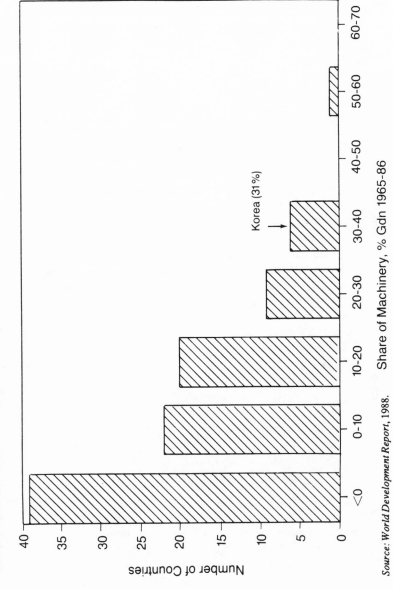

Source: World Development Report, 1988.

Table 4.2
Rate of Compositional Change of Exports

Time Period	Korea	Japan
1965–70	0.356	0.166
1970–75	0.357	0.196
1975–80	0.218	0.197
1980–85	0.236	0.117
Average	0.292	0.169

Source: United Nations Trade Statistics.
Note: Calculations are explained in the text.

modity categories) for each five-year interval between 1965 and 1985. The results, summarized in Table 4.2, show that roughly one third of exports shifted into "new" commodity categories between 1965 and 1975. Between 1975 and 1985 roughly one quarter of exports moved into new categories. These rates are very high by international standards; for example, they are roughly double the rates for compositional change calculated for Japanese exports over the same period.

Two somewhat cruder but more widely available measures of compositional change are reported in Figures 4.5 and 4.6. Figure 4.5 shows the international distribution of the increase in the share of *manufactures* in the export bundle, while Figure 4.6 reports the distribution of the increase in the share of *machinery and equipment* within manufactures. The data cover most countries over the 1965–86 period. During this period, Korea's manufactures share rose by 32 percentage points (from 59 to 91 percent) and its machinery and equipment share rose by 31 percentage points (from 8 to 39 percent). The figures show that these changes are also large when compared with those of other economies. Korea ranked in the upper decile on both measures, and would have ranked still higher had countries with anomalous results been omitted from the ranking.

Rapidly Changing Factor Endowments

Korean factor proportions have changed profoundly over the last 25 years. Investment in physical and human capital has been vigorous due to economic growth, international borrowing, and eventually high saving. Developments in education were particularly impressive. For example, Korea's rate of enrollment in secondary education (94 percent) is highest among developing countries and higher than in many high-income countries. At the same time, population grew at only 1.7 percent per annum between 1965and 1986, well below the average for upper-income developing countries (2.2 percent). Consequently, ratios of both physical and human capital to unskilled labor increased sharply relative to similar ratios elsewhere.[3] These changes, in turn, shifted comparative advantage and created pressure for trade adjustment.

Efficient Labor Markets

Widely regarded as efficient, Korean labor markets are characterized by great mobility from agriculture to industry, and from firm to firm within the industrial sector. There is little evidence of really sizable interfirm or intersectoral wage differentials such as those observed in Japan. A rapid inflow of workers from agriculture further facilitated industrial restructuring without dislocation—new people were absorbed in expanding activities. These characteristics help to explain how the labor market accommodated large structural changes from agriculture to industry and services, and within specific branches of the latter. At the same time, this high level of economic efficiency was apparently achieved with the help of policies that would have been politically unacceptable in more democratic countries. Until recently, Korea has had no significant unemployment insurance or social welfare support system and did not permit labor to organize.

Almost Efficient Capital Allocation

Unlike labor markets, Korean capital markets have been relatively repressed (Cole and Park, 1983). Large differentials have existed between interest rates on bank loans and in the unregulated curb market; the cost of capital has not been equal for different borrowers.

From the viewpoint of economic efficiency, however, the question is whether, and to what extent, different investment decisions were based on different rates of return. Suppose, for example, that the borrowers of bank credit were able to relend their funds through the competitive curb market. In this extreme case, those with access to bank credit would have earned substantial rents, but every investor would have still faced the market interest rate as the opportunity cost of capital. Thus, the fact that different people borrowed at different prices does not necessarily mean that there were similarly large differences in anticipated rates of return across different sectors or investments.

Although bank loans were indeed tied to sectoral policy objectives, they often went to large conglomerates that were involved in an unusually wide range of economic activities, including such inherently small-scale enterprises as laundries and restaurants. It is not unreasonable to suppose that capital allocation within conglomerates tended to circumvent the sectoral objectives of lending policy. In effect, the internal capital markets of large conglomerates may have "made up" for efficient formal capital markets by channeling capital into more efficient allocations than implied by the policy objectives guiding bank credit.

The empirical evidence on this issue is mixed. The data suggest that credit policy did have some effect on the intersectoral allocation of capital, but that its effect was more modest than suggested by the importance of bank credit in the Korean financial system (Cho, 1986). In the mid-1970s, for example, when credit rationing was extensive, preferred sectors showed lower rates of return (between 70 and 90 percent of the returns achieved by other sectors according to Leipziger et al., 1987, p. 43), but the differences were much smaller than would have been implied by the interest differentials observed between bank and curb market credit.

Efficient Allocation of Entrepreneurial Talent

The wide span of Korean conglomerates allowed management to shift not only financial but also entrepreneurial resources easily across different branches of economic activity. Conglomerates frequently entered new lines of business by startup rather than acquisition. The conglomerate's leading entrepreneur (or entrepreneurial team) typically was closely involved in the development of the new affiliate, which would eventually be turned over to others (often relatives) once under way. This strategy may have represented a uniquely efficient mechanism for allocating scarce and exceptional entrepreneurial talent (Jones and Sakong, 1980).

The story of Korean conglomerates is filled with examples of creative entrepreneurship, bold decisions, and strategic use of influence. The ability to shift resources across different economic activities is perhaps best illustrated by the remarkable story of the Handok Company, a conglomerate with 3,500 employees (Leipziger et al., 1987). In 1971, 95 percent of Handok's sales came from human-hair wigs. By 1976, its sales comprised paper products (51 percent), tuna (22 percent), wigs (16 percent) and watches (9 percent). In 1981 watches rose to 85 percent of sales. Watches were still important in 1985 (45 percent), but by then the company had also become involved in manufacturing computers (41 percent) and liquid crystal displays (10 percent). The experience of this company is a case study in the fluidity of Korean resource allocation and microeconomic agility.

UNUSUALLY DIVERSIFIED EXPORT PORTFOLIO

Rapid change in the Korean export bundle *might* have meant that the country's exports shifted from one narrow pattern of specialization to another. This was not the case. Instead, the export bundle expanded from a short list of labor-intensive goods to an uncommonly large variety of commodities, covering different factor intensities and levels of technology. Table 4.3 provides a quantitative measure of export diversification through "concentration ratios" showing the share of the largest export commodities (at the three-digit SITC level) in total manufactured exports. It shows, for example, that Japanese exports are quite concentrated, with 16.2 percent consisting of just one three-digit SITC commodity (passenger

Table 4.3

Share of Top SITC Categories in Total Manufactured Exports, Selected Countries, 1986

	Top Category	Top Three Categories	Top Ten Categories
Malaysia	42.5	55.7	70.1
Japan	16.2	26.1	48.7
Singapore	12.4	27.6	52.4
Germany	12.3	18.9	32.0
Thailand	11.0	26.5	55.2
Brazil	10.4	26.0	54.8
United States	9.9	21.4	46.2
Hong Kong	7.9	21.9	46.3
Korea	6.4	17.1	42.4

Source: UN International Trade Yearbook.

cars). Korea's export mix is the least concentrated among the countries shown in terms of either the top-one- or top-three-commodities measures, and is next-to-least concentrated by the top-ten-commodities measure. It should be noted that several of the countries included in the rankings—especially the United States, Germany, and Japan—have larger and more advanced economies and might have been expected to have far more diversified export patterns than Korea.

Diversification has permitted Korean trade to prosper under changing global economic conditions. In the late 1970s, for example, exports shifted sharply from labor-intensive consumer goods shipped to the United States and Japan toward capital goods and contract construction in developing countries. In the early 1980s Korea took advantage of the appreciation of the dollar to establish new positions in advanced consumer products in American markets. Since 1985, spurred by the high yen, Korean exports to Japan have grown at a 30+ percent annual rate, stressing a spectrum of goods ranging from textile products to consumer electronics.

Capital Rationing

While Korean conglomerates partially circumvented government targeting of credit, capital rationing did increase investment and lower rates of return in key targeted sectors. During the 1970s this meant primarily "heavy and chemical industry," including capital-intensive projects in basic chemicals, metals, and heavy machinery.

Investments in capital-intensive activities frequently created capacity for export and therefore help to explain the early appearance of capital-intensive products (such as metals and chemicals) in the Korean export basket. At the same time, it has been widely hypothesized that these same investments, by concentrating scarce capital in capital-using activities, also lowered the economy's wage rate below the level that would have prevailed otherwise. This (relatively) low wage rate, in turn, helps to explain the simultaneous importance of labor-intensive goods (apparel, plastics, toys) in the export bundle.

The dual bias toward more (subsidized) capital-intensive and more (cheap-labor-driven) labor-intensive exports offers one possible explanation for the diversity of Korean exports and for the unusually broad range of capital intensities involved in this trade. Exactly how important the bias was is a matter of debate; Krueger (1977) and Hong (1979) see it as a relatively important factor in Korean trade structure.

Shallow Specialization Niches

Free trade in the export sector and close economic relationships with Japan allowed Korea to specialize in narrow segments of the production process—that is, on narrow steps in the production ladders of various goods, rather than on many aspects of producing a few goods. These shallow niches often involve assembly operations and the manufacture of standardized or labor-intensive components. As a result of shallow specialization, Korean exports have become quite diversified across different types of products, even though they are probably less diversified across different types of production activities.

Shallow specialization patterns have been the subject of frequent criticism by Korean policymakers and, at times, have been targeted by specific initiatives designed to increase the local content of exports. From an economic perspective, however, Korean trade patterns suggest highly efficient specialization based on good access to foreign capital goods, components, and raw materials. Such trade patterns also help to ease the dislocations that might result from rapid changes in comparative advantage by allowing Korea to retain narrow, but still profitable, segments of declining industries.

KOREAN EXPORTS ARE UNUSUALLY PROTECTION PRONE

Korean trade has met with increasingly severe public criticism and administrative action in the United States, Canada, and Japan. Recent criticism has focused especially on Korean exchange rate policy, which permitted only slow and delayed appreciation of the won following the collapse of the dollar in 1985. While Korea was ultimately not singled out for retaliatory action under the new Super 301 section of the U.S. trade law, the threat of 301 and other trade actions has pressured Korea to liberalize imports, reduce the bilateral deficit with the United States, and mount aggressive lobbying and public relations efforts.

Table 4.4
Protection Faced by Exports to Developed Country Markets

Exporter	NTB Coverage (% value)	Tariff Rate
Korea	35.2	6.6
United States	16.1	3.8
Japan	18.2	3.9
Other Developed	20.3	4.1
East Asian NICs	29.2	6.1
East Asian LDCs	26.3	5.3
Other Developing	27.0	5.1
Average	20.9	4.3

Source: Petri, 1988.

To some extent, trade friction is the unavoidable result of Korea's enviable export record. More fundamentally, however, Korea's export basket is unusually protection prone. This fact emerges clearly in a quantitative comparison of the average tariffs and quantitative restrictions faced by Korea's and other countries' exports into developed country markets. Korean exports are heavily weighted toward commodities—such as apparel, steel, automobiles—that face high average rates of protection in such markets. Thus, even if all countries faced a common set of international barriers, the composition of Korean exports is such that the average tariff and nontariff barriers facing Korean exports would be higher than those facing the exports of other competitors (see Table 4.4).[4] What explains this adverse correlation between foreign protection and the Korean export mix?

Following Japan

The strategy of following Japanese companies into foreign markets is partly to blame. Rapid Japanese export growth had long ago triggered foreign resistance in several key markets that have recently become important to Korean trade. A simplified, but not inaccurate model of this process is that Japanese success in exporting caused foreign countries to erect anti-Japanese barriers, which in turn facilitated Korean entry. Quotas applied to particularly successful Japanese products, for example, were responsible for the initial surge of Korean exports of television sets, steel, and automobiles into U.S. and Canadian markets. Once Korea's ability to exploit these sheltered export opportunities was recognized, restrictions were also imposed on Korean products (Aggarwal et al., 1986).

Bilateral Imbalances

Korea has run a bilateral surplus with the United States since 1982, reaching $9.7 billion in 1987. Relative to GNP, this surplus was even larger than Japan's. At the same time, Korea has run a reasonably large bilateral deficit with Japan. These imbalances are closely tied to Korea's fundamental specialization pattern that, as already discussed, is similar to Japan's and requires imports of Japanese machinery and components. Yet these imbalances create continuing tensions with U.S. policymakers who see Korea as a "way station" for Japanese exports.

Whether or not bilateral trade imbalances are justified by the economics of international specialization, they attract intervention. The predominantly importing country—in this case the United States—tends to assume that the deficit is due to uneven access to markets. Since consumer interests are more diffuse than producer interests, the political balance in the importing country tends to favor import barriers. Moreover, in the case of substantially imbalanced trade, the exporting country cannot easily deter trade barriers since it does not possess a correspondingly painful threat. Thus imbalanced trade flows, such as those of Korea with the United States, are structurally vulnerable to policy pressure.

Korea has attempted to reduce its bilateral imbalances by providing subsidized loans to producers willing to switch sourcing from Japan to the United States. Partly as a result of these policies, the bilateral surplus with the United States and deficit with Japan were both reduced in 1988 by $1 billion. At the same time, these policies raised expectations abroad and may have reinforced perceptions that the Korean government is still firmly in charge of the economy's international sector.

History of Intervention

Because of government's active role in earlier phases of Korean industrialization, many observers of the Korean economy have been slow to accept the government's announced retirement from an active role in economic management. For example, a recent U.S. report designed to document U.S. perceptions about Korean trade quoted an American academic as saying that "Korea is a rare country in which everyone is a protectionist" and a U.S. official as saying that "Korea is the toughest nut to crack. They are worse than the Japanese" (USITC, 1989).

These perceptions are somewhat out of date. Some of the most effective tools of Korean intervention, including direct subsidies, preferential access to subsidized credit, extensive quantitative import restrictions, and high tariffs have been eliminated or reduced. At the same time, some explicit support and protection has been continued for key sectors such as computers under special laws, administrative guidance, and government procurement. Domestic trade associations continue to play influential roles in administering import policy. And new, divisive issues have arisen concerning exchange rate policy, investment barriers, agriculture, and intellectual property rights (USTR, 1989).

Recent exchange rate policy has led to particularly intense friction. In principle, Korea has been pegging the won to a weighted average of the special drawing rights (SDR) value of the dollar and a Korean trade-weighted basket of currencies since 1980. During the rise of the dollar in the early 1980s, the won did in fact depreciate relative to the dollar, as such a formula might have suggested. Between 1985 and 1987, however, the won appreciated very little—much less than would have been implied by any reasonable mechanical pegging rule (Kwack, 1988). Under pressure from the United States and even the International Monetary Fund, Korea accelerated its appreciation in late 1987 and the won in mid-1989 approached a level that will most likely reduce Korea's large current account surplus.

The potentially more significant response to the current account surplus has been Korea's renewed commitment to liberalization (Republic of Korea, MTI, 1989). The number of items scheduled for liberalization was expanded in both 1987 and 1988 and the government has promised a new plan to increase the automatic approval list between 1989 and 1991. A tariff reduction program has reduced average tariffs from 23.7 percent in 1983 to 12.7 percent in 1989 and will further cut tariffs to 7.9 percent by 1993. Special laws are under review and various other barriers have been eliminated.

The liberalization efforts of the mid-1980s, and especially those announced since 1987, are still too recent to have dramatically affected Korean trade or perceptions about trade management. However, they may have played a role in keeping Korea off 1989's Super 301 list. On paper, Korea's recent policy changes are impressive and, assuming they can be shown to bring results, should help to blunt criticisms of Korean policy in the longer term.

CONCLUSIONS

Korean trade has been shown to be an outlier in several important respects. Over the last 25 years, Korea's performance was remarkable in at least five important dimensions: exports grew faster, the economy achieved greater openness, export composition changed more rapidly, exports became more diversified than virtually anywhere else, and exports have succeeded despite the high level of protectionism.

A host of circumstances and policies appear to have been related to these special features of Korean trade. Certainly important were Korea's efficient factor markets, high-quality labor force, and enormous investments in physical and human capital. There is also little doubt about the importance of exceptionally able entrepreneurship, which helped to make the economy remarkably responsive to policy and market developments.

Among policies that encouraged rapid export growth, realistic exchange rate

valuation and measures that essentially freed the export sector from import barriers
were especially important. These and other export-promoting policies amplified
rewards to exporters and produced a trade regime that one might describe as
"reinforced comparative advantage." This regime did not significantly discriminate
among sectors, but it did sharply enhance the returns received by successful
exporters. Thus it helped to attract exceptional entrepreneurial talent into the export
sector but permitted private choices to govern the direction of trading activity.

Korea was also in "the right place at the right time." It simultaneously enjoyed
special relationships with Japan and the United States—in time to follow Japan's
successful export strategies and to take advantage of the sudden internationalization of the American economy. Korean growth occurred in the context of relatively
low and diminishing trade barriers, and in the presence of modest competition from
other developing countries. Korea used this opportunity to establish large-scale
trading enterprises that are now able to prosper also in a more challenging global
environment.

Next-tier NICs, such as Thailand, Malaysia, and China now face greater protection and more vigorous competition. While they too will benefit from opportunities
created by the upgrading of the trade patterns of Korea and other NICs, the
"economic wake" of these countries is much smaller than was Japan's. For these
and other reasons, the opportunities facing the next tier are more limited than those
that Korea faced in the 1960s and 1970s.

Even if Korea's trade miracle is the product of special circumstances, it still
provides valuable lessons on the mechanisms of internationalization and the
importance of effective policy. At least some of the many hypothesized linkages
among trade performance, policy, and resources sketched in this chapter must be
of great policy significance. Efforts to pin down which linkages were the most
critical should be vigorously pursued in future research.

NOTES

The author is grateful to Professors Anne Carter and Robert Stern for valuable
comments on an earlier draft.

1. The regressions used were

$$\text{Exports/GNP} = .117 + .049 \ln Y - .002 \ln Y2 - .032 \ln N - .004 \ln N2 - .468F$$
$$\quad\quad\quad (1.3)\quad (1.7)\quad\quad (0.8)\quad\quad (3.9)\quad\quad (2.2)\quad\quad (10.7)$$

$$\text{Imports/GNP} = .213 + .047 \ln Y - .002 \ln Y2 - .032 \ln N - .004 \ln N2 + .532F$$
$$\quad\quad\quad (1.4)\quad (1.5)\quad\quad (0.7)\quad\quad (3.9)\quad\quad (2.3)\quad\quad (12.1)$$

where Y is per capita GNP 1964 dollars, N is population in millions, and F is the net resource inflow (imports minus exports of goods and non-factor services) as a share of GNP (Chenery and Syrquin, 1975).

2. The measure was calculated as $x_{i,t} - x_{i,t-5}/2$, where $x_{i,t}$ is commodity i's share of exports in year t. This measure is sensitive to the level of commodity disaggregation used, but the relative rankings mentioned in the text seem to be robust; they are similar for a two-digit SITC disaggregation as for the three-digit results cited.

3. These calculations are based on data in World Bank (1988).

4. For details on these calculations, see Petri (1988).

REFERENCES

Aggarwal, Vinod K., Robert O. Keohane and David Yoffie, "The Dynamics of Negotiated Protectionism," Cambridge: Harvard University, 1986.

Balassa, Bela et al., *Development Strategies for Semi-Industrial Countries*, Baltimore: Johns Hopkins University Press, 1982.

Burton, Damon Scott, *The Effectiveness of Trade Liberalization in the Republic of Korea*, Unpublished senior honors thesis, Waltham: Brandeis University, 1989.

Chenery, Hollis, and Syrquin, Moises, *Patterns of Development*, London: Oxford University Press, 1975.

Cho, Yoon Je, "The Effects of Financial Liberalization on the Development of the Financial Market and the Allocation of Credit to the Corporate Sector: The Korean Case," Washington: World Bank, 1986.

Cole, David, and Park, Yung Chul, *Financial Development in Korea: 1945–1975*, Studies in the Modernization of the Republic of Korea, Cambridge: Harvard University Press, 1983.

Dervis, Kemal, and Petri, Peter A., "The Macroeconomics of Successful Development: What Are the Lessons?" *NBER Macroeconomics Annual 1987*, Cambridge: MIT Press, 1987.

Frank, Charles, Kim, Kwang Suk, and Westphal, Larry, *Foreign Trade Regimes and Economic Development: South Korea*, New York: Columbia University Press, 1975.

Hong, Wontack, *Trade, Distortions, and Employment Growth in Korea*, Seoul: KDI Press, 1979.

——, *Trade and Growth: A Korean Perspective*, Seoul: Seoul University, 1987.

Jones, Leroy, and Sakong, Il, *Government, Business, and Entrepreneurship in Economic Development: The Korean Case*. Studies in the Modernization of the Republic of Korea, 1945–1975, Cambridge: Harvard University Press, 1980.

Krueger, Anne, *Growth, Distortions, and Trade among Many Countries.* Princeton

Studies in International Finance No. 40, Princeton: Princeton University, 1977.

————, *The Development Role of the Foreign Sector and Aid.* Studies in the Modernization of the Republic of Korea, 1945–1975, Cambridge: Harvard University Press, 1979.

———— et al., *Export-Oriented Development Strategies: The Success of Five Newly Industrialized Countries*, Boulder: Westview Press, 1985.

Kwack, Sung Y., "Korea's Exchange Rate Policy in a Changing Economic Environment," *World Development, 16*, January 1988, 169–83.

Leipziger, Danny, et al., *Korea: Managing the Industrial Transition*, Washington: World Bank, 1987.

Petri, Peter A., "Korea's Export Niche: Origins and Prospects," *World Development, 16*, January 1988, 47–63.

Republic of Korea, Ministry of Trade and Industry, *Responsive and Responsible: Korea's Trade Partnership with the United States*, Pamphlet distributed by Reid and Priest, Washington, 1989.

Rhee, Yung Whee, Ross-Larsen, Bruce, and Pursell, Gary, *Korea's Competitive Edge: Managing the Entry into World Markets*, Baltimore: Johns Hopkins University Press, 1984.

United Nations, *Commodity Trade Statistics*, New York: United Nations, various issues.

————, *Yearbook of International Trade Statistics*, New York: United Nations, various issues.

U.S. International Trade Commission, *Foreign Industrial Targeting and Its Effects on U.S. Industries: Phase III, Brazil, Canada, The Republic of Korea, Mexico, and Taiwan*, USITC Publication No. 1632, Washington: USITC, 1985.

————, *The Pros and Cons of Entering into Negotiations on Free Trade Area Agreements with Taiwan, The Republic of Korea, and Asean, or the Pacific Rim Region in General*, USITC Publication No. 2166, Washington: USITC, 1989.

U.S. Trade Representative, *Foreign Trade Barriers*, Washington: USTR, 1989.

Westphal, Larry, and Kim, Kwang Suk, "Development Strategies for Semi-Industrial Countries," in Bela Balassa et al., eds., *Korea*, Washington: World Bank, 1982.

World Bank, *World Development Report*. Washington, D.C.: 1988.

Woronoff, Jon, *Korea's Economy: Man-Made Miracle*, Seoul: Si-sa-yong-o-sa Publishers, 1983.

5

Exchange Rate Policy in Korea

Bon Ho Koo and Won Am Park

INTRODUCTION

Since the collapse of the Bretton Woods system in the early 1970s, exchange rates between major currencies have moved frequently and on a large scale. In particular, the real exchange rates of the U.S. dollar have changed so often and to such a great degree over the past 15 years that one cannot easily explain these volatile movements by changes in market fundamentals or by standard exchange rate theories. Thus, recently, research on exchange rates has shifted toward focusing on the microeconomics of exchange rate movements. Given the apparent misalignment of major currencies, developing countries have adjusted their exchange rates both to cope with large external shocks such as oil price swings and high worldwide interest rates, and to manage problems of inflationary deficit finance and capital flight.

Latin American countries, in particular, have suffered from huge budget deficits, high inflation rates, and overvalued currencies. In those countries, capital flight has precluded consistent exchange rate policies (Diaz Alejandro, 1981). Widespread overvaluation of currencies has resulted from government concern over the standard of living and the inflationary impact of currency devaluation. Accelerated wage and price increases are especially likely to fuel overvaluation when a government adopts accommodating macroeconomic policies (Dornbusch, 1982).

Korea faces a different situation, having generally maintained sound public finance and strict capital controls. Wages in Korea are not indexed to past inflation. Therefore, the main concern has been how to mitigate the conflicts between competitiveness and real income growth. The rapid productivity gains spurred by Korea's comprehensive export-focused investment plan would seem to have provided a solution to this puzzle. Keeping these factors in mind, this chapter reviews the exchange rate policy in Korea.

THE KOREAN EXPERIENCE
WITH EXCHANGE RATES

A Brief Review of the Exchange Rate System

Before the government shifted from an import substitution to an export promotion policy in the early 1960s, the exchange rate remained overvalued. The overvaluation during the 1950s was allowed in order to avoid inflation, earn a greater amount of foreign exchange from won currency sales to UN forces, and increase the domestic purchasing power "counterpart" to aid flows. Currency overvaluation deterred exports, and excess demand for foreign exchange given the huge chronic deficit produced a black market where rates were substantially higher than official rates. As Korea's major exports were primary goods such as tungsten ore and agar-agar, policymakers overlooked devaluation as an export incentive. It was thought that a system of export incentives, tariffs, and strict quantitative restrictions on imports could effectively reduce the trade deficit (Krueger, 1982).

The exchange rate and trade regimes began to change in the early 1960s as the decline in foreign aid after 1957 set the stage for the new government's pursuit of export-driven growth. By that time, further pursuit of import substitution in machinery and consumer durables was thought to be ill advised due to the small domestic market and the large capital requirements.

In 1961, the official exchange rate increased 104 percent from 62.5 won to 127.5 won per dollar. This drastic devaluation contributed to absorbing the import premiums caused by quantitative controls and to unifying the multiple exchange rates for commodities. However, at the same time, expansionary monetary and fiscal policies by the military government accelerated inflation, which counteracted the real effects of currency devaluation, so that another devaluation was soon needed to depreciate the real exchange rate.

The second large devaluation from 130 won to 256 won per dollar was carried out in 1964, and was accompanied by fiscal and monetary reforms to reduce the inflationary pressure of devaluation. Although many difficulties emerged during this transition, including inflationary pressure, by implementing monetary and fiscal reforms the government firmly established its resolve to consistently pursue export-promotion polices. In fact, the year 1964 was really a watershed year after which the government was fully committed to a comprehensive export promotion policy (Koo, 1972).

By March 1965, the government had implemented a floating, unified exchange rate policy to maintain real exchange rate stability. It intervened, however, in this regime near the end of 1965. The exchange rate was maintained at about 271 won per dollar until 1968, when it began to depreciate again to maintain purchasing power parity (PPP). Until June 1971 the won was valued largely in consideration of the weighted percentage difference in inflation rates between Korea and her major trading partners. Table 5.1 confirms that purchasing power parity with other countries remained quite constant during this period. In the latter half of 1971, the exchange rate was allowed to float upward and then was pegged, a pattern which repeated itself until December 1974, when the exchange rate was devalued and pegged at 484 won per dollar.

The pegging of the won to the U.S. dollar at 484 won lasted until January 1980 when Korea devalued her currency by 20 percent. A new exchange rate regime was adopted in February 1980. Under the new system, the dollar exchange rate was determined by movements of the exchange rates of major trading partners as well as other factors affecting Korea's external position. This currency basket system is still in effect, and has allowed for more flexible management of the exchange rate to maintain external competitiveness.

It is notable that both of these major switches—one in 1974 and the other in 1980—took place in response to apparent real exchange rate misalignments and current account difficulties following oil shocks. Each included an approximately 20 percent one-shot devaluation. However, in contrast to the 1974 devaluation, which ended in a five year peg, the exchange rate floated more flexibly after 1980.

Exchange Rate Movements

Although the nominal exchange rate has been determined in different ways according to the regime, both PPP and the real effective exchange rate turn out to have relatively small variances over time (Table 5.1). This means that, for the most part, Korea has succeeded in maintaining external competitiveness since 1963 as a result of government efforts to consistently provide export incentives.

This contrasts sharply with the experiences of many Latin American countries. Table 5.2 shows the large fluctuations in real exchange rates in the major Latin American countries in which currencies experienced massive real appreciation during 1978–81, the years prior to the debt crisis. Although in Korea variations in the real effective exchange rate are minor compared with those in Latin America, Korea's real effective exchange rate has also varied to some degree.

Since Korea's trade with the United States and Japan has constituted more than 50 percent of her total trade, the large and persistent movements of the yen vis-à-vis the U.S. dollar have been strongly reflected in movements in Korea's nominal effective exchange rates. If relative price changes are also considered, the effects are seen in movements in the real effective exchange rate. Several points from Table 5.1 deserve mention.

First, the one-shot, approximately 20 percent devaluations in 1974 and 1980 were undertaken in the face of sharp real appreciations of the Korean won in the preceding years, mainly due to oil shocks. Second, the nominal effective depreciation of the won during 1971–73 and 1985–87 led to substantial real depreciation.

Table 5.1
Exchange Rates and Terms of Trade

Year	Nominal Exchange Rate[a]	Index of Exchange Rate	Nominal Effective Exchange Rate[b]	Purchasing Power Parity[b]	Real Effective Exchange Rate[b]	Terms of Trade
1963	130.00	21.40	18.20	95.42	81.16	111.00
1964	255.00	41.98	34.78	139.33	115.43	111.90
1965	271.00	44.61	36.96	138.11	114.40	114.40
1966	270.00	44.45	36.19	130.96	106.63	127.70
1967	268.00	44.12	35.32	123.83	99.12	132.20
1968	276.65	45.54	36.58	119.83	96.25	137.70
1969	288.16	47.44	37.88	119.81	95.66	132.60
1970	310.56	51.13	41.09	122.64	98.56	133.80
1971	347.15	57.15	46.78	127.16	104.09	132.70
1972	392.89	64.68	56.04	129.78	112.44	132.10
1973	398.32	65.58	60.40	141.76	130.58	125.40
1974	404.47	66.59	59.46	126.16	112.65	102.10
1975	484.00	79.68	70.57	125.90	111.50	92.10
1976	484.00	79.68	70.37	118.15	104.35	105.10
1977	484.00	79.68	74.15	113.34	105.47	112.40
1978	484.00	79.68	83.18	104.40	108.98	117.80
1979	484.00	79.68	80.38	96.31	97.15	115.30
1980	607.43	100.00	100.00	100.00	100.00	100.00
1981	681.03	112.12	110.04	98.85	97.02	97.90
1982	731.08	120.36	111.09	104.55	96.50	102.20
1983	775.75	127.71	118.55	111.34	103.35	103.10
1984	805.98	132.69	121.57	116.94	107.14	105.30
1985	870.02	143.23	129.63	125.34	113.45	105.90

82

1986	881.45	145.11	153.88	122.10	129.48	114.70
1987	822.57	135.42	155.35	113.36	130.05	118.08
Coefficient[c] of Variation		0.46	0.53	0.11	0.11	

[a]Yearly average.
[b]Using as weights each year's trade volume of seven major trading partners, i.e., U.S., Germany, Netherlands, Japan, U.K., Canada, France.
Purchasing power parity (PPP) = (index of exchange rate) × (relative wholesale price).
Real effective exchange rate = (nominal effective exchange rate) × (relative wholesale price).
[c]Standard deviation/mean.

Table 5.2
Real Exchange Rates in Latin America (index 1981–82 = 100)

	Argentina	Brazil	Chile	Mexico	Venezuela
1975	66.0	123.0	66.0	107.0	94.0
1976	81.0	122.0	74.0	106.0	97.0
1977	64.0	119.0	79.0	93.0	96.0
1978	74.0	108.0	72.0	94.0	93.0
1979	101.0	97.0	79.0	98.0	89.0
1980	115.2	83.8	94.4	102.6	90.1
1981	107.7	103.3	108.3	114.6	99.7
1982	77.0	113.0	97.3	82.7	110.2
1983	71.6	86.0	89.3	79.0	117.3
1984	80.2	85.7	90.1	91.9	85.9
1985	71.0	84.8	79.5	90.4	92.7
1986	60.9	74.3	68.5	65.0	85.6
1987	53.4	73.5	65.1	66.7	60.0

Source: Morgan Guaranty Trust Company, *World Financial Markets*, various issues.

Note: Higher values reflect real appreciation.

Third, with the adoption of a basket system in 1980, the real exchange rate started
to depreciate, peaking in the third quarter of 1986, after which it appreciated along
with the won appreciation vis-à-vis the U.S. dollar.

Since in developing countries exchange rate changes are often accompanied by
changes in export subsidies, tariffs, and quotas, commercial policies should also

Table 5.3
Changes in Commercial Policies (percent in average)

	1964-69	1970-73	1974-79	1980-85
Export Subsidies[a]				
Net[b]	8.6	4.7	2.3	--
Gross[c]	24.0	27.2	19.0	21.3
Actual Tariff Rate	9.0	6.2	6.5	5.9
Rate of Import Liberalization	56.5[d]	45.2	53.8	79.7

Source: K. S. Kim, 1986.

[a]Percentage subsidy per dollar foreign exchange.
[b]Preferential interest rate subsidy plus direct tax reduction.
[c]Includes exemption from indirect taxes and tariffs.
[d]Figure for 1967–69. In 1967, the government changed the import permit system from a positive list
system to a negative list system.

be described. This is done in Table 5.3. Net export subsidies, estimated as the percentage of subsidies per U.S. dollar of export, have declined, but fewer direct subsidies have been partially offset by indirect tax and tariff exemptions. On the import side, most studies distinguish three periods (K. S. Kim, 1986): 1967–68 was an early period of substantial liberalization, 1970-79 was a period of increasing restrictions, and since 1979, import liberalization has resumed as the government has moved away from interventionist policies. Actual tariff rates have generally fallen over time, although they increased somewhat during the second half of the 1970s. The period of real appreciation was a period of strengthened import restrictions, and the political economy behind this will be discussed below.

MACROECONOMIC STABILITY AND INFLATION

Under a managed floating exchange rate regime, the exchange rate is a policy instrument, but its successful management is possible only if there are sound fiscal and monetary policies as well as capital controls. The importance of budgetary and financial market policies stands out when we compare the Korean experience with those of Latin America with respect to macroeconomic policies and inflation.

First, depreciation usually brings on inflationary pressure, both because of its direct bearing on import prices and because it inflates the budget deficit if dollar-denominated debt service obligations are a substantial part of government outlays.

Second, exchange rate policies, which are more accommodating to price distur-bances, result in the increased persistence of wage and price movements. An accommodating monetary policy only exacerbates this price instability (Dornbusch, 1982).

Third, depreciation encourages capital flight rather than generating foreign exchange, especially when financial liberalization is accompanied by economic and political instability.

The importance of budgetary and financial policies to the success of exchange rate policies will be stressed by briefly describing Korea's experiences in macro-economic management. Microeconomic issues will be discussed in the following section. Figure 5.1 depicts monetary expansion and inflation in Korea. Despite the two oil shocks, both the wholesale price index (WPI) inflation rate and the M_2 growth rate remained below 45 percent even at their highest points, percentages modest by Latin American standards. Inflation seems to have had a weak relation-ship with monetary expansion, although both inflation and money growth have declined remarkably since 1982. This implies that inflation was caused by the high won prices of imported raw materials, especially oil, and other changes in cost variables, rather than by demand expansion (Corbo and Nam, 1986a; Park, 1987b).

Korean financial policies were designed to promote not only price stability but

Figure 5.1
M2 Growth Rate and WPI Inflation

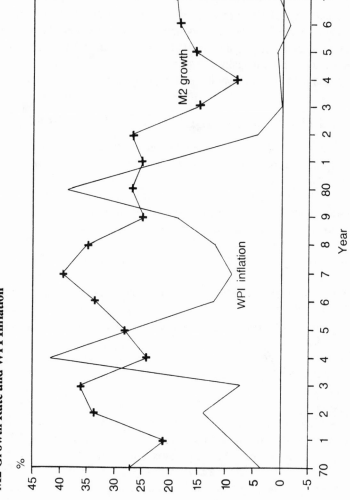

Source: Bank of Korea, *Economic Statistics Yearbook*, various issues.

also economic growth. The Korean government actively intervened in financial markets to promote growth objectives, preferential credit allocation serving as the main tool for industrial targeting (Collins and Park, 1988; World Bank, 1987). This system of credit allocation explains why monetary expansion did not directly lead to inflation in Korea.

The Korean government also controlled capital inflows and outflows. Compared with the 1970s, foreign capital became less attractive in the 1980s as both the interest rate differential between home and foreign markets and the real private cost of borrowing abroad became unfavorable, as shown in Table 5.4. Recently, however, the interest rate differential has grown to favor capital inflows given the nominal appreciation of the won since 1986. This has renewed concern over speculative capital inflows that might endanger economic stability in Korea. The speed and extent of financial liberalization will be adjusted to partly offset the negative aspects of such speculative capital inflows and to provide more incentives for investment abroad.

Fiscal policy in Korea is in striking contrast to those in Latin American countries. The budget deficit has been kept under control, remaining below 5 percent of the GNP. A tax reform including the introduction of a value-added tax (VAT) in the 1970s has enabled the steady expansion of tax revenues. Swings in the budget

Table 5.4
Cost of Foreign Capital (annual average, percent)

Item	1966-70	1971-75	1976-80	1981-83	1984-85	1986
1. Domestic Bank Lending Rate[a]	24.4	17.4	18.0	13.8	10.0	10.0
Curb Market Interest Rate	54.2	40.1	41.4	30.5	24.4	23.2
2. Foreign Interest Rate[b]	7.2	7.9	9.5	13.0	9.5	6.7
3. Exchange Rate Depreciation[c]	3.1	9.3	4.7	8.5	5.9	1.3
4. Domestic Inflation Rate (GDP Deflator)	15.4	18.8	20.9	8.5	4.0	1.4
5. Interest Rate Differential Between Home and Foreign Markets [(1) - (2) - (3)]	14.1	0.2	3.8	-7.7	-5.4	2.0
6. Real Private Cost of Borrowing Abroad [(2) + (3) - (4)]	-5.1	-1.6	-6.7	13.0	11.4	6.6

Sources: Bank of Korea, *Monthly Bulletin*, various issues; IMF, *International Financial Statistics*, various issues.

[a]Discounts on Bills of Deposit at Money Banks.
[b]90-day Eurodollar rate.
[c]Period average.

Figure 5.2
Fiscal Expenditures and Growth

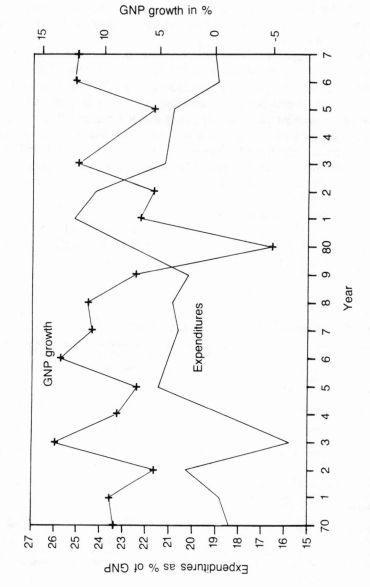

Source: Ministry of Finance, *Government Finance Statistics*, various issues.

deficit are caused by swings in public sector expenditures. Large deficits in 1975 and 1980–81 were caused mainly by increased outlays for the Grain Management Fund. In financing deficits, the government has depended increasingly on domestic debt. The diversification of budget financing between money creation, domestic debt, and external debt reduces the budgetary burdens of debt servicing, which has been one of the main causes for deficit expansion in Latin American countries, especially when world interest rates were rising and trade deficits were calling for real depreciation.

Fiscal policy has also been proven to be counter-cyclical (Corbo and Nam, 1986b), as seen clearly in the negative relationship between government expenditures and economic growth as shown in Figure 5.2.[1]

EXCHANGE RATES, WAGES, AND PRODUCTIVITY

An important issue in exchange rate policy is the linkage among real depreciation, competitiveness, and the standard of living. The relationship between real exchange rates and real wages is especially important because it embodies the trade-offs between competitiveness and the standard of living. Nominal depreciation may not result in real depreciation if accompanied by rises in domestic goods prices, though domestic real incomes will generally decline since nominal depreciation has little impact on the trade balance, and wage increases normally fail to offset the loss in purchasing power due to higher traded goods prices.

Productivity growth can reduce the sharp conflict between competitiveness and the standard of living. An increase in labor productivity reduces domestic prices while facilitating real depreciation and higher real wages. However, macroeconomic policies designed to reduce these conflicts are of limited use. Restrictive demand policies suppress inflation but cause unemployment. Loose demand policies stimulate employment at the cost of reduced competitiveness.

A number of unique aspects of the Korean economic experience emerge from Table 5.5, which shows the behavior of exchange rates, wages, and productivity during periods of real depreciation and real appreciation since 1964 (Park, 1987a). First, real wages grew throughout most of the period. Without any explicit backward-looking or indexation schemes in the wage-setting process as found in Latin America (Kim, 1982; Lindauer, 1984), Korea has succeeded in increasing real wages, the key factor being the constant increase in labor productivity made possible at least in part by the active role of government in promoting outward-oriented growth. The lack of wage indexation and collective action on the part of labor unions has also provided flexibility in wage adjustment. Korea's wage system, under which bonus payments make up a large share of workers' total compensation, has provided additional wage flexibility since bonus payments can be easily adjusted in accordance with economic swings.

Table 5.5
Exchange Rates, Wages, and Productivity in Manufacturing
(average annual percent change)

	1964-69	1969-73	1973-79	1979-85	1985-87
Nominal Exchange Rate	2.5	8.4	3.3	10.3	-2.8
Real Effective Exchange Rate	-3.7	8.1	-4.8	3.8	7.1
Nominal Wage	23.8	18.6	32.3	14.5	10.4
Consumer Price Index	11.9	11.0	17.9	10.4	2.7
Real Wage[a]	10.6	6.9	12.2	3.7	7.5
Labor Productivity[b]	6.6	11.3	7.5	3.3	4.2
Unit Labor Cost($)[c]	13.8	-1.8	19.1	0.5	9.0
Terms of Trade[d]	3.5	-1.4	-1.4	-1.4	5.6

[a]Nominal wage/consumer price index.
[b]Value added in manufacturing/number of workers employed
[c]Unit labor cost in won currency/nominal exchange rate.
[d]Export unit price/import unit price.

Second, Table 5.5 shows that real wages have grown more quickly during times of real appreciation. The periods of real appreciation, 1964–69 and 1973–79, saw high real wage increases of over 10 percent, while periods of real depreciation, 1969–73 and 1979–85, registered low real wage increases. Korea therefore seems to have experienced trade-offs between competitiveness and the standard of living in a variated form of the experience of Latin American countries, where real wages often declined with real depreciations.

Third, real wage growth was backed by rapid productivity growth. There is a consistent positive correlation between real wage gains and productivity growth in manufacturing, except for the period 1969–73. During 1973–79, accelerated wage growth with real appreciation worsened competitiveness, but this was offset partly by rapid productivity growth. On the other hand, during 1979–85 exchange rate policy was used to offset slowdowns in productivity growth and to maintain export competitiveness.

Fourth, the terms of trade continued to deteriorate on the average during 1969–85 regardless of changes in the real exchange rate. Terms of trade depend upon the pricing strategies of domestic exporting firms and foreign exporting firms, which will be discussed in the next section.

Finally, the period of 1985–87 is distinct from other periods in that with the substantial yen appreciation, for the first time in recent history, the effective exchange rate depreciated in spite of nominal won appreciation. The real depreciation is not associated with slowdowns in real wage growth or productivity growth. The favorable external developments of the low value of the dollar, low world interest rates, and low oil prices—dubbed the "three lows"—stimulated productivity growth and real wage growth without a loss in competitiveness. However, labor disputes and strikes, which have become increasingly frequent since 1986, may cause important changes to be made in wage determination and in the relationships among workers, managers, and the government.

EXCHANGE RATES, PRICES, AND PROFIT MARGINS

The U.S. experience of extreme and frequent exchange rate movements and misalignments has inspired new research on the microeconomic impacts of exchange rate movements.

The sluggish rise of import prices during the two-year fall of the U.S. dollar casts doubt on the "law of one price" (Baldwin, 1988; Krugman, 1986). A new approach emphasizing industrial organization introduces profit margins into the aggregate price equation in considering the pass-through of exchange rate changes to import prices. Profit margins change according to market structure, entry costs, and overall changes in the macroeconomic environment.

It should also be recognized that Korea's real exchange rate has varied greatly and moved frequently. The substantial real depreciation that went along with yen appreciation in 1985 has aroused recent interest in how exchange rate movements have been reflected in import and export price changes and how the behavior has changed since 1986 when Korea's current account moved into surplus. This section draws on the aggregate pass-through relationship between changes in exchange rates and changes in import and export prices and assesses the role of changing profit margins due to won appreciation.

Changes in Profit Margins

Changes in profit margins of exporting firms and domestic firms are shown in Figure 5.3.[2] The profit margins of exporting firms declined during 1973–79 when the real exchange rate appreciated, and has gone up since 1980 as the real exchange rate has depreciated. This negative correlation between the real exchange rate and the profit margins suggests that the pass-through rate for Korean firms is less than one. When the real exchange rate depreciates, exporters do not completely transmit these changes to export prices. Instead, export prices in foreign currency do not fall as much as the depreciation of the domestic currency, thereby raising profit margins. On the other hand, export prices in foreign currency also do not rise as much as domestic currency appreciation since exporters cut profit margins to maintain market shares abroad.

The profit margins of domestic firms moved in the same direction as those of exporting firms during most of the period, but sometimes moved in the opposite direction. These movements directly reflect domestic demand conditions and costs rather than movements in the exchange rate.

Figure 5.3
The Ratio of Normal Profit to Net Sales

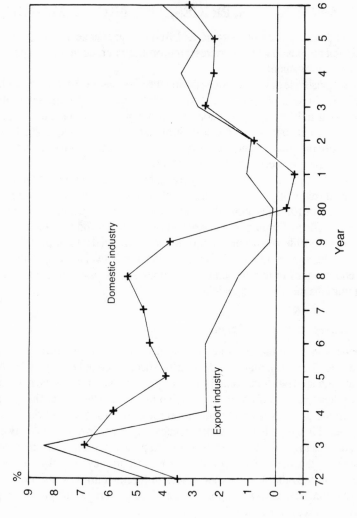

Source: Bank of Korea, *Financial Statement Analysis*, various issues.

An Estimation of Pass-through Rates

We regress the log of export prices in dollar terms and import prices in won currency terms on the log of domestic and foreign WPI's, nominal (effective) exchange rates, and non-oil raw material import prices for the period 1973:1–1985:4 using the second degree PDL with tail constraints. The Cochrane-Orcutt procedure is employed to correct the first-order serial correlation of error terms.

$$\log(PXGS) = -1.44 + 0.35 \log(WPI/E) + 0.33 \log(WPI_x^* \cdot EERX\$) \tag{1}$$
$$(-1.51) \quad (2.47) \qquad\qquad (1.58)$$

$$R^2 = 0.99 \quad \text{D.W.} = 1.13 \quad \rho = 0.84$$

$$\log(PMGSNO*E) = -4.47 + 0.57 \log(WPI_m^*) + 0.74 \log(EERM) + 0.04 \log(PC)$$
$$(-4.37) \quad (2.26) \qquad\qquad (6.15) \qquad\qquad (0.60)$$
$$+ 0.09 \log(PC_{-1}) + 0.12 \log(PC_{-2}) + 0.13 \log(PC_{-3})$$
$$(1.94) \qquad\qquad (3.12) \qquad\qquad (3.46)$$
$$+ 0.13 \log(PC_{-4}) + 0.10 \log(PC_{-5}) + 0.06 \log(PC_{-6}) \tag{2}$$
$$(3.37) \qquad\qquad (3.21) \qquad\qquad (3.08)$$

$$R^2 = 0.99 \quad \text{D.W.} = 1.80 \quad \rho = 0.82$$

where

PXGS: export unit price ($)
PMGSNO: non-oil import unit price ($)
E: nominal exchange rate (w/$)
WPI: wholesale price index
WPI_x^*, WPI_m^*: export-weighted and import-weighted wholesale price of seven major trading partners
EERX$: export-weighted nominal effective exchange rate of the dollar
EERM: import-weighted nominal effective exchange rate of the won
PC: non-oil commodity price index ($), from *International Financial Statistics*
and seasonal dummies are not reported.

Equation (1) shows that Korean exporters pass only about 35 percent of exchange rate changes through to the dollar price of exports without a lagtime. On the other hand, it was found in equation (2) that foreign firms immediately passed approximately 75 percent of exchange rate changes through to the won price of imports. Interestingly enough, commodity price changes also affect Korea's import prices with a lagtime of one and one-half years. Contracts with commodity exporters abroad, domestic reserve holdings of commodities, and utilization of forward markets seem to generate this lagged response.

The important finding is that Korean exporters' pass-through rate is only 35 percent, which is quite low, while foreign firms' pass-through rate amounts to 75 percent. Korean firms adjust their profit margins to avoid large fluctuations in foreign currency export prices, which determines their competitiveness with major trading partners. The pass-through rate of Korea's major competitors in the U.S. market was estimated to be 60 percent with the presence of a two-year lag (Mann, 1986).[3] Profit margins of foreign firms fall below normal levels as the dollar depreciates and rise above normal levels as it appreciates. To maintain competitiveness in foreign markets, Korean exporters must adjust profit margins just like other foreign firms. This adjustment on the part of Korean exporters is shown in Figure 5.3. Profit margins were cut when the won appreciated during 1973–79 and have increased since the won began depreciating in 1979. In contrast, the relatively mild competition in the domestic market among foreign exporters has resulted in small changes in profit margins and large fluctuations in the won price of imports in line with changes in Korea's real exchange rate.

We now turn to the question of how Korea's exchange rate pass-through relationships may have changed since the Plaza Agreement of September 1985. The test for a structural shift is to see whether regression errors are statistically larger in the postagreement period than in the preagreement period. Examining this property, we find little evidence that the pass-through of exchange rates has changed since 1986 (Park, 1988).

THE POLITICAL ECONOMY
OF EXCHANGE RATE POLICY

The movements of exchange rates on a large scale and in persistent ways, as well as frequent reforms of the exchange rate regime as reviewed in the previous section, have drawn attention to the political economy of exchange rate policy. Whatever the theoretical merits or actual outcomes of real depreciation or export-promotion policies may be, real appreciation and import-substitution strategies seem to attract policymakers. Persistent exchange rate misalignments have been consistent with the hypothesis of class conspiracy according to which interest groups lobby for distributional gains, with final policy decisions reflecting the balance of power among different interest groups (Sachs, 1985).

Korea's exchange rate policy has reflected both political reluctance to accept short-term costs for long-term benefits and the self-interests of powerful interest groups. In order for exchange rate depreciation to have a desirable impact on the trade balance, substitution effects should dominate. In reality, however, exchange rate depreciation cannot guarantee improvement of the trade balance in the short run. Nominal depreciation leads to domestic price increases so that the real exchange rate does not change enough to raise competitiveness. The depreciation gives rise to a reduction in the purchasing power of domestic goods or a reduction in the standard of living. Both the substitution and income effects of devaluation involve higher inflation and a decline in real income in the short run. Clearly, the devaluation is not a short-term prescription for winning popularity. Gradual improvement of the trade balance in response to devaluation necessitates a long-term view by policymakers willing to risk losing popularity in the short run.

Korea's impressive economic growth could not have been achieved without the adoption of export-oriented policies. But these export-oriented policies, coupled with inflation, have brought about a *de facto* multiple exchange rate system as well as the overvaluation of the Korean won. A variety of restrictions and subsidies have been imposed on both imports and exports. Trade theory contends that the unified floating of exchange rates is suboptimal in the presence of factor market distortions, externalities, and monopoly and infant industries, although the magnitudes of these market imperfections cannot be correctly estimated.

No matter how elaborate a theory celebrates a tariff-cum-subsidy policy as optimal, public intervention is likely to accentuate rather than offset market distortions and imperfections given the lack of correct information on the magnitudes of such imperfections, difficulties in adjusting by specific item, and temptations to subject adjustments to political manipulation (Koo, 1972).

In addition, the political influence of big firms with access to large foreign loans is substantial. Whenever there are large amounts of foreign loans outstanding, a devaluation increases debt service burdens. Thus, firms and individuals that will suffer financial losses due to the devaluation are likely to exert political pressure against devaluation. More importantly, big firms with large foreign debts are normally Korean exporters of manufacturing goods. Thus an overvaluation to avoid financial losses can bring about a loss in external competitiveness. Under these circumstances, big firms favor tariff-cum-subsidy policies, including quantitative restrictions, rather than devaluation. With the development of a black market for foreign exchange that accompanies overvaluation, some capitalists in industrial sectors are rationed scarce foreign exchange while others purchase foreign exchange on the black market. In this case, overvaluation normally results in additional distributional gains to big firms.

The above political factors have played a large role in determining exchange rates in Korea as well as in Latin American countries and even the U.S. The episodes of Korea's exchange rate system briefly introduced in section II are well-explained by the political economy of exchange rate policy.

The overvaluation during the 1950s arose from export elasticity pessimism. Primary exports were thought to be subject to low price and income elasticities of demand in advanced countries, so the typical menu of commercial policies—the barter system with some export incentives, tariffs, and strict quantitative restriction on imports—was strengthened. On the financial side, the Korean government was more concerned with obtaining foreign exchange through won sales and won "advances" to the United States and the United Nations. This was best facilitated by keeping the won overvalued.

The real appreciation during 1973–79 accompanied a shift of policy focus to import substitution strategies focusing on investment in heavy industries. Since huge investment projects had to be financed by foreign loans while being protected from competition, large firms gained political clout. Furthermore, the commodity boom of the early 1970s and the two oil shocks resulted in greater priority on price stability, which is threatened by devaluation.

Even the two major changes in the exchange rate regime, from unified float to dollar peg in 1974 and from dollar peg to basket system in 1980, occurred only when sustained real exchange rate misalignment following oil shocks became politically alarming.

Given the political economy of overvaluation, the International Monetary Fund (IMF) mission used to recommend devaluations that Korea's exchange rate policy could not realistically achieve. To them, Korean authorities seemed to prefer short-run popularity gains at the expense of long-run economic gains. However, once Korea's current account moved into surplus, the IMF strongly recommended appreciation of the Korean won, characteristically caring only for rapid achievement of long-term goals. This does not recognize that a realistic exchange rate policy consistent with the constraints of Korea's political economy (characterized by sluggish devaluation) was able (in harmony with commercial policies) to successfully bring about a structural current account surplus.

The political situation has changed with the emergence of current account surpluses as well as the new movement toward a more democratic society, which has drawn attention to the development of small and medium-sized enterprises, resulted in more labor disputes and accelerated wage increases, and in general promoted free market principles as the key to a competitive economy. The recent political turnaround will certainly have an impact on exchange rate determination. Therefore we recommend import liberalization to enhance market efficiency rather than rapid appreciation, which, combined with rapid wage growth, will badly affect the competitiveness of small firms.

CONCLUDING REMARKS

This study reviews exchange rate policy in Korea and attempts to explain its unique aspects in relation to the experience of Latin American countries. In Korea, sound fiscal and financial policies, accompanied by strict capital controls, provided the macroeconomic stability that prevented massive movements in real exchange rates. Korea solved the conflicts between competitiveness and the standard of living by focusing on productivity growth as the key to maintaining export competitiveness.

Estimating aggregate pass-through rates, we find that Korean firms adjust profit margins to avoid large fluctuations in the foreign currency price of exports so as to maintain their market shares abroad. Export prices in foreign currency terms will not rise as much as won appreciation, and so profit margins will decline with real appreciation. The political economy of exchange rate policy is characterized by the importance of short-term political popularity and the balance of political power among interest groups. Finally, increased liberalization of imports, rather than rapid real appreciation, should be chosen as the best means for reducing the large current account surplus.

NOTES

1. Total expenditures are an inadequate measure of fiscal policy because they include automatic stabilizers and respond to business cycles and because changes in tax policies are not considered. Corbo and Nam (1986b) have constructed a measure of "fiscal impulse" that adjusts for these factors. They found that in Korea "fiscal impulse" has an inverse relationship to economic growth over most of the period 1971–84.

2. The data are obtained from the Bank of Korea's *Financial Statement Analysis*. The data used in Figure 5.3 are the normal profit to net sales ratio. Other measures of profit rate such as normal profit to total assets ratio and net profit ratio yield similar results.

3. Experiments using a more broadly based exchange rate measure and bilateral trade weights produced a long-run pass-through estimate of around 90 percent.

REFERENCES

Baldwin, Richard, "Some Empirical Evidence on Hysteresis in Aggregate US Import Prices," NBER Working Paper No. 2483, 1988.

Bank of Korea, *Monthly Bulletin*, Seoul, various issues.

Collins, Susan M., and Park, Won Am, "External Debt and Macroeconomic Performance in South Korea," NBER Working Paper No. 2596, 1988.

Corbo, Vittorio and Nam, Sang Woo, (1986a) "Controlling Inflation: Korea's Recent Experience," KDI Working Paper No. 8608, Seoul, 1986.

——, (1986b) "The Recent Macroeconomic Evolution of the Republic of Korea: An Overview," KDI Working Paper No. 8610, Seoul, 1986.

Diaz Alejandro, C., "Southern Cone Stabilization Plans," in W. Cline and S. Weintraub, eds., *Economic Stabilization in Developing Countries*, Washington, D.C.: The Brookings Institution, 1981.

Dornbusch, Rudiger, "PPP Exchange Rules and Macroeconomic Stability," *Journal of Political Economy*, 90, February 1982, 158–65.

International Monetary Fund, *International Financial Statistics*, Washington, D.C., various issues.

Kim, Kwang Suk, "The Timing and Sequencing of a Trade Liberalization Policy—The Korean Case," Manuscript, March 1986.

Kim, Sookon, "Employment, Wages and Manpower Policies in Korea: The Issues," KDI Working Paper No. 8204, Seoul, 1982.

Koo, Bon Ho, "Korea's Foreign Exchange Policies: An Evaluation and Proposals," KDI Working Paper No. 7207, Seoul, 1972.

Krueger, Anne O., *The Developmental Role of the Foreign Sector and Aid*, Cambridge: Harvard University Press, 1982.

Krugman, Paul, "Pricing to Market When the Exchange Rate Changes," NBER Working Paper No. 1926, 1986.

Lindauer, D. L., "Labor Market Behavior in the Republic of Korea: An Analysis of Wages and Their Impact on the Economy," World Bank Staff Working Paper No. 641, World Bank, 1984.

Mann, Catherine, "Prices, Profit Margins, and Exchange Rates," *Federal Reserve Bulletin*, June 1986.

Morgan Guaranty Trust Company, *World Financial Markets*, New York, various issues.

Park, Won Am, (1987a) "Exchange Rates, Wages, and Productivity in Korea," *Korean Economic Review*, 2, September 1987, 17–34.

———, (1987b) "A Quarterly Macroeconometric Model for the Korean Economy," KDI Working Paper No. 8716, 1987.

———, "Exchange Rates, Wages, and Profit Margins," *KDI Quarterly Economic Outlook* (in Korean), 7, September 1988, 59–72.

Sachs, Jeffrey D., "External Debt and Macroeconomic Performance in Latin America and East Asia," *Brookings Papers on Economic Activity*, 2, 1985, 523-64.

World Bank, *Korea: Managing the Industrial Transition*, Washington, D.C.,1987.

6

Import Liberalization and Its Impact in Korea

Kwang Suk Kim

INTRODUCTION

The Republic of Korea has industrialized and grown rapidly since the early 1960s. It is generally accepted that the shift from an inward-looking import-substitution strategy to an export-oriented industrialization strategy has been largely responsible for the acceleration of industrialization and growth since the early sixties (Frank, Kim, and Westphal, 1975; Kim, 1975). Consequently, exports served as the engine of growth in Korea.

Korea did not begin its conscious effort to liberalize imports until 1965 when it gained some confidence in export expansion. The first episode of import liberalization consisting primarily of loosening quantitative restrictions (QRs) on imports, continued until 1967. After that, however, the liberalization effort was virtually suspended for a decade due to an unfavorable balance of payments and other reasons. The second episode of import liberalization took place in 1978–85, mainly in the forms of both loosening QRs and reducing tariff barriers on imports. Unlike the earlier episode, the second episode continued for a long period of time and provided the basis for continuous progress in import liberalization.

A LONG-TERM PATTERN OF IMPORT LIBERALIZATION

A long-term pattern of Korea's import liberalization is described by estimating the overall degree of import liberalization for the period 1955–85. As shown in Table 6.1, the two main factors—the average legal tariff rate and the degree of import QRs—are taken into account in the estimation of the overall degree.

Table 6.1
Estimate of Overall Degree of Import Liberalization for Korea, 1955–85 (in percent)

Year	Average Rate of Legal Tariffs Regular[a] (1)	Average Rate of Legal Tariffs Total[b] (2)	Inverted Total Tariff Rate (3)=(1)/(1)+(2)	Degree of Liberalization from QRs[c] Trade Program Only (4)	Degree of Liberalization from QRs[c] Trade Program Plus Special Laws (5)	Overall Degree of Liberalization Average of (3)&(4) (6)	Overall Degree of Liberalization Average of (3)&(5) (7)
1955	27.4	27.4	78.5	1.0	1.0	39.3	39.3
1956	27.4	27.4	78.5	3.5	3.5	41.0	41.0
1957	35.4	35.4	73.9	6.4	6.4	40.2	40.2
1958	35.4	42.9	70.0	6.3	6.3	38.2	38.2
1959	35.4	66.5	60.1	4.7	4.7	32.4	32.4
1960	35.4	58.0	63.3	5.0	5.0	34.2	34.2
1961	35.4	36.0	73.5	4.0	4.0	38.8	38.8
1962	49.5	49.6	66.8	5.4	5.4	36.1	36.1
1963	49.5	49.5	68.3	0.4	0.4	34.4	34.4
1964	49.5	51.0	66.2	2.0	2.0	34.1	34.1
1965	49.5	52.7	65.5	5.9	5.9	37.8	37.8
1966	49.5	52.3	65.7	9.1	9.1	37.4	37.4
1967	49.5	52.6	65.5	58.8	48.7	62.2	57.1
1968	56.7	58.9	62.9	56.0	46.6	59.5	54.8
1969	56.7	58.3	63.2	53.6	43.8	58.4	53.5
1970	56.7	58.5	63.1	52.8	43.0	58.0	53.1
1971	56.7	57.9	63.3	53.5	43.7	58.4	53.5
1972	56.7	57.5	63.5	49.5	40.1	56.5	51.8
1973	48.1	48.2	67.5	50.7	41.3	59.1	54.4

Year						
1974	48.1	48.1	67.5	49.3	40.5	58.4	54.0
1975	48.1	48.1	67.5	47.8	38.5	57.7	53.0
1976	48.1	48.1	67.5	49.6	40.9	58.6	54.2
1977	41.3	41.3	70.8	49.9	40.8	60.4	55.8
1978	41.3	41.3	70.7	61.3	52.2	66.0	61.5
1979	34.4	34.4	74.4	69.1	58.8	71.8	66.6
1980	34.4	34.4	74.4	70.6	60.1	72.3	67.3
1981	34.4	34.4	74.4	75.5	63.4	75.0	68.9
1982	34.4	34.4	74.4	77.4	65.4	75.9	69.9
1983	34.4	34.4	74.4	81.2	69.6	77.8	72.0
1984	26.7	26.7	78.9	85.4	78.3	82.3	78.6
1985	26.4	26.4	79.1	88.6	81.7	83.9	80.4

Source: K. S. Kim, 1987b, p.33.

[a]The average rate of regular tariffs, weighted by the value of 1975 production.

[b]Includes the average foreign exchange tax rate and special tariff rate on imports in addition to the regular tariffs.

[c]Represents the degree of import liberalization from QRs for the second half of each year in 1955–79, and that for the second half of the year indicated and the first half of the following year in 1980–85. The degree is adjusted to make it comparable over time on the basis of the same system of classification as the four digit CCCN codes (1079 items)used during 1977–79 (until the first half).

Figure 6.1
Overall Degree of Import Liberalization for Korea, 1955–85

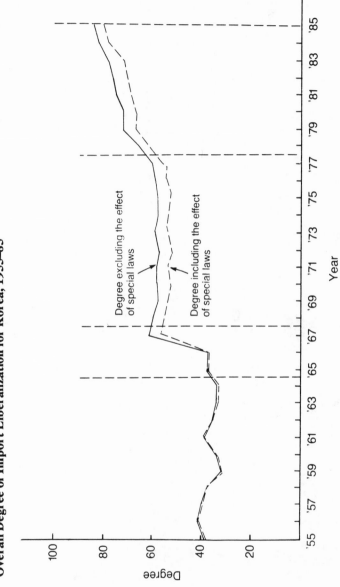

Source: Table 6.1

First, the degree of import liberalization in terms of tariffs was estimated. To accomplish this, the annual series of average legal tariff rate was calculated by adding the average rates of both the foreign exchange tax and special tariffs to the average legal rate of regular tariffs, since such tax and special tariffs were imposed on imports on top of the regular tariffs during 1958–73 (see Kim, 1987a, for statistical data). The average legal rate of regular tariffs for 1955–85 was obtained by weighting legal rates on commodity groups by the value of domestic production in 1975 (see column 1).[1]

The average legal tariff rate, however, may have an upward bias in two respects. For one, this legal rate has been substantially higher than the average actual tariff rate because of the tariff exemptions and reductions granted for various purposes.[2] In addition, the average legal rate weighted by the value of domestic production may have an upward bias, since high protection on a sector tends to raise the nominal value of that sector's production above the level obtainable without such protection. For this reason, the average legal rate should be taken as an indicator of potential protection, reflecting the upper boundary of Korea's tariff protection.

In any case, the annual series of the average legal tariff rate is inverted in percentage form to show the degree of import liberalization in terms of tariffs (see column 3). These series indicate that the degree of import liberalization rises as the average rate of legal tariffs declines.

Second, turning to the degree of import liberalization from QRs, two different series are estimated. One is the degree of import liberalization based only on the semiannual or annual trade program without including the trade-restricting effects of special laws. For the period 1967–85, the degree represents the ratio of automatic approval (AA) items to total commodity items, based on United Nations' Standard International Trade Classification (SITC) or the Customs Cooperation Council Nomenclature (CCCN), which was adjusted to make it comparable over time on the basis of the same system of classification. For the period prior to 1967, an index of the number of AA items (with the first half of 1967 as 100) was estimated and used to extrapolate the adjusted degree for 1967–85.[3] The annual series so obtained for the entire period is shown in column 4 of Table 6.1. The other series is the degree estimated by consolidating the trade-restricting effects of special laws with the QRs based only on the trade program (see column 5).[4] The only difference between the two series is the trade-restricting effects of special laws on import liberalization.

Finally, the degree of import liberalization in terms of tariffs and the alternative figures representing the degree of import liberalization from QRs are simply averaged to obtain two alternative, overall degrees of liberalization: one using the degree of import liberalization based only on the trade program (column 6), and the other using the degree based on both the trade program and the special laws (column 7).

The two alternative "overall degrees of import liberalization" are shown in

Figure 6.1 for visual comparison. The figure shows that the overall degree including the effects of special laws was identical to the overall degree excluding them during 1955–66, as expected. During the latter period (1967–85), when the special laws provided for additional QRs on top of those based on the trade program, the overall degree consolidating the effects of the special laws was significantly lower than that excluding them. Still, the two moved together.[5]

It is clear from the two degrees that conscious efforts to liberalize imports were made in Korea during the two periods, 1965–67 and 1978–85. The import liberalization for the first period was not very successful, and it did not assure continued progress in liberalization. The second period appears to have been rather successful, since import liberalization has continued, although slowly, for a long period of time. The successful liberalization in the second period has provided the basis for continued liberalization even after 1985.

ECONOMIC IMPACT OF IMPORT LIBERALIZATION

Economic literature on the economic impact of import liberalization tends to emphasize static welfare gains arising from production and consumption effects of such liberalization, since such gains are easily identifiable. The liberalization may also produce dynamic effects that are more difficult to measure than the static effects. One of the important dynamic effects is that the liberalization reduces X-inefficiency and enhances the international competitiveness of domestic industries by increasing competition in domestic markets (Greenaway, 1983). All of these positive economic effects actually originate from the fact that the liberalization provides easier access to imports and reduces import costs compared with the preliberalization period. If, however, the liberalization leads to too rapid an increase in imports, the production and employment of import-competing industries may decline, thereby causing some serious industrial adjustment problems.

As discussed in the preceding section, some significant progress was made in Korea's import liberalization during two periods, 1965–67 and 1978–85. The two liberalization episodes, however, did not have any discernible negative impact on the growth rates of important macroeconomic variables for the country: GNP, employment, investment, exports, imports, balance of payments, and so forth. It seems, at least, more obvious at the aggregate level than at the sectoral level that the import liberalization did not have any major negative impacts. On the other hand, it is not actually possible to measure the positive impact of the liberalization on the macroeconomic variables. This section, therefore, attempts to deal with the impact of liberalization at the sectoral level.

Kim (1987a) attempted to estimate the actual imports of the specific commodity items liberalized from QRs during 1965–67 and 1978–79 and to compare them with annual aggregate imports. He found that those imports liberalized from QRs generally accelerated in the same year and the year following the liberalization.

Table 6.2
Degrees of Import Liberalization by Sector, Selected Years (Consolidating both QRs and Tariffs) (in percent)

	Sector Title	1966	1970	1975	1980	1983	1985
01	Agr., forestry & fishery	41.4	54.0	52.8	56.3	63.0	69.1
02	Mining	51.0	89.5	87.8	85.2	92.2	94.1
1	Processed food	40.3	37.4	46.2	56.5	54.8	70.2
2	Beverage	20.5	20.8	21.5	22.3	28.8	40.8
3	Tobacco	0.8	27.3	27.3	29.3	33.8	38.8
4	Textile yarn & fabric	40.5	50.9	52.3	80.7	82.6	87.1
5	Knitted goods	25.8	18.0	34.1	51.7	65.7	89.2
6	Carpets & other textile products	32.2	32.4	39.6	77.2	75.4	88.5
7	Wearing apparel	26.0	25.9	33.4	70.3	57.4	87.9
8	Leather products	41.5	46.2	53.4	68.9	71.6	88.3
9	Footwears	27.0	26.5	31.3	85.0	85.0	91.3
10	Wood & cork products	43.6	65.9	72.1	88.3	89.9	94.0
11	Furnitures & fixtures	30.8	36.7	38.9	37.0	67.3	89.8
12	Paper & its products	37.0	53.0	45.0	71.9	84.5	86.8
13	Printing & publishing	42.5	56.9	70.8	91.7	96.3	97.3
14	Industrial chemicals	55.0	64.3	62.0	60.3	67.3	78.3
15	Other chemical products	44.4	60.9	66.1	70.0	72.3	77.2
16	Petroleum products	51.5	46.3	50.8	53.0	72.4	73.5
17	Other petroleum & coal products	58.9	96.5	97.0	98.5	98.5	98.5
18	Rubber products	32.5	49.7	62.0	82.4	84.6	89.0
19	Plastic products	40.5	25.0	33.8	88.8	88.8	93.0
20	Pottery, china & earthenwares	34.5	67.2	67.2	75.7	77.0	82.3
21	Glass & its products	40.4	59.5	66.8	74.7	77.6	81.7
22	Other nonmetallic mineral products	41.7	78.7	79.2	92.5	92.5	94.5
23	Iron & steel	44.0	72.8	74.6	86.1	90.7	92.6
24	Nonferrous metal products	47.8	76.5	76.0	87.1	86.2	87.8
25	Fabricated metal products	35.9	46.9	49.9	75.7	86.3	90.1
26	Engines & turbines	51.4	76.4	71.5	76.5	80.0	85.3
27	Industrial machinery	52.4	67.8	58.9	78.9	76.6	82.9
28	Office & other machines	41.0	82.9	51.1	51.1	76.8	78.3
29	Electrical machinery & apparatus	41.8	57.7	48.6	54.9	65.4	73.8
30	Sound & communication equipment	39.3	52.9	48.8	57.1	60.8	72.4
31	Electrical appliances & housewares	30.0	40.1	44.1	39.0	68.1	77.5
32	Other electrical products	41.5	50.5	56.3	71.1	80.8	87.1
33	Shipbuilding	44.3	34.0	78.6	78.3	63.7	76.0
34	Railroad equipment	50.0	98.3	99.0	98.0	98.0	96.0
35	Motor vehicles	34.8	51.5	48.6	54.1	50.2	62.0
36	Aircrafts & others	50.0	100.0	100.0	98.8	98.8	97.8
37	Medical, optical & measuring equip.	40.0	60.6	54.0	59.5	76.3	82.5
38	Other manufacturing	31.8	39.5	38.7	58.2	65.4	76.1

Note: The sectoral degrees of import liberalization given in this table are obtained by simply averaging the sectoral degrees of import liberalization from QRs and the sectoral degrees of liberalization in terms of tariffs. These sectoral degrees are prepared by using data given in Ministry of Commerce and Industry (various years), and Korean Traders Assiciation (various years), Ministry of Finance (various years) reports, and Choi (1983).

Table 6.3

Overall Degrees of Import Liberalization by Major Industry, Selected Years (Consolidating Both QRs and Tariffs) (in percent)

	By Major Industry[a]	1966	1970	1975	1980	1983	1985
I.	Primary industry (01-02)	42.0	56.2	55.1	58.8	65.3	71.2
II.	Food, beverage & tobacco (1-3)	30.0	32.4	38.4	49.6	49.6	64.1
III.	Textiles, clothing & leather products (4-9)	34.7	36.6	43.8	74.0	74.3	87.8
IV.	Wood & its products (10-11)	24.2	64.0	69.1	76.5	82.7	92.4
V.	Paper, paper products and printing & publishing (12-13)	39.5	54.7	54.5	78.4	88.8	90.8
VI.	Chemicals, petroleum, coal, rubber & plastic products (14-19)	47.9	57.1	58.4	65.9	75.2	80.0
VII.	Nonmetallic mineral products (20-22)	41.0	77.0	76.8	89.1	89.2	91.7
VIII.	Basic metal products (23-24)	44.7	73.3	74.8	86.2	90.1	92.0
IX.	Metal products, machinery & equipment (25-37)	41.0	59.3	55.4	63.6	69.7	77.8
X.	Other manufacturing (38)	31.8	39.5	38.7	58.2	65.4	76.1
	All manufacturing (II-X)	37.5	47.7	52.6	66.8	71.3	79.8
	Light industry (II-V,X)	33.7	38.2	43.7	62.3	63.8	76.8
	Heavy & chemical industry (VI-IX)	44.5	62.5	61.2	70.5	76.5	81.7
	All industry average (I-X)	39.6	50.8	52.3	65.6	70.4	78.5

Note:This table gives the degrees of import liberalization by major industry which are obtained by averaging the sectoral data given in Table 6.2, weighted by the current price value of domestic production for respective years.

[a]Numbers in parentheses indicate the sector numbers matched to each industry. See Table 6.2 for the title of each sector.

Although the imports of items liberalized in the first half of 1978 and in the same period of 1979 did not follow this tendency, the increase in imports of those items liberalized in other periods was generally much higher than the growth of aggregate imports in one or both of the first two years following liberalization.

A research report by the Korea Institute for Economics and Technology (KIET) generally supports Kim's findings, although it covered a different period, 1982–84. The KIET report disclosed that the imports of those items liberalized from QRs generally showed a higher rate of increase over the past trend within the six months to one year immediately following liberalization, but they tapered off after that. The report concluded that over the entire period, from the second half of 1982 to the first half of 1985, the loosening of QRs could not have contributed to the

Table 6.4

Pearson's Correlation Coefficients Between Changes in Sectoral Degrees of Import Liberalization and Other Related Variables, 1966–1970

	ML_i	RM_i	RE_i	P_i	X_i	L_i	$(X/L)_i$	AX_i
ML_i	1.0	0.136	-0.305	0.352	-0.359	-0.443	0.027	-0.103
RM_i		1.0	-0.310	-0.084	-0.149	-0.199	0.083	0.082
RE_i			1.0	-0.080	0.295	0.279	0.082	0.070
P_i				1.0	-0.577	-0.562	-0.251	0.056
X_i					1.0	0.865	0.563	0.524
L_i						1.0	0.088	0.453
$(X/L)_i$							1.0	0.307
AX_i								1.0

Source: Data for 38 manufacturing sectors used for estimation of these correlation coefficients are available from the KDI data bank.

Note: Correlation is statistically significant at the 5 percent level if the coefficients exceeded 0.32. Subscript "i" represents sectors (i = 1, 2, 3 . . . 38).

Definition:
ML = increment in the degrees of import liberalization
RE = increment in the ratio of exports to production
RM = increment in the ratio of imports to domestic production
P = percentage increase in domestic wholesale price
X = percentage increase in domestic production
L = percentage increase in employment
X/L = percentage increase in gross output per worker
AX = percentage increase in total factor productivity index (production basis), estimated by Kim and Park (1988).

Table 6.5

Pearson's Correlation Coefficients Between Changes in Sectoral Degrees of Import Liberalization and Other Related Variables, for 1975–85

	ML_i	RM_i	RE_i	P_i	X_i	L_i	$(X/L)_i$	OR_i
ML_i	1.0	0.349	0.144	-0.210	0.011	-0.099	0.074	-0.657
RM_i		1.0	-0.119	0.135	-0.487	-0.436	-0.328	-0.382
RE_i			1.0	0.004	0.047	0.219	-0.116	0.141
P_i				1.0	-0.597	-0.414	-0.682	0.053
X_i					1.0	0.838	0.740	-0.053
L_i						1.0	0.302	-0.038
$(X/L)_i$							1.0	0.109
OR_i								1.0

Source: Data for 38 manufacturing sectors used for estimation of these correlation coefficients are available from the KDI data bank.

Note: Correlation is statistically significant at the 5 percent level if the coefficients exceeded 0.32.
Definition: OR = percentage increase in capacity utilization ratio. For other variables, see Table 6.4.

increase in imports above the level expected from the pattern of increases in the three years prior to liberalization. It gave four reasons for this unusual result. (1) Domestic economic activities were, in general, sluggish in 1982–85. (2) A considerable number of those items liberalized from QRs during this period had already been imported, even before the liberalization. (3) Domestic industries producing those items liberalized from QRs had enough supply capacity and international competitiveness. (4) Other import restriction measures (such as an increase in the tariff rate, the designation of items subject to diversification of import origins, and the designation of import-observation items) on some selected items were effective.

The results of the two previous studies mentioned above are actually related to the impact of loosening QRs by the trade program, not taking into account the changes in tariff rates and special law QRs that may have replaced the QRs based on the trade program. The degree of import liberalization should be measured by consolidating both the levels of all QRs (including special law QRs) and tariffs, to examine the full impact of liberalization. Table 6.2 presents such degrees of import liberalization for 40 tradable sectors for selected years, whereas Table 6.3 shows the same data averaged at the level of ten major industry classifications.

The degrees of import liberalization (consolidating the effects of all QRs and tariffs) as of 1985 varied widely by sector, ranging from the minimum of 38.8 percent for tobacco manufacturing to the maximum of 98.5 percent for other petroleum and coal products (see Table 6.2). An average degree of liberalization for all tradable sectors, weighted by domestic production, increased from 39.6 percent to 78.5 percent between 1966 and 1985[6] (see Table 6.3). Comparing the degrees of liberalization as of 1985, the average degree for all manufacturing industries was 79.8 percent—significantly higher than the average of 71.2 percent for primary industries. Among the nine major manufacturing industries, the degrees of liberalization for wood & wood products (IV), basic metal products (VIII), nonmetallic mineral products (VII), and paper, paper products, and printing & publishing (V) reached around 91–92 percent, the highest as of 1985. On the other hand, the average for the food, beverage & tobacco industry was the lowest, 64.1 percent in 1985.

To examine the impact of import liberalization on individual sectors, it might be desirable to analyze the annual time-series of major economic variables for the respective sectors. Since such annual time-series are not usually available by sector on a consistent basis, however, a cross-section analysis was attempted by using the Bank of Korea's input-output data for selected years. In fact, a correlation analysis was conducted by relating changes in sectoral degrees of liberalization to changes in those sectors' major economic variables over the periods of liberalization.

Table 6.4 presents the matrix of Pearson's correlation coefficients estimated between changes in the sectoral degrees of liberalization and changes in the sectors' other economic variables for the period 1966–70, which covers the first liberalization episode. Table 6.5 shows the same matrix of Pearson's correlation coefficients estimated for the period 1975-85, which covers the second liberalization episode.[7] It should be noted that the correlation coefficients were estimated by using the data for 38 manufacturing sectors, excluding two primary sectors, out of a total of 40 tradable sectors (shown in Table 6.2).

According to Table 6.4, a simple correlation coefficient between changes in the degrees of import liberalization (ML_i) and changes in the ratio of imports to domestic production of final goods (RM_i) estimated for 1966–70 was positive, as expected, but it was not high enough to be statistically significant (at the 5 percent level). However, the correlation coefficient between the degrees of liberalization (ML_i) and domestic production (X_i) and that between ML_i and employment (L_i) turned out to be negative and statistically significant, indicating that the liberalization in the latter half of the 1960s had an adverse impact on domestic production and employment. It should be noted that the correlation coefficient between the ratio of imports to domestic production (RM_i) and domestic production (X_i) and that between RM_i and employment (L_i) were both negative as expected, although they were statistically insignificant. The liberalization of the 1960s did not seem to significantly affect industrial productivity, since the correlation coefficients between MLi and gross output per worker $(X/L)_i$ and between ML_i and total factor productivity indices (AX_i) were statistically insignificant.

Interestingly, the correlation analysis for the 1966–70 period showed that the degree of liberalization (ML_i) is negatively correlated with the ratio of exports to production (RE_i) and positively correlated with domestic wholesale prices (P_i). The marginally significant, negative correlation between ML_i and RE_i seems to indicate that, in the latter half of the sixties, import liberalization was promoted mainly giving priority to the sectors in which Korea did not have a comparative advantage in production. On the other hand, the significant positive correlation between ML_i and P_i reflects the result that the liberalization was promoted more strongly in the late sixties for those commodity items whose domestic prices were increasing most rapidly than for others, partly to stabilize domestic prices.

The correlation analysis for the later period (1975–85) indicates that the degree of import liberalization (ML_i) was positively correlated with the import ratio to domestic production (RM_i) as in the earlier period, and the coefficient of correlation turned out to be statistically significant in contrast to the earlier period in which the coefficient was insignificant. Although the correlation coefficients between RM_i and domestic production (X_i), and between RM_i and employment (L_i) both turned out to be negative, as expected, and statistically significant, the direct correlation coefficient between ML_i and X_i or L_i turned out to be statistically insignificant. However, the correlation coefficient between ML_i and the capacity utilization ratio (OR_i) was negative and statistically significant, indicating that the liberalization tended to adversely affect capacity utilization ratios during 1975–85. On the other hand, there is no indication that the liberalization was pushed during 1975–85 to the extent that domestic industrial productivity could be enhanced.

In contrast to the earlier period, the correlation coefficient between ML_i and P_i turned out to be negative, as expected, in the latter period, although it was not statistically significant. The coefficient of correlation between ML_i and export ratios (RE_i) was positive, in contrast to the earlier period, but statistically insignificant.

SUMMARY AND CONCLUDING REMARKS

Korea's record of import liberalization policy can be divided into two periods: 1965–67 and 1978–85. The first period mainly took the form of loosening QRs, whereas the second period consisted of loosening QRs and gradually reducing tariffs. Since it is more obvious at the aggregate level than at the sectoral level that the two liberalization episodes did not have any discernible impact on the economy, an attempt was made to examine the impact of liberalization at the sectoral level.

Our analysis suggests that import liberalization had some tendency to increase imports during the two periods, 1966–70 and 1975–85. But the positive correlation coefficient between the degrees of liberalization and the ratios of import to domestic production at the level of 38 manufacturing sectors for the first period was not statistically significant. It seems that the liberalization clearly had some adverse impact on domestic production and employment during the earlier period, while it had no significant, direct impact during the latter period. On the other hand, there is no clear indication that the liberalization had any significant impact on domestic industrial productivity during both periods.

This difference in the impact of liberalization over the two periods may be attributable to two factors. First, the approach to liberalization changed between the two periods. In other words, the liberalization in the latter half of the sixties was, in effect, a one-stage approach in the sense that the degree of liberalization made a sudden jump by loosening QRs in 1967 but made no further progress for the rest of the period, whereas the liberalization beginning in 1978 followed a gradual, multistage approach by using the system of "advance notices." Second, the stage of Korea's industrialization progressed significantly between the two periods and domestic manufacturing industries became internationally more competitive by the late seventies and eighties than in the earlier period. The fact that the country could maintain a more realistic exchange rate in the eighties than in the late sixties was, of course, helpful for strengthening the international competitiveness of domestic industries.

Korea achieved a current-account surplus beginning in 1986 after a long history of chronic deficits in its balance of payments. Due to this drastic change in the country's balance-of-payments situation, Korea is in a much better position than ever before to actively promote import liberalization. In addition, there are strong pressures from the United States and other countries to expedite liberalization in Korea. It seems that the country can now dismantle most of the remaining QRs, including those by special laws, without much adverse impact on the economy, as experienced in the past.

It is advisable to dismantle first the regime of special law QRs, which are inconsistent with the General Agreement on Tariffs and Trade (GATT) rules but not readily visible, and then move on to the other QRs. It is also suggested that the average legal rate of tariffs be reduced substantially by giving priority to lowering the legal rates higher than 10 percent. As long as the programs of import liberalization are carried out gradually by making use of the "advance notices" system, the country's experience suggests that any adverse impact of liberalization may be kept at a minimum, if it is not entirely negligible.

NOTES

1. A simple average tariff rate was first estimated for each of the two-digit CCCN groups (99 groups), and then the simple average rate was weighted by the value of each group's production in 1975 to obtain the average legal rate for all items in respective years.

2. The average actual tariff rate had been quite high during 1958–62 due to the effect of the foreign exchange tax, but the actual rate generally ranged between 5 and 10 percent during 1963–85. See Kim (1987a), p. 58.

3. The ratio of AA items to total commodity items based on SITC and CCCN codes could not be estimated for the period prior to 1967, since no consistent system of commodity classification was used during that period.

4. Of the 33 trade-related special laws effective as of the second half of 1985, the trade restricting effects of 11 laws that are not consistent with the GATT rules are consolidated with the QRs based on the trade program. For a detailed description of import restriction by the special laws, see Kim (1987b).

5. The special laws provided for additional QRs beginning in 1967 due to the adoption of a new "negative-list system" of the trade program in that year. The semiannual trade program had previously been formulated as a "positive-list system," under which only those items listed in the program could be imported with or without government approval. Under the new system, the trade program listed only those items whose import was prohibited or restricted, implying that all items not listed are AA items.

6. This average degree of liberalization weighted by domestic production turned out to be slightly lower than the simple average degree given in Table 6.1.

7. Spearman's rank correlation coefficients were also estimated by using the same data for the two periods. But the results are not reported here because they are not very different from the Pearson's correlation coefficients given in Tables 6.4 and 6.5.

REFERENCES

Bank of Korea, *Korea's Input-Output Tables*, Seoul: BOK, various years.

Choi, Kwang, ed., *Facts and Figures on the Public Sector in Korea* (in Korean), Seoul: KDI Press, 1983.

Frank, Charles R. Jr., Kim, Kwang Suk, and Westphal, Larry E., *Foreign Trade Regimes and Economic Development: South Korea*, New York: National Bureau of Economic Research, 1975.

Greenaway, David, *International Trade Policy*, London: Macmillan, 1983.

Kim, Kwang Suk, "Outward-looking Industrialization Strategy: The Case of Korea" in Wontack Hong and Anne Krueger, eds., *Trade and Development in Korea*, Seoul: KDI Press, 1975.

———, (1987a) "The Timing and Sequencing of a Trade Liberalization Policy: The Case of Korea," (Unpublished paper submitted to the World Bank), Kyung Hee University, Seoul, 1987.

———, (1987b) "The Nature of Trade Protection by Special Laws in Korea," Discussion paper No. 87-01, Graduate School of Business Administration, Kyung Hee University, Seoul, 1987.

————, and Park Sung Nok, *Productivity Growth of Korean Manufacturing and Its Causes, 1966–83* (in Korean), Seoul: KIET, 1988.

Korea Institute for Economics and Technology, *Analysis of Effects of Import Liberalization* (in Korean), Seoul: KIET, 1986.

Korean Traders Association, *Guidelines on Exports and Imports by Commodity Item* (in Korean), Seoul, various years.

Ministry of Commerce and Industry, *Semi-annual (or Annual) Trade Program* (in Korean), Seoul, various years.

Ministry of Finance, *Tariff Schedules of Korea* (in Korean), Seoul, various years.

7

Market Distortions and Polarization of Trade Patterns: Korean Experience

Wontack Hong

INTRODUCTION

In the two-factor, multicommodity trade models of Jones (1971 and 1974), Krueger (1977), and Deardorff (1979), capital accumulation in a small open economy tends to raise the wage rate and the capital intensity and leads to greater increases in the outputs of capital-intensive sectors than in the labor-intensive sectors. In Korea, however, during 1966–83, we observed a fairly rapid expansion of outputs and exports not only in some highly capital-intensive sectors but also in some highly labor-intensive sectors such as footwear and electronics (assembling).

In a simple multicountry model by Deardorff (1979), the expansion of outputs and exports of highly labor-intensive sectors is possible in a country whose degree of factor abundance lies at the intermediate range relative to others, provided that the country excessively protects the highly capital-intensive import-competing sectors. The domestic production of highly capital-intensive commodities behind a high protectionist wall will lower the wage rate and will induce the production of highly labor-intensive commodities in place of the commodities with intermediate capital intensities that are not very different from the country's overall capital-labor endowment ratio. Then these highly labor-intensive commodities become the export goods of the country.

Furthermore, in a Deardorff (1979) type of multicommodity trade model, all importables can be produced domestically, and the necessary level of tariff protection will increase monotonically as the commodities (in terms of their relative capital intensities) lie further away from the country's capital-labor endowment ratio. The export of highly capital-intensive goods, however, is not possible without introducing subsidies.

Krueger (1977, p. 314) has suggested that the policy-cum-structural factor market distortions in the form of lower rental-wage rates applied to the capital-intensive manufacturing sectors would result in expanded production and "exports" of the very capital-intensive commodities that are produced with highly capital-intensive techniques of production. At the same time, the relatively higher rental-wage rates that would result for the labor-intensive manufacturing sectors would make the very labor-intensive sectors become profitable with highly labor-intensive techniques of production.[1] This implies that, across the countries, we should expect to observe more significant disparities (or polarization) in the capital intensities of sectoral production and exports of a country with substantial factor-market distortions than in those of a country with only moderate distortions in factor markets. In addition, within a country with substantial factor-market distortions, we should expect the disparities to become more conspicuous as time passes.

The object of this chapter is to examine the polarization effect of market distortions by examining the relationship between the distortions in commodity and factor markets and the patterns of manufacturing production and trade in Korea during the period 1960–83.

COMMODITY AND FACTOR MARKET DISTORTIONS

According to Table 7.1, the effective rate of protection (ERP) on the (moderately capital-intensive) intermediate manufacturing group amounted to about 52 percent, while the rates on both the relatively labor-intensive and the relatively

Table 7.1
Effective Rates of Protection by Sectors: Balassa Method (in percent)

Sectors	1970	1975	1978
Labor-Intensive	20.0	-30.5	- 8.1
Intermediate	52.0	-12.4	5.1
Capital-Intensive	15.7	274.6	72.5
All-Manufacturing	32.7	- 8.0	7.8
Agr., For. & Fishery	30.2	38.9	98.1
Mining	2.9	1.9	33.5

Source: Kim and Hong (1982).

Note: The original 217-sector classification of Kim and Hong (1982) was regrouped into 66 sectors (see Hong, 1988). The labor-intensive manufacturing represents sectors from 1 to 19, the intermediate manufacturing represents sectors from 20 to 36, and the capital-intensive manufacturing represents sectors from 37 to 52.

capital-intensive groups of manufacturing sectors amounted to less than 20 percent on the average in 1970. By 1975, however, the ERP on the relatively capital-intensive group of manufacturing sectors amounted to as high as 275 percent, while the ERP on the intermediate group and the relatively labor-intensive group amounted to about –12 percent and –31 percent, respectively. In 1978, the ERP on the relatively capital-intensive group amounted to about 73 percent vis-à-vis 5 percent for the intermediate group and –8 percent for the relatively labor-intensive group. That is, by the late 1970s, the vigorous government policy to promote the capital-intensive "heavy & chemical industries" was reflected in the drastically raised effective rates of protection accorded to these sectors.

To see the relationship between the sectoral protection and the capital intensity of each sector, we conducted a simple regression analysis as follows: $Y = a + bX$ where Y_i represents the effective rates of protection and X_i the physical capital intensities of Korean manufacturing sectors in 1978 (where $i = 1 \dots 52$). The results are as shown below:

$$Y = 10.5 + 5.9X \qquad R^2 = 0.12$$
$$(0.55) \ (2.35)^*$$

where the figures in parentheses represent t values and * represents significance at the 5 percent level. As expected, we found a significant positive relation between the sectoral capital intensities and the sectoral rates of effective protection.

The short-term export credits in Korea have been allocated to exporters in proportion to their gross export earnings, and hence have not discriminated against the manufacturing sectors according to their capital intensities. The export credits, however, take less than 15 percent of total domestic bank loans. The government has rationed, directly or indirectly, most of the remaining domestic bank loans and foreign loans among the selected sectors. In the 1970s, and especially in the late 1970s, the Korean government concentrated its interest-rate-subsidized loan allocations on the loosely defined heavy and chemical industries, which were mostly very capital-intensive industries. See Hong and Park (1986).

Table 7.2 shows that the magnitude of total domestic bank loans expanded from about 11 percent of GNP in 1954–61 to about 52 percent of GNP in 1980–85. We have approximated the rate of return on capital in Korea by the gross real rate of return on investment in the manufacturing sector. If we take the difference between the estimated rate of return on capital and the weighted-average real interest rate on domestic bank loans to be the subsidy rate associated with credit rationing, the annual provision of interest subsidies in Korea expanded from about 3 percent of GNP in 1962–71 to about 10 percent of GNP, on the average, in 1972–79. At 10 percent of GNP, the domestic credit subsidy must be judged large enough to significantly affect the pattern of Korea's output and trade. Furthermore, the

Table 7.2
Interest Subsidy Associated with Credit Rationing in Korea, 1954–1985 (in percent)

Annual Average	Loan GNP Ratio[a] (L)	Average Nominal Interest Rate	Average Annual Rate of Inflation	Real Interest Rate[b] (I)	Gross Rate of Return[c] (R)	Rate of Interest Subsidy (R)-(I)	Subsidy/ GNP Ratio L(R-I)
1954-61	11.1	17.2	22.3	-5.1	10.9	16.0	1.8
1962-66	14.7	14.4	19.7	-5.3	15.2	20.5	3.0
1967-71	26.8	20.7	15.0	5.7	17.7	12.0	3.2
1972-76	35.1	14.6	20.9	-6.2	23.1	29.3	10.3
1977-79	34.0	15.7	19.2	-3.5	23.0	26.5	9.0
1980-85	52.4	13.7	9.8	3.9	8.2	4.3	2.3

Sources: Bank of Korea, *Economic Statistics Yearbook*, *National Income Accounts, 1984; New National Accounts, 1986; Input-Output Tables of Korea*, various issues.

[a]Loan represents total domestic bank loans provided through the deposit money banks (DMB), the Korean Development Bank (KDB), the Korea Export-Import Bank (EXIMB), and the Korea Long Term Credit Bank (KLTB).

[b]The difference between the nominal weighted average interest rate on loans provided by the DMB, KDB, EXIMB, and KLTB and the rate of change in GNP deflator in each year.

[c]Gross-incremental-value-added/fixed-capital-formation ratio multiplied by the nonlabor share in gross value added (at factor cost), taking account of the existence of net working capital and capital gains (or losses). See Hong and Park (1986) for the method of estimation.

government directly allocated interest subsidies on the foreign loans to entrepreneurs; these averaged about 6 percent of GNP each year in the 1970s.[2]

Table 7.3 shows that in the 1970s (1971–81), the average bank-loan to value-added ratio for the relatively capital-intensive group of manufacturing sectors exceeded that for the relatively labor-intensive group by about 20 to 32 percent. If we include foreign borrowing, however, the average total-loan to value-added ratio for the relatively capital-intensive group of manufacturing sectors was about 170 to 120 percent larger than that for the relatively labor-intensive group. As a result, the average "real" interest cost of total borrowing (that is, the ratio of total financial expenses to total borrowings) of the capital-intensive group of manufacturing sectors amounted to –9.9 percent per annum in 1971–76 and –6.7 percent per annum in 1977–81, while that of the labor-intensive group of manufacturing sectors amounted to –5.6 percent and –1.1 percent, respectively.[3]

According to the 1978 *Report on Occupational Wage Survey*, the average wage rate of female workers amounted to about 44 percent of the average wage rate of male workers. On the other hand, the wage rate of lowly educated workers (workers with or less than high school education) amounted to about 34 percent of the wage

Table 7.3
Sectoral Loan/VA Ratios and Financial Costs

Annual Average	Bank Loans[a] Value Added	Total Loans[b] Value Added	Fin. Expense[c] Total Borrowing
	Labor-Intensive Sectors (1-19)		
1971-76	0.84	0.91	13.98%
1977-81	0.82	0.89	18.53%
1982-86	0.88	0.94	14.38%
	Intermediate Sectors (20-36)		
1971-76	1.41	1.90	11.65%
1977-81	1.03	1.27	15.69%
1982-86	1.03	1.20	14.30%
	Capital-Intensive Sectors (37-52)		
1971-76	1.01	2.46	9.66%
1977-81	1.08	1.97	12.97%
1982-86	0.98	1.45	13.45%

Source: The Bank of Korea, *Financial Statements Analysis*, various issues.

[a]Total short-term and long-term loans from domestic banks divided by value-added.
[b]Domestic bank loans plus foreign loans (excluding trade credits) divided by value-added.
[c]Financial expenses to total borrowings that bear interest payments such as corporate bonds, borrowings from banks and curb markets, etc. It represents the average "nominal" interest cost in percent.

rate of highly educated workers (workers with or more than junior college education). As suggested by the structuralists, sex and education seem to have constituted the two major causes of dual labor markets in Korea.[4]

In 1978, the proportion of female workers in the total number of workers in the labor-intensive manufacturing sectors amounted to about 55 percent on the average, while that in the capital-intensive sectors amounted to only about 14 percent, on the average. Although we do not have comparable data for the lowly educated workers, it seems that, in Korea, the higher the capital intensity of a manufacturing sector, the smaller is the proportion of female workers and lowly educated workers. These factors must have, at least partly, contributed to the significant positive relationship between the capital intensity and the average wage rate of the sector as shown below (that is, the higher the capital intensity, the higher the sectoral average wage rate):

$$Y = 0.93 + 0.06X \qquad R^2 = 0.68$$
$$(17.76)** \ (10.19)**$$

where ** represent significance at the 1 percent level. These are the results for 1978, but similar results were obtained for 1983 also.

SHIFTING PATTERNS OF MANUFACTURING PRODUCTION AND TRADE

Uneven Expansion in the Sectoral Share of Exports and Employment

During 1966–83, Korea's total commodity exports expanded by about 92 times, growing from $0.25 billion to $22.9 billion in current dollar prices; the proportion of manufactures in commodity exports increased from about 82 percent to about 96 percent; manufacturing employment expanded by 3.9 times; the average physical capital intensity (physical capital per worker) of the whole manufacturing sector increased by 3.4 times; and the average real manufacturing wage (applying the GNP deflator) rose by 5.3 times in constant prices. The sectoral share of exports and employment, however, expanded somewhat unevenly.

Among the highly capital-intensive group of manufacturing sectors, the share of fertilizers, chemical fibers, and organic chemicals (Sectors 46, 47, and 48) in total manufactures exports expanded from 0.1 percent in 1966 to 2.9 percent in 1983. Their share in total manufacturing employment also expanded from 0.6 percent to 1.1 percent during the same period. The share of iron and steel (Sector 44) in total manufactures exports expanded from 0.04 percent to 3.7 percent, and its share in total manufacturing employment expanded from 0.5 percent to 1.5 percent. Among the moderately capital-intensive group of manufacturing sectors, the share of ships in total manufactures exports expanded from 0.4 percent to 11.0 percent (to about 5 percent excluding the repaired ships), and the share of shipbuilding in total manufacturing employment expanded from 1.4 percent to 3.3 percent.

Among the highly labor-intensive group of manufacturing sectors, the share of artificial wigs in total manufactures exports declined from 7.6 percent in 1966 to 0.25 percent in 1983, and its share in total manufacturing employment also declined from 1.3 percent to 0.3 percent during the same period. The share of both textiles and wearing apparels in total manufactures exports declined slightly during the period (from 7.2 percent to 7.0 percent and from 12.8 percent to 10.1 percent, respectively).

Not surprisingly, in a rapidly growing country like Korea, the share of many labor-intensive sectors in outputs and exports declined—some slowly, some rapidly. One might be surprised, however, to find a rapidly expanding share of highly labor-intensive sectors. Indeed, among the highly labor-intensive sectors, the share of miscellaneous manufactures (excluding artificial wigs) in total manufactures exports expanded from 0.6 percent in 1966 to 5.0 percent in 1983; its share in total manufacturing employment also expanded from 2.4 percent to 3.8 percent during the same period. The share of footwear in total manufactures exports expanded from 3.9 percent to 5.5 percent. The shares of precision instruments and metal products expanded from 0.2 percent to 1.3 percent, and from 1.2 percent to 4.6 percent, respectively. Furthermore, the share of communication equipment, electronic parts, electronic appliances, and semi-conductors and integrated circuits (Sectors 16, 17, 18, and 19) in total manufactures exports expanded from 1.2 percent in 1966 to 13.0 percent in 1983; their share in total manufacturing employment expanded from 0.6 percent to 7.5 percent during the same period.

Increasing Disparities in Capital Intensities of Production and Exports

The next point for consideration is whether or not the disparities in capital intensities of manufacturing sectors and of manufactured exports became more conspicuous in Korea over the period 1966–83. We have estimated the (standardized) deviations of the sectoral physical-capital intensities from the manufacturing mean value by computing $k_i^* = (k_i/k) - 1$ [where $k_i = K_i/N_i$, $k = K/N$, and K and N represent total physical capital and total number of workers in manufacturing, respectively], and then multiplying each of them with the share of exports (x_i or $\bar{x}_i$) or employment (n_i) of each sector in total manufactured exports or in total manufacturing employment. And then two dispersion indices (DI) were computed by summing up (i) the numbers with negative values only, and (ii) the numbers with positive values only. We also have estimated the positive and negative DI

Table 7.4

Dispersion Indices (DI) of Capital Intensities for Manufactured Exports and Manufacturing Employment in Korea, 1966 and 1983

Weighted by Relative Share of Sectoral--	Physical Capital Intensities (k_i^*)		Total Capital Intensities (c_i^*)	
	1966	1983	1966	1983
--Gross Exports	$\sum k_i^* x_i$		$\sum c_i^* x_i$	
Negative DI	-0.27	-0.33	-0.29	-0.23
Positive DI (1)	0.52	1.05	0.60	0.96
(Tobacco Products)	(0.05)	(0.00)	(0.12)	(0.01)
(Cement)	(0.13)	(0.07)	(0.07)	(0.02)
(Refined Petroleum)	(0.23)	(0.39)	(0.33)	(0.71)
Positive DI (2)	0.11	0.59	0.08	0.22
--Net Exports	$\sum k_i^* \overline{x}_i$		$\sum c_i^* \overline{x}_i$	
Negative DI	-0.29	-0.35	-0.31	-0.25
Positive DI (1)	0.53	0.76	0.62	0.48
(Tobacco Products)	(0.07)	(0.00)	(0.17)	(0.01)
(Cement)	(0.16)	(0.08)	(0.08)	(0.03)
(Refined Petroleum)	(0.20)	(0.12)	(0.29)	(0.22)
Positive DI (2)	0.10	0.56	0.08	0.22
--Employment	$\sum k_i^* n_i$		$\sum c_i^* n_i$	
Negative DI	-0.20	-0.34	-0.24	-0.26
Positive DI	0.20	0.34	0.24	0.26

using the value added per worker (c_i) as an index of the total capital intensity of each sector. The shares of sectoral exports were estimated by using the gross export values (x_i) presented in the I-O Tables as well as the net values ($\overline{x}_i$). The net export figures were estimated by applying the sectoral value-added coefficients (where the sectoral value-added coefficient and induced import coefficient add up to unity) computed from the I-O data.

When we apply the physical-capital intensities, we can see that the negative DI and the positive DI of Korea's (gross or net) manufactured exports and employment have all increased significantly during 1966–83. Interestingly, however, the results presented in Table 7.4 do not show any significant increases in the disparities of capital intensities during 1966–83 when we apply the per worker sectoral value added (as an index of total capital intensity of each sector). Such a result may be attributed to the fact that the distortions in Korea's factor market have been very concentrated on the use of physical capital only and consequently have generated increasing disparities mostly in the physical-capital intensities of manufactures exports and manufacturing employment.

Table 7.4 shows that manufactured tobacco products, cement, and particularly the refined petroleum products contributed most significantly to enhance the magnitude of positive DI of manufactures exports in 1966 as well as in 1983. However, the I-O export data and the export data based on customs clearance differed enormously in 1966. The differences represent the military procurements by the UN Command that were recorded as exports in the I-O Tables. For instance, the cigarettes purchased by the UN Command (with U.S. funding) were consumed almost entirely by the Korean soldiers under the UN Command (or in Vietnam), and yet, since they generated foreign-exchange earnings to the Korean government, they were recorded as exports. The same is true with fuel oils. On the other hand, the I-O export data and the customs clearance data differed only slightly in 1983, since the UN Command no longer made such procurements. That is, in 1966, the so-called exports of tobacco products, cement, and refined petroleum represented mostly domestic consumption while those in 1983 represented real exports. The positive DI excluding these three items [that is, positive DI(2) in Table 7.4] show more than doubling disparities in capital intensities during 1966–83.

When we apply the "total" capital intensities, c_i^*, to the gross export values, the negative DI declines in absolute magnitude. Furthermore, the DI for manufacturing employment shows a very small increase during 1966–83. When we apply total capital intensities to the "net" export values, both positive and negative DI decrease significantly. The positive DI increases significantly if we take out tobacco, cement, and petroleum products, but we still have the declining negative DI. Therefore, we can conclude that during 1966-83 only the disparities of "physical" capital intensities increased substantially. We cannot be so sure about the general trends of shift for "total" capital intensities.

Differential Rates of Sectoral Capital Deepening

If we examine Table 7.5, we can see that the real wage rate increased by 10 percent per annum on the average during 1966–83 in Korean manufacturing sectors. However, the physical-capital intensity of the relatively labor-intensive manufacturing sectors increased by only about 5 percent per annum on the average during the period, while that of relatively capital-intensive sectors increased by about 11 percent per annum. The estimated point elasticity of substitution (assuming no change in rental price of capital) between 1966 and 1983 amounted to about 0.5 in labor-intensive sectors while that in capital-intensive sectors amounted to about 1.2. Such a difference may at least partly be explained by the differences in total-loan/value-added ratios (0.9 versus 2.1) and in real interest costs (–1.6 percent versus –5.8 percent). That is, the fact that the capital-intensive manufacturing sectors were provided with more than twice larger (domestic bank and foreign) loans per value added activity at more than three times cheaper (overall) financial

Table 7.5
Factor Substitution in Korean Manufacturing Sectors (in 1985 dollar price[a])

	Physical Capital Intensity (k)	Total Capital Intensity (c)[b]	Real Wage Rate (w)	Elasticity of Substitution[c] $\frac{(dk/k)}{(dw/w)}$	$\frac{(dc/c)}{(dw/w)}$	Total-Loan/ Value-Added Ratio (1971-83)	Average Real Interest Rate[d] (Percent, Per Annum) 1971-83 1972-80 1981-86
					Labor-Intensive Sectors		
1966	$2,181	$1,591	$ 523				
1983	$5,182[e]	$7,857	$2,787				
(83-66)[e]	(5.2%)	(9.9%)	(10.3%)	0.51	0.96	0.9	-1.6% -5.5% 9.1%
					Intermediate Sectors		
1966	$ 4,237	$ 2,756	$ 628				
1983	$13,782	$14,043	$ 3,542				
(83-66)[e]	(7.2%)	(10.1%)	(10.7%)	0.67	0.94	1.5	-3.6% -8.1% 8.9%
					Capital-Intensive Sectors		
1966	$ 9,265	$ 5,820	$ 1,051				
1983	$54,163	$30,425	$ 4,853				
(83-66)[e]	(11.0%)	(10.2%)	(9.4%)	1.17	1.09	2.1	-5.8% -10.2% 8.1%

Sources: Economic Planning Board, *Report on Mining and Manufacturing Census*; Bank of Korea, *Financial Statements Analysis*, various issues.

[a] 1985 won values were obtained by applying the GNP deflators for capital formation and value added in manufacturing. 1985 dollar prices were obtained by applying the exchange rate of 777.63 won per dollar.

[b] Per worker value added.

[c] Assuming no change in real interest rates.

[d] Total-financial-expenses/Total-borrowing ratio minus rate of change in GNP deflator.

[e] Average annual rate of change during the period 1966–83.

costs must be responsible for such a differential in the rates of capital deepening between labor-intensive sectors and capital-intensive sectors.

An interesting fact is that when we used the per worker value added as an index of total capital intensity, we could not observe very significant differences between the labor-intensive sectors and capital-intensive sectors. The per worker value added of both groups of sectors increased by about 10 percent per annum during 1966–83. The elasticity of substitution estimated by using per worker value added amounted to about 1.0 for the labor-intensive sectors and about 1.1 for the capital-intensive sectors. It seems that there has been significant deepening of non-physical-capital intensities, say, in the form of skill and other human capital formation, in the labor-intensive group of manufacturing sectors. On the other hand, since the capital-intensive sectors were provided with relatively abundant funds for physical-capital formation at low financial costs, they seem to have paid less attention on the non-physical-capital formation activities.

CONCLUDING REMARKS

We observed that, in the 1970s, the Korean economy maintained significant distortions in commodity and factor markets in favor of the capital-intensive manufacturing sectors. Capital accumulation is expected to raise both the wage rate and the capital intensity of the production processes of the manufacturing sectors in general, and at the same time it is expected to expand the output and the employment of capital-intensive sectors more rapidly than those of the labor-intensive sectors (see Hong, 1975, 1976, 1979, 1987). Commodity and capital market distortions in favor of the capital-intensive sectors should accelerate the speed of capital deepening and the speed of the expansion of the capital- intensive manufacturing sectors. In Korea the real wage rate increased by about 10 percent per annum, on the average, during 1966–83 in both labor-intensive and capital-intensive sectors. And yet, the physical-capital intensity of capital-intensive sectors increased at more than twice the rate of the labor-intensive sectors. Such a difference may be partly explained by the credit rationing and interest cost differentials in favor of capital-intensive manufacturing sectors.

On the other hand, we also observed fairly rapid rates of expansion in the output and exports of some highly labor-intensive sectors such as wearing apparel and electronics and telecommunications equipment. These sectors, however, showed very low rates of capital deepening during the 1966–83 period. That is, we could observe increasing disparities in the physical-capital intensities of manufacturing sectors and of manufactured exports in Korea. This polarization phenomenon is consistent not only with the commodity market distortions but also with the double-factor-market-distortion model, that is, relatively low wage rates paid in the labor-intensive sectors together with a subsidized credit rationing in favor of the capital-intensive sectors. We observed that in Korea the higher the capital intensity of a sector, the higher the sectoral average wage rate was. Furthermore, we observed a significant positive relation between the capital intensity of a sector and the rate of effective protection accorded to the sector.

One may contend that the increased polarization of Korea's export pattern must be, at least partly, explained by the "protection" of Korea's established export markets for labor-intensive commodities by the established quota system of advanced countries that discriminates against the "later comers" (such as China) that have even lower wage cost than Korea. One may also contend that the rapid expansion of some labor-intensive manufactures exports does represent the growing diversification of Korea's exports into the high-quality, skill-intensive commodities instead of an increasing polarization in terms of capital-intensive commodities vs. simple unskilled labor-intensive commodities.

We could not determine to what extent the higher real wage rates in capital-intensive sectors reflected the return on human capital (such as higher education and higher on-the-job skill training). Furthermore, we only examined the factor market distortions in Korea and made no attempt to examine whether Korea's factor markets were more or less distorted in comparison with its major competing countries such as Taiwan. Perhaps one may argue that Korea's labor market has operated efficiently on the basis of supply and demand and has not been any more dualistic than the labor markets of Taiwan. One may, however, still argue that Korea's capital market has been more distorted in favor of capital-intensive sectors than that of Taiwan, and that a more amplified Krueger mechanism has operated in Korea, polarizing its export pattern more than in Taiwan. Unless one can substantiate the merit of polarized growth, however, we should expect that the reduction in market distortions would enhance the allocative efficiency of the Korean economy.

NOTES

1. In a two-factor two-sector Magee (1976) model, too much subsidy on the use of capital in the capital-intensive sector will raise (the wage rate and) the capital intensities of the capital-intensive as well as the labor-intensive sectors; but will somewhat oddly expand the output of the labor-intensive sector at the given endowment of capital stock. That is, with an extreme capital market distortion, the substitution effect will more than offset the output-expansion effect of the subsidy to the capital-intensive sector. If we further add the labor market distortion in the form of dual labor markets that pay lower wages in the labor-intensive sector, the net output-expansion effect becomes ambiguous, but instead we get a clear substitution effect: the labor-intensive sector becomes more labor intensive and the capital-intensive sector becomes more capital intensive than we would have expected in the absence of such double factor-market distortions.

2. The weighted-average real interest rate on foreign loans amounted to 2.1 percent per annum during 1967–71 and –7.4 percent per annum during 1972–76. See Hong and Park (1986). The Eurodollar (LIBOR) interest rates were about 13.2 percent per annum on average during 1977–81, and the domestic currency (won) depreciated by about 7 percent per annum on the average. Meanwhile, the rate of inflation in Korea (approximated by the rate of change in GNP deflator) was about 19.6 percent per annum on the average during the period. Therefore, the average real interest cost of foreign borrowing to Korean businesses could not have exceeded 1 percent per annum during 1977–81. During 1981–86, the LIBOR rate was 8.6 percent per annum on the average and domestic currency depreciated by about 5.3 percent per annum, while the rate of inflation in Korea was only about 4.2 percent per annum. Therefore, the real interest cost of foreign borrowing amounted to about 10 percent per annum during 1982–86.

3. Since 1982, however, Korea has been able to keep the rate of inflation below 5 percent per annum (which raised the real rate of interest on domestic bank loans to about 4 percent per annum on the average, and the real interest cost of foreign borrowing to about 10 percent) and has reduced the degree of concentration in credit rationing in favor of capital-intensive industries. As a result, the average bank-loan to value-added ratio and total-loan to value-added ratio of the capital-intensive sectors became only 11 percent and 54 percent larger than those of the labor-intensive sectors, respectively, and the average real interest cost of total borrowing of the labor-intensive group exceeded that of the capital-intensive group by only 7 percent per annum on the average during 1982–86.

4. The wage differentials according to sex and education were significantly reduced by 1985, that is, the wage rate of female workers amounted to 49 percent of that of male workers, and the wage rate of lowly educated workers amounted to 46 percent of that of highly educated workers.

REFERENCES

Deardorff, Alan V., "Weak Links in the Chain of Comparative Advantage," *Journal of International Economics*, 9, May 1979, 197–209.

Hong, Wontack, "Capital Accumulation, Factor Substitution, and the Changing Factor Intensity of Trade: The Case of Korea (1966–72)," in Wontack Hong and Anne O. Krueger, eds., *Trade and Development in Korea*, Seoul: KDI Press, 1975.

———, *Factor Supply and Factor Intensity of Trade in Korea*, Seoul: KDI Press, 1976.

———, *Trade, Distortions and Employment Growth in Korea*, Seoul: KDI Press, 1979.

———, "A Comparative Static Application of the Heckscher-Ohlin Model of

Factor Proportion: Korean Experience," *Weltwirtschaftliches Archiv, 123*, 1987, 309–24.

———, Market Distortions and Trade Patterns of Korea: 1960-85, KDI Working Paper No. 8807, Seoul, 1988.

———, and Park, Yung Chul, "Financing Export-Oriented Growth in Korea," in A. Tan and B. Kapur, eds., *Pacific Growth and Financial Interdependence*, Sydney, Australia: Allen and Unwin, 1986.

Jones, Ronald W., "A Three-Factor Model in Theory, Trade and History," in J. Bhagwati et al., eds., *Trade, Balance of Payments and Growth*, Amsterdam: North Holland, 1971.

———, "The Small Country in a Many-Commodity World," *Australian Economic Papers, 13*, December 1974, 225–36.

Kim, Kwang-Suk, and Hong, Sung-Duck, Long-Term Shifts in the Structure of Nominal and Effective Rates of Protection in Korea, KDI Report No. 82-02, Seoul, 1982.

Krueger, Anne O., *Growth, Distortions and Patterns of Trade Among Many Countries*, Princeton Studies in International Finance, No. 41, Princeton, N.J.: Princeton University, 1977.

Magee, Stephen P., *International Trade and Distortions in Factor Markets*, New York: Marcel Dekker, 1976.

8

Changing Comparative Advantage and Productivity Growth in the Manufacturing Industries

David Dollar and Kenneth Sokoloff

INTRODUCTION

Over the last two decades Korea has been transformed from an exporter of light manufactures, especially textiles, to a major exporter of heavier industrial products, such as steel and automobiles, and of higher-technology consumer goods, such as televisions. In this chapter we argue that both the Heckscher-Ohlin and Ricardian models of international trade provide important insights into these changes in comparative advantage. As Korea has accumulated capital much more rapidly than the world as a whole, its exports have shifted from light to heavy manufactures, as predicted by the Heckscher-Ohlin model. It is also the case that the particular industries in which exports have grown rapidly have generally exhibited rapid total factor productivity growth, suggesting that industry-specific technological advance is also an important source of comparative advantage, as implied by the Ricardian model.

SOURCES OF CHANGING COMPARATIVE ADVANTAGE: A THEORETICAL FRAMEWORK

The Heckscher-Ohlin (HO) and Ricardian models of international trade both provide insight into potential sources of changing comparative advantage. In each model it will be seen that the *proximate* source of changes in a nation's comparative advantage is differential rates of labor productivity growth across industries. The models, however, present different hypotheses concerning the underlying cause of these differential rates of labor productivity growth.

The Heckscher-Ohlin model hypothesizes that the underlying source of comparative advantage is a country's endowment (or supplies) of basic factors of production—land, minerals, capital, labor, and so on. In the case of Korea in the 1960s, for instance, the economy was poorly endowed with land, minerals, and capital, relative to its labor supply. Hence it is no surprise that during that decade, once an appropriate exchange rate was established and trade somewhat liberalized, exports consisted primarily of labor-intensive manufactures while imports were concentrated in capital- and natural-resource-intensive products.

Within this framework, changing comparative advantage results from changes in a country's supply of basic factors. Since endowments of natural resources do not change much over time, the key alteration in relative factor supplies is growth in the overall capital-labor ratio. To the extent that an individual economy is accumulating capital more rapidly than the world as a whole, its comparative advantage should be shifting toward more capital-intensive manufactures.

There are a number of ways in which this change in comparative advantage can be brought about at the industry level. The most plausible scenario is that capital deepening will be occurring in every industry as a result of the greater availability of capital in the economy.[1] This capital deepening tends to raise average labor productivity in every industry, but it raises it more in heavy industries than in light industries. To see this formally, consider a standard growth decomposition for an industry i, which exhibits constant returns to scale:

$$\hat{Y}_i = \alpha_i \hat{K}_i + (1 - \alpha_i)\hat{L}_i \tag{1}$$

where Y, K, and L are value added, capital input, and labor input, and "^" denotes relative rate of change. If factors are paid their marginal products then α_i is capital's distributional share (and $1 - \alpha_i$ is labor's distributional share); across industries, α_i increases with capital intensity. Equation (1) can be rearranged to provide a relationship between labor productivity growth and capital deepening:

$$(Y_i \widehat{/L_i}) = \alpha_i (K_i \widehat{/L_i}) \tag{2}$$

Hence it can be seen that average labor productivity rises more rapidly in capital-intensive industries for a given rate of growth of the capital-labor ratio. It is also the case that in Korea the capital-labor ratio has tended to rise more rapidly in the heavy industries than in the light (as documented below).

Real wages should also be rising as a result of this capital deepening, at a rate that reflects average productivity growth for the whole economy and which is the same across industries if labor markets are fairly competitive. In this situation production costs in heavy industries will be declining relative to costs in light industries.[2] This process is the micro foundation of changing comparative advantage.

It is well known that in a model with more industries (products) than factors of production, the HO model cannot predict specifically which industries will increase their shares of total exports.[3] The model rather makes the general prediction that, in a country undergoing rapid growth in the overall capital-labor ratio, exports should be shifting from light to heavy industries.

The Ricardian trade model focuses alternatively on relative technology levels, both across industries and across countries.[4] The model predicts that a country's exports will be concentrated in industries in which its technology level is relatively high. It might be argued that technology is a kind of productive factor, and that hence this theory is not really different from the HO model. The HO model, however, focuses on productive factors that can be used in any sector of the economy, whereas technology tends to be specific to a particular sector. In this sense the Ricardian model, as well as its later offshoots such as the Ricardo-Viner model, locates the source of comparative advantage in factors that are industry specific.

According to Ricardian analysis, Korea's comparative advantage in the 1960s lay in manufacturing industries with standardized technologies that could easily be adopted by a developing economy. This notion is not mutually exclusive with the HO prediction of comparative advantage in light industries; and can even be viewed as helping to resolve some of the indeterminacy in the multi-industry version of the HO model. There are in reality a large number of light industries, and yet many different developing countries have followed the same route of first concentrating exports in clothing and textiles, industries with easily accessible technologies.

In the Ricardian framework, changing comparative advantage naturally arises from technological change occurring at different rates in different industries. Once again, we can analyze these changes in terms of their effects on labor productivity. Other things equal, industries with rapid technological change will exhibit rapid labor productivity growth and hence declining relative costs (assuming as before that labor markets are competitive and that wages are rising at similar rates across industries). From the Ricardian point of view, equation (2) above ignores total factor productivity (TFP) growth, which is the residual that results from attempting to fit equation (1) to real world data.[5] Taking account of TFP growth, equation (2) becomes

$$(\hat{Y_i/L_i}) = \alpha_i(\hat{K_i/L_i}) + \hat{TFP}_i \qquad (3)$$

There is no reason in principle not to integrate the HO and Ricardian theories. Both trade models imply that changing comparative advantage is linked to differential rates of labor productivity growth across industries; specifically, they imply that exports should be shifting toward industries with rapid productivity growth. This is a general proposition that will be tested empirically against Korean data, below. Furthermore, the decomposition of labor productivity growth in equation

(3) will be carried out industry-by-industry to provide evidence of the source of changing Korean comparative advantage.

A final note about the Ricardian model is that it is ultimately somewhat dissatisfying in that it leaves unaddressed the question of what is the source of technological innovation and why its pace varies across industries. Hence in industries in which rapid TFP growth is found to be of importance, it will be interesting to speculate on its origins.

CHANGES IN KOREA'S PATTERN OF TRADE, 1970–83

In this section we examine changes in Korea's pattern of trade between 1970 and 1983. Unfortunately, the highly aggregated character of Korean trade data from the 1960s makes it difficult to extend this analysis back before 1970. Even for the more recent period, trade data tend to be more aggregated than production and employment data. Hence we are able to examine exports and imports disaggregated into 14 manufacturing categories plus several other categories that we have lumped together under the heading "Natural Resource Industries" (primarily food products and petroleum).

Table 8.1 lists the 14 manufacturing industries and ranks them in descending order of the capital-labor ratio (using 1979 data, the most recent year for which industry-level capital stock data were available to us). The seven most labor-intensive industries have been separated into a "Light Industries" category. We found it useful to divide the seven most capital-intensive industries into two categories, "Heavy" and "Medium," because the productivity performance of these two groups has been quite different.

The interindustry distribution of Korean exports in 1970, 1978, and 1983 is presented in Table 8.2. Exports in 1970 were overwhelmingly concentrated in light industries, with four fifths of exports originating in this sector. Furthermore, one industry in this group (textiles, clothing, footwear) alone accounted for almost half of all exports. These data confirm the earlier assertion that in the 1960s Korean comparative advantage clearly lay in labor-intensive, low-technology products.

Table 8.2 also indicates that Korea's comparative advantage has slowly been evolving away from the light industries, toward the medium and heavy industries. By 1978 the light industries' share of exports had declined to .66. Over the same period the medium industries increased their share from .04 to .15, while the heavy industry share rose from .05 to .10. The trend continued in the 1978–83 period, with light industry exports declining to .53 of total exports. Over these five years the share of the medium industries nearly doubled, to .26, while the heavy industry share rose to .13. The medium and heavy industries together, which accounted for only 9 percent of Korean exports in 1970, generated almost 40 percent of exports in 1983.

Table 8.1
Characteristics of Korean Manufacturing Industries

Industries	Index of Capital Intensity, 1979 (Mfg=100)	Value Added Share 1963-1979 (percent)
Heavy Industries	282[a]	29.7
Iron and Steel	590	7.9
Nonferrous Metals	210	1.2
Nonmetal Products, n.e.c.	169	6.2
Chemicals	168	14.4
Medium Industries	121[a]	17.1
Transport Equipment	139	8.5
Machinery	127	4.5
Metal Products, n.e.c.	79	4.2
Light Industries	57[a]	53.2
Wood Products	69	3.9
Textiles, Clothing, Footwear	61	28.8
Electrical Goods	53	11.0
Rubber Products	51	3.9
Leather Products	50	1.0
Furniture	40	0.6
Manufactures, n.e.c.	33	4.0
All Industries	135[a]	100.0

Sources: The information on value added and employment were drawn from the relevant years of the *United Nations Yearbook of Industrial Statistics*. The estimates of the net value of the capital stock were prepared by the Economic Planning Board, and appear in *Preliminary Data on Korean Capital Stock by Industry, 1960-1979*, Seoul: KDI, 1987.

[a]Weighted average, using value added shares from Table 8.1, Column 2.

Between 1970 and 1983 seven individual industries experienced large changes in their share of total exports. (We somewhat arbitrarily define "large change" as a shift of 4 percentage points, either positive or negative.) The four industries that undergo large increases are iron and steel, transport equipment, metal products n.e.c., and electrical goods. It is interesting that in terms of capital intensity, the four are distributed rather evenly among Korean manufacturing industries: steel is by far the most capital-intensive industry; transport equipment and metal products are of medium intensity; while the electrical goods industry is less capital-intensive than textiles. Hence it is not simply the case that capital-intensive industries are expanding their export shares, while labor-intensive industries are contracting

Table 8.2
Distribution of Korean Exports by Industry,
1970, 1978, and 1983

Industries	(percent of total exports)		
	1970	1978	1983
Heavy Industries	4.8	9.8	13.1
Iron and Steel	1.7	4.6	7.6
Nonferrous Metals	0.8	0.3	0.6
Nonmetal Products, n.e.c.	0.3	2.2	1.8
Chemicals	1.5	2.7	3.1
Medium Industries	3.9	14.9	26.1
Transport Equipment	1.2	9.0	17.3
Machinery	1.1	1.7	3.0
Metal Products, n.e.c.	1.6	4.2	5.8
Light Industries	79.9	65.7	53.1
Wood Products	12.1	4.3	0.7
Textiles, Clothing, Footwear	46.0	39.0	30.6
Electrical Goods	5.6	10.0	12.3
Rubber Products	0.5	1.8	1.6
Leather Products	0.1	0.4	0.2
Furniture	0.2	0.3	0.3
Manufactures, n.e.c.	15.5	9.9	7.4
Natural-Resource Industries	11.4	11.6	7.7

Source: Bank of Korea, *Economic Statistics Yearbook*, various issues.

theirs. It is true, however, that the three industries that experienced large declines in their shares of total exports are all light industries: wood products, textiles, and manufactures, n.e.c. The latter industry is the least capital-intensive and includes toys and other simple manufactured goods.

Table 8.3 presents the interindustry distribution of Korean imports in 1970, 1978, and 1983. In 1970 imports consisted primarily of chemicals, machinery (including transport equipment and electrical goods), and natural-resource-based products like food and petroleum. It may seem surprising that imports of textiles were so substantial, but this reflects the fact that Korea imported synthetic fiber and fabric to be processed into clothing, much of which was subsequently exported.

Between 1970 and 1983 the structure of imports did not change as much as the structure of exports. Only four industries experienced as much as a four-percentage-point swing in their share of total imports. The share of machinery in imports

Table 8.3
Distribution of Korean Imports by Industry,
1970, 1978, and 1983

Industries	(percent of total exports) 1970	1978	1983
Heavy Industries	15.5	19.1	16.2
Iron and Steel	4.9	7.2	3.8
Nonferrous Metals	1.1	1.9	1.9
Nonmetal Products, n.e.c.	0.5	0.7	1.0
Chemicals	9.0	9.3	9.5
Medium Industries	27.6	27.7	21.8
Transport Equipment	8.3	7.7	9.1
Machinery	16.9	18.6	11.4
Metal Products, n.e.c.	2.4	1.4	1.3
Light Industries	31.0	28.0	26.0
Wood Products	7.0	4.8	2.8
Textiles, Clothing, Footwear	13.7	7.2	5.6
Electrical Goods	7.3	9.3	10.9
Rubber Products	0.1	0.1	0.3
Leather Products	0.3	2.7	2.5
Furniture	0.1	0.0	0.1
Manufactures, n.e.c.	2.5	3.9	3.8
Natural-Resource Industries	25.9	25.2	36.0

Source: Bank of Korea, *Economic Statistics Yearbook*, various issues.

declined most dramatically, from .169 in 1970 to .114 in 1983, reflecting the fact that Korean demand for machinery is increasingly met from domestic supply. Wood and textile imports also declined; this resulted from the relative decline of these industries as exporters and the consequently diminished need for imported inputs. The big increase in import share is realized by the natural-resource products, reflecting a growing need for petroleum and also a large increase in the relative price of that commodity.

LABOR AND TOTAL FACTOR PRODUCTIVITY GROWTH, 1963–79

In this section we examine the extent to which changing Korean comparative advantage can be explained by interindustry differentials in labor productivity growth and also investigate the underlying sources of that productivity growth. To do this we draw on our earlier work on the growth of labor and total factor productivity in Korean manufacturing industries over the period 1963–79 (Dollar and Sokoloff, forthcoming). It will be seen that both the HO and Ricardian trade models can help us understand the alterations in Korea's trade patterns described in the previous section.

Table 8.4 summarizes our main findings concerning the growth rates of real value added per worker, net capital per worker, and TFP in 14 manufacturing industries.[6] Labor productivity in general was rising very rapidly during this period, at a (weighted) average rate of 12.2 percent per annum for these industries. There are significant inter-industry differentials in growth rates. Productivity in transport equipment, for instance, rose at an average rate 4 percentage points greater than the rate of growth in textiles, clothing, and footwear. Over 17 years this necessarily

Table 8.4

Rates of Growth of Labor Productivity, Capital Intensity, and TFP in 14 Korean Manufacturing Industries, 1963-79 (annual rates of growth in percent)

	Valued Added Per Worker	Net Capital Per Worker	TFP
Heavy Industries[a]	12.4	10.9	4.4
Iron and Steel	14.1	15.4	2.5
Nonferrous Metals	14.9	9.3	8.1
Nonmetal Products, n.e.c.	10.0	13.4	0.1
Chemicals	12.3	7.4	6.9
Medium Industries[a]	14.5	8.3	8.5
Transport Equipment	14.5	7.9	8.7
Machinery	13.6	10.2	6.2
Metal Products, n.e.c.	15.3	6.9	10.4
Light Industries[a]	11.3	6.1	7.0
Wood Products	6.6	5.1	3.0
Textiles, Clothing, Footwear	10.3	6.4	5.7
Electrical Goods	14.7	6.1	10.4
Rubber Products	11.2	4.2	8.3
Leather Products	12.6	-0.1	12.7
Furniture	10.4	1.7	9.2
Manufactures, n.e.c.	13.9	8.6	8.0
Natural-Resource Industries[a]	12.2	7.9	6.5

Source: Dollar and Sokoloff, forthcoming.

[a]Weighted average, using value added shares from Table 8.1, column 2.

resulted in a large change in relative labor costs for the two industries (assuming as before that labor markets are fairly competitive).[7]

It is interesting, however, that the heavy industries as a group do not experience higher than average labor productivity growth. The medium industries in fact have the most rapid average growth rate, 14.5 percent, compared with 12.4 percent for the heavy industries. The light industries as a group do experience slower than average labor productivity growth.

The average rate of growth of the capital-labor ratio differs substantially across industries. Capital deepening occurs at average annual rates of 10.9 percent in the heavy industries, 8.3 percent in the medium industries, and 6.1 percent in the light industries. On the basis of this, one would expect more dispersion in industry labor productivity growth rates than we observe. However, total factor productivity growth has been much more rapid in the light and medium industries than in the heavy. In fact, for the former two categories, TFP growth is the main source of labor productivity growth, accounting for more than half of it. Only in the heavy industries is capital deepening the main source of labor productivity growth.

We have also addressed the question of whether changes in Korea's pattern of exports can be explained by these interindustry differentials in productivity growth. As noted earlier, trade data before 1970 are too aggregated to be of use for our purposes. Hence we are left trying to explain changes in trade patterns between 1970 and 1978 with data on productivity growth over a longer period, 1963–79. This approach can be justified on the grounds that interindustry differences in productivity growth are likely to change slowly over time and that hence average productivity growth in 1963–79 is bound to be highly correlated with productivity growth during the shorter period 1970–78 (especially if the latter were corrected for cyclical factors, as it should be).

We take as our measure of changing comparative advantage the difference between an industry's share of exports in 1978 and its share in 1970, which is positive (negative) for an industry whose exports are expanding more (less) rapidly than exports as a whole.[8] Our correlation analysis reports the (weighted) correlation, across the 14 industries, of this measure with the growth rates of labor productivity, capital intensity, and TFP. Most important is the very high, positive correlation (.76) between increased export share and labor productivity growth: it is true that changing comparative advantage is related to labor productivity growth.

All four of the industries identified in the previous section as having large increases in export share have labor productivity growth in excess of 14 percent per annum, well above the average for the manufacturing industries. Wood products, textiles, clothing, and footwear, on the other hand, are industries with declining export shares and lower than average labor productivity growth. Manufactures n.e.c. is the only aberration, with high labor productivity growth and a large decline in export share.

Our correlation analysis also indicates that increased export share is positively correlated with TFP growth (.33) and capital deepening (.30), though the latter correlations are only of moderate strength.[9] It is also the case that there is a very strong negative correlation (-.65) between TFP growth and capital deepening, indicating that in general rapid labor productivity growth results from above average TFP growth or above average capital deepening but rarely both. Hence it appears that in some industries expanding export share results from rapid capital deepening, whereas in others it is caused by technological advance. Steel is the best example of the former, while electrical goods is an example of the latter. Transport equipment and metal products are also industries with above average TFP growth, but rates of capital deepening at or below the average for all industries.

We also estimated a cross-section regression "explaining" increased export share by TFP growth and capital deepening. Both explanatory variables are significantly positive, and the R^2 is surprisingly high, at .57, so that most of the change in the pattern of Korean exports can be explained by a simple eclectic model focusing on capital deepening and TFP growth.

Our data on productivity growth end in 1979, hence we cannot relate them formally to changes in export shares between 1978 and 1983. However, the correlation between increased export share 1970–78 and increased export share 1978–83 is .92. What we observe in the 1980s is apparently a continuation of trends in the pattern of trade begun in the 1970s.

Hence we reach the eclectic conclusion that the HO and Ricardian models both inform our understanding of changing Korean comparative advantage. There is a strong positive relationship at the industry level between labor productivity growth and increasing export share, as trade theory in general predicts. As the HO model would suggest for a country undergoing rapid growth in the overall capital-labor ratio, the light industries do experience relatively slow labor productivity growth and lose export share. Electrical goods, however, is one very labor-intensive industry that goes against this trend in a major way, experiencing rapid labor productivity growth driven by technological development and consequently earning an expanded export share.

It is also the case that the medium industries, despite slower capital deepening than that achieved in the heavy industries, experience very rapid labor productivity growth, and again it is TFP growth that accounts for this result. Thus we find that changing Korean comparative advantage is not simply a case of shifting from light to heavy industries; technological development seems to play a major role in determining which industries are increasing their share of exports.

CONCLUSIONS

It has been established then that changing comparative advantage is related to differential rates of labor productivity growth across industries. Furthermore, the latter has been decomposed into the contribution of capital deepening plus a residual, labeled TFP growth. The task that naturally arises next is to explain these inter-industry differentials in capital deepening and TFP growth.

In the absence of government intervention, different rates of capital accumulation across industries should reflect differences in industry production functions, specifically the elasticity of substitution between labor and capital. As wages rise in response to overall capital accumulation, some technologies admit of easier substitution away from the factor whose cost is rising, and consequently will exhibit more rapid rise in the capital-labor ratio.

In the case of Korea, especially during the 1970s, we must also take into account the intervention of the government, which was very active in directing credit to certain industries under its industrial policy of promoting the "Heavy and Chemical Industries" (HCI). Among the industries under consideration here, iron and steel, chemicals, transport equipment, machinery, and electrical goods were the major beneficiaries of subsidized investment funds. It should be noted that the program was specifically aimed at diversifying Korean trade through the promotion of heavy industrial exports.

The HCI program no doubt explains the extremely rapid rate of growth of the capital-labor ratio in heavy industries. In economic terms the program met with mixed success. Results in petrochemicals and machinery were very poor; steel has become a successful international competitor, but the amount of subsidized capital injected into this industry was enormous; transport equipment is the only unqualified success from the program. The electrical goods industry has grown very impressively, but not in the sub-sectors targeted by the HCI program. Very labor-intensive assembly operations fueled much of the growth in this industry, and despite its inclusion in the HCI program the capital-labor ratio in this industry grew much less rapidly than in manufacturing as a whole.

If there were important externalities that justified government subsidization of these industries, one would expect to see especially rapid TFP growth in the targeted industries. In fact, of the five main industries subsidized, only transport equipment and electrical goods exhibited higher than average TFP growth.[10] It is interesting that these are the two industries with the greatest increases in their export shares. A balanced assessment of the HCI program is that it facilitated industrial restructuring in the direction in which Korea's comparative advantage was likely to go, but that the program was overambitious and hence unnecessarily costly. This is the view taken in the World Bank's recent study of Korean industrial policy (Leipziger et al., 1987, p. 47).

While the HCI program no doubt explains some of the large interindustry differences in rates of capital deepening, trying to account for the differences across industries in the rate of TFP growth is necessarily more speculative. In our earlier work we showed that rapid TFP growth is associated with growth in the average number of workers per plant. This suggests that TFP growth may be driven by the

adoption of more modern, large-scale production techniques with a finer division
of labor. The extent to which this is feasible in a particular industry depends on
many things, including whether or not there are production techniques in use in
developed countries that can be easily borrowed or licensed. It is also the case that
in certain industries production can be easily broken down into different activities,
which can then take place in different countries. Electrical goods and transport
equipment are both examples of industries with this kind of technology, and in both
cases Korea has tended to specialize in particular niches and to engage in cooperative production with firms in the United States and Japan, under many different
institutional arrangements (direct foreign investment, joint ventures, licensing, and
so on). It seems plausible that the successful transfer of new technology to Korea
would be easier in industries where the production process can be decomposed in
this way.[11] In steel and petrochemicals it is much more difficult to divide up the
production process, and that may be one reason why investment in those industries
has not been as successful and why TFP growth has been sluggish.

One thing that does emerge clearly from the Korean experience is that the
government cannot simply choose to "create comparative advantage" in a particular manufacturing industry. If the government directs investment to an industry
for which the country does not have the necessary technological capability, the
likely outcome is that rapid growth in the capital-labor ratio will be offset by
relatively poor TFP performance and that the country's firms will not emerge as
successful exporters. (Korean petrochemicals is an example.) On the other hand,
in industries where the country's firms can develop the necessary technological
base, targeted investment will accelerate the shift in comparative advantage in the
direction of these industries. It is another question altogether whether this kind of
government support is necessary or cost effective. After the fact, the extremely
rapid TFP growth in transport equipment and electrical goods seems to indicate the
existence of major externalities that would justify government targeting of these
industries. But, as the Korean experience with industrial policy in the 1970s makes
clear, it is extremely difficult to know beforehand which industries to support.

NOTES

1. In the HO model with factor-price equalization across countries, accumulation of capital by a small country would not result in capital deepening in any
industry; rather, the industry mix would shift toward more capital-intensive industries without any change in the capital-labor ratio in any industry. This prediction
does not fit the Korean data at all. On the HO model with factor-price equalization,
see Leamer (1984, ch. 2); on the HO model without factor-price equalization, see
Deardorff (1984).

2. The cost of producing value added includes capital cost in addition to labor

cost. But the increased availability of capital will also be reducing capital costs in heavy industries relative to capital costs in light industries. This follows because the cost of using capital will be declining and naturally this provides a relatively greater saving for industries that use capital intensively. This is another reason why production costs in heavy industries will be declining relative to costs in light industries.

3. See, for instance, Leamer (1984, ch. 2).

4. Recent technology-based models in the Ricardian tradition include Krugman (1979) and Dollar (1986).

5. As measured TFP growth is a residual, it may be capturing other (omitted) factors in addition to technological advance. Some might argue that it is capturing growth of human capital, which is a general productive factor that can be included in the HO framework. Such an argument does not fit the Korean data very well: across industries measured TFP growth has no correlation with wage growth, as would be expected if measured TFP growth is picking up increases in human capital and such increases are reflected in wages.

6. Unfortunately, several industries covered by our productivity study are aggregated together in the trade statistics. In compiling Tables 8.1 and 8.4, which match the industry classification used in the trade tables, we aggregated the productivity results for several subindustries, and did so by calculating weighted averages, using value added shares (1963–79) as the weights.

7. Across Korean industries, wages have grown at remarkably similar rates, implying that the labor markets are in fact very competitive.

8. Empirical work on changing comparative advantage is ideally done using net exports. The problem with applying this approach to Korea is that the country has shifted from having a large overall trade deficit in the 1970s to having a large surplus in the 1980s, so that in fact all manufacturing industries have experienced large increases in net exports. Since, as noted above, the structure of Korean imports has changed relatively little in the period under examination, changes in the structure of exports seems to us to be a good proxy for changing comparative advantage.

9. Nishimizu and Robinson (1984), working with industry-level data from Korea, Turkey, and Yugoslavia, also find a positive relationship between TFP growth and export expansion, and discuss several hypotheses that may explain this result. Their estimates of TFP growth for Korean manufacturing disaggregated into 16 industries are derived from a gross output rather than value added framework, and consequently tend to be lower than our estimates. The pattern of interindustry variation, however, is broadly similar.

10. The poor TFP performance of the petrochemical industry is not obvious from Table 8.4 because we have aggregated industrial chemicals and other chemicals in order to be consistent with the trade data. TFP growth in industrial

chemicals, which includes petrochemicals, was 1.2 percent per annum during the 1963–79 period.

11. For an interesting discussion of technological development in Korean manufacturing industries and its relation to trade and investment, see Westphal, Rhee, and Pursell (1981).

REFERENCES

Deardorff, Alan V., "Testing Trade Theories and Predicting Trade Flows," in Ronald Jones and Peter Kenen, eds., *Handbook of International Economics*, vol. 1, Elsevier Science Publishers, 1984.

Dollar, David, "Technological Innovation, Capital Mobility, and the Product Cycle in North-South Trade," *American Economic Review*, 76, March 1986, 177–90.

————, and Sokoloff, Kenneth, "Patterns of Productivity Growth in South Korean Manufacturing Industries, 1963–1979," *Journal of Development Economics* (forthcoming).

Krugman, Paul R., "A Model of Innovation, Technology Transfer, and the World Distribution of Income," *Journal of Political Economy*, 87, April 1979, 253–66.

Leamer, Edward E., *Sources of International Comparative Advantage*, Cambridge: MIT Press, 1984.

Leipziger, D. M., et al. "The Conduct of Industrial Policy," *Korea: Managing the Industrial Transition*, vol. 1, World Bank, 1987.

Nishimizu, Mieko and Robinson, Sherman, "Trade Policies and Productivity Change in Semi-Industrialized Countries," *Journal of Development Economics*, 16, September–October 1984, 177–206.

Westphal, L., Rhee, Y. W., and Pursell, G., "Korean Industrial Competence: Where It Came From," World Bank Staff Working Papers, No. 469, World Bank, 1981.

Part Three

FACTOR SUBSTITUTION
AND PRODUCTIVITY GROWTH

Change in productivity is both the cause and the consequence of the evolution of dynamic forces operating in an economy, that is, technical progress, accumulation of human and physical capital, entrepreneurship, and institutional arrangement. Also, the information regarding the elasticity of substitution between factor inputs is important from the policy standpoint. If, for example, the elasticity of substitution between labor and capital is high, it is relatively easy to expand employment opportunities without sacrificing output growth by manipulating relative factor prices (that is, the reduction of the wage-rental ratio). The high elasticity of substitution also allows a flexible response to external changes—a factor price change in the international market.

In Korea during the period of rapid growth, the displacement of labor was successfully averted (in the face of a rising wage-rental ratio and nearly unitary elasticity of substitution between labor and capital) through the rapid growth of output and exports. In the future, however, as the growth rates of output and exports decline, the prevention of labor displacement will not be possible without altering the wage-rental ratio.

In their efforts to address some of these issues J. K. Kwon and K. Yuhn examine, in the first chapter of this section, the production structure and productivity growth of Korean manufacturing. They examine three specific issues: (a) the pattern of substitution among factor inputs (capital, labor, energy, and materials); (b) the measurement and analysis of the multifactor productivity (MFP) growth with special emphasis on the labor productivity growth; and (c) the existence of a value-added aggregate implicit in GNP statistics.

The principal findings of their study are that: (1) the elasticity of substitution between capital and labor is higher than the previous results; (2) contrary to common notion, capital services and energy are substitutes while energy and labor are complements; (3) technical change biases are toward labor saving and capital using; (4) the analysis of productivity growth suggests a relatively small total multifactor productivity change and that capital and material inputs were the dominant sources of the growth of output; (5) labor productivity growth is largely attributable to the growth of capital stock.

One of the most striking features of Korean manufacturing observed from their study is the rapid growth of factor inputs—especially capital and materials—as the predominant sources for the growth of output, and the relatively small role played by technological progress. The slowdown in TFP (MFP) growth in Korean manufacturing is attributable to the overambitious investment policy of the government, which has frequently ignored the market mechanism and the concomitant inefficiency associated with rapid capital formation caused by double distortions (that is, in factor prices and factor proportions). Meanwhile, the relatively high elasticity of substitution between capital services and labor, together with the factor price distortion, is responsible for the shift toward capital-using and labor-saving technological change.

In an attempt to examine the effect of different development approaches in Korea and Taiwan on their respective production (or cost) functions and productivity growth, in the second chapter J. P. Choi compares the production technology of manufacturing in Taiwan and Korea. His estimates are based on the translog function approach developed by Christensen, Jorgenson, and Lau, and is basically the same approach as that of Kwon and Yuhn, but with different data. The general conclusion of Choi is that for both Korea and Taiwan, the respective growth rates of TFP are low, concurring with the findings of Kwon and Yuhn. While the rates of TFP growth for Korean manufacturing estimated by Kwon and Yuhn and by Choi are considerably lower than the rates estimated by others, they seem to be in concurrence with the low rates estimated by others for Japan, the United States, Singapore, and Taiwan, all of which show a negligible contribution of TFP and a more substantial contribution of capital and materials.

9

Analysis of Factor Substitution and Productivity Growth in Korean Manufacturing, 1961–1981

Jene K. Kwon and Kyhyang Yuhn

INTRODUCTION

The objective of this study is to investigate empirically the production technology of Korean manufacturing at the aggregate level. We are specifically interested in three issues: The first involves the pattern of substitution among factor inputs. This issue is of special interest in view of substantial controversy in the literature concerning the complementarity or substitutability between capital and energy and between labor and energy—issues that are of considerable importance for policy purposes. The second concerns the measurement and analysis of multifactor productivity growth in Korean manufacturing, with specific reference to various aspects of its industrialization in the past two decades. Finally, to link the two analyses, we test for the existence of value-added aggregate to see if the traditional measure of value-added output is appropriate for the analysis of productivity growth. The double deflation techniques used in Korea as in other countries to measure value-added output for subsectors of the economy are based on the assumption of strong partial separability of capital and labor from intermediate inputs.[1]

The present study employs the translog function approach developed by Christensen, Jorgenson, and Lau (1973). It provides a flexible functional form that permits the test of factor substitution and input separability.

The principal findings of the study are: (1) The elasticity of substitution between capital and labor is higher than previous results. Given the factor distortions caused by government policies, this poses an ominous sign for the policymakers. (2) Contrary to the common notion, capital and energy are found to be substitutes while energy and labor are complements. (3) In contrast with the results of others, our analysis of productivity growth suggests a relatively small contribution of multifactor (total) productivity (MFP or TFP) change on the real output growth. (4) The strong separability hypothesis that underlies input and output measurements in the conventional GNP framework of output is clearly rejected.

THE MODEL

We specify a nonhomothetic translog cost function to evaluate the nature of production technology. The total cost is related to four inputs—labor (L), capital (K), energy (E), and raw materials (M) as:

$$\ln C = \alpha_0 + \alpha_Q \ln Q + \frac{1}{2}\gamma_{QQ}(\ln Q)^2 + \sum_i \alpha_i \ln P_i + \frac{1}{2}\sum_i \sum_j \gamma_{ij} \ln P_i \ln P_j$$

$$+ \sum_i \gamma_{Qi} \ln Q \ln P_i + \sum_i \theta_{it} \ln P_i \ln T + \theta_{Qt} \ln Q \ln T + \beta_t \ln T + \frac{1}{2}\beta_{tt}(\ln T)^2 \quad (1)$$

where C is total cost; Q, output; P's, the prices of the factor inputs; and T, the index of "technology" that is a simple time function. We assume that the cost function as specified in equation (1) is well behaved.

Differentiating the translog cost function logarithmically with respect to input prices yields the cost share equations

$$S_i = \alpha_i + \sum_j \gamma_{ij} \ln P_j + \gamma_{Qi} \ln Q + \theta_{ti} \ln T \quad (2)$$

for $i, j = $ K, L, E, M, where S_i is the cost share of the ith input.

Following Berndt and Christensen (1973), the Allen partial elasticities of substitution between inputs i and j for the translog cost function can be expressed in terms of the parameters of the cost function and cost shares as

$$\sigma_{ij} = (\gamma_{ij} + S_i S_j)/S_i S_j \quad (3)$$

The own price elasticity of demand for the ith-factor of production is

$$\eta_{ii} = \sigma_{ii} S_i \quad (4)$$

The translog specification has other advantages. We can describe various types of production technology by imposing parametric restrictions to equation (1).[2] We consider four models with parametric restrictions in addition to the nonhomothetic functional form as shown in equation (1).

For the estimation of the translog cost function and, particularly, for the analysis of productivity growth, it is critically important to investigate the existence of a value-added $(K - L)$ aggregate in Korean manufacturing sector. As Norsworthy and Malmquist (1983) noted, the incorrect choice of the value-added framework of output for productivity analysis can distort the magnitude and sometimes even the direction of productivity growth. In order for a value-added aggregate to exist, there must be separability of K and L from E and M. We distinguish two separability conditions that are based on Denny and Fuss (1977).

(a) Connective weak separability:

$$\frac{\gamma_L}{\gamma_K} = \frac{\gamma_{LM}}{\gamma_{KM}} = \frac{\gamma_{LE}}{\gamma_{KE}} \tag{5}$$

(b) Additive weak separability:

$$\gamma_{LM} = \gamma_{KM} = 0, \, \gamma_{LE} = \gamma_{KE} = 0, \, \gamma_{LL} = -\gamma_{LK}, \, \gamma_{KK} = -\gamma_{LK} \tag{6}$$

The practical advantage of distinguishing these two types of separability is that the double deflation method used in most national income accounting is permissible only under strong partial separability. However, for the purpose of productivity analysis, the distinction between the two has no special importance.

Technical change biases also have direct relevance to the analysis of Korean industrialization. Technical change can be measured on the cost side of the production dual by $\frac{\partial \ln C}{\partial \ln T}$. Given the existence of technological advancement, the measure of technical change bias (TCB) is then

$$\text{TCB}_i = \frac{\partial S_i}{\partial \ln T} = \theta_i \tag{7}$$

$\text{TCB}_i > 0$ implies that technological change is relatively ith-factor using; $\text{TCB}_i < 0$, a relative ith-factor saving; and $\text{TCB}_i = 0$, neutrality.

Finally, the rate of growth of multifactor productivity (MFP) is defined as

$$\dot{MFP} = \dot{Q} - \dot{F} \tag{8}$$

where F is the total factor input, and a dot represents a rate of growth.[3] The conventional Divisia index of F is the cost-share weighted average of the growth rates of inputs:

$$\dot{F} = \sum_i \frac{P_i X_i}{C} \dot{X}_i \tag{9}$$

where X_i is the quantity of the ith factor.

In estimating the parameters of the cost function, we jointly estimate the total cost function and three cost share equations. A nonlinear iterative Zellner (1962) estimation procedure was used to estimate the parameters.

DATA AND EMPIRICAL RESULTS

Data

Data consist of annual time-series for Korean manufacturing, 1961–81. They are measures of aggregate output, and the quantities and prices of labor, capital, energy, and materials. The index of manufacturing production is used as a measure of aggregate output while the quantity of labor input is represented by the total man-hours worked. Total costs are defined as the sum of four elements: nominal expenditures on labor, energy, materials, and the value of flow services of capital. (See chapter Appendix A.)

The data for output, employee remunerations, the number of man-hours worked, and expenditures on capital, energy, and materials are available from the *Report on Mining and Manufacturing Survey*; and the price indices for energy and materials are available from the *Economic Statistics Yearbook*.

The wage rate is computed by dividing employee remunerations by the total man-hours. The total man-hours are obtained by multiplying the number of workers by the total hours worked during the year. The *Annual Report on the Economically Active Population Survey* (EPB) contains the average (annual) hours worked per week. The total hours for the year are calculated by multiplying the average hours per week by 42 weeks. The computation of the rental price of capital is based on the Christensen and Jorgenson (1969) formula.[4]

Since Korean firms are known to depend heavily on bank credits as well as loans from the unregulated money market (UMM) to finance their investment and working capital, we found it necessary to separately account for the bank interest rates and the UMM interest rates in the calculation of the interest rate charged to the firms. The commercial banks' discount rate on bills was used as a measure of the bank interest rate. In the computation of the weighted interest rate, a variable weight was assigned to the discount rate as well as the UMM interest rate to reflect relative importance.[5]

Results

Parametric Estimates of the Cost Function

After having obtained the parametric estimates of the translog cost function with and without parametric restrictions (see chapter Appendix B), we performed a likelihood ratio test to see which model best describes the technology of Korean manufacturing.[6] The test statistics are presented in Table 9.1.

Table 9.1
The Likelihood-Ratio Test Statistics
Under Alternative Specifications of Technology

	Restrictions on Nonhomothetic Model			
	Homothetic	Neutral	Homogeneous	Cobb–Douglas
Number of Restrictions	3	3	4	7
Critical χ^2 (1%)	7.82	7.82	9.49	14.07
Actual χ^2	5.26	15.38	10.22	84.74

First, the homotheticity restriction cannot be rejected at the 0.01 level, while neither the homogeneity nor the neutrality nor the Cobb-Douglas hypothesis is consistent with any of the data sets. This result indicates that using the Cobb-Douglas form to describe features of the Korean manufacturing technology is inappropriate.

Elasticities of Substitution and Own Price Elasticities

Next, Allen partial elasticities of substitution and own price elasticities were estimated. A positive estimate σ_{ij} indicates that input pairs are substitutes whereas a negative estimate indicates that they are complements. Results in Table 9.2 indicate that, except for σ_{LE} (labor and energy), all estimates are positive regardless of the specifications. Since there has been a substantial controversy in the literature regarding the issue of complementarity or substitutability between capital and energy, our finding, namely, the substitutability between capital service flow and energy, is of particular interest.[7]

In general, studies using time-series data have found energy and capital service flow to be complements. By contrast, pooled-cross-section time-series studies have found energy and capital service flow to be substitutes. The conventional explanation for these sharply contrasting sets of results is that the time-series studies tend to reflect short-term relationships while the cross-section studies capture the long-term effects.

However, Berndt and Wood (1979) argue that this rationalization is unsatisfactory, noting that a pooled-cross-section time-series study by Fuss (1977) also shows energy-capital service flow complementarity and that the different estimates of the elasticity of substitution/complementarity between energy and capital service flow cannot be reconciled simply on the basis of a long-run/short-run distinction based on the use of pooled or time-series data.

We propose an explanation for energy-capital service flow substitutability that is different from others. It is based on the proposition that capital stock and its utilization are substitutes in generating the capital service flow (which is an argument in the production function) and that the utilization of capital stock and energy inputs are complements. This proposition leads directly to energy-capital stock substitutability, and suggests energy-capital service flow substitutability as evidenced by our empirical results. Thus capital stock-energy substitution is consistent with the finding of capital service flow-energy substitution.

This explanation is more plausible in the economic setting of Korean manufacturing, in which capacity utilization played a significant role in its growth process. It was estimated that for Korean manufacturing the rate of capacity utilization grew

Table 9.2
Estimated Elasticities of Substitution (t-ratios in parentheses)

	σ_{KL}	σ_{KM}	σ_{KE}	σ_{LM}	σ_{LE}	σ_{ME}
Non-homothetic						
1961	0.6051 (5.6542)	0.8019 (11.1355)	0.6692 (2.3379)	0.5848 (6.6932)	-2.1494 (-2.3166)	-0.0264 (-0.0560)
1966	0.5836 (5.1699)	0.8261 (13.0716)	0.6596 (2.2413)	0.4665 (4.1524)	-3.7453 (-2.6800)	-0.2872 (-0.4866)
1971	0.6495 (6.8400)	0.8174 (12.3140)	0.5765 (1.5734)	0.5728 (6.3714)	-3.5013 (-2.6411)	0.5238 (-0.7493)
1976	0.5121 (3.8749)	0.8062 (11.4489)	0.6341 (2.0024)	0.5218 (5.1874)	-3.1026 (-2.5673)	-0.0584 (-0.1203)
1981	0.4812 (3.4238)	0.7855 (10.0768)	0.6838 (2.4979)	0.5573 (7.5413)	-1.9655 (-2.2489)	0.2036 (0.5568)
Homothetic						
1961	0.9454 (11.5430)	0.7041 (13.9111)	1.1670 (4.3029)	0.7599 (7.5984)	-3.6534 (-4.6876)	0.2056 (0.4867)
1966	0.9415 (10.7365)	0.7398 (16.6175)	1.1723 (4.1930)	0.1916 (1.4926)	-6.0103 (-5.1263)	0.0174 (0.0334)
1971	0.9493 (12.4832)	0.7321 (15.9720)	1.2338 (3.2435)	0.7435 (6.9599)	-6.6865 (-5.1861)	-0.2799 (-0.4107)
1976	0.9314 (9.0532)	0.7103 (14.3324)	1.1875 (3.8942)	0.7229 (6.2691)	-5.1598 (-5.0002)	0.1809 (0.4150)
1981	0.9228 (7.9737)	0.6866 (12.8061)	1.1718 (4.1961)	0.7280 (6.4324)	-4.1195 (-4.8047)	0.3453 (0.9913)

at the average annual rate of 6.9 percent during the 1961–80 period, and accounted for 17 percent of the multifactor productivity growth.[8]

Table 9.2 also shows that energy and labor are complements. While this contradicts most findings, there are some studies including the ones by Hudson and Jorgenson (1974), Halverson and Ford (1979), and Turnovsky et al. (1982) that do support it. Some have attributed this result to the aggregation of production and nonproduction workers, whose elasticities of substitution with respect to capital differ. In fact, Berndt and Wood (1979) show that according to U.S. data, production workers are substitutes for energy while non-production workers are complements with energy.

Our results of energy-labor complementarity are also consistent with the proposition regarding the substitutability of capital stock and its utilization. Because labor inputs (in man-hours) and the utilization of capital stock (in machine-hours) are complements and also because energy inputs and the utilization of capital stock are complements, it follows that energy and labor are expected to be related as complements in our empirical results. Since energy is complementary to labor and a substitute for capital, an increase in the price of energy may not only affect the demand for energy, but also may result in an increase in unemployment and more intensive use of capital stock.

Finally, our estimate of $\sigma_{LK} = .93$ is only slightly higher than other previous estimates for Korean manufacturing and has an important policy implication.[9] Relatively high elasticities of substitution (for example, ratios greater than, say, 0.7) indicate that factor-price adjustment can have a substantial impact on the factor proportion. In such cases, factor-price modifications may be an important means of generating more employment opportunities. In Korean manufacturing, given the $\sigma_{LK} = .93$, the rapid growth of employment in the face of the rapid increase of the wage-rental ratio (13.3 percent average annual rate) has been possible primarily through the rapid growth of its output.[10] It implies that either the economy will have to continue to grow fast, or the wage-rental ratio will have to decrease if we are to expect continuing growth of employment. Further discussion of the wage-rental ratio will be made shortly in conjunction with the productivity growth.

The estimates of price elasticities of demand for various factors are presented in Table 9.3. The negative sign for most of the own price elasticities suggests that the demand for a factor input is responsive to a change in own price.

Technical Change Biases

From Appendix B we find that there was capital-using ($\theta_K > 0$), labor-saving ($\theta_L < 0$) technical change during the 1961–81 period. The estimates of θ_M and θ_E are also positive, but none of these estimates are significant even at the 0.01 level of significance.

Table 9.3
Own Price Elasticities (t-ratios in parentheses)

	η_{KK}	η_{LL}	η_{EE}	η_{MM}
Non-homothetic				
1961	- 0.5610 (-13.3839)	- 0.4040 (- 8.7786)	-0.0607 (0.2673)	- 0.2741 (-14.7887)
1966	- 0.5394 (-11.1658)	- 0.3052 (- 5.3346)	0.2686 (0.9763)	- 0.2884 (-15.0499)
1971	- 0.5472 (-14.6425)	- 0.4059 (- 8.8622)	-0.4894 (1.5011)	- 0.2883 (-15.0450)
1976	- 0.5632 (-13.1195)	- 0.3205 (- 5.7757)	0.1385 (0.5647)	- 0.2530 (-14.2968)
1981	- 0.5703 (-11.7828)	- 0.3490 (- 6.6674)	-0.1045 (-0.5557)	- 0.2441 (-14.0493)
Homothetic				
1961	- 0.5640 (-24.3339)	- 0.5160 (-15.4800)	-0.0360 (-0.1938)	- 0.2803 (- 8.3310)
1966	- 0.5434 (-27.3716)	- 0.4434 (-10.6416)	0.1433 (0.6408)	- 0.2915 (- 8.4370)
1971	- 0.5490 (-26.6973)	- 0.5033 (-14.4279)	-0.4764 (0.6219)	- 0.2890 (- 8.4153)
1976	- 0.5670 (-23.6860)	- 0.4536 (-11.1888)	0.0404 (0.1997)	- 0.2561 (- 8.0289)
1981	- 0.5736 (-21.5193)	- 0.4498 (-10.9826)	-0.1268 (0.7622)	- 0.2422 (- 7.8153)

The Test of Separability

We now test the null hypothesis—the separability of capital and labor from energy and material inputs. To do this we use a likelihood ratio test. Table 9.4 provides the test statistics for various constraints. The constraints are rejected in both cases of separability. Since the strong partial separability of primary inputs from energy and materials inputs is not accepted, we conclude that the separability conditions necessary for the double deflation method of obtaining real value-added are not met. Real value-added obtained by this method is inappropriate as a measure of output for Korean manufacturing.

Table 9.4
Separability Test Statistics

	Number of Restrictions	Critical χ^2	Actual χ^2
Weak Separability			
Non-homothetic	2	5.99	12.24
Homothetic	5	11.07	28.86
Strong Partial Separability			
Non-homothetic	4	9.48	33.56
Homothetic	7	14.07	50.38

Productivity Growth in Korean Manufacturing

Table 9.5 presents the growth rates of multifactor productivity (MFP) as well as the growth rates of single-factor productivity. These results provide an interesting interpretation of what accounted for a spectacular success of industrialization in Korea in the past two decades.

Our division of the sample period into three subperiods highlights the different phases of industrialization in Korea. The 1961–71 period is marked as the early stage of industrialization. During this period, the allocation of investment among competing activities was relatively well balanced. The period of 1971–78 was the time of maximum enthusiasm for industrialization. The massive effort to build up heavy industries enabled the Korean economy to grow continuously, but, by the end of the same period, some difficulties surfaced that stemmed from the distortion of the price mechanism. Finally, the 1978–81 period was the period of external and

Table 9.5
Productivity Measures in Gross Output Basis
(average annual rates of growth)

Years	Multi-Factor Productivity	Capital Services Productivity	Labor Productivity	Energy Productivity	Materials Productivity
1961–71	1.90	1.03	9.34	3.88	0.90
1971–78	1.08	-7.64	8.78	10.78	3.33
1978–81	-2.54	-19.06	5.65	-6.17	3.12

Table 9.6
Growth of Gross Output and Factor Inputs (average annual rates of growth)

Year	Gross Output	Capital Services	Labor	Energy	Material
1961–71	19.00	17.97	9.66	15.12	18.10
1971–78	22.90	30.54	14.12	12.12	19.57
1978–81	2.99	22.05	-2.66	9.16	-0.13

internal turmoil that reduced the speed of industrialization below what it should have been.

Our results unravel what has remained a mystery in explaining the tremendous growth of the Korean economy. The immediate impression from Table 9.5 is that the outstanding feature of the Korean economy under investigation is the mixture of the low growth of multifactor productivity and the high growth of labor productivity. The average annual growth rates of MFP are 1.90 in 1961–71, 1.08 in 1971–78, and –2.54 during the 1978–81 period, whereas labor productivity grew at the rates of 9.34, 8.78, and 5.65 during the respective periods. This observation suggests that much of industrialization in Korea in the past two decades is attributable to the rapid growth of factor inputs, rather than the "technological" progress attributed to MFP, and this trend has accelerated as further industrialization has progressed. In particular, the rapid growth of capital (services), together with a larger quantity of material input, accounted for much of the spectacular growth of the Korean economy (see Table 9.6).

The impressive growth of capital services is hardly surprising in the light of historically high wage-rental ratios in Korea. The wage-rental ratio grew at the annual rate of 20 percent during the 1971–81 period. According to the "induced innovation" hypothesis elaborated by Kennedy (1964), Samuelson (1965), Hayami and Ruttan (1970), and others, capital-using, labor-saving innovations are precipitated by rapidly rising wage-rental ratios. Our study, which confirms capital-using, labor-saving technical change biases, lends support to the thesis of induced innovation.

It should, then, come as no surprise that workers equipped with a greater volume of capital could enhance their capacity to process a larger quantity of materials input. Thus, a higher growth rate of capital combined with a sufficient amount of materials was the major source that contributed to the high growth of labor productivity, which, in turn, worked as a prime engine for industrialization. This result is readily discernable from Table 9.7. Growth in capital and materials outweighs growth in multifactor productivity in contributing to the growth of labor productivity. These findings are in agreement with Norsworthy and Malmquist

(1983), who have studied productivity growth in the U.S. and Japanese manufacturing sectors.

Finally, the slowdown in the growth of MFP during the periods of 1971–78 and 1978–81 relative to the first period warrants an explanation, especially in relation to the different phases of industrialization. In general, the growth of MFP may be affected by many market and nonmarket factors such as economies of scale, capacity utilization, physical characteristics of factor inputs, production environment, and organization principles that determine the combination of various inputs. However, none stands out more prominently than the overly ambitious investment policy of the government as an underlying cause of slowdown in MFP growth in Korean manufacturing during the 1971–81 period. The government's big push for investment in heavy and chemical industries occurred in two thrusts—one in 1968–76 and the other in 1977–79, which brought about a rapid buildup of capital services at a dizzying pace of over 28 percent per annum during the 1971–81 period as shown in Table 9.6 and Appendix A. This rapid accumulation of capital stock took place concurrently with massive investment subsidies granted to these businesses in the form of low interest rate loans and other incentive devices.[11] The resultant factor price distortion, in turn, has led to technical as well as allocative inefficiencies in Korean manufacturing.

The negative growth of MFP (–2.5) during the 1978–81 period is not all that surprising in view of the fact that there was a slowdown in the output growth in the same period (see Table 9.6). During the recession of 1980, in particular, GNP declined 6.2 percent due largely to (a) the 1979 oil shock, (b) political instability following the assassination of the president, and (c) the sudden policy shift from growth promotion to price stabilization in the aftermath of the oil shock. During this period, the inefficiencies in the manufacturing sector became increasingly

Table 9.7
Components of Labor Productivity Growth Based on Factor Intensities Relative to Labor (relative contributions in percent in parentheses)

Year	Labor Productivity Growth	Capital Service Effect	Energy Effect	Materials Effect	Multi-Factor Productivity Effect
1961–71	9.34	2.46 (26.33)	.22 (2.35)	4.77 (51.07)	1.90 (20.34)
1971–78	8.79	4.55 (51.75)	–0.08 (–0.90)	3.25 (36.97)	1.08 (12.28)
1978–81	5.65	6.12 (108.13)	.54 (9.54)	1.54 (27.21)	–2.54 (–44.88)

evident. The majority of the plants built during the 1977–79 push for large-scale projects in heavy and chemical plants met with serious shortages in demand.

Comparison of MFP (or TFP) Measures

Our findings concerning the contribution of MFP to the real output growth deserve special attention in that they are in such clear contrast with the prevailing view that total productivity (TFP) growth has been a crucial determinant of rapid economic growth in Korea.

Our estimates of MFP growth are considerably smaller than the estimates by Rhee (1982), Nishimizu and Robinson (1984), Kwon (1986), and Kim and Park (1988), but quite similar to the results by Choi (1987). Comparison with other findings is presented in Table 9.8.

Our findings are also roughly in parallel with those obtained by Norsworthy and Malmquist (1983) and Nishimizu and Hulten (1978) for the Japanese economy, by Tsao (1985) for the Singapore economy, and by Choi (1987) for Taiwan, all of which show negligible contribution of TFP growth and more substantial contribution of capital and materials growth to real output growth (see Table 9.9).

The differences between our results and those of others can be ascribed mainly to the differences in the measurement of output (that is, value-added output or gross output), specification of production technology, and the treatment of factor inputs, especially capital input. This study used the capital service flow: the flow of capital services is not a constant proportion of the capital stock employed in the actual production activities. Most studies on Korean factor productivity are based on the

Table 9.8
Comparison of Major Studies on TFP Growth in Korean Manufacturing

Studies by	Period Covered	TFP Growth (%)
Rhee (1982)	1961–77	3.98
	1967–77	4.67
Nishimizu and Robinson (1984)	1960–77	3.71
Kwon (1986)	1961–72	1.79
	1972–78	4.80
Kim and Park (1988)	1966–73	3.60
	1973–79	1.40
	1973–83	1.00
Choi (1988)	1963	0.21
	1974	-0.10
	1981	-0.09
Kwon and Yuhn (1989)	1961–71	1.90
	1971–78	1.08
	1978–81	-2.54

Table 9.9
Intercountry Comparison of Major Studies on TFP Growth in Manufacturing

Studies by	Countries	Period	TFP Growth (%)
Nishimizu and Hulten (1978)[a]	Japan	1955-71	2.04
Norsworthy and Malmquist (1983)	Japan	1965-73	0.83
Tsao (1985)	Singapore	1970-79	0.08
Choi (1988)	Taiwan	1963	0.02
		1974	0.00
		1981	0.00

[a]10 sectors of the economy

notion of capital stock.[12] In addition, a distinction between value-added output and growth output is not fully spelled out in those studies.

SUMMARY AND CONCLUSION

Korean manufacturing in the 1960s and 1970s can be characterized by (a) relatively high elasticity of substitution between capital services and labor, (b) rapid growth of capital input and output, (c) relatively low MFP growth and high labor productivity growth, and (d) factor price distortions. However, the most striking feature of the Korean economy drawn from this study is the rapid growth of factor inputs—especially, capital and materials as the predominant sources of the growth of output in Korean manufacturing, and the relatively small role for "technological" progress in the industrialization process. The latter finding is manifest in the low growth of MFP.

Many factors may be responsible for the slowdown in MFP growth in Korean manufacturing. However, none stands out more prominently than the overambitious investment policy of the government, which has frequently ignored the market mechanism. In Korea, the funds for capital investment are not acquired in a strictly competitive market due to massive investment subsidies granted by the government. No consistent cost-benefit methods were used to rank projects according to their profitability. At the same time, there is no effective provision against the misuse of capital assets. Relatively small MFP growth that occurred in the face of rapidly growing output is, at least partly, attributable to the misallocation of resources.

On the other hand, the relatively high elasticity of substitution between capital services and labor combined with the factor price distortion is responsible for the shift toward capital-using and labor-saving technological change evidenced in this study. This presents policymakers a difficult choice: high growth policy (to maintain the level of employment) and/or the policy of reduced wage-rental ratio. The latter, in turn, entails two options: that of wage controls and/or the realignment of the price of capital services with their true social cost.

The energy-capital substitutability and energy-labor complementality observed in the study also have an important policy implication: whereas the energy-capital substitution points to the potential for continued economic growth even under moderately severe energy supply shocks, the labor-energy complementarity may lead to a pessimistic outlook for the employment environment.

Finally, our productivity analysis was carried out based on the gross measure of output. The rationale for this approach is provided by the rejection of the hypotheses of weak local separability and strong partial separability of capital and labor from energy and materials.

NOTES

1. Gross output and materials inputs are deflated by their respective price indices and the difference in the deflated values is called real value-added. It is implicitly assumed that the production function is additively separable of the form $Q = VQ + M$ where Q is gross output and VQ is real value-added while M is materials.

2. $\gamma_{Qi} = 0$ for homotheticity, $\gamma_{Qi} = 0$, $\gamma_{QQ} = 0$ for homogeneity, $\theta_{ti} = 0$ for Hicks neutrality, and $\gamma_{Qi} = 0$, $\gamma_{QQ} = 0$, $\gamma_{ij} = 0$ for Cobb-Douglas restrictions.

3. The KLEM representation of equation (8) would be

$$\dot{MFP} = \dot{Q} - (S_K \dot{K} + S_L \dot{L} + S_E \dot{E} + S_M \dot{M}),$$

and the labor productivity can be deduced as

$$(\dot{Q} - \dot{L}) = (\dot{K} - \dot{L})S_K + (\dot{E} - \dot{L})S_E + (\dot{M} - \dot{L})S_M + \dot{MFP}.$$

4. The rental price of capital, P_K, is

$$P_K = [\alpha DR + (1 - \alpha)UMMR - \pi^e + d]P_K^p$$

where

α	=	the weight for DR and $(1 - \alpha)$, the weight for UMMR
DR	=	the commercial bank discount rate on bills (*Economic Statistics Yearbook*, BOK, various years)
UMMR	=	unorganized money market rate (internal data, Ministry of Finance)
π^e	=	the expected rate of inflation. Three-year moving average of the rate of change of the GNP implicit price deflator was used as a measure of π^e. In this way, $\alpha DR + (1 - \alpha)UMMR - \pi^e$ constitutes the expected real interest rate.

d   = the depreciation rate of capital stock; the constant rate of 12 percent per year was used. Available data (*Financial Statements Analysis*, BOK) show that between 1972 and 1981 the depreciation rate fluctuated between 11 percent and 13.6 percent.

P_K^p = the purchase price of capital equipment. The wholesale price index of capital goods was used (*Major Statistics of Korean Economy*, EPB, various years).

5. The study by Byeon (1985) shows that the ratio of UMM loan and bank loan declined from 1.73 in 1963 to 0.55 in 1982.

6. The likelihood ratio is the maximum value of the likelihood function for the constrained case divided by the maximum value for the unconstrained case. Hence λ = L (constrained)/L (unconstrained).

7. Our finding is consistent with the result of Turnovsky, Folie, and Ulph (1982), Griffin and Gregory (1976), Pindyck (1979), and Halvorsen and Ford (1979); but not with the results of Berndt and Wood (1979), Hudson and Jorgenson (1974), and Norsworthy and Malmquist (1983). Our result is also consistent with a number of engineering studies that show that increases in energy efficiency are possible through increased investment either by improving existing plant and equipment or through new engineering designs. One might expect capital stock and energy to be substitutes since new equipment could be designed to achieve higher thermal efficiencies but at greater capital costs.

8. See Kwon (1986) and Kim and Kwon (1977).

9. On the basis of two-factor (*K,L*) translog production function, Pyo (1984) produced $\sigma_{LK} = 0.8$, and Kwon and Williams (1982) using 1973 cross-section data for seven manufacturing subsectors show the overall average of $\sigma_{LK} = 0.7$. Based on the two-factor CES function Kim (1984) finds elasticities of substitution between capital and labor, in the large and small-medium manufacturing industries (eight subsectors), to be significantly different from zero. Using an alternative definition,

$$\sigma_{LK} = \frac{d\dfrac{K}{L} \Big/ d\dfrac{w}{r}}{\dfrac{K}{L} \Big/ \dfrac{w}{r}},$$

Hong (1976) shows 0.4 for the 1967–73 period and 0.8 by adjusting it for the utilization of capital stock.

10. See Hong (1979) and Kim and Roemer (1979) for further discussion of wage-rental ratio and factor distortion.

11. Government subsidies on business investment include low interest rate loans, favorable exchange rates, low tariffs on imported capital goods, tax holidays on new investment, and accelerated depreciation on capital goods. See Hong (1979), Westphal (1979), and Westphal and Kim (1977).

12. The potential impact of choice of capital input between stocks and flows on the computed MFP growth rates cannot be overlooked. For example, Nishimizu and Robinson (1984) identified 12.98 (1960–77) and Rhee (1982) reported 14.67 (1961–77), respectively, as the growth rate of capital stocks; and Kwon (1986), using the capital stock data constructed by Choo et al. (1982), shows the growth rate 18.38 (1961–78). On the other hand, the growth rate of capital services in this chapter comes out to be 23.33 for the 1961–78 period and 30.54 for the 1971–78 period.

Appendix A
Input Price Indices and Input Costs—Korean Manufacturing, 1961-81

	Price Indices				Input Costs (Billions of Current Won)			
	P_K	P_L	P_E	P_M	K	L	E	M
1961	.400	.0713	.1060	.1410	25.0	9.7	4.6	55.2
1962	.456	.0846	.1160	.1550	35.9	12.9	5.7	76.9
1963	.434	.1064	.1190	.1720	45.7	18.1	6.9	98.4
1964	.798	.1202	.1330	.2290	76.3	23.2	10.0	137.4
1965	1.361	.1322	.1530	.2740	101.2	29.8	14.1	187.8
1966	1.567	.1497	.1650	.2940	118.8	37.8	17.6	243.6
1967	1.530	.1883	.1910	.3020	177.4	53.4	19.2	301.9
1968	1.499	.2371	.2080	.3150	224.2	77.1	30.4	437.2
1969	1.510	.3007	.2250	.3290	319.9	106.8	36.9	548.7
1970	1.512	.3833	.2420	.3610	412.6	137.8	48.2	736.5
1971	1.406	.4518	.2720	.3870	529.9	161.5	53.2	928.9
1972	1.040	.4981	.3280	.4400	688.6	211.5	74.7	1,267.2
1973	.958	.5948	.3560	.4970	937.6	310.6	105.2	2,216.5
1974	.983	.7640	.7630	.8070	1,419.5	451.3	217.3	3,619.3
1975	1.000	1.0000	1.0000	1.0000	2,176.5	651.6	398.1	4,943.7
1976	1.379	1.2785	1.0860	1.1010	3,066.6	1,009.1	478.6	7,124.9
1977	1.572	1.6847	1.1860	1.1700	4,135.6	1,460.6	563.0	9,279.1
1978	1.868	2.3127	1.3050	1.2280	5,970.9	2,222.0	677.6	12,289.1
1979	1.738	3.0395	1.7750	1.6520	6,286.4	2,922.0	1,092.6	16,389.0
1980	2.593	3.8936	3.2990	2.3720	8,386.2	3,471.0	1,844.8	22,577.0
1981	1.821	4.6598	4.2783	2.8474	11,279.5	4,133.3	2,924.4	28,380.3

Note:P_K = rental price of capital; P_L = price of labor; P_E = price of energy; P_M = price of raw materials; K = cost of capital service; L = cost of labor; E = cost of energy; and M = cost of raw materials

Appendix B
Cost Function Parameter Estimates (t-ratios in parentheses)

Parameter	NHOMOTH	HOMOTH	HOMOG	NEUTRA	COB-DOG
α_O	13.4352	-12.4015	-1.4453	25.7842	0.4819
	(1.7484)	(-2.0893)	(-2.2859)	(2.8260)	(0.5576)
α_Q	6.2250	-2.0982	1.1126	10.6785	0.9405
	(2.5691)	(-1.1296)	(11.0732)	(3.6566)	(6.0614)
Υ_{QQ}	0.6745	-0.4048	-----	1.2417	-----
	(2.2224)	(-1.7259)	-----	(3.3608)	-----
α_L	0.1073	0.1869	0.1945	0.0864	0.1109
	(3.0594)	(13.6018)	(14.1749)	(43.6780)	(10.1503)
α_E	-0.0095	0.0347	0.0458	0.0450	0.0439
	(-0.3323)	(3.1713)	(3.7376)	(23.4346)	(4.2176)
α_K	0.2003	0.1856	0.1740	0.2473	0.3344
	(2.3919)	(6.3042)	(6.0619)	(45.6593)	(9.6511)
α_M	0.7019	0.5928	0.5857	0.6213	0.5108
	(8.6335)	(19.3725)	(18.9547)	(115.055)	(16.1136)
Υ_{LE}	-0.0150	-0.0241	-0.0210	-0.0108	-----
	(-3.3843)	(-5.9775)	(-4.9099)	(-2.5344)	-----
Υ_{LK}	-0.0110	-0.0016	-0.0028	-0.0083	-----
	(-3.6883)	(-0.6762)	(-1.3785)	(-3.2089)	-----
Υ_{LM}	-0.0252	-0.0150	-0.0166	-0.0298	-----
	(-4.7456)	(-2.4086)	(-2.7201)	(-5.3189)	-----
Υ_{EK}	-0.0040	0.0021	-0.0047	0.0003	-----
	(-1.1419)	(0.6043)	(-1.3341)	(0.0859)	-----
Υ_{EM}	-0.0274	-0.0219	-0.0038	-0.0288	-----
	(-2.1801)	(-1.8771)	(-0.3262)	(-2.2049)	-----
Υ_{KM}	-0.0308	-0.0456	-0.0376	-0.0417	-----
	(-2.7470)	(-5.8411)	(-4.8898)	(-4.6601)	-----
Υ_{LL}	0.0512	0.0470	0.0404	0.0489	-----
	(10.6667)	(13.3056)	(10.6316)	(14.8182)	-----
Υ_{EE}	0.0464	0.0439	0.0295	0.0393	-----
	(4.4616)	(4.9326)	(3.2065)	(4.0515)	-----

Appendix B (continued)

Parameter	NHOMOTH	HOMOTH	HOMOG	NEUTRA	COB-DOG
Υ_{KK}	0.0458 (4.0893)	0.0451 (7.2742)	0.0451 (7.3934)	0.0497 (5.9167)	----- -----
Υ_{MM}	0.0834 (7.7222)	0.0825 (4.2526)	0.0580 (3.1016)	0.1003 (4.9167)	----- -----
Υ_{LQ}	- 0.0198 (-3.2825)	----- -----	----- -----	- 0.0210 (-8.1446)	----- -----
Υ_{EQ}	-0.0120 (-2.0410)	----- -----	----- -----	-0.0033 (-1.4174)	----- -----
Υ_{KQ}	0.0066 (0.4457)	----- -----	----- -----	0.0120 (2.3523)	----- -----
Υ_{MQ}	0.0252 (1.6913)	----- -----	----- -----	0.0123 (2.3654)	----- -----
θ_L	-0.044 (-0.5733)	-0.0223 (-7.2615)	-0.0238 (- 7.6257)	----- -----	-0.0038 (-1.4389)
θ_E	0.0127 (1.9889)	0.0028 (1.1147)	0.0008 (0.2931)	----- -----	-0.0008 (-0.3198)
θ_K	0.0107 (0.5636)	0.0136 (2.1750)	0.0160 (2.6119)	----- -----	-0.0137 (-1.6536)
θ_M	-0.0190 (-1.0270)	0.0059 (0.8806)	0.0070 (1.0448)	----- -----	0.0183 (2.4079)
θ_Q	-1.0125 (-2.0363)	0.6892 (1.7831)	----- -----	-1.8718 (-3.0800)	----- -----
B_t	-4.2887 (-1.4492)	5.5655 (2.3528)	0.9948 (1.9475)	-8.3180 (-2.3138)	-0.5103 (-0.6355)
B_{tt}	0.5813 (1.0277)	-1.2559 (-2.6366)	-0.3061 (-1.8039)	1.1625 (1.6419)	0.1663 (0.6122)

REFERENCES

Bank of Korea, *Economic Statistics Yearbook*, Seoul, various issues.
——, *Financial Statements Analysis*, Seoul, various issues.
Berndt, E. R., and Christensen, L. R., "The Translog Function and the Substitution of Equipment, Structures, and Labor in U.S. Manufacturing, 1929–68," *Journal of Econometrics, 1*, March 1973, 81–114.
——, and Wood, C. M., "Income Redistribution and Employment Effects of Rising Energy Prices," Resources paper 30, Department of Economics, University of British Columbia, Vancouver, Canada, 1979.
——, "Engineering and Econometric Interpretations of Energy-Capital Complementarity," *American Economic Review, 69*, June 1979, 342–54.
Byeon, Yangho, "Effects of Financial Liberalization and Monetary Policy in the Presence of Unregulated Money Market," Ph.D. dissertation, Department of Economics, Northern Illinois University, DeKalb, 1985.
Choi, Jeong P., "Productivity Comparison in the Manufacturing for Korea and Taiwan," *Han Kook Kyong Je Yon Goo*, Seoul, November 1987, 73–92.
Choo, H. C., Kim, Y.S. and Yoon, J. H., "Estimates of the Value of Capital Stock in Korea (1960–77)", Monograph, KDI, Seoul, 1982.
Christensen, L. R., and Jorgenson, D. W., "The Measurement of U.S. Real Capital Input, 1929–1967," *Review of Income and Wealth, 14*, December 1969, 293–320.
——, Jorgenson, D. W., and Lau, L. J., "Transcendental Logarithmic Production Frontier," *Review of Economics and Statistics, 55*, February 1973, 28–45.
Denny, M. and Fuss, M., "The Use of Approximation Analysis to Test for Separability and the Existence of Consistent Aggregates," *American Economic Review, 67*, June 1979, 404–18.
Economic Planning Board, *Report on Mining and Manufacturing Survey*, Seoul, various issues.
Fuss, M. A., "The Demand for Energy in Canadian Manufacturing," *Journal of Econometrics, 5*, January 1977, 89–116.
Griffin, J. M., and Gregory, P. R., "An Intercountry Translog Model of Energy Substitution Responses," *American Economic Review, 66*, December 1976, 845–57.
Halvorsen, R., and Ford, J., "Substitution among Energy, Capital, and Labour Inputs in U.S. Manufacturing," in R. S. Pindyck, ed., *Advances in the Economics of Energy and Resources*, Greenwich: JAI Press, 1979, 51–75.
Hayami, Y., and Ruttan, V. W., "Factor Prices and Technical Change in Agricultural Development: The United States and Japan, 1880–1960," *Journal of Political Economy, 78*, September/October 1970, 1115–41.
Hong, W. T., *Trade, Distortion and Employment*, Seoul: Korea Development Institute, 1979.

Hudson, E. A., and Jorgenson, D. W., "U.S. Energy Policy and Economic Growth, 1975/2000," *Bell Journal of Economics and Management Sciences*, 5, Autumn 1974, 461–514.

Kennedy, C., "Induced Bias in Innovation and the Theory of Distribution," *Economic Journal*, 74, September 1964, 541–47.

Kim, J. W., "CES Production Function in Manufacturing and Problems of Industrialization in LDC: Evidence from Korea," *Economic Development and Cultural Change*, 33, October 1984, 143–65.

Kim, K. S., and Roemer, R., *Growth and Structural Transformation*, Cambridge: Harvard University Press, 1979.

————, and Park, S. R., *Analysis of Changing Productivity and Its Causes for S. Korean Manufacturing* (in Korean), Seoul: Korea Institute for Economics and Technology, 1988.

Kim, Y. C., and Kwon, J. K., "The Utilization of Capital and the Growth of Output in a Developing Economy: The Case of South Korean Manufacturing," *Journal of Development Economics*, 4, September 1977, 265–78.

Kwon, J. K., "Capacity Utilization, Economies of Scale and Technical Change in the Growth of Total Factor Productivity: An Explanation of South Korean Manufacturing Growth," *Journal of Development Economics*, 24, November 1986, 75–90.

————, and Williams, M., "The Structure of Production in South Korea's Manufacturing Sector," *Journal of Development Economics*, 11, October 1982, 215–26.

Nishimizu, M., and Hulten, C. R., "The Sources of Japanese Economic Growth," *Review of Economics and Statistics*, 60, August 1978, 351–61.

————, and Robinson, S., "Trade Policies and Productivity Change in Semi-Industrialized Countries," *Journal of Development Economics*, 16, September-October 1984, 177–206.

Norsworthy, J. R., and Malmquist, D. H., "Input Measurement and Productivity Growth in Japanese and U.S. Manufacturing," *American Economic Review*, 73, December 1983, 947–1067.

Pindyck, R. S., *The Structure of World Energy Demand*, Cambridge: MIT Press, 1979.

Pyo, H. K., "Elasticities of Substitution and Technical Progress in a Developing Economy: The Case of Korea (1963-81)," Paper presented at the 1983 Korean Economic Association Meeting, Seoul, 1984.

Rhee, S. Y., "Total Factor Productivity Analysis: A Disaggregated Study of the Korean Mining and Manufacturing Sectors with Explicit Consideration of Intermediate Inputs," Mimeo, Korea Development Institute, Seoul, 1982.

Samuelson, P. A., "A Theory of Induced Innovation along Kennedy Weisacker Lines," *Review of Economics and Statistics*, 47, November 1965, 343–56.

Tsao, Y., "Growth without Productivity: Singapore Manufacturing in the 1970s," *Journal of Development Economics, 19,* September/October 1985, 25–38.

Turnovsky, M., Folie, M., and Ulph, A., "Factor Substitutability in Australian Manufacturing with Emphasis on Energy Inputs," *Economic Record, 58,* March 1982, 61–72.

Westphal, L. E., "Manufacturing," in P. Hasan and D. C. Rao, eds., *Korea: Policy Issues for Long-Term Development,* Baltimore: Johns Hopkins University Press, 1979, 233–80.

———, and Kim, K. S., "Industrial Policy and Development in Korea," World Bank Staff Working Paper, No. 263, Washington, 1977.

Zellner, A., "An Efficient Method for Estimating Seemingly Unrelated Regression and Tests for Aggregation Bias," *Journal of the American Statistical Association, 57,* June 1962, 348–68.

10

Factor Demand and Production Technology in Korean and Taiwanese Manufacturing

Jeong Pyo Choi

INTRODUCTION

The objective of this study is to compare the production technologies of Korean and Taiwanese manufacturing.

Korea and Taiwan have been viewed as the two most successful cases of economic development over the last three decades. At the same time, the two countries are notable for some basic differences in their respective approach to economic development and for the differences in their industrial structure. For example, (a) Korean industries are subject to far more active government intervention than Taiwanese industries; (b) Korean industries tend to be considerably more highly concentrated than those in Taiwan; (c) Korean manufacturing has a higher proportion of heavy industry than that of Taiwan; and (d) the heavy subsidies to business by the Korean government have created massive distortions in factor prices and factor proportions. This problem does not seem to exist in Taiwan. Therefore, it is not difficult to see that the production technologies of the two countries can be rather different.

In this chapter the production technology of Korea and Taiwan is compared in terms of price elasticities of factor demand, elasticities of substitution, and productivity growth.[1]

Since it is assumed that all inputs are employed at an optimum level so as to minimize total costs, the estimation of the technological characteristics can be based on the duality theorem between production and cost under which, as shown by Binswanger (1974a), the cost function can be applied more usefully than the production function. This chapter uses the translog total cost function model, following various techniques developed by Binswanger (1974a), Berndt and Wood (1975), Christensen and Greene (1976), Norsworthy and Malmquist (1983), and others. Based on the gross output approach, the model identifies the four major inputs, namely, capital, labor, energy, and materials. The aggregate manufacturing data are applied to the model, covering the period between 1964 and 1984 for Korea and 1961 and 1981 for Taiwan. These periods include two oil shocks that caused drastic changes in relative factor prices and high growth in real output.

METHODOLOGY

Suppose that production occurs at a full equilibrium point in which total cost is minimized, and there is a production function with traditional, neoclassical curvature properties. Then a translog total cost function that is dual to the production function can be specified as

$$\ln C = a_0 + a_Y \ln Y + \sum_i a_i \ln P_i + \frac{1}{2} b_{YY} (\ln Y)^2 + \frac{1}{2} \sum_i \sum_j b_{ij} \ln P_i \ln P_j$$

$$+ \sum_i b_{Yi} \ln Y \ln P_i + a_T T + b_{YT} \ln YT + \sum_i b_{iT} \ln P_i T + \frac{1}{2} b_{TT} T^2 \qquad (1)$$

$$i, j = K, L, E, M$$

where C is the total cost, Y the output, P_i the price of ith input service, K the service of capital, L the service of labor, E the service of energy, M the service of materials, and T the state of technology. In equation (1), b_{iT} represents the technical change biases. Thus, if $b_{iT} = 0$ for all i, the technical change is Hicks neutral, and $(a_T + b_{TT} T)$ is the Hicks neutral technological progress rate.

The application of the Shephard's lemma to the partial derivative of $\ln C$ with respect to $\ln P_i$ provides the share equation of input factor i. Thus the share equation can be given from equation (1) as:

$$S_i = \frac{\partial \ln C}{\partial \ln P_i} = a_i + b_{Yi} \ln Y + \sum_j b_{ij} \ln P_j + b_{iT} T \qquad (2)$$

$$i, j = K, L, E, M$$

The theory requires the cost function specified in equation (1) to be linearly homogenous and symmetric in factor prices. Thus, the following restrictions are imposed on the parameters a priori for the homogeneity and symmetry.

$$b_{ij} = b_{ji}, \quad \sum_i a_i = 1$$

$$\sum_i b_{ij} = \sum_j b_{ij} = 0, \ \sum_i b_{Yi} = 0$$

$$\sum_i b_{iT} = 0, \ i, j = \text{K,L,E,M}$$

In addition, it is assumed that constant returns to scale is satisfied by the following restrictions on the parameters:

$$a_Y = 1, \ b_{YY} = 0, \ b_{YT} = 0, b_{Yi} = 0$$
$$(i = \text{K, L, E, M})$$

Technical Change Biases

The partial derivative of the share equation with respect to T determines the direction of technical change biases (see Binswanger, 1974a and b).

$$\frac{\partial S_i}{\partial T} = 0 : \text{factor } i \text{ neutral technical change} \tag{3a}$$

$$\frac{\partial S_i}{\partial T} > 0 : \text{factor } i \text{ using technical change} \tag{3b}$$

$$\frac{\partial S_i}{\partial T} < 0 : \text{factor } i \text{ saving technical change} \tag{3c}$$

Productivity Growth

The cost share of factor i is defined as $S_i = P_i X_i / C$ where X_i is the amount of factor i. For the given factor price, the logarithmic derivative of the share equation with respect to T provides $\dot{S}_i = \dot{X}_i - \dot{C}$ where a dot represents the growth rate of its respective variable. Therefore the productivity growth rate of factor i can be represented as:

$$\frac{\partial \ln X_i}{\partial T} = \frac{\partial \ln S_i}{\partial T} + \frac{\partial \ln C}{\partial T}$$

$$= \frac{b_{iT}}{S_i} + a_T + b_{YT} \ln Y + \sum_i b_{iT} \ln P_i + b_{TT} T \tag{4}$$

$$i = \text{K, L, E, M}$$

The rate of growth of total factor productivity is a cost-share weighted average of the productivity growth rates of individual factors that is equivalent to $(\partial \ln C)/\partial T$:

$$\frac{\partial \ln C}{\partial T} = a_T + b_{YT} \ln Y + \sum_i b_{iT} \ln P_i + b_{TT}T \tag{5}$$

$$i = K, L, E, M$$

Elasticities of Substitution

The Allen partial elasticities of substitution between inputs i and j ($\sigma_{ij} = \sigma_{ji}$) are defined as:

$$\sigma_{ij} = \frac{CC_{ij}}{C_i C_j} \tag{6}$$

where subscripts of C represent first and second partial derivatives of C with respect to P_i and P_j (see Uzawa, 1962). From the translog cost function defined in equation (1), the elasticity of substitution can be derived as:

$$\sigma_{ij} = \sigma_{ji} = \frac{1}{S_i S_j} b_{ij} + 1 \qquad \text{for all } i, j \tag{7a}$$

$$\sigma_{ii} = \frac{1}{S_i^2} (b_{ii} + S_i^2 - S_i) \qquad \text{for all } i \tag{7b}$$

Price Elasticities of Demand

The own and cross price elasticities of factor demand are defined and derived from equation (1) as:

$$\eta_{ij} = \frac{\partial X_i}{\partial P_j} \frac{P_j}{X_i} = \frac{b_{ij}}{S_i} + S_j \tag{8a}$$

$$\eta_{ii} = \frac{\partial X_i}{\partial P_i} \frac{P_i}{X_i} = \frac{b_{ii}}{S_i} + S_i - 1 \tag{8b}$$

ESTIMATION RESULTS
AND ECONOMIC INTERPRETATIONS

The translog total cost function in equation (1) was estimated in simultaneous equations system with share equations (2) using the aggregate manufacturing data covering the 1963–84 period for Korea and the 1961–81 period for Taiwan.[2] The data set in use is briefly summarized in Table 10.1. The rate of growth of real output is higher in Korea than in Taiwan. The cost share of materials is the highest of the four inputs in both countries, but higher in Taiwan than in Korea. The cost share of energy is 4 percent in both countries. The cost share of capital is much higher in Korea than in Taiwan, but the cost share of labor is higher in Taiwan than in Korea. That is, Korea's manufacturing is capital-intensive whereas Taiwan's manufacturing is labor-intensive. The rates of growth of input price indices are higher for all inputs in Korea than in Taiwan.

The estimated parameters of the translog total cost function in equation (1) are presented in Table 10.2, along with their standard errors in parentheses. They satisfy the regulatory conditions for the nondecreasing and concave cost function in factor prices that are required by the theory of production and cost.[3]

First of all, in estimating the translog cost function, Hicks neutral technical change hypothesis was tested. The test results are reported in Table 10.3. The hypothesis of Hicks neutrality is rejected for Korea, but accepted for Taiwan. Thus, for Taiwan, the rate of growth of Hicks neutral technological progress can be computed after imposing the restrictions of Hicks neutral technical change. The computed value of Hicks neutral technological progress rate was zero. This means that, in Taiwan, the productivity of each input grew without a significant bias toward any specific input, but the improvement in overall efficiency was negligible.

Table 10.4 reports the estimated average annual percentage growth rates of individual and total factor productivities for Korean and Taiwanese manufacturing for the years 1961, 1963, 1974, 1981, and 1984, respectively. The productivity growth of individual factors was estimated using equation (4).[4] The growth rate of the total factor productivity is a cost-share weighted average of the productivity growth rates of the four individual factors that is equivalent to the value of the logarithmic partial derivative of total cost with respect to T, as defined in equation (5).[5]

In Korea, the productivities of labor and energy increased at high rates while those of capital and materials declined. By contrast, in Taiwan, the productivities of capital and labor increased at moderate rates, while those of energy and materials declined. On the whole, no significant change was observed over time in the rates of growth of individual factor productivities. However, the total factor productivity growth rates were very low for both countries.[6] They became even lower after 1974.

The rate of growth of labor productivity is around 6 percent per year for Korea, while it is only around 1 percent for Taiwan. This difference could possibly be the

Table 10.1
Description of Korean and Taiwanese Aggregate
Manufacturing Data (average annual values before and after 1973)

Years[a]	Countries	Output Index[b]	Total Costs[c]	Capital Share	Labor Share	Energy Share	Materials Share	Capital Price Index[d]	Labor Price Index[e]	Energy Price Index[f]	Materials Price Index[g]
1961-1973	Korea	0.26	1,133.43	0.29	0.10	0.04	0.57	0.30	0.21	0.18	0.36
	Taiwan	0.36	173.70	0.13	0.15	0.04	0.69	0.45	0.27	0.41	0.51
1974-1984	Korea	1.54	32,303.40	0.25	0.10	0.04	0.61	1.45	2.51	2.38	1.49
	Taiwan	1.18	1,410.48	0.09	0.13	0.04	0.74	1.24	1.36	1.42	1.21

[a]The pre-1973 period for Korea is 1963-73 and the post-1973 period for Taiwan is 1974-81.
[b]The base year is 1976.
[c]The numbers represent Billion Won for Korea and Billion N.T. Dollars for Taiwan.
[d]The base year is 1976.
[e]The base year is 1976.
[f]The base year is 1976.
[g]The base year is 1976.

result of the relatively capital-intensive production in Korea and relatively labor-intensive production in Taiwan. Labor equipped with greater volume of capital would be more productive. On the other side, capital with a greater amount of working labor would be more productive. Thus, in contrast to the rate of growth of labor productivity, the rate of growth of capital productivity is higher in Taiwan than in Korea.

The rate of growth of energy productivity is high in Korea, but negative in Taiwan. This result could be explained by the fact that the capital-intensive technology in Korea tends to increase the productivity of energy, whereas the labor-intensive technology in Taiwan would not significantly affect the productivity of energy. The rate of growth of materials productivity is consistently negative in both countries. Since this negative value is weighted by the highest cost share of materials in the calculation of the total factor productivity growth rate, the rate of growth of total factor productivity is estimated to be very low in both countries.

The estimated results of technical change biases defined in equations (3) are reported in Table 10.5. Korean manufacturing shows the capital and materials using but labor and energy saving technological progress, whereas Taiwanese manufacturing shows energy and materials using but capital and labor saving technological progress.

Table 10.6 reports the estimated values of own and cross price elasticities of demand for capital, labor, energy, and materials. All of them are less than 1 in absolute value for both countries. Furthermore, it is very interesting to note that all of them are consistently higher for Taiwan than for Korea. This indicates that the response of factor demand is more sensitive in Taiwan than in Korea to changes in factor prices, suggesting a freer market mechanism in Taiwan than in Korea. Accordingly, Taiwanese manufacturing is more vulnerable to the shock in factor prices than Korean manufacturing in the sense that the effects of the shock in factor prices on the structure of factor demand are greater in Taiwan than in Korea. The estimated values of price elasticities of factor demand are relatively stable over time in both countries. There is no strong evidence in either country that the production technology has significantly changed over the period under this study.

Concerning the own price elasticity of demand, capital is most elastic (between –0.46 and –0.47) and energy is most inelastic (between –0.06 and –0.22) in Korea, while capital and labor are equally very elastic (between –0.82 and –0.84 for both inputs) and energy and materials are equally inelastic (between –0.36 and –0.54 for both inputs) in Taiwan. Demand for labor is very own price inelastic (between –0.14 and –0.19) in Korea. On the other hand, demand for materials is relatively own price elastic (between –0.29 and –0.35) in Korea.

Furthermore, it is worth noting that a change in materials price has a strong effect on the demand for each input in both countries. Demand for capital, labor, and energy is affected more strongly by a change in materials price than by a change in own price. Thus, it is important to stabilize the materials price in order to keep

Table 10.2
Parameter Estimates of Translog Total Cost Function
for Korean and Taiwanese Manufacturing (standard errors in parentheses)

Parameter	Korea Biased Technical Change	Korea Hicks Neutral Change	Taiwan Biased Technical Change	Taiwan Hicks Neutral Change
AO	17.5468	17.4096	20.6634	20.6521
	(0.0874)	(0.0031)	(0.0822)	(0.0061)
AK	0.2003	0.2113	0.0955	0.0928
	(.0207)	(0.0101)	(0.0501)	(0.0034)
AL	0.2198	0.1117	0.1456	0.1242
	(0.0592)	(0.0037)	(0.1008)	(0.0069)
AE	0.0882	0.0491	0.0364	0.0407
	(0.0340)	(0.0028)	(0.0340)	(0.0022)
AM	0.4919	0.6279	0.7225	0.7422
	(0.0822)	(0.0139)	(0.1730)	(0.0099)
AT	-0.0149	-0.0007	-0.0018	-0.0005
	(0.0085)	(0.0004)	(0.0105)	(0.0099)
BKK	0.0711	0.0696	0.0065	0.0041
	(0.0214)	(0.0410)	(0.0230)	(0.0085)
BKL	-0.0336	-0.0334	-0.0388	-0.0403
	(0.0119)	(0.0107)	(0.0315)	(0.0067)
BKE	-0.0220	-0.0186	-0.0212	-0.0205
	(0.0156)	(0.0103)	(0.0059)	(0.0053)
BKM	-0.0155	-0.0176	0.0535	0.0567
	(0.0218)	(0.0370)	(0.0493)	(0.0079)
BKT	0.0009		-0.0002	
	(0.0014)		(0.0031)	
BLL	0.0692	0.0273	0.0041	-0.0137
	(0.0139)	(0.0042)	(0.0625)	(0.0104)
BLE	-0.0073	-0.0235	0.0028	0.0046
	(0.0168)	(0.0038)	(0.0287)	(0.0048)
BLM	-0.0283	0.0296	0.0319	0.0495
	(0.0251)	(0.0129)	(0.1129)	(0.0096)
BLT	-0.0056		-0.0013	
	(0.0030)		(0.0064)	
BEE	0.0398	0.0345	0.0225	0.0264
	(0.0101)	(0.0038)	(0.0232)	(0.0115)
BEM	-0.0105	0.0076	-0.0042	-0.0106
	(0.0277)	(0.0093)	(0.0302)	(0.0115)
BET	-0.0019		0.0003	
	(0.0017)		(0.0020)	
BMM	0.0542	-0.0195	-0.0812	-0.0956
	(0.0522)	(0.0309)	(0.1694)	(0.0223)
BMT	0.0066		0.0012	
	(0.0036)		(0.0108)	
BTT	0.0008	0.0001	0.0001	0.0000
	(0.0004)	(0.0000)	(0.0007)	(0.0001)
Log of Likelihood Function	367.081	345.221	334.670	333.935

Table 10.3
Test Result of Hicks Neutral Technical Change Hypothesis
in Korean and Taiwanese Manufacturing

Hypothesis	Countries	Test Statistic -2 x (R-U)	Test Result
Hicks Neutral	Korea	43.72	Rejected
Technical Change	Taiwan	1.47	Accepted

Note: The test statistic in which R and U are the logs of the likelihood functions of restricted and unrestricted estimates respectively has chi-square distribution and thus provides the likelihood ratio test.

the structure of factor demand undisturbed. However, the effects of a change in energy price on the demand for other inputs are very low in both countries. If such is the case, the energy crises that occurred during the periods under this study would not significantly influence the structure of factor demand. Other cross price elasticities of factor demand are also low. Except for the cross price elasticities from the change in materials price, own price elasticities are higher than cross price

Table 10.4
Productivity Growth Rates of Capital, Labor, Energy, Materials, and Total Factor in Korean and Taiwanese Manufacturing

Inputs	Countries	1961	1963	1974	1981	1984
Capital	Korea	--	-0.08	-0.44	-0.47	-0.56
	Taiwan	0.19	0.18	0.21	0.32	--
Labor	Korea	--	5.98	6.16	5.87	5.97
	Taiwan	0.74	0.82	1.02	1.02	--
Energy	Korea	--	4.49	3.89	3.36	4.17
	Taiwan	-0.54	-0.64	-0.71	-0.50	--
Materials	Korea	--	-0.98	-1.20	-1.16	-1.24
	Taiwan	-0.17	-0.16	-0.17	-0.16	--
Total Factor	Korea	--	0.21	-0.10	-0.09	-0.19
	Taiwan	0.02	0.02	0.00	-0.00	• --

Table 10.5
Technical Change Biases in Korean and Taiwanese Manufacturing

Inputs	Countries	
	Korea	Taiwan
Capital	U	S
Labor	S	S
Energy	S	U
Materials	U	U

Note: U and S stand for "using" and "saving" respectively.

Table 10.6
Price Elasticities of Demand for Capital, Labor, Energy, and Materials in Korean and Taiwanese Manufacturing

Quantities	Years	Capital		Labor		Energy		Materials	
		Korea	Taiwan	Korea	Taiwan	Korea	Taiwan	Korea	Taiwan
Capital	1961	--	-0.82	--	-0.11	--	-0.11	--	0.72
	1963	-0.46	-0.82	-0.01	-0.13	-0.03	-0.12	0.53	0.75
	1974	-0.47	-0.83	-0.04	-0.24	-0.04	-0.16	0.58	0.80
	1981	-0.46	-0.84	-0.05	-0.44	-0.04	-0.25	0.59	0.82
	1984	-0.46	--	-0.05	--	-0.05	--	0.60	--
Labor	1961	--	-0.08	--	-0.80	--	0.06	--	0.82
	1963	-0.04	-0.11	-0.19	-0.82	-0.03	0.06	0.26	0.87
	1974	-0.12	-0.21	-0.14	-0.84	-0.03	0.06	0.29	0.99
	1981	-0.13	-0.24	-0.17	-0.84	-0.02	0.08	0.32	1.01
	1984	-0.13	--	-0.15	--	-0.04	--	0.32	--
Energy	1961	--	-0.30	--	0.23	--	-0.49	--	0.55
	1963	-0.19	-0.37	-0.07	0.23	-0.06	-0.42	0.32	0.57
	1964	-0.20	-0.44	-0.06	0.20	-0.12	-0.38	0.38	0.62
	1981	-0.17	-0.31	-0.04	0.18	-0.22	-0.54	0.43	0.68
	1984	-0.27	--	-0.08	--	-0.05	--	0.39	--
Materials	1961	--	0.22	--	0.23	--	0.04	--	-0.49
	1963	0.28	0.21	0.05	0.21	0.03	0.04	-0.35	-0.45
	1974	0.23	0.18	0.04	0.17	0.03	0.03	-0.31	-0.38
	1981	0.21	0.14	0.05	0.17	0.04	0.05	-0.29	-0.36
	1984	0.21	--	0.05	--	0.03	--	-0.28	--

Table 10.7
Elasticities of Substitution in Korean and Taiwanese Manufacturing

Input-input	Countries	1961	1963	1974	1981	1984
Capital-Capital	Korea	--	-1.52	-1.80	- 1.99	-1.96
	Taiwan	- 6.08	-6.14	-7.91	-12.23	--
Capital-Labor	Korea	--	- 0.14	-0.45	- 0.55	-0.57
	Taiwan	- 0.63	- 0.85	-1.95	- 3.57	--
Capital-Energy	Korea	--	- 0.63	-0.78	- 0.72	-1.13
	Taiwan	- 2.22	- 2.81	-4.22	- 4.59	--
Capital-Materials	Korea	--	0.91	0.90	0.89	0.90
	Taiwan	1.62	1.60	1.69	2.04	--
Labor-Labor	Korea	--	- 1.96	-1.53	- 1.80	-1.62
	Taiwan	- 4.52	- 5.18	-6.75	- 6.79	--
Labor-Energy	Korea	--	- 0.69	-0.71	- 0.41	-0.84
	Taiwan	1.33	1.43	1.59	1.41	--
Labor-Materials	Korea	--	0.48	0.48	0.51	0.51
	Taiwan	1.28	1.30	1.35	1.34	--
Energy-Energy	Korea	--	- 1.37	-2.49	- 4.04	-1.05
	Taiwan	-10.04	-10.04	-9.79	- 9.72	--
Energy-Materials	Korea	--	0.58	0.64	0.69	0.62
	Taiwan	0.87	0.85	0.85	0.90	--
Materials-Materials	Korea	--	- 0.63	-0.51	- 0.47	-0.45
	Taiwan	- 0.76	- 0.68	-0.52	- 0.47	--

elasticities. Therefore, in summary, the estimated price elasticities of factor demand show that demand for each input has been mainly affected by a change in the own price or materials price.

The technological characteristics of factor substitution described by the sign of the cross price elasticities of factor demand reported in Table 10.6 are analyzed in depth by the elasticities of substitution reported in Table 10.7. Capital is complementary to labor and energy, and materials are substitutes for capital, labor, and energy in both countries. However, labor and energy are complements in Korea, but substitutes in Taiwan.

The capital-energy relationships have been an important issue in the investigation of production technology because capital-energy complementarity has been interpreted to mean a vulnerability of the production structure in the presence of an energy crisis. If capital and energy are complements, energy will not be able to be substituted efficiently by capital when there is an energy crisis. Berndt and Wood (1975) and Norsworthy and Malmquist (1983) showed that capital and energy are complements in U.S. and Japanese manufacturing. The estimated results in this chapter also show that capital and energy are complements in Korean and Taiwanese manufacturing. Given these empirical results, the adoption of efficient capital would not be considered a good choice for energy policy. More importantly, Taiwan's manufacturing is more vulnerable in the sense that the capital-energy complementarity is greater in Taiwan than in Korea.

The labor-energy relationship is different in Korea and Taiwan. Labor is a complement to energy in Korea whereas labor is a substitute for energy in Taiwan. Korea and Taiwan are labor-abundant countries. However, due to the labor-energy complementarity, the abundance of labor would not be able to help Korea overcome the energy crisis through factor substitution in manufacturing production. Furthermore, the labor-energy substitutability in Taiwan could be a reason why the rate of growth of energy productivity was very low in the labor-intensive production of Taiwan's manufacturing.

The estimated elasticities of substitution are also consistently higher in Taiwan than in Korea. Thus, it can be pointed out that substitution between inputs could take place more sensitively in Taiwanese manufacturing than in Korean manufacturing when there is a change in relative factor price. The change in relative factor price has greater effects on the structure of factor demand in Taiwan than in Korea. It is also worth noting that the estimated elasticities of substitution are mostly shown to be slightly increasing over time.

CONCLUDING REMARKS

This chapter has shown several notable differences in the production technology of Korean and Taiwanese manufacturing.

First of all, the pattern of technological progress could be explained by Hicks neutrality for Taiwan but not for Korea. The rate of growth of individual factor productivity is high for labor and energy, but low for capital and materials in Korea. However, it is relatively low for all four inputs in Taiwan. Despite these differences in the pattern of the growth rate of individual factor productivity, the growth rate of total factor productivity is equally low in both countries. Thus, it could be pointed out that the rapid growth of output achieved in Korean and Taiwanese manufacturing is largely attributable to the movement along the given production function rather than the shift in the production function.[7]

Compared with Taiwanese manufacturing, Korean manufacturing is characterized by a high proportion of heavy industries with large-scale firms using capital-intensive technology. By contrast, Taiwanese manufacturing is characterized by a high proportion of light industries with small and medium-sized firms, using labor-intensive technology. Furthermore, capital is complementary to labor and energy in both countries. However, labor is complementary to energy in Korea while it is a substitute for energy in Taiwan. Consequently, in Korea, labor equipped with a greater volume of capital that is complementary to labor could become more productive than in Taiwan. In addition, the greater volume of capital that is also complementary to energy would raise the productivity of energy in Korea. However, the greater amount of labor in Taiwan's labor-intensive production is not likely to raise the productivity of energy because energy is a substitute for labor in Taiwan. And, in Taiwan, labor equipped with less capital is less productive than in Korea.

Capital-energy complementarity is also an important finding. Many countries were interested in developing the efficient capital that was substitutive for energy when the energy crises took place in the 1970s. In particular, the substitution of capital for energy was an important issue in Korea and Taiwan because both of them relied heavily on imports for much of their energy. However, the observed capital-energy complementarity indicates that energy cannot be efficiently substituted by capital in these countries.

More importantly, on the whole, various elasticities investigated in this chapter are consistently higher for Taiwan than for Korea. This result indicates that the structure of production is more market oriented and therefore more sensitive to the shock in factor prices in Taiwanese manufacturing than in Korean manufacturing. The change in factor prices will influence the pattern of factor demand more in Taiwan than in Korea.

NOTES

1. Although no comparison of technological characteristics between the two countries has ever been made, various analyses are available for Korea (see Kwon and Williams, 1982; Kwon, 1986; Kim and Park, 1988; Kwon and Yuhn, above).

2. The Korean data set used in this research was mostly constructed by the author. The Taiwan data were provided by Chi-Yuan Liang, Institute of Economics, Academia Sinica, Taiwan. For Korea, most of the raw data used in this research are available from *Report on Mining and Manufacturing Survey* and *Economic Statistics Year Book*, and various capital stock estimates (from which one series is used for this research) are reported in Pyo and Song (1987). The construction of data for each variable basically follows the KLEM data concepts discussed in Norsworthy and Malmquist (1983).

3. The concavity condition was violated in energy prices for several years in Korean data. But this violation did not significantly affect the subsequent analyses.

4. The estimated sign of equation (4) will be negative if the prductivity of input *i* improves, because the required input quantity to produce the selected constant output level would decrease as productivity of the input improves. However, the sign is changed when it is reported in Table 10.4, in order to make the positive sign to represent increase in productivity.

5. The estimated sign of equation (5) will also be negative if the total factor

productivity improves. Thus, for by the same reason as in note 4, this sign is also changed when it is reported in Table 10.4.

6. The estimate of the growth rate of the total factor productivity by Kwon and Yuhn (above) is also low for Korea, whereas the one by Kim and Park (1988) is high.

7. For some discussion on the sources of real output growth in Korean and Taiwanese manufacturing, see Choi (1988).

REFERENCES

Bank of Korea, *Economic Statistics Yearbook*, Seoul, various years.

Berndt, Ernst R., and Wood, David O., "Technology, Prices and the Derived Demand for Energy," *Review of Economics and Statistics, 57*, August 1975, 259–68.

———, "Engineering and Econometric Interpretations of Energy-Capital Complementarity," *American Economic Review, 69*, June 1979, 342–54.

Binswanger, Hans P., (1974a) "A Cost Function Approach to the Measurement of Elasticities of Factor Demand and Elasticities of Substitution," *American Journal of Agricultural Economics, 56*, May 1974, 377–86.

———, (1974b) "The Measurement of Technical Change Biases with Many Factors of Production," *American Economic Review, 64*, December 1974, 964–76.

Choi, Jeong Pyo, "Productivity Growth and the Sources of Output Growth in Korean and Taiwan's Manufacturing; A Temporary Equilibrium Approach," Mimeo, Department of Economics, Kon-Kuk University, June 1988.

Christensen, L. R., and Greene, W. H., "Economies of Scale in U.S. Electric Power Generation," *Journal of Political Economy., 84*, August 1976, 655–676.

———, Jorgenson, D. W., and Lau, L. T., "Conjugate Duality and the Transcendental Logarithmic Production Function," (abstract), *Econometrica,39*, July 1971, 255–56.

———, ———, and ———, "Transcendental Logarithmic Production Frontiers," *Review of Economics and Statistics, 55*, February 1973, 28–45.

Economic Planning Board, *Report on Mining and Manufacturing Survey*, Seoul, various years.

Jorgenson, D. W., and Fraumeni, B. M. "Relative Prices and Technical Change," in E. R. Berndt and B. C. Field, eds., *Modeling and Measuring Natural Resource Substitution*, Cambridge: MIT Press, 1981.

Kim, K. S., and Park, S. R., *Analysis of Changing Productivity and Its Causes for S. Korean Manufacturing* (in Korean), Seoul: Korea Institute for Economics and Technology, 1988.

Kwon, J. K., "Capacity Utilization, Economies of Scale and Technical Change in the Growth of Total Factor Productivity: An Explanation of South Korean Manufacturing Growth," *Journal of Development Economics, 24*, November 1986, 75–90.

————, and Williams, M. "The Structure of Production in South Korea's Manufacturing Sector," *Journal of Development Economics, 11*, October 1982, 215–26.

Norsworthy, John R., and Malmquist, David H., "Input Measurement and Productivity Growth in Japanese and U.S. Manufacturing," *American Economic Review, 73*, December 1983, 1066–79.

Pyo, H. K., and Song, C. Y. "Estimates of Capital Stocks in South Korea, 1960-1984," The Annual Conference of the Korean Economic Association, February 13, 1987, Book 2.

Solow, R. M., "Technical Change and the Aggregate Production Function," *Review of Economics and Statistics, 39*, August 1957, 312–20.

Uzawa, H., "Production Functions with Constant Elasticity of Substitution," *Review of Economic Studies, 30*, October 1962, 291–99.

Part Four

MACRO-DYNAMICS

A. Financial System and Monetary Aggregates

In Korea, the government's control of the financial system was an integral part of the government-led economic development. Korea's financial sector played a significant role in this development by mobilizing domestic savings for capital formation. Yet the development of the financial system in Korea has been somewhat eventful due largely to the government's repression of the financial sector. At least until well into the 1980s, the innovation in Korea's financial system had not kept pace with the growth in other sectors.

In an effort to present a thorough review of Korea's financial development, P. J. Kim in his chapter has marshaled a considerable array of information and knowledge on the financial institutions and the interplay of policy and circumstances as background for analysis. As Kim points out, the single most significant aspect of the banks' role during the decades of economic growth was to serve as the major source of government-directed loans to Korean businesses. This delicate nexus between the government, banks, and business constitutes the unique characteristics of Korea's economic development. On the other hand, the 1980s are notable for the beginning of the policy switch from government-led to private-led management of the national economy.

One of the major issues in the Korean monetary-finance sphere is the relative accuracy of various monetary aggregates as measures of the flow of monetary services in the economy. All the monetary aggregates currently in use in Korea have overlooked the fact that different monetary components have different degrees of moneyness and that aggregating monetary components as the simple-sum does not provide an adequate measure of the flow of monetary services to the economy.

To rectify this imperfection, T. H. Lee, in the second chapter in this section, used the Fisher Ideal index number in the aggregation of monetary quantities as measures of monetary services to the economy. Since the Fisher Ideal index is based on a flexible utility function of holding monetary assets, it takes into account the degrees of moneyness among the monetary components even when the structure of interest rates is determined by the government.

Upon comparing various monetary aggregates, Lee reaches a conclusion that the Fisher Ideal index with M2 components is superior to all the rest including the conventional simple-sum index number for monetary aggregates. He also points out that the proposed approach is especially useful for countries such as Korea where the alternative costs of holding monetary assets are relatively high and variable due to the presence of a curb market.

In the third chapter, Y. J. Cho examines the differences in the financial policies between Korea and Taiwan. He shows that although the financial systems in both countries are regulated by the government, the degree of control was much less in Taiwan in the 1960s and 1970s. In Taiwan, the price mechanism (that is, interest rates) and the allocation of funds have been, in general, more closely related to the market principle than in Korea. Taiwan consistently maintained a high interest rate policy with a very low and stable inflation during this period. In Korea, the interest rates were kept artificially low. Consequently, in Taiwan the growth of financial savings as well as national savings was remarkable. On the other hand, in Korea, the substantial part of investment to achieve a high growth rate had to be financed through foreign capital.

11

Korea's Financial Evolution, 1961–1986

Pyung Joo Kim

INTRODUCTION

Over the last quarter century or so, the Korean financial sector has made a significant contribution to Korea's economic development by mobilizing domestic savings for capital formation. The growth of the financial sector, however, has not always kept pace with the rapidly changing economic needs. More often than not, changes were instituted in an ad hoc fashion without carefully weighing their long-run consequences; government control of the financial system has been ubiquitous and often blatant.

The objective of this study is to review the evolution of the financial system while assessing the impact of some of the major financial policies.

THE MAJOR DEVELOPMENTS PRIOR TO 1961

Three major developments in the period immediately preceding 1961 deserve special attention. The first was the privatization of commercial banks that had previously been nationalized in the process of divesting Japanese interests. The government shares of commercial banks were put on the block beginning in 1954 and on a massive scale in 1957. The auctions were conducted in such a fashion that the result was the high concentration of stock in a few hands. The second development worthy of mention was the establishment in 1959 of the Bank of Seoul as a bank exclusively funded with private capital. The Bank of Seoul was the first new entry into commercial banking since liberation.

The third new development was the initiation of the Financial Stabilization Program beginning in 1957 on the recommendation of the United States aid agency and the International Monetary Fund. In the preceding period, the fiscal and monetary policies of the Korean government had been highly dependent upon the magnitude and direction of U.S. aid and grants, and therefore were not stable and systematic. The late 1950s saw a trend of dwindling economic aid and grants, and the Korean government was notified of their imminent termination. Thus the Financial Stabilization Program signified the start of meaningful self-management of economic policies. The target variable of monetary policy was Ml, a narrowly defined monetary aggregate: currency in circulation plus demand deposits. The annual and quarterly targets of Ml were set by the monetary authorities—that is, the Ministry of Finance and the Bank of Korea—and in order to curb monetary increases within pre-set targets, direct and selective control instruments were used. Direct control on bank credit was necessitated by the fact that the indirect control instruments, such as open market operations, rediscount policy, and reserve requirement manipulation, were, by and large, inappropriate to an economy with undeveloped financial markets.

FINANCIAL EXPERIMENTS AND REVERSALS (1961–71)

The vision and determination of C. H. Park's military regime was different from that of his predecessors. The "government-led growth policy" represents the main tenor of economic policies during this period. The growth during this period, which was remarkable, was sustained largely at the expense of repressing the financial institutions and their development.

The character of financial-sector development during this early phase of Park's regime may be described as a flow of waters, the main currents of which were Japanese influences (that is, government control and interference with financial institutions as well as preference toward market segmentation such as specialized banks). During this period a host of U.S. advisers visited Korea frequently under the auspices of USAID and international organizations. Their recommendations were put into practice with much fanfare and had an apparently dramatic effect for a while. These experiments, imbued with American ideas and implemented by officials more susceptible to U.S. influence, made ripples on the surface of Korea's financial structure. In most cases, these experiments were short lived, distorted, ignored, and eventually overwhelmed by the main currents flowing steadily under the surface. However, there were some major developments in the financial sector during this period.

Subjugation of the Central Bank

The strengthened control of the government over the financial system is most evident in its relationship to the central bank and the Monetary Board. In May 1962, the Bank of Korea Act was amended. The official Korean appellation of the Monetary Board was changed from *gumyung tongwha wiwonhui* (monetary board) to *gumyung-tongwha unyong wiwonhui* (monetary management board). This titular change has since been interpreted as an expression of the government's intention to downgrade the function of the board from policy deliberation to policy management discussion.

The board's membership was expanded to nine by adding two appointed members to the existing seven. The power of the finance minister was strengthened; the minister could request that the board reconsider a resolution previously passed. If the request was overruled by the board with a two-thirds majority, the final decision would be made at a cabinet meeting, at which the minister's view would be ensured a hearing. However, the process of appointing the governor of the Bank of Korea and the seven non-ex-officio members was such that the strengthening of the position of the minister in the board was unnecessary. The board was divested of the function of formulating foreign exchange policy; this task was transferred to the finance minister.

This singular division of monetary policies between those directly related to domestic currency and those related to foreign exchange might have been made with an intention of expediting the introduction of foreign savings through bypassing the possibly cumbersome deliberation process of the board. The absurdity of this artificial division has increased as the significance of the foreign sector has become more pronounced and the inseparability of factors affecting money supply has become more evident. As final proof of its subordination, the central bank was made subject to examination by the finance minster at least once a year, and its annual budget was to be approved by the cabinet.

Nationalization and Comprehensive Control of Commercial Banks

Korean entrepreneurs, perennially short of funds, are heavily dependent upon external financing for their operation and expansion. The "over-loaning" of commercial banks has been the mirror image of their client firms' "over-borrowing." In other words, the commercial banks of Korea have been confronted with a chronic excess demand for funds throughout the four decades since 1945. To cover the shortage of funds they have had recourse to the discount window of the central bank. As a result, a door has been opened wide for the central bank's application of "window guidance" to restrict increases in bank lending.[1]

In addition, those commercial banks privatized in the late 1950s were once again nationalized as a result of confiscating "illicit" wealth accumulated under the previous regime immediately after the military coup. Furthermore, it was legislated that the voting power of major shareholders (except the government) owning 10 percent or more of the total outstanding stocks of a bank should be circumscribed. The annual budgets of commercial banks were made subject to the approval of the finance minister, although there was neither binding statute nor legislated rule to that effect. The case was the same with the top management of banks. The organizational structures of banks were made identical. In essence, the presence of the government was felt in commercial banks almost to the same extent as in special banks, which were fully government owned and controlled. In sum, the role of banks, whether commercial or special, was to be that of credit-rationing outlets at the behest of the government.

Specialization of Banks

The compartmentalization of financial institutions, namely, special banks, was a colonial legacy.[2] This specialization in finance meshes well with the aim of Korea's economic planners to encourage economic growth in selected projects and industries with policy-directed loans.

The specialized banks of Korea were established mostly during the 1960s for purposes specifically defined by their respective statutes. One feature of specialized banks is that they are owned, directed, and supervised by the government and, in principle, are outside the purview of the Monetary Board. However, some areas of their business operations are subject to the control of the Monetary Board. Minimum reserve requirements and maximum interest rates decided by the Monetary Board and the governor of the Bank of Korea are universally applied to the specialized banks as well as to the commercial banks. Specialized banks are also subject to the Bank Superintendent's Office, empowered by the finance minister. Another feature is that their major sources of financial resources are borrowing from the government, debentures issues, and deposits received from the public.

The Korea Development Bank was founded in 1954 to supply long-term credit for key industries. In the latter half of the 1950s the bank contributed to the rehabilitation of industrial facilities destroyed during the Korean War. The bank was reoriented to financing major development projects in line with the First Five-Year Economic Development Plan launched in 1962. The Small and Medium Industry Bank was established in 1961 to reinforce financial support for small- and medium-sized firms, since they had difficulty in competing with large-sized firms for the limited funds of banks. A number of mutual finance companies were consolidated into the Citizen's National Bank of Korea in 1962; a year later this was reorganized as the Citizen's National Bank. This bank was to specialize in small loans to small-sized firms with poor credit standing as well as to households. The National Agricultural Cooperative Federation and its affiliated cooperatives were reorganized in 1961 via the merger of the former Agricultural Cooperatives and the Agriculture Bank. Similarly, the National Federation of Fisheries Cooperatives and its affiliated cooperatives were established in 1962 to meet the financial needs of fishers and fisheries manufacturers.

The hectic year for establishing specialized banks was 1967. First, the Korea Exchange Bank was established in 1967 with the specific task of supporting foreign exchange transactions of firms, which had previously been handled mainly by the Bank of Korea. The need for a bank specializing in this field had increased with the rapid growth of foreign trade volume beginning in 1966. The Korea Housing Bank was also founded in 1967 to finance housing for low-income households. As rural-to-urban migration increased with the pace of industrialization, the housing shortage in urban areas became an acute issue, and the establishment of a specialized bank was deemed necessary to mitigate this problem. A third bank, established in 1969, was the Korea Long Term Credit Bank (reorganized from the Korea Development Finance Corporation). It was empowered to extend medium- and long-term credit to firms in the form of loans, discounts, equity investments, and guarantees. This bank is unique, in that it is a privately funded institution with specialized functions assigned to it.

Booming exports necessitated the inauguration of the Export-Import Bank of Korea in 1969, with its paid-in capital funded by the government, the Bank of Korea, and the Korea Exchange Bank. Its main business is financing of medium- and long-term export-import transactions; investing overseas, including natural resources development projects abroad; underwriting export insurance for domestic corporations and foreign institutions; and extending credit to foreign buyers for importing capital goods and technical services from Korea.

The initiation of a local banking system also took place in 1967. As mentioned previously, the Bank of Seoul was founded in 1959 and regionally restricted to the Seoul area, but in 1962 it became a nationwide bank. During the period from 1967 to 1971, ten local banks were established, one for each province. This was most likely an echo of the "one-bank-in-each prefecture" principle from Japan (Bank of Japan, 1978, p. 64). The branch network of these banks is allowed within each province, in which their head offices are located. These local banks have been privately owned from the outset, in contrast to the nationwide commercial banks.

The year 1967 was noteworthy in yet another respect because it witnessed the inauguration of foreign bank branch offices. The Seoul branch office of the Chase Manhattan Bank was the first, and the other foreign bank branches soon followed. The major purpose of allowing foreign banks into Korea was to facilitate foreign capital inflow and to give incentives for domestic banks to improve their banking practices and managerial skills by borrowing ideas from their international competitors.

Financial Experiments

One of the major characteristics of economic policies during the Park regime was the unabashed adventurism manifested in frequent trials and errors or sudden starts and abrupt reversals. Most of the drastic experiments were attempted in the sphere of finance. To illustrate the experiment-happy spirit during this period, the following example may be cited:

The interest rate reform enacted on September 30, 1965 was the best known and most well documented event during this period. In May 1964, the exchange system was unified, and the won was depreciated from 130 per U.S. dollar to 255 per U.S. dollar. This was followed by the interest rate reform of 1965 that doubled the maximum rate on one-year time deposits from 15 percent to 30 percent per annum. This was done to increase private savings while simultaneously discouraging unproductive use of bank credit. To make up for losses to the banks due to inverted rates (that is, loan rates set below deposit rates), interest at the rate of 3.5 per annum was paid to banks on reserve deposits with the central bank.

During the three-year period from 1966 to 1969, deposits and loans grew rapidly, at annual rates of 72.5 and 26.5 percent respectively. Real GNP increased at the average annual rate of 12 percent during the same period. Meanwhile, inflation was running at the average annual rate of 3.5 percent, providing a remarkable respite from the rate of 17.5 percent in the preceding five years.[3]

At this time, a package of readjustment or "realization" policies, including interest rate reform, which had originally been recommended by U.S. advisers (Gurley, Patrick, and Shaw 1965, pp. 58–59), was adopted by the Korean government. One goal was to encourage foreign capital inflow through creating a wider spread of domestic interest rates in excess of foreign money market rates. The dramatic increase in bank deposits and loans was brought about by the combination of the reform itself, inflow of foreign capital, and strengthened restrictions on real estate speculation.

In this heady environment, cases of insolvency and bankruptcy became more frequent and noticeable. Firms long accustomed to an inflationary milieu could not adjust to the stabilizing overall prices and the shifting demand pattern that had developed since 1965. Recipients of relatively cheap foreign loans in the form of plant and equipment were often selected irrespective of their net worth and debt-servicing capacities. They had to resort to borrowing from domestic sourses, including the curb market, to make up for the shortages in working capital. The ratio of current liabilities to net worth of manufacturing firms soared precipitously from 56 percent in 1965 to 113.3 percent in 1968. In addition, a brake was applied on bank credit expansion beginning in the last quarter of 1969 in connection with the Financial Stabilization Program. The configuration of these forces eventually paved the way for the Emergency Decree Concerning Economic Stability and Growth, promulgated on August 3, 1972.

It should be noted at this point that the reform of 1965 was not an unmixed success (which is definitely not the case) but that a policy posture of financial liberalization was not maintained for a period long enough to alter the basic texture of accustomed practices of financial repression. Financial liberalization culminating in the interest rate reform of 1965 remained a short episode in the midst of financial repression, rather than an epoch-making event ushering in a new phase of financial liberalization.

Relations between the Government and the Banks

As for the relationship between the Korean government and the banks, the government's role may be summarized as one of direction and management. The weight of policy-directed loans was increasingly heavy; the magnitude and allocation of commercial loans was tightly controlled; and other aspects of bank management such as personnel management, budgeting, and organization were also subject to the approval of the government. Consequently, commercial banks were virtually credit-rationing outlets of the government to nearly the same extent as the specialized banks.

A useful way to examine Korean finance may be to see the tripartite relationship between the government, business, and financial institutions rather than a bilateral relationship of the government versus banks.

During the drive-to-high-growth period, the primary objective of enterprises was growth (or sales) maximization rather than profit maximization. The goal was for enterprises to grow at top speed to achieve a critical minimum size, at which the government would be unable to allow insolvency or bankruptcy. After all, widespread unemployment ignited by the failure of large corporations would cause social unrest and loss of reputation overseas for the Korean economy. Fuel for the rapid expansion of firms was provided by high leverage or heavy dependence on debt financing. Firms raced to the brink of bankruptcy with one eye ever fixed on the government, which played the role of referee in this game of brinkmanship. It exercised discretionary power for determining which firm would get the benefit of financial credit and thus be saved from going over the edge. Thus, the maintenance of a good relationship with the government was the most crucial element for success in business. The stance of banks was a passive one; they simply responded to the commands of the government to extend or withdraw credit to designated firms. A natural and inevitable consequence of this tripartite relationship was the increase in insolvent firms or nonperforming assets on the balance sheets of the banks.

FINANCIAL REPRESSION REINFORCED (1972–79)

The period under discussion contained a number of serious internal and external disturbances, that is, (a) a political shift toward more authoritarian leadership, (b) rampant inflation, (c) a temporary slowdown in growth, and (d) the oil crisis in 1973–74, which aggravated balance of payment deficits, causing a scramble for foreign capital.

This string of events had inevitable repercussions for Korea's finance system;

namely, reinforced financial repression, proliferation of policy-directed loans, and endeavors to devise mechanisms to facilitate foreign capital inflows. The general characteristics of the earlier phase became intensified.

Freeze on Curb Markets

Korea's official (or organized) financial markets have always suffered from excess demand for funds. Aggravating this situation was negative interest charged to borrowers as a result of high inflation and interest rates of financial institutions artificially held below a market-clearing level. For many applicants obtaining access to bank credit was very difficult. Thus, frustration at official financial markets abounded, and borrowers sought other sources of funds. On the supply side, Koreans in every walk of life have had close contact with unorganized money markets (notably *kyes*), and under protracted inflation and low official interest rates, the preference for this type of market instead of official institutions was strong. Thus fertile ground was created for unorganized money markets.

As economic growth began to sour in 1970 and worsened in the first half of 1972, business leaders began to blame their troubles on mounting financial burdens and voiced their demand for lower interest rates (partly as a delayed reaction to the interest rate reform of 1965) through organizations representing their interests such as the Federation of Korean Industries. The Park regime, never sympathetic to the financial community, was ready to accommodate the alleged needs of business. The Emergency Decree Concerning Economic Stability and Growth was promulgated on August 3, 1972. The thrust of this decree was to stop loans to businesses originating from the unofficial and unregulated private money market (curb market) sources.

The emergency decree was designed to reduce the financial costs of businesses, primarily by removing the burden of loans from unorganized money markets. In addition, measures were taken to lower the interest rates of banking institutions; to convert portions of outstanding bank loans into long-term, low-interest loans; to establish a credit guarantee fund; and to improve the financial structure of firms. According to the decree, it was the obligation of both the creditors and the debtor firms to report to the tax offices or the banking institutions the total amount of curb loans plus unpaid interest as of August 2, 1972. Incentives and penalties were combined to enhance reporting. Reported curb loans were to be converted into long-term loans having a three-year grace period and thereafter a five-year repayment period with an equal amount (corresponding to 10 percent of the loan amount) to be repaid every six months.

The total amount of curb loans reported within the seven-day reporting period was staggering: 357.1 billion won reported by the creditors and 345.6 billion won by the debtor firms. Even using the lower figure, this was tantamount to 88 percent of M1 (currency in circulation plus demand deposits) and 32.4 percent of outstanding loans and discounts of the demand deposit banks as a whole.

From a longer-term perspective, the emergency decree had only a small effect on the operation and magnitude of the unorganized money markets. In the early 1980s, a decade after the emergency decree, the curb markets were still in operation, and they sometimes erupted into major financial scandals. However, the steady growth of official financial institutions has made the curb markets relatively insignificant.

The Proliferation of Nonbank Financial Institutions

In connection with the emergency decree, a trio of nonbank financial institutions was created in 1972 to absorb curb market funds into the official financial markets: (1) investment and finance companies, (2) mutual savings and finance companies, and (3) credit unions and mutual credits (the mutual credit facilities of agricultural and fisheries cooperatives), of which the first deserves some elaboration.

Investment and finance companies (*danja hoisa*) were officially created in 1972 with the promulgation of the Short-Term Financing Business Act. These companies were designed to attract funds from the curb market and to develop the money market. The model for these kinds of finance companies was the investment banks of the United States, and the International Finance Corporation promoted this idea to the Korean government. The idea was to allow a fairly wide range of financial activities, including securities business. However, the types of businesses specifically listed in the act were narrowed, and in the actual practice it was restricted further, especially after the creation of another financial institution comprising a comprehensive range of businesses. The principal function of these finance companies consists of meeting short-term financial needs of the business community with funds raised through selling papers drawn on themselves and trading in papers issued by other firms. Subject to the authorization of the finance minister, these finance companies may engage in securities transactions such as underwriting, buying and selling, and acting as brokers or agencies. For a long time, these securities transactions have not been fully allowed; for instance, the finance companies have not been authorized to participate in the management of underwriting securities. The companies also serve as dealers in treasury bills issued by the government. Until the door was opened to new entries again in 1982, 24 of these companies (of which 7 were located in Seoul) were operating. They had only the head office; no branch offices were allowed.

After the initiation or reorganization of the three institutions just mentioned, another nonbank financial institution was introduced in 1976—the merchant banking corporation. The oil crisis exacted a heavy toll on Korea's foreign exchange reserves. The existing channels were inadequate to replenish the coffers, and new ones had to be found to facilitate foreign capital inflows. The Merchant

Banking Corporation Act was promulgated to meet this task. The official title for these institutions was *jong-hap kumyung hoisa* (literally, comprehensive finance companies). The range of business allowed to these firms is indeed comprehensive and includes (1) brokerage of foreign capital inducement, overseas investment, and international financing for enterprises or inducement of foreign capital inflows on their own account and subleasing to enterprises; (2) loans for working and equipment capital; (3) discounts, purchases, sales, acceptance, and guarantee of papers issued by enterprises; (4) underwriting and brokerage of securities sales; and (5) consulting services including business management guidance. In addition, securities investment trusts and leasing are permitted by the finance minister. In short, these firms are "department stores" for financial commodities. The model for this type of financial institution was the merchant banking institutions of Great Britain.

Merchant banking represents a unique deviation from the accepted financial structure of Korea, which has the same compartmentalized structure as in Japan. The merchant bank in Great Britain is a counterpart to the investment bank in the United States, and Korea has two types of financial institutions that play virtually the same roles under different names. There appears to be a tendency for a newly appointed minister to try to leave his imprint on the institutions and conventions under his control. A trend frequently noted in the Korean bureaucracy is that a new institution conceived by the current minister is often nurtured at the expense of other institutions initiated by former ministers.

Accordingly, short-term financing of businesses with funds raised through issuance of a financial company's own papers (one of the main businesses of investment and finance companies) was permitted to merchant banking corporations on a limited basis. Securities-related transactions of investment and finance companies were restricted, to the benefit of merchant banking corporations and securities companies.

Development of the Capital Market

The Korean Stock Exchange came into existence in 1956, and the Securities and Exchange Law was enacted in 1962. For more than a decade afterward, the major business of the securities market was transactions of government and public debentures; hence, the market was of only minor significance as far as corporate financing was concerned. The number of listed companies was limited, and returns on securities investment were much lower than those on alternative investment opportunities. In September 1968, the Law on Fostering the Capital Market was enacted, and under this law the Korea Investment Corporation was established to induce firms to go public and to encourage public participation in the securities market. In 1969 regular-way transactions were instituted in place of forward transactions, which were prone to encouraging excessive speculation.[4]

However, it was after the enactment of the Public Corporation Inducement Law in 1972 that the securities market really began to put on steam. The intent of the law was to invest the government with the power to designate firms eligible to go public and to issue ordinances to that effect. The Securities and Exchange Commission and its executive body, the Securities Supervisory Board, were established in 1977.

A glimpse at securities market activities during the 1970s shows that the number of listed companies in the stock market increased sluggishly from 48 at the beginning of 1970s to 66 at the end of 1972. This number began to grow sharply, reaching 355 at the end of 1979 after being stimulated by the new government policy. The total amount of listed stocks increased 18.4 times (from 119.9 billion won to 2,202.3 billion won) during the 1970s. The increase in the total amount of listed public and corporate bonds in this period was more spectacular, increasing by 88.1 times (from 17.5 billion won to 1,541.5 billion won). The stock market experienced a boomlet from 1976 to 1978; the composite stock price index rose from 104.04 at the end of 1976 to 144.86 by the end of 1978. Then a crash occurred, and the composite stock price index plummeted to 118.97 at the end of 1979. Meanwhile, the bond market picked up steadily, with the value of transactions soaring 14.3 times between 1976 and 1979.

Policy-Directed Loans

Policy-directed loans have been an indispensable channel by which the government has directed the flow of funds into selected sectors such as export-related industries and heavy and chemical industries. These sectors were deemed strategic to economic development. The government was determined to steer the economy through the development of heavy and chemical industries after the Yushin measure, and the need for mobilizing and directing funds greatly increased in magnitude. The conventional method of credit extension to selected industries via specialized banks was not sufficient for the new task. A set of measures had to be designed to bring other financial institutions (especially commercial banks), in addition to specialized banks, into the process. The participation of commercial banks in policy-directed loans had previously been limited primarily to export-supporting finance with the aid of rediscount facilities at the central bank.

Thus, the National Investment Fund was instituted in January 1974 to meet the challenge of supporting investment in major industries including heavy and chemical industries. The formulation of an annual program of fund raising and lending for the National Investment Fund is prepared by the Ministry of Finance, and the actual operation of the fund is entrusted to the Bank of Korea. Its resources are raised by (1) compulsory deposits from banking institutions, national savings associations, insurance companies, and various public funds managed by central and local governments and other public entities, and (2) transfers from various

government budgetary accounts. The compulsory contributions of banking institutions make up the bulk of the fund's resources; they are required to deposit 13
percent of the increase in time and saving deposits to the fund. This required
contribution rate varies over time. National savings associations, which channel
mandatory savings by public and private employees, also contribute a minor
portion by depositing 100 percent of their savings with the fund.

The line of demarcation between commercial banks and specialized banks has
become increasingly blurred because of (1) the increased role of commercial banks
in policy-directed loan activities, and (2) the allowance of deposit-taking to
specialized banks and subsequently the increased weight of deposits as a source of
their funds. With commercial banks and specialized banks steadily being homog-
enized, the profitability of commercial banks declined, and the gap between the
profitability of commercial banks and that of nonbank financial institutions widened.

Commercial Banks under Financial Repression

Until privatization, the government was the unchallenged single major shareholder in all nationwide commercial banks. The top management of banks (whether
commercial or specialized) was largely hand picked by the government. Annual
budgeting and other major activities of the banks were subject to approval by the
Ministry of Finance. Under these circumstances, it is natural that the overriding
concern of the top management of banks has been not to maximize profits or operate
efficiently but rather to obtain a higher "grade" from the government. The rate of
increase in deposits has been a key criterion in this grading for a long time. Thus,
annual and quarterly targets of deposits are established for each bank, and these
are disaggregated into targets for each branch office. (This practice in banking
institutions reflects the growth-oriented, sales-maximizing behavior of private
enterprises as previously described.) The top management of banks has paid little
heed to profitability but has placed a great emphasis on achieving deposit goals and
extending credit as directed by the government. Government-controlled finance is
doubly harmful, in that it causes repression of the evolution of banks as autonomous
business entities as well as protection of personnel unfit for the banking business.
Top managers have not been held accountable for poor profits by the major
shareholder (i.e., the government), private shareholders' views have been regarded
as nothing more than a nuisance, and banks' profits have been illusory, sometimes
being manipulated by the payment of interest on deposits with the central bank.

ATTEMPTS AT FINANCIAL LIBERALIZATION (1980–86)

At the beginning of the 1980s, opinion within and outside the government began
to shift toward changing economic helmsmanship, that is, switching from govern-

ment-led to privately led management of the national economy. The preamble of the Fifth Five-Year Economic and Social Development Plan was noteworthy for (1) frankly admitting mistakes that had arisen from the government-led mode of economic development involving comprehensive planning, and (2) expressing the need to promote private initiative and steer the national economy along the lines of indicative planning.

Price Stability

At the start of the 1980s the Korean economy plunged into serious stagflation, registering a slow and negative growth of GNP (7.0 percent in 1979 and –4.8 percent in 1980 after double-digit growth performance in the previous three years) and soaring price levels (18.8 and 38.9 percent per year as measured by the WPI in 1979 and 1980, respectively, after an inflationary but relatively stable period). Three factors contributed to this situation: (1) the OPEC-engineered second worldwide oil crisis; (2) a poor rice harvest in 1980; and (3) the turbulent atmosphere of the nation's political and social scenes in the aftermath of President Park's death in 1979. On the economic scene, a relaxation of the authoritarian government's grip began to be manifested in various ways. In particular, cases of labor unrest became more frequent.

An external concomitant of this poor economic performance was a deterioration of the international balance of payments. The current account deficit increased sharply from US $1.1 billion in 1978 to US $4.1, US $5.3, and US $4.6 billion in 1979, 1980, and 1981, respectively. Consequently, the nation's foreign indebtedness began to increase rapidly from US $14.8 billion at the end of 1978 to US $46.8 billion at the end of 1985.

The new regime of Chun affirmed its will to stem runaway inflation and to maintain price stability. On one hand, the resort to market mechanisms has allegedly been the basic posture of the government in bringing about an overall balance of supply and demand. On the other hand, the Price Stabilization and Fair Trade Act of 1975 was enforced primarily to control the prices of basic commodities and products of monopolistic and oligopolistic industries.[5] Moreover, the government has maintained a system of listing commodities under price watch as well as a means of direct control over prices of goods produced by government-controlled enterprises. Therefore, the government's direct and indirect control of prices has been very much in effect in the 1980s. Some examples can be cited to demonstrate the government's emphasis on price stability.

In January 1980, interest rates on deposits and loans of banking institutions were increased.[6] It was significant that this unpopular contractionary measure—almost anathema to the heavily indebted business community—was taken in the politically most difficult period. Another example was a freeze on the government's general fiscal budget in 1984. This measure was noteworthy because a general election for the National Assembly was scheduled to be held the following January. The government party sustained a major setback in that election, in part because of that budget freeze. Government stabilization measures and stabilizing forces overseas (a steady fall in oil prices and international money market rates) contributed to sustained price stability in the period after 1982—a remarkable achievement for a nation long accustomed to an inflationary milieu. In contrast with double-digit inflation for a decade, WPI rose 2.4 percent in 1982 and maintained that level in the subsequent three years, then fell by 2.6 percent in 1986. The movement of the CPI showed a similar trend but remained a few percentage points higher. In 1986 the CPI crept up by 1.4 percent. Price stability was essential for a great surge of exports and domestic savings, and thus the way had been paved to financial liberalization.

Privatization of Nationwide Banks

A tentative first step toward the denationalization of nationwide commercial banks was taken in 1973 when government-owned shares in the Commercial Bank of Korea were transferred to the Korea Traders Association. Earnest privatization endeavors had to await a change of position on the part of the government. The process of privatization was accelerated in the early 1980s as a result of a shift in the government's views on economic helmsmanship, with a greater role being assigned to the private sector. Government-owned shares in the remaining four nationwide commercial banks were put on the block. A ceiling of 8 percent was placed on individual shareholding in nationwide commercial banks to prevent the concentration of economic power.

Forced Changes in the Financial Sector

The evolution of the financial sector in Korea has rarely proceeded smoothly or in accordance with a program well prepared in advance with an overall grasp of the outcomes. More often than not, changes have been forced on financial institutions in tandem with the government's hasty response to unexpected turns of events. Financial institutions and money markets were rocked to their foundations by large-scale irregularities and scandals on several occasions in the early 1980s.

The frequent occurrence of large-scale financial irregularities in such a short span of time (three major scandals in as many years) was rooted in the financial pressures caused by the government's stabilization posture during this period, which adversely affected those enterprises still tied to the accustomed way of doing business in an inflationary milieu.

One of the changes that was instituted during this period was a drastic reduction of interest rates on a whole spectrum of bank loans; the rates of discount on commercial bills were slashed from 14 to 10 percent per annum. Reduction of loan rates was deemed necessary to alleviate the debt service burden of financially besieged firms. The second was the measure to phase out financial transactions via anonymous accounts and to require that every financial transaction be carried out on a real-name basis. However, the idea of making real-name financial transactions mandatory turned out to be premature. Thus, the law making the real-name financial transactions mandatory was promulgated, but, wisely, not enforced immediately.

The third was the measure to attract and absorb curb market funds into official financial institutions; doors sprang open for curb market dealers to start new financial institutions. The government's resorting to market mechanisms and stimulation of competition—slogans often repeated and also abused by officials during this period—was congruent with this open-door policy.[7] The new open-door policy was aimed primarily at nonbank financial institutions familiar to curb market dealers, namely, investment and finance companies and mutual savings and finance companies. After the barriers to entry were lowered, 12 new firms were added to 20 existing investment and finance companies, and 41 new mutual savings and finance companies were added to the existing 199 by the end of 1983. Branch offices of financial institutions were also allowed to expand in number. Finally, amid outcry over excessive competition, the open-door period was phased out.

With more competitors in the market, with financial services overlapping and contractionary monetary policies in full swing, financial institutions found it increasingly difficult to attract funds from the public. Funds shifted, sometimes with great volatility, from one type of financial institution to another, and even between different institutions of the same type, in the search for a better deal. In particular, "disintermediation" (that is, the shift of funds away from banking institutions and toward nonbank financial institutions) became an increasingly serious problem. Naturally this situation caused a clamor for new financial instruments with attractive terms. From time to time the Finance Ministry was inclined to calm the furor by issuing a new commodity to any institution that marshalled greater influence and presented a more pressing case at a given moment. Sooner or later it would become evident that while the new commodity was a boon to one type of financial institution, it was a curse to another. This usually occasioned another cycle of outcry and assuagement. By and large, the clamor for new commodities and better terms for existing commodities came from three sources: commercial and special banks, investment and finance companies, and securities companies. Negotiable certificates of deposit (CDs), a new breed of commercial papers (CPs), sale of bonds on repurchase agreements (RPs), and cash management accounts (CMAs) were the major commodities newly created or reactivated in the early 1980s. CPs were authorized for investment and finance companies in June 1981 and extended to the five large securities companies in April 1984. At the same time, CMAs were issued to investment and finance companies, partly to compensate them for the "inequity" caused by the extension of CPs to other financial institutions. Securities companies were allowed to engage in RP business as of February 1980, and banks joined this business in September 1982. CDs, which had been created in 1974 and then lay dormant, were reactivated in June 1984 to help staunch the outflow of funds from commercial banks to nonbank financial institutions.

Financial Liberalization

The need for reforming financial institutions as a main method for streamlining the national economy began to gain credence as early as the late 1970s. At the start of the 1980s it became widely accepted both inside and outside the government. Eventually the idea was anointed by the Finance Ministry, and the culminating rite was the formation of the Financial Development Committee as an advisory group to the finance minister in 1982. Financial Development Committee meetings were frequent in its first two years, and its agenda covered a wide range of issues on financial liberalization and development.

Against the backdrop of this realignment in the government's mood and allocation of human resources, four developments paved the way for further liberalization.

First, a feeble but significant first step was taken toward the deregulation of interest-rate determination. In January 1984, a measure of this was put into force, as a narrow band of rates ranging from 10 to 10.5 percent a year was introduced to permit banks to charge different rates on the basis of borrowers' creditworthiness. The band was widened and the upper limit was raised to 11.5 percent a year in November 1984. In addition, the ceilings were lifted on interbank call rates and issuing rates of unsecured corporate bonds.

Second, in the previous decades of financial repression, financial institutions were nearly suffocated with a multitude of regulations, ordinances, instructions, and directives issued by the Finance Ministry and the Bank Superintendent's Office. Commercial banks were particularly entangled in the web of regulations. In the early 1980s hundreds of regulations and directives were abolished or simplified. Moreover, efforts were made to pry the power to appoint top-level bank officials out of the government's hands.[8]

Third, policy-directed loans made in previous decades had turned sour in many cases. Insolvent firms became nonperforming assets (that is, more or less irredeemable loans to be written off in due course) of commercial banks. Unless this burden was somehow relieved, autonomous and profitable operation of banks would be difficult. Determined efforts were made in the early 1980s to reduce policy-directed credit (for example, by limiting further growth of the National Investment Fund to which commercial banks are obligated to contribute) and to adjust the backlog of insolvent firms with the aid of the central bank's facility as lender of last resort. Although this adjustment and drastic consolidation of insolvent cases inevitably bred charges of favoritism and inequity, it is fair to say it went a long way toward clearing the way for further liberalization of commercial banks.

Fourth, also during this time, the allocation of credit for large-scale projects in the heavy and chemical industries was deemphasized. In contrast, the promotion of small- and medium-sized firms was highlighted. Commercial banks were required to extend at least 35 percent of their loans to small- and medium-sized firms. The required ratios for local banks and foreign bank branches were 55 to 25 percent, respectively. In addition, nonbank financial institutions (notably investment and finance companies) were also assigned specific target credit ratios for small- and medium-sized firms.

Financial Internationalization

To facilitate the ever-expanding export and import activities of the national economy and in the name of motivating domestic banks to improve their banking services and skills, financial internationalization has been one of the major directions the government has pursued in the 1980s. Another 24 foreign bank branches have been allowed to operate in Korea while 3 foreign bank branches have folded since 1981, bringing the total number to 53 by the end of 1986. Korea's financial internationalization has proceeded partly in response to competition from overseas. The success of Korean commodity exports brought about the United States' demand for reciprocity in service industries. Financial businesses have become the primary target of U.S. demands for reciprocity or "national treatment" and lowered entry barriers. In this atmosphere, discriminatory restrictions on foreign banks in the domestic financial market have been gradually phased out. In 1985 foreign banks were permitted to handle trust business and to make use of rediscount facilities at the Bank of Korea for export financing. In 1986, the rediscount facilities of the central bank were made available for all operations of foreign bank branches. In the spirit of "national treatment," foreign bank branches have been asked to comply with requirements such as the obligatory ratio of loans to small- and medium-sized firms (that is, 35 percent or more, effective August 1, 1986—the same as the ratio required of domestic nationwide commercial banks). As of the end of 1986, the opening of foreign life insurance and securities businesses remained a hot issue on the agenda for trade talks between Korea and the United States.

Development in the Securities Market

Efforts to upgrade the securities market continued to gain momentum in the 1980s. In January 1980, bond transactions on RPs were institutionalized to enlarge the scope of the bond-issuing market. Furthermore, in July 1983, the securities authorities announced the Measures for Reinforcement of Capital Market Function, the main intent of which was to induce corporations in good credit standing to sell stock and help stimulate security issuance at the market price. As a measure for liberalizing securities markets further, two open-ended types of investment trusts exclusively for foreigners, namely, the Korea International Trust (KIT) and the Korea Trust (KT), were established and sold for US $15 million each in November 1981.[9]

An overview of securities market activities during the period from 1980 to 1986 may be gained from surveying the following facts. The composite stock price index did not rebound to the level of 1978 until 1985. Because of this slackness of the stock market, which in turn reflected a sluggish national economy, the number of listed companies dwindled to 328 at the end of 1983 and then increased again to 355 (the same as in 1979) at the end of 1986. The total paid-in capital of listed companies increased only 2.6 times (from 2,202.3 billion won to 5,649.7 billion won), whereas that of listed public and corporate bonds jumped 11.1 times (from 1,541.5 billion won to 17,112.6 billion won) in the seven-year period up to the end of 1986. Meanwhile the stock market has turned increasingly bullish from mid 1985 on, bringing the year-end composite stock price index up from 14.246 in 1984 to 163.37 in 1985 and 272.61 in 1986. The boom was sustained and eventually peaked in late 1987, with the composite stock price index hovering at 509.05 by the end of October. The total market value of listed stocks amounted to 11,994.2 billion won at the end of 1986, 1.8 times the level of one year earlier.

AN OVERVIEW OF THE FINANCIAL SYSTEM

Financial institutions in Korea can be classified into the central bank (Bank of Korea) and two other broad categories—banking institutions and nonbank financial institutions. Banking institutions (or deposit-money banks, to be more specific) comprise commercial banks and specialized banks. The former category is composed of 7 nationwide banks, 10 local banks, and 55 foreign bank branches (as of the end of 1987); the latter includes the Korea Exchange Bank, the Small and Medium Industry Bank (most recently renamed the Industrial Bank of Korea), the Citizen's National Bank, the Korea Housing Bank, the National Agricultural Cooperatives Federation, the National Federation of Fisheries Cooperatives and member cooperatives, and the National Livestock Cooperatives Federation. The Korea Development Bank, the Export-Import Bank of Korea, and the Korea Long-Term Credit Bank are also specialized banks, in that they were established under special laws, but they are classified functionally as nonbanks, because their primary source of funds is not deposits but issuance of debentures, borrowings, and so on.

Nonbank financial institutions subsume five categories of institutions: development institutions, savings institutions, investment institutions, insurance companies, and other financial institutions. Development institutions are the three specialized banks functionally classified as nonbanks. Savings institutions include 40 trust accounts of banking institutions, 238 mutual savings and finance companies, 5,772 credit unions, 1,685 mutual credits, and postal savings at post offices. Investment companies include 32 investment and finance companies and six merchant banking corporations. Insurance companies consist of 6 life insurance companies, 15 non-life insurance companies, and postal life insurance through post offices. Other financial institutions include securities market institutions and the institutions not classified elsewhere—25 securities companies, 8 leasing companies, 4 venture capital companies, a credit guarantee fund, and a credit administration fund.

Notwithstanding the retardation of their development under governmental control, Korean financial institutions are highly diversified and specialized, though to a lesser degree than those of Japan. Nonbank financial institutions were rather insignificant in the early 1970s. Since then they have grown rapidly and have substantially eclipsed the dominance of banking institutions due to preferential interest rates and less interference of the government in the earlier phases of their existence. At the beginning of the 1980s, government control in the sphere of nonbank financial institutions was increased with a view to correcting the relatively disadvantaged position of banking institutions. Deregulation has been steadily progressing in banking institutions, but the market share of nonbank financial institutions in terms of deposits has climbed from 16 percent in 1971 to slightly over 50 percent in 1986.

The shortage of national savings relative to gross investment has been a chronic feature of the financial scene of Korea. In 1986, however, for the first time a surplus was recorded in the national savings-investment balance. The ratio of national savings to GNP increased to 32.6 percent (a big rise from 28.6 percent in 1985), while the gross investment ratio was 29.8 percent (a decline from 31.1 percent in 1985). A primary impetus came from the remarkable growth in savings of the business sector, reflecting a sizable surplus in the international trade balance. The household savings ratio also inched up a bit but still remained at a considerable distance from that of either Japan or Taiwan. National savings relative to gross investment were 109.4 percent in 1986, as compared with 92 percent in 1985, and a mere 73.1 ercent in late 1982. In 1987 the national savings ratio rose to about 35.6 percent, again outstripping the gross investment ratio. As a result, the need for net inflow of foreign savings waned, and the size of foreign debts diminished rapidly from the peak of US $46.8 billion at the end of 1985 to US $35.6 billion at the end of 1987.

NOTES

This chapter is an abbreviated and revised version of P. J. Kim, "The Evolution of Financial Institutions in Korea," East Asia Economic Policy Studies, no. 5, East-West Population Institute, East-West Center, Hawaii, 1988.

1. The terms "over-loan," "over-borrowing," and "window guidance" were endemic to the Japanese prewar and postwar financial experience until the period of balance of payments surpluses in the early 1970s. See, for instance, Wallich and Wallich (1976, p. 284ff.), Bank of Japan (1978, p. 64), Goldsmith (1983, p. 162), and Horiuchi (1984, p. 28ff.). I have used this terminology deliberately to indicate a strong similarity between the two countries' experiences for much of the postwar period.

2. Specialization in finance takes several forms (Wallich and Wallich, 1976, pp. 278–90). One form of specialization is based on the types of financial operations, particularly lending, underwriting and trading in securities, and trust administration. A second form of specialization defines finance on the basis of maturity terms, that is, short- and long-term credit. Other forms of specialization involved concentration on selected areas of the economy (such as agriculture, housing, and exports); on the size of client firms (such as small- and medium-sized versus large-sized firms); and on the region of business (such as nationwide versus local banks). Most of these forms of specialization are well represented in the financial system of Japan.

3. This episode of interest rate reform and its consequences was regarded as "financial reform without tears" and as a good example of "financial deepening" (McKinnon, 1973, pp. 105–11; Shaw, 1973, ch. 5).

4. In regular-way transactions, the settlement or delivery of stock is to be made on the second business day following the contract date as against within two months in the case of forward transactions.

5. Although the Anti-Monopoly and Fair Trade Act was enacted in 1980, a part of the 1975 act concerning direct control of the prices of basic commodities has been kept intact.

6. Interest rates on deposits over one year were raised from 18.6 to 24 percent a year.

7. In this climate, the Shinhan Bank (funded exclusively by Korean residents in Japan) and the KorAm Bank (a joint venture between Korean interests and the Bank of America) were established in July 1982 and March 1983, respectively.

8. At first, bank executives were unconvinced and wondered whether their new option was a blessing or a trap. Reportedly they went to the Finance Ministry, and the minister made news by turning them away with unopened envelopes containing lists of candidates. However, suspicion of outside interference persisted.

9. The amount of KIT and KT funds was increased by US $10 million each two years later. Buoyed by their popularity among foreign investors, three additional

investment trusts of US $30 million each were sold to foreigners in March and April 1985, namely, Korea Growth Trust (KGT), Seoul International Trust (SIT), and Seoul Trust (ST). A most significant event was the establishment in New York in May 1984 of the Korea Fund, a closed-end, company-type investment vehicle of US $60 million. Later this company was listed on the New York Stock Exchange. The aim of the Korea Fund was to allow some leeway for foreigners to participate in capital appreciation through long-term investment in equity securities of fast-growing Korean enterprises, yet without prematurely opening the domestic capital market.

REFERENCES

Bank of Japan, Research Institute, *The Financial System in Japan* (In Japanese) Tokyo, 1978.

Goldsmith, Raymond W., *The Financial Development of Japan, 1868–1977*, New Haven: Yale University Press, 1983.

Gurley, John G., Patrick, Hugh T., and Shaw, E. S., *The Financial Structure of Korea*, Seoul: Bank of Korea, 1965.

Horiuchi, Akiyoshi, "Economic Growth and Financial Allocation in Postwar Japan," Discussion paper, University of Tokyo, Tokyo, 1984.

McKinnon, Ronald I., *Money and Capital in Economic Development*, Washington, D.C.: Brookings Institution, 1973.

Ranis, Gustav, "Economic Development and Financial Institutions," in Bela Balassa and Richard Nelson, eds., *Economic Progress, Private Values and Public Policy: Essays in Honor of William Fellner*, Amsterdam: North Holland, 1977.

Shaw, Edward S., *Financial Deepening in Economic Development*, New York: Oxford University Press, 1973.

Wallich, H. C., and Wallich, Mable I., "Banking and Finance," in Hugh Patrick and Henry Rosovsky, eds., *Asia's New Giant*, Washington, D.C.: Brookings Institution, 1976.

12

Monetary Aggregates in the Presence of a Curb Market

Tong Hun Lee

INTRODUCTION

Different monetary assets provide different degrees of "monetary" or transaction services as well as the store-of-value services to the economy. For this reason it has been pointed out in the recent literature on monetary aggregation (see, for example, Barnett, 1980; Clements and Nguyen, 1980; Spindt, 1985) that the simple-sum index, currently used to aggregate over monetary components, does not appropriately capture the contribution of monetary assets to the economy's flow of transaction services. This is particularly true in the case of developing countries like Korea where the government sets interest rates in the regulated sector of money markets while the market interest rate is determined in the underground or curb market (see, for example, Lee, 1985, 1988). For instance, with a given monetary base, official changes in the rate structure between the bank and the non-bank liabilities would shift the composition of liabilities held by the public, thereby changing the flows of monetary services. Thus, it is important to take into account such an effect on substitutability in aggregating monetary assets. Moreover, since the alternative costs of holding monetary assets are relatively high and variable due to the presence of a curb market, it becomes even more important to take into account the effects of curb market changes on aggregating monetary assets.[1] The purpose of this chapter is to incorporate these effects in monetary aggregation by constructing a statistical index number for monetary quantities, following a procedure similar to that of Barnett (1980).

Barnett's (1980) approach assumes that the consumer maximizes a flexible utility function that has as its arguments quantities of various monetary assets held. The solution of this problem provides an exact aggregator function for monetary quantities that depends on unknown parameters. To remove the unknown parameters, the user costs of monetary assets are substituted in the aggregator function, using the theory of index numbers by Diewert (1976). The user cost of a monetary asset is defined by the opportunity cost of holding the monetary asset in lieu of the benchmark asset that is accumulated to transfer wealth between periods rather than to provide monetary service in the current period of the consumer decision. Thus, the index number for monetary aggregate includes the yield but not the quantity of benchmark asset. Although Barnett initially derived both Divisia and Fisher Ideal index number formulas for monetary aggregation, he has advocated the use of the former rather than the latter in aggregating monetary components for the United States (see, for example, Barnett, 1980; Barnett and Spindt, 1982; and Barnett et al., 1984).

In this study, we shall derive the Fisher Ideal index number for aggregating monetary components in the presence of a curb market and examine its usefulness for developing countries, using the case of Korea as an example. Our approach is to utilize the curb market yield as the benchmark rate of return in constructing the index for monetary quantities. Since the curb market yield is the highest rate of return available in a developing country like Korea, it may be regarded as the opportunity cost of holding monetary assets or the benchmark rate of return.[2] Moreover, the use of a curb market rate enables the monetary index to reflect the impact of curb market changes on monetary aggregate when the volume of such activities is not even observable.

The plan of this study is as follows: first to outline the theoretical model of Fisher Ideal index numbers using the curb market yield as the benchmark rate, then to evaluate the desirability of this index for developing countries. The next section actually constructs such an index for Korea and shows that the Fisher Ideal index number in aggregating monetary components is indeed superior to the simple-sum index currently used in Korea. The last section completes the chapter with some concluding remarks.

INDEX FOR MONETARY QUANTITIES

To provide the theoretical analysis for the monetary index proposed in this chapter, we first define the variables as follows:

q_{is} consumption of good i ($i = 1, \ldots, n$) during period s; q_s = vector of n goods for period s.

p_{is} price of consumer good i ($i = 1, \ldots, n$) during period s; p_s = vector of n prices for period s.

m_{is} planned real balance of monetary asset i ($i = 1, \ldots, k$) during period s; m_s = vector of k real asset balances for period s.

r_{is} nominal holding period yield on monetary asset i ($i = 1, \ldots, k$) during period s.

A_s planned holding of curb market asset during period s.
R_s yield on curb market asset during period s.

To derive the formula for the monetary index following Barnett (1980), we initially assume that the consumer has a two-period planning horizon, $s = t$ and $t + 1$, in which he allocates the consumption of goods and the holdings of real monetary assets including the terminal curb market asset, A_{t+1}.[3] We further assume that the consumer's overall utility function at time t is homothetic, weakly separable and monotonically increasing in each period's consumption of goods and monetary assets and the terminal curb market asset. This may be written in symbolic form

$$U_t = U_t[u_t(m_t), v_t(q_t); u_{t+1}(m_{t+1}), v_{t+1}(q_{t+1}), A_{t+1}] \qquad (1)$$

where the curb market asset for period t is omitted as the benchmark asset. The subutility functions of u's and v's are specified by functions of the quadratic mean of order two:

$$u_s(m_s) = (m_s'Am_s)^{1/2} \qquad (s = t, t+1) \qquad (2)$$

and

$$v_s(q_s) = (q_s'Bq_s)^{1/2} \qquad (s = t, t+1) \qquad (3)$$

which are assumed to be positive for $m_s > 0$ and $q_s > 0$ and strictly quasiconcave with nonsingular symmetric matrices of parameter A and B. These functional forms are sufficiently flexible to provide a second-order differential approximation to any linear homogenous function (see, for example, Diewert, 1976). Thus, they take into account various degrees of substitutability, particularly among different monetary components.

To formulate the problem of utility optimization involving monetary assets, we define the user-cost of the real balance of the ith monetary asset, π_{is}, by

$$\pi_{is} = \frac{P_s^*[R_s - r_{is}(1 - \tau_s)]}{\rho_s} \qquad (s = t, t+1) \qquad (4)$$

where $\rho_s = (1 + R_t)$ for $s = t$ and $\rho_s = (1 + R_t)(1 + R_{t+1})$ for $s = t + 1$; P_s^* is the true cost of living index to be defined later; and τ_s is the rate of proportional tax on interests imposed in Korea.[4] Thus, the real user-cost of the ith nominal asset

(π_{is}/P_s^*), may be interpreted as the discounted opportunity cost of holding the ith nominal monetary asset $(P_s^* m_{is})$ for its monetary service in lieu of holding the curb market asset. According to Barnett et al. (1984, p. 1054), the freedom from default that is implied by the store of value of monetary assets should be valued in the utility function and hence, certainty-equivalence theory on which the user-cost concept is based requires that any risk premium be left in the rate structure. This suggests that all of the interest rates including the curb market rate in our user-costs should be measured with risk premium intact in the yields.[5]

Following Barnett (1978, 1980), the wealth constraint W_{ot} at time t can be equated to the sum of the expenditures on monetary assets as well as consumer goods for two periods within the planning horizon and the consumer's provisions for later periods as[6]

$$W_{ot} = p'_t q_t + (1/\rho_t) p'_{t+1} q_{t+1} + \pi'_t m_t + \pi'_{t+1} m_{t+1}$$
$$+ \sum_{i=1}^{k} (1/\rho_{t+1})(1 + r_{it+1}) P_{t+1}^* m_{it+1} + (1/\rho_t) P_{t+1}^* A_{t+1} \qquad (5)$$

where π_t and π_{t+1} are respectively the vectors of user-costs of m_t and m_{t+1}.

Since the overall utility function is homothetic and blockwise weakly separable, the consumer can maximize utility function (1) subject to wealth constraint (5) as if he is making decisions in two stages.[7] In the first stage, the consumer allocates the given wealth among each period's aggregate monetary asset expenditure and aggregate consumer good expenditure, and the terminal curb market assets. In the second stage, he further allocates each aggregate expenditure separately over the individual monetary components or over the individual consumer goods. Thus, our problem of optimizing the holdings of monetary assets at time t is to maximize $u_t(m_t) = (m'_t A m_t)^{1/2}$ in (2) subject to the constraint

$$\pi'_t m_t = E_t \qquad (6)$$

where E_t is the aggregate monetary asset expenditure selected in the consumer's first stage decision.

Using the first-order condition of this maximization, the demand for monetary assets in real terms may be derived as

$$m_t = \frac{E_t}{(\pi'_t A^{-1} \pi_t)} A^{-1} \pi_t \qquad (7)$$

With the first-order condition, the aggregate monetary asset expenditure can be broken down into two parts

$$E_t = (\pi_t' A^{-1} \pi_t)^{1/2} (m_t' A m_t)^{1/2} = \Pi_t u_t(m_t) \tag{8}$$

where $u_t(m_t)$ now denotes the aggregator function for monetary assets and Π_t denotes the unit cost function as a dual to $u_t(m_t)$.

To eliminate the unknown parameter A in the aggregator function, we apply the method of Diewert (1976), also used by Barnett (1980) in monetary indexing. The method is to apply the first-order condition of utility optimization to reduce a ratio of the aggregator functions to a parameter-free index number formula. The index number so derived for two adjacent periods is

$$\frac{u_t(m_t)}{u_{t-1}(m_{t-1})} = \left[\frac{(\pi_t' m_t)(\pi_{t-1}' m_t)}{(\pi_t' m_{t-1})(\pi_{t-1}' m_{t-1})} \right]^{1/2}$$

$$= \left[\frac{\sum_{i=1}^{k} \pi_{it} m_{it} \sum_{i=1}^{k} \pi_{it-1} m_{it}}{\sum_{i=1}^{k} \pi_{it} m_{it-1} \sum_{i=1}^{k} \pi_{it-1} m_{it-1}} \right]^{1/2} \tag{9}$$

This is the Fisher Ideal index number in chain form which is applied to the real quantities of monetary assets. By setting the nominal monetary aggregate at base year, $P_0^* u_0(m_0)$, equal to 1, and multiplying through the subsequent chain index numbers, we can generate the fixed-base index number for nominal monetary assets, M^F, for any time period.[8]

PROPERTIES OF THE MONETARY INDEX

An important feature of our monetary index is that although the volume of curb market activities is not observable due to the illegal nature of the transactions, their effect on the index can be taken into account by including the curb market interest rate. We may theoretically examine this effect by the comparative static analysis in the first stage of the consumer decision.

Since the second stage decisions are blockwise separable in deriving aggregator functions, we may consider the first stage decision by maximizing the overall utility function (1) subject to the budget constraint (5), expressed in terms of the aggregator functions. The budget constraint in terms of aggregator functions is

$$W_{ot} = \Pi_t u_t(m_t) + P_t^* v_t(q_t) + (1/\rho_t) P_{t+1}^* \Phi u_{t+1}(m_{t+1})$$
$$+ (1/\rho_t) P_{t+1}^* v_{t+1}(q_{t+1}) + (1/\rho_t) P_{t+1}^* A_{t+1} \tag{5'}$$

where the aggregator functions and their respective unit cost functions are

$$v_t(q_t) = (q_t' B q_t)^{1/2}; \qquad\qquad P_t^* = (p_t' B^{-1} p_t)^{1/2}$$

$$u_{t+1}(m_{t+1}) = (m_{t+1}' A m_{t+1})^{1/2}; \qquad P_{t+1}^* \Phi = P_{t+1}^* (\iota' A^{-1} \iota)^{1/2}$$

$$v_{t+1}(q_{t+1}) = (q_{t+1}' B q_{t+1})^{1/2}; \qquad P_{t+1}^* = (p_{t+1}' B^{-1} p_{t+1})^{1/2}$$

Analogous to equation (8), we have here derived P_t^* and P_{t+1}^* as the unit cost functions of the respective aggregator functions $v_t(q_t)$ and $v_{t+1}(q_{t+1})$ and have also obtained $P_{t+1}^* \Phi$ as the unit cost function of aggregator function $u_{t+1}(m_{t+1})$.[9]

The first-order condition for the consumer's first-stage optimization is

$$[\partial U_t / \partial u_t(m_t)] = \lambda \Pi_t$$

$$[\partial U_t / \partial v_t(q_t)] = \lambda P_t^*$$

$$[\partial U_t / \partial u_{t+1}(m_{t+1})] = \lambda (1/\rho_t) P_{t+1}^* \Phi$$

$$[\partial U_t / \partial v_{t+1}(q_{t+1})] = \lambda (1/\rho_t) P_{t+1}^*$$

$$[\partial U_t / \partial A_{t+1}] = \lambda (1/\rho_t) P_{t+1}^*$$

$$W_{ot} = \Pi_t u_t(m_t) + P_t^* v_t(q_t) + (1/\rho_t) P_{t+1}^* \Phi u_{t+1}(m_{t+1})$$
$$+ (1/\rho_t) P_{t+1}^* v_{t+1}(q_{t+1}) + (1/\rho_t) P_{t+1}^* A_{t+1} \tag{10}$$

where λ is the Lagrangian multiplier.

By taking the total differential of the first-order condition in (10) while holding the overall utility level constant, we can solve for the comparative static results with respect to changes in each exogenous variable. In particular, with the constant level of overall utility, we may derive the comparative static derivative of $u_t(m_t)$ with respect to R_t as

$$\left(\frac{\partial u_t(m_t)}{\partial R_t} \right)_c = \left(\frac{\partial u_t(m_t)}{\partial \Pi_t} \right)_c \left(\frac{\partial \Pi_t}{\partial R_t} \right)$$

$$+ \left(\frac{\partial u_t(m_t)}{\partial (P_{t+1}^*/\rho_t)} \right)_c \left(\frac{\partial (P_{t+1}^*/\rho_t)}{\partial R_t} \right) \tag{11}$$

In other words, the wealth-compensated effect on the monetary aggregate of a change in the curb market yield consists of two parts: One is through the compensated own-price effect of Π_t and the other through the compensated cross-price effect of (P^*_{t+1}/ρ_t). Since the compensated own-price effect is always negative and since its multiplicat, $(\partial \Pi_t/\partial R_t)$, is $[u_t(m_t)]^{-1}m'_t(\partial \pi_t/\partial R_t) > 0$, the first term on the right side of equation (11) is negative.10 The second term is also negative because $[\partial(P^*_{t+1}/\rho_t)/\partial R_t] = (-P^*_{t+1}/\rho_t^2)$ is negative and because the compensated cross-price effect is always positive due to the homothetic and completely separable properties of Ut.11 Therefore, the comparative static derivative in (11) has a negative sign, indicating that there is an indirect substitution between the monetary aggregate and the curb market asset.12 Thus, our index number formula in (9) provides a measure of the economy's monetary services that are adversely affected by the presence of curb market assets.13

There are a number of other advantages in using the Fisher Ideal index number for monetary quantities as formulated in the preceding section. To start with, the interest rate control in the regulated sector usually raises the user-cost of the regulated monetary asset to above the equilibrium rate. The holdings of monetary assets, therefore, always lie on the demand functions based on the subutility function even when the regulated market is out of equilibrium. Since the subutility function (2) underlying the index is quite general, such an index would properly allow the various degrees of substitutability among monetary components that would result from the government rate control. On the other hand, if the subutility function is restricted with parameter $A = (\iota\iota')$, it becomes the simple-sum index as in the case of Korea, which assumes the perfect substitutability among monetary components. Although an assumption of perfect substitutability is not appropriate, particularly when the interest rates are often shifted by the government, it is subsumed as a special case of the Fisher Ideal index number.

Secondly, as pointed out by Diewert (1976), the Fisher Ideal index number satisfies the axiom of the revealed preference theory that does not require a specific form of the utility function. In our case, if $(\pi^T_{t-1}m_t) > (\pi^T_{t-1}m_{t-1})$ and $(\pi^T_t m_{t-1}) \leq (\pi^T_t m_t)$, then the portfolio of monetary assets mt is revealed preferred to mt-1 and the index number is greater than unity. On the other hand, if $(\pi^T_{t-1}m_t) < (\pi^T_{t-1}m_{t-1})$ and $(\pi^T_t m_{t-1}) \geq (\pi^T_t m_t)$, then the portfolio of monetary assets mt-1 is revealed preferred to mt and also the index number is less than unity. This means that even if the utility function is not homothetic as in equation (2), our index number will correctly indicate the direction of changes in the monetary aggregate due to changes in the interest rates, including curb market rate.

Finally, the Fisher Ideal index unlike Divisia satisfies Fisher's so-called determinate test and hence, it does not go to zero or infinity when the component series become discontinuous (see, for example, Diewert, 1976). Thus, we can calculate a chain index for the monetary aggregate even when the composition of monetary aggregate changes over time due to financial development. All of these properties indicate the desirability of using our monetary index for developing countries.

APPLICATION TO KOREA

Since the curb market is widespread in Korea, it would be interesting to construct a Fisher Ideal monetary index for Korea and to examine its usefulness in compar-

Table 12.1
Fisher Ideal and Simple-Sum Indices for
Nominal Quantities of Monetary Assets: 1980-I to 1986-II

Year-Qt.	M_1^F	M_1	M_2^F	M_2	M_3^F	M_3
1980 I	1.000	1.000	1.000	1.000	1.000	1.000
II	0.924	0.923	1.025	1.041	1.047	1.065
III	1.001	1.004	1.084	1.095	1.118	1.135
IV	1.094	1.089	1.175	1.186	1.206	1.223
1981 I	1.173	1.174	1.257	1.271	1.300	1.320
II	1.145	1.149	1.289	1.320	1.359	1.399
III	1.049	1.032	1.334	1.380	1.420	1.471
IV	1.134	1.110	1.444	1.491	1.549	1.612
1982 I	1.218	1.197	1.543	1.600	1.652	1.726
II	1.270	1.281	1.614	1.687	1.753	1.848
III	1.542	1.547	1.738	1.821	1.908	2.015
IV	1.709	1.718	1.843	1.933	2.060	2.187
1983 I	1.729	1.747	1.896	1.996	2.141	2.274
II	1.711	1.739	1.943	2.057	2.235	2.386
III	1.800	1.823	2.025	2.145	2.343	2.505
IV	1.965	1.989	2.109	2.233	2.469	2.644
1984 I	2.037	2.067	2.160	2.289	2.562	2.751
II	1.869	1.901	2.129	2.269	2.653	2.859
III	1.919	1.946	2.181	2.324	2.788	3.008
IV	2.031	2.046	2.271	2.417	2.949	3.183
1985 I	2.054	2.078	2.321	2.461	3.107	3.355
II	1.900	1.918	2.367	2.513	3.220	3.482
III	1.939	1.944	2.459	2.647	3.343	3.643
IV	2.124	2.135	2.561	2.769	3.530	3.861
1986 I	2.126	2.150	2.605	2.838	3.660	4.022
II	2.164	2.201	2.716	2.981	3.863	4.262

Note: Quarterly nominal quantities are given relative to the respective base period figure of unity for 1980-I

Table 12.2
Biases of Simple-Sum Indices in Measuring the
Annual Rate of Increase in Monetary Services: 1980-I to 1986-II

Def. of Bias	Average Absolute Bias	Range	
$\%\Delta M_1 - \%\Delta M_1^F$	1.13%	-1.86%	4.07%
$\%\Delta M_2 - \%\Delta M_2^F$	1.66%	-0.46%	3.91%
$\%\Delta M_3 - \%\Delta M_3^F$	1.87%	0.44%	3.76%

ison with the official simple-sum index for monetary quantities. To make direct comparisons, we compose Fisher Ideal indices, each with identical monetary components as those of the simple-sum indices of M_1, M_2, and M_3.[14] Unlike the M_1 and M_2 series, however, published data on M_3 are not sufficient for constructing the Fisher Ideal index number. One of the deficiencies in M_3 data is the lack of information on the different types of savings accounts held by non-bank financial institutions. Since the savings deposits of nonbank financial intermediaries are likely to be held in time deposit accounts at commercial banks (see, for example, Bank of Korea, 1984), we assume this to be the case in adjusting deposits among bank and non-bank financial intermediaries for constructing M_3 components. Another deficiency in M_3 data is that the M_3 components are available, not by daily balances, but by the seasonally unadjusted end-of-month figures that start only from 1980. Thus, to make an overall comparison among different monetary aggregates on the basis of the same data, we have used the quarterly average of seasonally unadjusted end-of-month figures for all monetary components for the period of 1980-I to 1986-II.[15]

In deriving the user costs, we have calculated and used the after-tax rates of return on monetary components including the implicit rate of return on demand deposits at commercial banks.[16] For the benchmark rate of return, we use the curb market rate that is the highest rate of return observed in Korea. Since Barnett et al. (1980, 1982, 1984) define the benchmark rate of return as the maximum yield on any asset available in the economy, our choice of curb market yield is quite reasonable. All of these yields in user-costs are then transformed to a one-month holding period basis by making the appropriate allowance for the holding periods as well as the methods of interest payments and compounding associated with each monetary component.[17]

Using these data, Fisher Ideal indices of M_1^F, M_2^F, and M_3^F for nominal quantities of monetary assets are calculated in Table 12.1 along with the respective official simple-sum indices of M_1, M_2, and M_3. In general, the simple-sum monetary index tends to exceed the corresponding Fisher Ideal index. For instance, in the second

Table 12.3
Variabilities of Income Velocities of Different Monetary Aggregates:
1980-I to 1986-II

Monetary Aggregates	Coeff. of Var. in Income Velocity	S.D. of Annual Growth Rates of Income Velocity
M_1^F	0.1873#	13.73#
M_1	0.1948	14.69
---	------	------
M_2^F	0.1749#	8.07#
M_2	0.1861	8.20
---	------	------
M_3^F	0.2392#	7.24#
M_3	0.2596	7.31

Note:# indicates a smaller value of the two statistics that are calculated for the monetary aggregates consisting of identical components.

quarter of 1986, the size of M_2 exceeds that of M_2^F by a large magnitude of 26.5 percent [$= (2.981 - 2.716) \times 100$]. Since this difference is caused by the simple-sum index for its inability to properly account for monetary services, it may be considered a bias in measuring the true monetary services, particularly in relation to curb market assets.

To examine the extent of such a bias on the annual basis, we have calculated the biases measured in each quarter by the annual growth rates of M_1, M_2, and M_3 in Table 12.2. As may be noted in the second column of this table, the average absolute size of the biases in measuring the annual growth rates of monetary aggregate is not trivial. For each measure of M_1, M_2, and M_3, the magnitude of the average absolute bias exceeds 1 percentage point. More crucial, however, is the variability of the biases over time. For instance, the range of the biases in M_3 reported in the third column of Table 12.2, exceeds 3 percentage points, whereas the range of the biases in M_1 or M_2 turns out to be even worse. Thus, it is important to examine whether such a bias in measuring the money supply growth would actually affect the performance of the index as a monetary indicator.

According to the quantity theory of money, if income velocity is either constant or at least predictable, changing the money supply would result in a predictable change in nominal income. Therefore, one way of selecting an appropriate concept of money is to choose a monetary aggregate that provides a relatively stable income velocity (see, for example, Anderson, 1975).[18] To analyze the stability of income velocity, we first calculate the coefficients of variation in income velocity for each monetary aggregate in the second column of Table 12.3. Comparing each pair of the monetary aggregates consisting of identical components, we find that the coefficient of variation in M_1^F is smaller than that in M_1, as is the coefficient for M_2^F compared to the M_2 coefficient, and we find the same pattern when comparing the M_3^F coefficient with the M_3 coefficient. Thus, the Fisher Ideal index number for monetary aggregate appears to be better than the simple-sum index used in Korea.

Since monetary components have different seasonal as well as trend factors, the coefficients of variation containing these factors cannot be used to make a direct comparison among the monetary aggregates consisting of different components. To remove both the seasonal and trend factors, we calculate the annual growth rates of income velocity for each quarter relative to the corresponding quarter of the preceding year and obtain their standard deviations. These results are reported in the last column of Table 12.3. They again show that the Fisher Ideal index is superior to the simple-sum index as it provides a smaller standard deviation. Moreover, the results indicate that for broader monetary aggregates, the gain from using the Fisher Ideal index number is greater. This follows from the fact that the income velocity becomes more stable with a smaller standard deviation of its growth rates.

Even when the income velocity is volatile, if it can be predicted, the monetary authority can adjust money supply to exert a predictable change in nominal income. Thus, the predictability of income velocity may be used as a guide for selecting an appropriate monetary aggregate on which the income velocity is defined.

According to Peltzman (1969) and Jaffee (1970), changes in income velocity may be explained by a logarithmic partial adjustment model. The actual change in velocity $(Y/M)_t$ occurs in response to a spread between the desired velocity $(Y/M)_t^d$ and the actual velocity of the preceding period $(Y/M)_{t-1}$:

$$\Delta \ln(Y/M)_t = \alpha[\ln(Y/M)_t^d - \ln(Y/M)_{t-1}] \tag{12}$$

where α is the adjustment coefficient between 0 and 1. The desired velocity may be assumed to depend on real national income (Y_t), the rate of inflation (P_t^*/P_{t-1}^*), the curb market interest rate (R_t) and seasonal dummy D_2, D_3, and D_4 with the following specification:

$$\ln (Y/M)_t^d = a_1 + a_2 D_2 + a_3 D_3 + a_4 D_4 + b \ln (Y_t) + c \ln (P_t^*/P_{t-1}^*) + d \ln (R_t) \tag{13}$$

Table 12.4
Estimates of the Velocity Equation Using Different
Monetary Aggregates: 1980-I to 1986-II

Exp. V.	$\ln(Y/M_1^F)$	$\ln(Y/M_1)$	$\ln(Y/M_2^F)$	$\ln(Y/M_2)$	$\ln(Y/M_3^F)$	$\ln(Y/M_3)$
Const.	-10.91^b	-10.97^b	-12.04^b	-12.35^b	-13.54^b	-13.82^b
	(6.96)	(6.63)	(12.5)	(12.1)	(11.7)	(11.3)
D_2	$.2636^b$	$.2701^b$	$.1673^b$	$.1720^b$	$.2072^b$	$.2131^b$
	(3.57)	(3.47)	(3.98)	(4.00)	(4.15)	(4.13)
D_3	$.1849^b$	$.1953^b$	$.1103^b$	$.1091^b$	$.1394^b$	$.1410^b$
	(3.71)	(3.65)	(3.93)	(3.72)	(3.94)	(3.79)
D_4	.1146	.1553	.0622	.0561	.0855	.0805
	(1.85)	(1.85)	(1.48)	(1.24)	(1.58)	(1.39)
$\ln(y)$	$.9096^b$	$.9120^b$	1.020^b	1.044^b	1.055^b	1.078^b
	(6.78)	(6.43)	(12.2)	(11.7)	(10.2)	(9.71)
$\ln(P^*/P_{-1}^*)$	1.066^b	1.106^b	$.7597^b$	$.7421^b$	$.9137^b$	$.9096^b$
	(3.46)	(3.36)	(4.57)	(4.21)	(4.43)	(4.14)
$\ln(R)$	$.3644^a$	$.3844^a$	.1662	.1643	.2034	.1985
	(2.81)	(2.80)	(1.89)	(1.74)	(1.77)	(1.60)
Lagged Dep. V.	$.3183^a$	$.3367^a$	$.2893^a$	$.3253^b$	$.3848^b$	$.4202^b$
	(2.06)	(2.14)	(2.68)	(2.91)	(3.10)	(3.24)
ρ	$.8168^b$	$.8033^b$	$.9842^b$	$.9857^b$	$.9871^b$	$.9859^b$
	(7.06)	(6.64)	(47.9)	(52.3)	(58.1)	(53.6)
R^2	.9596	.9540	.9894	.9880	.9829	.9804
SEE	$.0519^\#$	.0554	$.0282^\#$	.0300	$.0359\#$	.0383

Note: Figures in parentheses are t-statistics; #indicates a smaller value of the two standard errors of estimates calculated for the aggregates consisting of the identical monetary components.
[a]indicates statistical significance at the .05 level.
[b]indicates statistical significance at the .01 level.

Inserting equation (13) and adding the disturbance term ε_t, we derive an estimable equation:

$$\ln (Y/M)_t = \alpha a_1 + \alpha a_2 D_2 + \alpha a_3 D_3 + \alpha a_4 D_4 + \alpha b \ln (Y_t)$$
$$+ \alpha c \ln (P_t^*/P_{t-1}^*) + \alpha d \ln (R_t) + (1 - \alpha) \ln (Y/M)_{t-1} + \varepsilon_t \qquad (14)$$

Assuming that the disturbance term ε_t has the first-order autocorrelation of

$$\varepsilon_t = \rho\varepsilon_{t-1} + \eta_t \tag{15}$$

where the random variable η_t is normally distributed with $E(\eta_t) = 0$, $E(\eta_t\eta_{t-1}) = 0$, and $E(\eta_t^2) = \sigma^2$, we can estimate equation (14) by the maximum likelihood method.[19] The results are reported in Table 12.4.

All of the velocity equations in Table 12.4 appear to fit the data well with high values of R^2. In addition, most of the coefficients are statistically significant with expected signs, indicating an appropriate specification of the partial adjustment model for income velocity. Since the Standard Error of Estimates (SEE) is a measure of the unexplained variation in income velocity, we may assume that the smaller the value of SEE, the more appropriate is the monetary aggregate corresponding to that income velocity.[20] Comparing the SEEs between a pair of monetary aggregates consisting of identical components, we find that in all cases the Fisher Ideal index number yields a smaller SEE than does the simple-sum index. Furthermore, among the Fisher Ideal index numbers, M_2^F provides the smallest SEE, followed by M_3^F and M_1^F. In other words, a change in national income can best be predicted by Fisher Ideal index numbers and, in particular, by the Fisher Ideal index with M_2 components.

In short, all of our analyses in this section, though limited in data, lead to the same conclusion that the Fisher Ideal index for monetary quantities is superior to the simple-sum index. In addition our analyses show that the Fisher Ideal index for a broad monetary aggregate such as M_2^F or M_3^F outperforms the narrow concept of M_1^F.

CONCLUDING REMARKS

Since different monetary components have different degrees of moneyness, aggregating monetary components as the simple-sum does not provide an adequate measure of the flow of monetary services to the economy. This may be particularly true in developing countries where the interest rates in the regulated market are set by the government while the market rate is determined in the unregulated or curb market. For these reasons, we have proposed the Fisher Ideal index number for monetary quantities and applied it to Korea as an example of its usefulness.

There are a number of advantages in using the Fisher Ideal index number for monetary quantities as the measure of monetary services to the economy. Since the Fisher Ideal index is based on a flexible utility function of holding monetary assets, it takes into account the various degrees of moneyness among the monetary components even when the structure of interest rates is determined by government control. Moreover, the Fisher Ideal index is consistent with the axioms of revealed preference theory, implying that the underlying utility function may be even more general. Furthermore, since the curb market yield is used as the benchmark rate of return, the Fisher Ideal index correctly reflects an adverse impact of curb market changes on the flow of monetary services. Finally, since the Fisher Ideal index number satisfies Fisher's so-called determinate test, it does not take on extreme values of zero or infinity even when some component series become discontinuous due to financial development. Thus, the Fisher Ideal index for monetary quantities is more suitable to developing countries than the simple-sum index or even the Divisia index.

Although the data in Korea is limited, we have constructed the Fisher Ideal monetary index for Korea and examined the stability and predictability of income velocities based on such index numbers. For each money total, the Fisher Ideal index number has always outperformed the official simple-sum index, thus confirming our prior expectation. Among the Fisher Ideal index numbers, a broad concept of either M_2^F or M_3^F performs clearly better than the narrow concept of M_1^F. Although the broadest concept of M_3^F may be even better than M_2^F, the difficulty of obtaining reliable data on M_3^F components in Korea precludes a definite answer.

Therefore, given the existing data in Korea, we propose the use of the Fisher Ideal index with M_2 components. Even though the government is now attempting to revise M_2 to M_2B, our analysis appears to indicate that despite changes in monetary components, the Fisher Ideal index number will turn out to be better than the conventional simple-sum index number for monetary quantities.[21] Furthermore, a bias incurred by such a simple-sum index in measuring the monetary service is not likely to be negligible. We have confirmed this in calculating the money supply increases with the existing simple-sum index numbers.

NOTES

1. The importance of a curb market in the developing country can be measured by a method recently developed by Lee and Han (forthcoming). In the case of Korea, the ratio of the size of the curb market to that of the regulated market was .21 in mid 1986.

2. The conventional procedure in monetary indexing (see, for example, Barnett et al., 1980, 1982, 1984) is to use the maximum yield on any asset available in the economy as the benchmark rate of return. Since there are no records in Korea of yields higher than the curb market rate, it is quite reasonable to choose such a yield as the benchmark rate of return.

3. While Barnett assumes a planning horizon of n periods, we take only a two-period horizon to simplify our analysis without losing generality.

4. Since the curb market transactions take place underground, they would undoubtedly evade taxes on their interest earnings.

5. Thus, the curb market yield should contain all premiums including the risk premium for forgoing the monetary services provided by the monetary assets.

6. Our expenditure constraint is derived from the n-period constraint of Barnett (1978, pp. 147–48). The last two terms of our constraint represent the nominal value of the consumer's provisions for the later planning period,

$$\Sigma\,(1 + r_{i,t+1})P^*_{t+1}m_{i,t+1} + (1 + R_{t+1})P^*_{t+1}A_{t+1}$$

whereas the initial wealth of W_{ot} contains aside from labor incomes the nominal value of assets carried over from the prior planning period,

$$\Sigma\,(1 + r_{i,t-1})P^*_{t-1}m_{i,t-1} + (1 + R_{t-1})P^*_{t-1}A_{t-1}$$

7. The theory of multistage budgeting with blockwise weakly separable utility function was originally developed by Green (1964). In this paragraph, we closely follow the exposition of Barnett (1980) who applied the theory to monetary aggregation and indexing.

8. It should be noted that in the transformation to nominal quantities, the true costs of living index, P^*_t and P^*_{t-1}, are not required as they are cancelled out in equation (9).

9. Since the vector of prices for consumption goods q_t is p_t, analogous to equation (8), the unit cost function for the quantity aggregator function $(q'_t Bq_t)^{1/2}$ is $(p'_t B^{-1}p_t)^{1/2}$. Similarly, the unit cost function of the aggregator function $(m_{t+1}Am_{t+1})^{1/2}$ is $P^*_{t+1}(\iota'A^{-1}\iota)^{1/2}$, derived from the total nominal value of monetary assets, $P^*_{t+1}\iota'm_{t+1}$, which combines two terms of m_{t+1} without the discounting factor in budget constraint (5).

10.
$$(\partial\Pi_t/\partial R_t) = [\partial(\pi'_t A^{-1}\pi_t)^{1/2}/\partial R_t] = (\pi'_t A^{-1}\pi_t)^{-1/2}\pi'_t A^{-1}(\partial\pi_t/\partial R_t) = [u(m_t)]^{-1}m'_t(\partial\pi_t/\partial R_t)$$
where the last equality is derived using equations (7) and (8). Since $(\partial\pi_{it}/\partial R_t) = P^*_t(1 + r_{it})/(1 + R_t)^2 > 0$ for all i, $(\partial\pi_t/\partial R_t)$ is a vector of positive elements along with $[u(m_t)]^{-1}m'_t > 0$ and hence, $(\partial\Pi/\partial R_t)$ is positive.

11. Blackorby et al. (1978, p. 267) shows that if the utility function is blockwise completely separable as in (1), the Allen's partial elasticities of substitution between blocks have the equality condition that $\sigma_{1i} = \sigma_{1j}$ for $i \neq j$. Since $\sigma_{11} < 0$ and $\Sigma_i k_i\sigma_{1i} = 0$ with k_i a positive value of the expenditure share of the ith block, the equality condition implies that $\sigma_{1i} > 0$ for $i \neq 1$. In other words, the monetary aggregate at time t is a substitute for other aggregates in different blocks. Since the

Hicksian cross-price effect is positively related to Allen's partial elasticity of substitution, the compensated cross-price effect in our case must also be positive.

12. This may be called an indirect effect of substitution in the sense that a fall in the curb market yield increases the holding of current monetary assets while it decreases all future expenditures for consumption, monetary assets, and curb market assets at time $(t + 1)$ through a decreased holding of the current curb market assets.

13. Since the user costs are commonly viewed as the prices of services of monetary assets rather than their stocks, the user-cost evaluated monetary stocks in the Fisher Ideal index may be viewed as an index for expenditures on the services of monetary assets.

14. M_1 is the sum of cash and demand deposits; M_2 is M_1 plus time and savings deposits at commercial banks; and M_3 includes, in addition to M_2, negotiable certificates of deposits, time and savings deposits at nonbank financial institutions, debentures issued by bank and nonbank financial intermediaries, and sales of commercial bills by commercial banks. For calculating Fisher Ideal index numbers, a further decomposition of each monetary component is required. For instance, M_3 is broken down into 32 categories for the Fisher Ideal index number formula in (9). For the details of these breakdowns, see Lee (1988, pp. 7–8).

15. The source and description of the data are provided in detail elsewhere. (See Lee 1988, pp. 19–23.)

16. The after-tax rates of return are calculated from the unpublished data provided by the Bank of Korea on various interest rates and taxes paid. Since commercial banks pay minimal interest on demand deposits that cannot be regarded as a competitive market rate, we instead calculated the implicit rate of return by assuming that all marginal profits from demand deposits are indirectly passed on to deposits holders. The formula used is $r(1-R/D)$, suggested by Klein (1974), where r is the marginal return on investment derived from demand deposits and (R/D) is the average reserve deposit ratio. Since commercial banks mostly engage in commercial lending at the fixed rate controlled by the government, we used the lending rate as the measure of r. Also since the individual households are not likely to receive the implicit returns, we further adjusted the implicit rate of return by multiplying the fraction of total demand deposits held by private business and public corporations.

17. One-month holding period yields for each monetary asset were derived elsewhere by Lee (1988), following a procedure similar to that of Barnett and Spindt (1982).

18. Because of the limited number of observations, we omitted other tests such as the leads and lags of the money-expenditure relationship.

19. Using equations (14) and (15), we obtain the final estimating equation:

$$\ln V_t = \alpha a_1 (1 - \rho) + \alpha a_2 D_2 + \alpha a_3 D_3 + \alpha a_4 D_4$$
$$+ \alpha b [\ln (Y_t) - \rho \ln (Y_{t-1})]$$
$$+ \alpha c [\ln (p_t/p_{t-1}) - \rho \ln (p_{t-1}/p_{t-2})]$$
$$+ \alpha d [\ln (R_t) - \rho \ln (R_{t-1})]$$
$$+ (1 - \alpha)[\ln (V_{t-1}) - \rho \ln (V_{t-2})] + \rho \ln (V_{t-1}) + \eta_t$$

20. Because of the limited number of observations, we did not carry out the predictions of the income velocity outside the sample period.

21. Although we have experimented with the several different combinations of monetary components elsewhere (see Lee, 1988), the Fisher Ideal index number always turned out to be superior to the simple-sum index or the fixed-weight index that had previously been proposed in Korea.

REFERENCES

Anderson, L., "Selection of a Monetary Aggregate for Economic Stabilization," *Federal Reserve Bank of St. Louis Review*, October 1975, 9–15.

Bank of Korea, *Money and Banking Statistics*, Seoul, 1984.

Barnett, William A., "The User Cost of Money," *Economic Letters*, *1*, October 1978, 145–49.

———, "Economic Monetary Aggregates: An Application of Index Number and Aggregation Theory," *Journal of Econometrics*, *14*, September 1980, 11–48.

———, and Spindt, Paul A. "Divisia Monetary Aggregates, Compilation, Data, and Historical Behavior," Federal Reserve Board Staff Studies No. 116, Washington, D.C.: Board of Governors of the Federal Reserve System, 1982.

———, Offenbacher, Edward K., and Spindt, Paul A. "The New Divisia Monetary Aggregates," *Journal of Political Economy*, *92*, December 1984, 1049–85.

Blackorby, D., Primount, D., and Russell, R. R., *Duality, Separability, and Functional Structure*, Amsterdam: North-Holland, 1978.

Clements, Kenneth W., and Nguyen, Phuong, "Economic Aggregates–Comment," *Journal of Econometrics*, *14*, September 1980, 49–53.

Diewert, Erwin W., "Exact and Superative Index Numbers," *Journal of Econometrics*, *4*, May 1976, 115–45.

Green, H. A. J., *Aggregation in Economic Analysis*, Princeton: Princeton University Press, 1964.

Jaffee, Dwight M., "The Structure of the Money-Expenditure Relationship: Comment," *American Economic Review*, *60*, March 1970, 216–19.

Klein, Benjamin, "Competitive Interest Payments on Bank Deposits and the

Long-Run Demand for Money," *American Economic Review, 64*, December 1974, 931–49.

Lee, Tong Hun, "The Appropriate Monetary Indicators for the Korean Economy," *Yonsei Business Review, 22*, August 1985, 177–85.

———, "Utility Monetary Aggregates in Case of Korea," Ilhae Institute Research Paper Series No. 88-08, Seoul: Ilhae Institute, 1988.

———, and Han, Sil, "On Measuring the Relative Size of the Unregulated to the Regulated Money Markets," *Journal of Development Economics*, forthcoming.

Peltzman, S., "The Structure of the Money-Expenditures Relationship," *American Economic Review, 59*, March 1969, 129–37.

Spindt, Paul A., "Money Is What Money Does: Monetary Aggregation and the Equation of Exchange," *Journal of Political Economy, 93*, February 1985, 175–204.

13

The Financial Policy and Financial Sector Developments in Korea and Taiwan

Yoon Je Cho

INTRODUCTION

The economies of Korea and Taiwan have been widely studied as most successful examples of economic development. In fact the growth of both economies during the last two or three decades has been spectacular. Around 1960 both countries switched their industrialization strategy from that of import substitution to export promotion. At the same time, their respective governments have played significant roles in the process of economic development.

However, there were also substantial differences between the two countries' economic policies. The financial sector policy is one example. The two countries' financial systems started with very similar structures in the early 1950s that were inherited from the period of Japanese rule. The banking sector was dominant in both countries' financial systems and the banks have been owned by the governments during most of the post-war period.[1] Their operations also have been strongly regulated by the government. However, the degree of financial repression by the government has been much stronger in Korea than in Taiwan until very recently. The interest rates and credit allocation have been more strongly controlled in Korea than in Taiwan.

As a result, the growth of Taiwan's financial sector has been more rapid than that of Korea, especially in the 1960s and 1970s. Taiwan consistently maintained a high interest rate policy with a very low and stable inflation during this period. In Korea, on the other hand, the level of interest rates fluctuated with the changes in the government's interest rate policy, and with the relatively high and volatile inflation rate.

Korea has reoriented its financial policy toward financial liberalization in the 1980s. Although financial reform has been gradual, the overall growth of the

Table 13.1
Interest Rates and Inflation Rates: Korea

	Curb Market[a]	Corporate Bond	Bank Loan — General	Bank Loan — Export	Bank Loan — MIPF[b]	Bank Deposit[c] — NIF	Foreign Loan[d]	Inflation (GNP Deflator)
1968	--	--	26.0	6.0	--	25.2	--	--
1971	46.4	--	22.0	6.0	--	20.4	12.7	12.9
1972	39.0	--	19.0	6.0	--	12.0	5.2	16.3
1973	33.3	--	15.5	7.0	10.0	12.0	31.8	12.1
1974	40.6	--	15.5	9.0	12.0	15.0	12.5	30.4
1975	41.3	20.1	15.5	9.0	12.0	15.0	26.6	24.6
1976	40.5	20.4	17.0	8.0	13.0	16.2	5.6	21.0
1977	38.1	20.1	18.0	8.0	13.0	16.2	6.1	15.9
1978	41.2	21.1	19.0	9.0	15.0	18.6	8.8	21.6
1979	42.4	26.7	19.0	9.0	15.0	18.6	12.1	20.0
1980	44.9	30.1	20.0	15.0	20.0	19.5	39.7	25.3
1981	35.3	24.4	18.0	15.0	11.0	16.2	29.0	15.4
1982	33.1	17.3	10.0	10.0	10.0	8.0	20.6	6.7
1983	25.8	14.2	10.0	10.0	10.0	8.0	15.8	3.9
1984	24.8	14.1	10.0-11.5	10.0	10.0-11.5	10.0	14.8	3.8
1985	24.0	14.2	10.0-11.5	10.0	10.0-11.5	10.0	16.3	4.1
1986	--	12.8	10.0-11.5	10.0	10.0-11.5	10.0-11.5	--	2.3

Sources: Bank of Korea, Economic Statistics Yearbook, various issues; and IMF, International Financial Statistics, various issues.
[a]BOK data.
[b]Machinery Industry Promotion Fund.
[c]One year time deposit,
[d]An export effective interest rate of foreign loans which was derived by adding up the rate of changes in exchange rate with LIBOR.

financial sector has been very rapid in this decade, thus bringing the pattern of financial growth in the 1980s closer to that of Taiwan in the 1960s and 1970s. Both countries, due primarily to the continuing large current account surplus, are now facing greater internal and external pressure to further liberalize their financial systems.

The purpose of this study is to compare financial policy and the development of the financial sectors in both countries.

FINANCIAL POLICY AND FINANCIAL SECTOR DEVELOPMENT IN THE 1960s AND 1970s

Korea

Until the early 1960s, the domestic financial market in Korea was poorly developed and fragmented. A substantial part of industrial investment had to be financed by foreign aid and an unorganized money market. Resource mobilization through the banking system was very poor. The military government, which took over in 1961, repossessed the commercial banks that were then owned by private industrial groups.

In 1965 the government implemented a major interest rate reform. The interest rates on time deposits were doubled and bank loan rates, although subsidized, were also raised. The purpose of these changes was to stimulate the growth of the financial system, and through this, to contribute to growth in output. The policy was implemented following the recommendation of the report of the U.S. aid mission written by Gurley, Patrick, and Shaw.[2]

The growth of financial savings was very rapid during the second half of the 1960s owing to the interest rate reform of 1965. However, its growth slowed drastically in the 1970s because the government went back to a low interest rate policy in the early 1970s. Throughout the 1970s, the real interest rates of bank loans and deposits had been fluctuating around zero (Table 13.1). If we include the interest rates of preferential loans, the average real interest rate of bank loans in the 1970s must have been significantly negative. Consequently, the growth of the financial sector was stagnated in the 1970s after its rapid growth in the latter half of the 1960s (Table 13.2). The M2-GNP ratio increased from 12.1 to 35.0 from 1965 to 1970, while it stayed in a level of about 32 percent throughout the 1970s.

This low interest rate policy, in a sense, reflects the economic philosophy of the Korean government. The Korean government was very reluctant to leave the determination of interest rates and resource allocation to the market function. It continuously controlled the cost and allocation of capital. And it chose to fill any gap between domestic savings and investment through foreign borrowings rather than enthusiastically pursuing the domestic resource mobilization through encouraging competition and liberalization of the domestic financial system.

Table 13.2
Growth of Financial Sector: Korea

	$\dfrac{M_1}{GNP}$	$\dfrac{M_2}{GNP}$	$\dfrac{M_3}{GNP}$	Corporate Bond/GNP	Domestic Credit/GNP	Deposit Share(%) Banks	Deposit Share(%) NBFIS	National Saving (% of GNP)	Stock Market Capitalization /GNP
1965	--	12.1	--	--	--	--	--	7.4	--
1970	--	35.0	--	--	--	--	--	15.7	--
1975	11.7	31.3	36.0	--	39.5	82.1	17.9	19.1	--
1977	12.3	33.1	42.4	1.6	33.7	78.5	21.5	27.5	--
1979	10.7	32.1	43.5	3.6	38.5	73.3	26.7	28.1	--
1981	8.8	34.7	51.5	5.2	48.8	65.3	34.7	21.7	6.6
1983	11.5	38.9	63.8	7.4	54.0	58.2	41.8	24.8	5.9
1985	10.4	39.2	75.2	10.0	58.4	53.7	46.3	28.6	9.0
1987	10.4	41.3	94.4	10.2	57.9	48.7	51.3	--	26.8

Sources: Bank of Korea, *Economic Statistics Yearbook*, various issues; Ministry of Finance, Korea, *Fiscal and Financial Statistics*, various issues.

With the low interest rate ceiling there has been severe excess demand for bank credit, and the government-controlled banks had to ration credit under the criteria set by the government. Under these circumstances, a stable access to low-cost funds (that is, bank credit and government-distributed foreign loans) was considered to be crucial for firm performance. Being disfavored by government, which owned the banks and controlled their loans (as well as foreign banks), could easily lead to a firm's demise, particularly since firms are highly indebted.[3]

In the process of an aggressive and centrally controlled economic development strategy since the early 1960s, the Korean government has made extensive and forceful use of a wide range of incentives designed to assure private industry's close compliance with its plans. Among them, probably the most forcefully and persistently used one has been selective credit allocation and low interest rate ceilings by commercial banks as well as specialized banks under government control.

In essence, the Korean government provided two strong incentives for the development of strategic industries that had an important bearing on private firms' investment decisions. First, the government changed the expected rate of profit of investment by controlling the interest rates and allocation of bank loans. By favorably allocating cheap bank credit to a strategic sector, the government could reduce the cost of investment and increase the expected rate of return in that sector or its firms. Second, the government changed the perceived risk of investment by assuring a stable flow of bank loans to selected industries regardless of their short-term financial performance. Thus, if a firm followed government policy by investing in the projects in which government put high priority, its bankruptcy risk was reduced, perhaps even eliminated. In other words, the government, by controlling the financial sector, became a risk partner of firms, encouraging them to undertake projects that might have been declined otherwise.

Among the domestic bank loans, the most forceful tool to encourage investment in the priority sectors was those policy loans that were earmarked to specific sectors or industries with much lower cost than the already highly subsidized general bank loans. Indirect information on the relative magnitude of policy loans can be found in Table 13.3, which shows the decomposition of the uses of commercial banks' deposit funds. According to this table, more than half of the net increase of bank deposits in 1981 was used for directed credit by government. However, the real amount of loans of which allocation has been influenced by government has been larger than the figures shown in the tables, although we cannot figure out the exact amount of it. According to one recent study (Chung, 1987), the policy loans accounted for about 50 to 70 percent of the total domestic bank loans in the 1960s and 1970s.

It is also difficult to figure out the exact amount of subsidy that policy loans have generated to their borrowers, since it depends on what has been the level of the equilibrium market interest rate, which again is not exactly known in a country like Korea where the major part of the financial sector has been regulated by interest

Table 13.3
The Uses of Commercial Banks Net Increase of Deposit, 1981

	Amount (100 Million Won)	Share (%)
Net Deposit Increase (A)	16,664	100.0
Directed Uses (B)	9,445	56.7
Reserve Requirement	917	5.5
Contribution to NIF	2,176	13.1
Policy Loan	6,352	38.1
(Export Credit)	(780)	(4.7)
(Other)	(5,572)	(33.4)
Undirected Uses (A) - (B)	7,219	43.3

Source: Kim and Park (1984).

rate ceilings. However, the relative degree of subsidy that various types of policy loans generate can be seen by comparing the preferential interest rates with other interest rates as was shown in Table 13.1. Throughout the 1970s the real interest rates of bank loans were negative, while the real rate of the informal credit market was quite high and stable around 20 percent. The degree of subsidy was highest in the case of policy loans such as export credit, whose real interest rate was often lower than –10 percent in the 1970s.[4]

Foreign borrowing was also quite favorable to borrowers in the 1970s when the exchange rate was fixed with a much higher domestic inflation rate than that of the rest of the world. Since the nominal interest rate of foreign loans was lower than the domestic bank loans in the 1970s and the exchange rate was fixed in the latter half of the 1970s, it was even cheaper than the domestic bank loans (Table 13.1).

In summary, the Korean government's low interest rate policy and heavy intervention in credit allocation generated a tremendous amount of rent involved in the bank (and foreign) loans. Through its power of distributing rents the government could maintain strong control over business firms, and the rent-seeking behavior had been an essential part of business activities in Korea. On the other hand, the repressive financial policy hindered the growth of the financial sector. The growth of financial savings had been sluggish relative to the growth of GNP in the 1970s. As a result, a substantial part of domestic investments to achieve high economic growth during this period had to depend heavily upon foreign savings, as will be discussed later. The banking system played the passive role of allocating credit, following the government's direction, and had little room for commercialism to work. Little incentive was given to banks for private innovations and improvement of efficiency. Many of the government-directed policy loans also turned out to be nonperforming loans that further burdened the growth of the banking sector.

Taiwan

The structure of the financial system in Taiwan was similar to that of Korea in the 1960s and 1970s (except that the Central Bank of China was established in 1961 while the Bank of Korea was established in 1950).

However, the government's intervention in the banking system has been moderate in the case of Taiwan compared with Korea in the following regards. First, although the interest rate ceilings were imposed by the government, they generated a substantially high positive real rate. Second, the selective credit program was mostly limited to the export sector. The proportion of it in the total credit was also very small relative to Korea. For example, export credit was about 11.3 percent of the total loans in Korea while it was only 1.5 percent of the total loans in Taiwan in 1985. If we consider the export credit to be only a part of directed credit programs in Korea, the extent of selective credit control in Taiwan has been quite moderate compared with Korea.

Taiwan adopted a high interest rate policy in the early 1950s when most developing countries adopted a low interest rate policy (given the influence of Keynesian economics) to promote industrial growth. Originally, the policy was devised, outlined, and advocated to curb high inflation after the civil war, following the influence of S. C. Tsiang and T. C. Liu. Despite its government-owned and controlled financial system, the Taiwanese monetary policy seems to have consistently kept actual interest rates close to that equilibrium level (Scitovsky, 1985). As is shown in Table 13.4, the real deposit rate at banks has been substantially high during the last three decades except for some turbulent years of oil shocks. Furthermore, it was much higher than those of most industrialized economies such as the United States, Japan, and Germany for the same period.

The high interest rate policy, in a sense, reflects that the Taiwanese government, compared with the Korean government, has shown greater respect for the market forces in the financial sector. Taiwan, like Korea, also has had an active informal credit market despite this high level of interest rates, which implies that there has been credit rationing in the formal banking sector. However, the Taiwanese government has been generous about the operation of the informal credit market and implicitly regarded it as a safety valve of credit rationing of banks, while the Korean government has continuously tried to abolish or reduce it by several means including the presidential special decree in 1972 (Scitovsky, 1985). Also, in terms of government intervention in credit allocation, the Taiwanese case has been more moderate compared with that involving the Korean government.

Consequently, the degree of interest rate subsidy through preferential lending was also smaller in the case of Taiwan than in the case of Korea. The difference between the general lending rate and the preferential loan rates (for example, the export loan rate) in the case of Korea was more than 8–15 percentage points, while in Taiwan it was about 5–7 percent in the 1960s and 1970s (Tables 13.1 and 13.4). In real terms, Korea's preferential loan generated significantly negative interest rates (about –5 percent to –10 percent in the 1960s and 1970s), while in Taiwan, even preferential loans had significantly positive real interest rates except for a couple of years of oil shock. The high and stable real interest rates have been owed, in great extent, to the stable macroeconomic environment in Taiwan, which again is owed to prudent monetary policy. In Korea, monetary expansion to support industrial investment has often been permitted, which again ended up with relatively high and volatile inflation rates. This further reduced the level of real interest rates of formal financial institutions, and consequently increased the degree of financial repression.

The steadily high real interest rates in Taiwan have encouraged a remarkable growth of the financial sector. Financial savings (M2) has grown at a much higher rate than the GNP, which resulted in continuous growth in the M2/GNP ratio (Table 13.5). The M2/GNP ratio in Taiwan has grown much faster than that of Korea. At

Table 13.4
Interest Rates and Inflation Rates: Taiwan (in percent)

End of Year	"Curb Market" Unsecured Loan	At Banks			Consumer Price Inflation
		Savings Deposit[a]	Unsecured Loan	Export Loan	
Average					
1956-62	41.1	17.0	20.9	11.2	8.4
1963-73	25.4	10.1	14.1	7.7	3.4
1974	29.3	13.5	15.5	9.0	47.5
1975	26.4	12.0	14.0	7.0	5.2
1976	27.6	10.7	12.7	7.0	2.5
1977	25.6	9.5	11.5	6.5	7.0
1978	27.2	9.5	11.5	6.5	5.8
1979	30.1	12.5	15.2	10.5	9.8
1980	31.3	12.5	16.2	10.5	19.0
1981	30.1	13.0	15.2	11.0	16.3
1982	27.7	9.0	10.7	8.2	3.3
1983	26.8	8.5	8.5 -10.2	8.0	1.8
1984	29.9	8.0	8.0 -10.0	7.7	1.7
1985	27.4	7.0	6.5 - 9.5	6.25	-0.2
1986	24.3	5.0	5.0 - 9.0	5.75	0.5

Sources: The Central Bank of China (Taiwan), *Financial Statistics Monthly*, various issues, and Cheng (1986).

[a]One-year savings deposits.

Table 13.5
Growth of Financial Sector: Taiwan

	GNP[a] Growth Rate	M$_2$[a] Growth Rate	M$_2$/GNP
1961-65	--	--	30.8
1966-70	-	--	42.5
1971-74	24.9	29.8	48.3
1976	19.8	26.0	59.3
1978	19.9	31.0	73.0
1980	24.3	22.7	65.0
1982	6.9	24.3	75.6
1984	11.4	20.3	93.9
1985	5.3	24.1	109.8

Source: The Central Bank of China, *Financial Statistics Monthly*, various issues.

[a]Nominal

Table 13.6
Savings and Investment[a]

	Korea			Taiwan		
	Gross Investment	Domestic Savings	Foreign Savings	Gross Investment	Domestic Savings	Foreign Savings
1964	15.6	8.7	6.9	17.0	16.3	0.7
1967	20.2	11.4	8.8	25.4	23.2	2.2
1971	25.1	14.5	10.5	26.4	29.0	- 2.6
1972	20.9	15.7	5.2	25.8	32.3	- 6.5
1973	24.7	21.4	3.4	29.3	34.6	- 5.3
1974	31.8	19.3	11.9	39.5	31.8	7.7
1975	27.5	16.9	10.5	30.8	29.0	3.8
1976	25.7	22.2	3.5	31.1	32.7	- 1.6
1977	27.7	25.4	2.3	28.6	32.9	- 4.3
1978	31.9	27.3	4.5	28.6	34.8	- 6.2
1979	36.0	26.5	9.5	33.3	33.8	- 0.5
1980	32.1	20.8	11.3	34.3	32.7	1.6
1981	30.3	20.5	9.8	30.5	31.8	- 1.3
1982	28.5	20.9	7.9	25.2	30.1	- 4.9
1983	29.9	25.3	4.6	23.0	32.0	- 9.0
1984	31.9	27.9	4.0	21.3	33.4	-12.1
1985	31.1	28.6	3.5	17.9	31.6	-13.7
1986 (P)	30.2	32.8	-2.6	--	--	--

Source: Economic Planning Board, *Korean Economic Indicators*, Korea, 1987.

[a]Ratio of GNP

the end of 1970s, M2/GNP in Taiwan was 66.2 percent while it was 31.6 percent in Korea. This high M2/GNP ratio of Taiwan was even close to that of Japan in the 1950s and 1960s.[5] Among the developing countries, Taiwan showed the highest degree of financial deepening in the 1960s and 1970s.[6]

The high interest rate also seems to have encouraged domestic resource mobilization through the higher national savings rate. Taiwan's savings rate has been among the highest in the world. As a result, Taiwan's domestic investment was more than fulfilled by domestic savings. Owing to this, Taiwan, since the late 1960s, became a net foreign lender while Korea has continuously been a big net foreign borrower (Table 13.6).

SOME IMPLICATIONS OF FINANCIAL POLICY FOR THE REAL SECTOR DEVELOPMENT

A Conceptual Framework

The government-controlled low interest rate ceilings generate a substantial degree of rents associated with bank loans. That is, if the real cost of bank credit is set below the real rate of return of capital investment, borrowing from banks entails rent. In the case of financial intermediation, this rent is usually divided among three groups: lenders (depositors), borrowers (firms), and financial intermediaries (banks). If the financial system is competitive, most of the returns out of investment go to the depositors except those normal profits that allow firms and banks to stay in business. However, if the price of capital is regulated, most rents go to the privileged borrowers, that is, firms.

This was largely the case in Korea. Once the privileged borrowers could secure a continuous flow of bank credit, they could grow much faster than otherwise. They also grew much faster than their competitors, or potential entrants, who do not have as good an access to bank loans. This contributed to a high economic concentration that has been developed through the following courses. First, the government-favored firms could grow much faster than the rest of the firms with huge rent associated with bank credit. Second, the favored firms that were supported by government's continuous commitment of bank loans could enjoy little risk of bankruptcy while the rest of the firms often went bankrupt as the external and internal environment changed against them. Third, large incumbent firms with favored access to credit could easily bar entry of new firms by building up excess capacity (Dixit, 1980; Spence, 1977), and could take over small incumbent firms through various means such as predatory pricing, with their easy access to cheap loans.

The small firms that were rationed out of bank credit grew slowly and faced a high risk of bankruptcy for the following reasons. First, they had to depend on other sources of borrowing, the costs of which were even double or triple the bank loan. Second, because of poor access to capital, they had difficulty in quickly responding to the opportunity of profitable investment. Third, the unfavored firms in credit rationing often had to operate under a suboptimal input mix, since the opportunity cost of input (that is, capital) was misrepresented and had to incur higher cost than otherwise. Fourth, with poor access to capital they had to keep their asset structure very liquid in order to reduce bankruptcy risk, which again gave lower rates of return on their assets than otherwise. All these factors have strengthened the degrees of efficiency loss and economic concentration. And the degrees have been increased as the deviation of interest rates from the market rate increased and as the degree of credit rationing became pervasive.

The low interest rate ceilings and government intervention in credit allocation, in which favoritism was often involved, also negatively affected income distribution. This practice works in such a way that it taxes the depositors and gives subsidy to loan recipients. In today's newly industrialized economies where typical depositors are small household savers and typical borrowers are large corporations, which are typically owned by small groups of families, the repressed financial system works against the fair distribution of income. It also induces the method of production in a more capital-intensive way and tends to reduce the wage share of the total output of the economy (Scitovsky, 1985).

The Comparison of the Cases of Korea and Taiwan

Economic Concentration

One of the most notable differences between the two countries' economic growth patterns is the different degree of economic concentration. In short, Korea's economic growth has been based on an expansion of the size of firms while that of Taiwan has been based on an increase in the number of establishments. The average annual number of manufacturing companies rose at an annual rate of 0.9 percent in Korea, and 9.6 percent in Taiwan during the period of 1966–81.

Among many factors that brought about these different patterns of business concentration, the two countries' different approaches to financial policy may have played a substantial role. In Korea, 100 of the largest firms borrowed about 35 percent of total financial institutions' loans and 400 of the largest firms borrowed about 50 percent of the total loans as of February 1983.[7] Since most large firms in Korea belong to the industrial group, this means that a smaller number of big conglomerates have occupied a major proportion of bank loans. In the case of Taiwan, 97 firms got loans more than NT$0.5 billion and 333 firms got loans more than NT$0.2 billion, which means that the top 97 firms got 11.6 percent and the top 333 got 18.0 percent of total loans at the end of 1981.[8] This means that there has been much less loan concentration in Taiwan than in Korea, which again partially explains the different patterns of business concentration.

Income Distribution

It is true that in Korea and in Taiwan income distribution is relatively equitable compared with other developing countries in the static context. However, if we look at the development of income distribution of the two countries in the dynamic context, we find a difference.

Both Korea and Taiwan went through civil war, which left them to start with a very equal income distribution in the 1950s as there was very poor wealth accumulation and a very weak industrial base. The land, which was the major part of wealth in that period, was redistributed through land reforms in the 1950s in both countries. However, Taiwan came up with even improved income distribution since 1960 while Korea experienced aggravated distribution of income in the 1970s. By 1980, Taiwan's GINI Index was .303 as compared with .389 for Korea. These outcomes again may have been affected by many factors. Among them there may have been the financial sector policies as discussed above. For example, in Korea, the repressive financial policy that created high rent and subsidy must have worked against fair distribution of income.

Financial Structure of Corporate Sector

The misrepresented cost of debt by interest rate ceilings also encouraged the corporate sector to get highly leveraged. Under highly subsidized interest rates, the firms that borrowed more from banks became better off since they were more heavily subsidized. As the market share of these favored firms grew in Korea's corporate sector, the debt ratio of the overall corporate firms in Korea also became higher. Korean corporate firms are leveraged higher than in any other country. As of 1984 the debt-equity ratio for Korean manufacturing was 342.7 percent, as compared with 309.8 for Japan, 134.5 for Taiwan, and 110.1 for the United States.[9] This left the corporate firms in Korea very vulnerable to changes in economic conditions, and this again has called for continued government intervention in the financial system. Compared with Korean firms, Taiwanese firms have a lower debt ratio, which also implies more stability of the corporate sector with changes in the internal and external economic environment.

POLITICAL ECONOMY OF FINANCIAL POLICY

Both Korea and Taiwan have had strong and authoritarian government during the last two or three decades. Yet, the economic philosophy of the two governments seems to have been different. In Korea, the military government pushed industrialization in the early 1960s and was strongly involved in picking the winners and losers. Once it had created a favored group of industrialists, the government and industrialists began reinforcing each others' interests. The government continuously kept strong leverage over the industrial sectors through maintaining the power of rent distribution, while the favored industrial groups retained the privileged relation with the government by various rent-seeking behavior. The more the industrial groups became indebted to the banking sector, the stronger was their need for maintaining good relations with the government. Under the highly leveraged financial structure of firms mentioned above, the control of credit by the government was crucial to their business and survival.

The authoritarian government, which did not have strong public support, also needed strong support from industrialists. As a result, the government and industrial groups became a mutually supportive group through rent distribution and rent seeking for survival. The continuation of repressive financial policy by the government seems to have been nurtured under this political environment in Korea.

On the other hand, Taiwan's government pursued a distinctly different financial policy. At least two factors contributed to this policy orientation in Taiwan. First, the philosophy of the Kuo Min Dang government has been based on the teachings of Sun Yat-sen, who emphasized equity and respect for public decision. This philosophy of the Taiwanese government might have made itself eschew the concentration of economic power, and pay greater respect to the market mechanism as compared with the Korean government. In Taiwan, the firm or industry that benefited from economies of scale and thus became a monopoly was usually held as a public enterprise, while in Korea private firms became monopolies in these industries.

Another strong political factor that might have affected the economic policy in Taiwan is the division of political power and economic power between groups of different ethnic background. The political power in Taiwan has been held by those who moved from mainland China after the civil war in the late 1940s, while the commercial activity was dominated by indigenous Taiwanese people. This political group may have been reluctant to allow the local economic elites to eventually become a threat to their political power. This may have caused the government to be less enthusiastic about creating rent and subsidy to support industrialists.

FINANCIAL REFORMS IN THE 1980s

Korea

The adverse impact of government intervention in the financial system, which was intensified in the latter half of the 1970s through governmental promotion of heavy and chemical industries, became apparent by the end of the 1970s. Partly in reaction to this trend, the Korean government changed direction in the 1980s and reoriented its financial policies. The intent of the financial policy shift was to liberalize—to give financial institutions greater freedom to set their own prices and to attract and allocate funds. Accomplishing this shift turned out to be more difficult and gradual than anticipated, especially in the banking sector, which had been the most pervasively controlled part of the financial system and had carried the major burden of financing heavy industry investments.

A central feature of the liberalization policy was the sale of the government's shares in the large commercial banks, which occurred between 1981 and 1983. However, continued government control of interest rates at all banks, along with the high proportion of non-performing bank loans and the heavy dependence on the Bank of Korea for low-cost funds to support their outstanding loans, has left the privately owned banks very vulnerable. A substantial part of their outstanding loans is still policy related. Highly indebted firms, declining industries such as shipping, shipbuilding, construction, and industrial restructuring, have continued to be seen by the government as justifying intervention in credit allocation despite its intention to deregulate.

In contrast to the plight of commercial banks, nonbank financial intermediaries (NBFIs) have always been privately owned and have been both less controlled and less protected by the government.[10] They were allowed higher interest rate ceilings than banks so that they could absorb informal credit market funds since their establishment in the mid 1970s. In the 1980s, the government allowed greater competition among NBFIs through the relaxation of entry barriers and encouraged competitive development in the financial subsector.

The growth of the financial sector in the 1980s has been very rapid compared with that of the 70s. This expansion occurred predominantly among the NBFIs, a pattern that has resulted in a sharp decline in the relative importance of commercial banks.

In recent years, the informal credit markets also seem to have declined in relative importance, although this trend cannot be quantified with any precision. The growth and changing structure of the financial sector are depicted in Table 13.2. There was modest decline of M1 relative to GNP; a moderate increase of M2 relative to GNP; and nearly a doubling of the M3 to GNP ratio. Since M3 roughly approximates the size of NBFI deposits, this finding confirms the important role of the NBFIs in the growth of the regulated financial system. The deposit share of NBFIs increased from less than 20 percent in the mid 1970s to more than 50 percent by 1987.

The rapid growth of Korea's financial sector in the 1980s is owed to several factors. The most important factor among them may have been the increased real interest rates through reduced inflation. In 1982, the rate of inflation dropped below 10 percent for the first time in many years and has stayed very stable since then. In addition, increased competition among financial institutions with privatization and relaxed entry barriers also helped to attract more financial savings.

Another important policy change, introduced in June 1982, was the elimination of the preferential low bank loan rates, with few exceptions (Table 13.1). This change was accomplished primarily by reducing the general loan rate to the prevailing levels of preferential loans. This process was made easier by the decline in the rate of inflation. Also recently, the government has gradually reduced the amount of export credit because the Korean economy started having a current account surplus, and consequently the need to subsidize the export sector has diminished. There still exists a substantial amount of policy loans and the borrowers in the strategic sector continue to have preferential access to bank loans, but since 1982 they have not benefited from special interest rates as they once did in the 1970s.

The financial reforms in the 1980s also had some impact on the efficiency of credit allocation to the industrial sector. As a result of the expansion of NBFIs, which are a more liberalized and competitive financial subsector, the cost of capital among different types of borrowers has been gradually equalized since 1982. For example, the variance of average borrowing costs of 18 manufacturing industries has been reduced from 21.4 in 1979 to 5.9 in 1984 (Cho, 1988). The gaps in the cost of capital between large and small firms also have been reduced. The flow of funds also has been affected through financial liberalization in such a way that the source of funds for the corporate sector has become more extended and diversified.

In summary, the patterns of financial sector growth in Korea in the 1980s became similar to those of Taiwan and Japan in the 1960s and early 1970s. The controlled interest rate that generated a substantially high real positive rate under stable prices attracted financial savings and achieved the rapid growth of the financial sector. The reduced degree of government intervention in credit allocation also helped to improve the overall efficiency of credit allocation compared with the 1970s.

Taiwan

Most commercial banks in Taiwan are still owned by the government and their operation suffers many typical problems of public enterprises. On the other hand, there has been some effort to foster the short-term money market, especially by allowing free market interest rates in this market. This has facilitated the development of markets for commercial papers, bank acceptance, and CDs. As a result, the sources of the corporate sector's liability have become diversified. The share of funds raised via the money market kept increasing from 0.04 percent in 1975 to 10.9 percent in 1983. However, there have not been significant changes in the financial system in Taiwan in the 1980s except for a substantial expansion of postal savings in the total deposit (Cheng, 1986). Yet, the majority of short-term monetary market assets issued by firms are purchased by commercial banks and such transactions, in fact, are equivalent to indirect bank financing.[11]

This relatively slow progress of liberalization in the 1980s in Taiwan compared with that in Korea may reflect the different internal and external environment it faced relative to Korea in the early 1980s. Taiwan, as a net international creditor country, probably has been less compelled to liberalize the financial system in order to facilitate domestic resource mobilization than Korea, which was a big debtor country. Debt crisis and world economic recession in the early 1980s have compelled Korea to reconsider its development strategy, and pushed it into a stability-oriented and more domestic savings dependent one. In Korea, this external environment added the urgency of financial liberalization, which was already recognized through the adverse impact of financial repression such as the misallocation of capital and the inefficiencies of the financial institutions.

As the industrial sectors became more mature in both countries, a more diversified and competitive financial system was needed to provide more diversified sources of finance within the corporate sectors. However, in Taiwan, with a high domestic savings rate and a declining investment rate since 1982, domestic resource mobilization was not a high priority. Rather, the impending issue was to reduce the monetary pressure from external surplus. This environment probably necessitated that Taiwan concentrate its liberalization strategy more on immediate concerns, that is, the liberalization of the external account rather than the domestic liberalization of the financial system. Since 1986, Korea has faced a similar problem. Korea's current account turned out to be a large surplus in contrast to a long period of deficit, thus initiating great pressure for monetary management. Now it also faces great pressure for the liberalization of foreign exchange and capital account transactions.

CONCLUDING REMARKS

The Korean financial system had been more strongly repressed than the Taiwanese system in the 1960s and 1970s. Under the relatively high and unstable inflation, the nominal interest rate ceiling imposed by the government often generated negative real interest rates in Korea. The government created various types of policy loans that entailed high rent and exercised a strong control over the allocation of it as well as general bank loans. This resulted not only in poor domestic resource mobilization through the financial system but also in poor overall efficiency of resource allocation of the economy. It also ended up with a very inefficient banking system with a large burden of bad loans.

The banking system in Taiwan has been owned and controlled by the government as well. Nevertheless, the price mechanism (that is, interest rates) and the allocation of credit have been, in general, more closely related to the market principle compared with the Korean case. Consequently, in Taiwan the growth of financial savings as well as national savings was remarkable, which made it possible for the country to achieve rapid growth without recourse to foreign capital. In Korea, the substantial part of investment to achieve high growth rate had to be financed through foreign capital.

Comparison of the Korean and the Taiwanese cases suggests that financial policy might have played some significant role in shaping the current business structure and income distribution in both countries. The control of interest rates and credit allocation in Korea was used as a major tool for government industrial policy, and in the process it must have affected the shaping of the current structure of business and industry. In this regard, the notable differences in business concentration and income distribution may also have been affected by different approaches of the two countries in financial sector policy as discussed above.

In the 1980s, Korea has moved toward financial liberalization and achieved a rapid growth of financial savings. The most significant factors contributing to this development were the price stability achieved since 1981, and the rapid development of nonbanking financial institutions and the securities market. Compared with the Korean case, domestic financial reform in Taiwan has been moderate in the 1980s. This probably reflects the fact that Taiwan already had a relatively more liberal financial sector before the 1980s than Korea, and that the adverse impact of financial repression was less serious. Nevertheless, Taiwan is facing strong pressure for deregulation and improvement of the efficiency of the banking system through, for example, allowing more private initiation in the financial sector. The development of a more diversified financial market through further development of NBFIs and the securities market is also needed.

Both countries face strong pressure of internationalization of the domestic capital market under the large current account surplus. If the current size of trade surplus continues, they will soon have to move toward liberalization of the domestic financial market. This again will result in more pressure for further liberalization of the domestic financial system since, without a competitive and liberalized domestic financial system, opening the domestic financial market might be very costly. This implies that both countries are now facing a big challenge of setting up an appropriate monetary and financial policy that not only secures continuous price stability but also leads to a more competitive and efficient financial system.

NOTES

1. Korea has privatized commercial banks recently. See below.
2. However, this financial reform was not a typical financial liberalization as often has been cited. See McKinnon (1973) for example.
3. Korean firms are very heavily indebted. Under the low cost of borrowing, those firms that had access to bank loans tended to expand their asset structure and to be highly leveraged.
4. The Korean government, however, abolished the preferential lending rate

in June 1982 as part of the liberalization program. The favor in terms of accessibility still exists, generating a certain degree of subsidy to the borrowers of policy loans.

5. The M2/GNP ratio in Japan was 63.3 percent in 1955, 7.8 percent in 1960, and 9.59 percent in 1970.

6. For example, M2/GNP in 1969 was 29 percent in Argentina, 18 percent in Chile, 29 percent in Turkey, and 25 percent in India.

7. *Dong-A*, daily newspaper, November 9, 1983.

8. Staff estimates of Council for Economic Planning and Development, Republic of China.

9. According to a recent study by Kim (1985), big firms in Korea have a debt ratio (debt/equity) close to 1,000 percent.

10. Investment and finance companies, investment and trust companies, mutual savings and credit companies, life insurance companies are among NBFIs.

11. In Korea, nonbank financial institutions take this major role.

REFERENCES

Cheng, Hang-Sheng, "Financial Policy and Reform in Taiwan, China," in H. S. Cheng, ed., *Financial Policy and Reform in Pacific Basin Countries*, Lexington: Lexington Books, 1986.

Cho, Yoon Je, "The Effect of Financial Liberalization on the Efficiency of Credit Allocation—Some Evidence from Korea," *Journal of Development Economics*, 29, September 1988, 101–10.

Chung, Un-Chan, "Economic Growth and Financial Developments in Korea, 1962–81," Paper presented at the conference on "Economic Development of Japan and Korea: A Parallel with Lessons for Economic Development," East-West Center, Hawaii, 1987.

Dixit, Avinash, "The Role of Investment in Entry-Deterrence," *Economic Journal*, 90, March 1980, 95–106.

Horiuchi, Akiyoshi, "The Low Interest Rate and Economic Growth in Postwar Japan," *Developing Economies*, 24, December 1984, 349–71.

Kim, E. Han, "Corporate Financial Structure in Korea: Theory, Evidence and the Need for Reform," Mimeo, Graduate School of Business Administration, University of Michigan, August 1985.

Kim, P. J., and Park, Y. C., *The Korean Economy and Its Finance* (in Korean), Seoul: Phak Young Sa, 1984.

Kohsaka, Akira, "Financial Liberalization in Asian NICs—A Comparative Study of Korea and Taiwan in the 1980s." Manuscript, Harvard University, June 1987.

McKinnon, Ronald I., *Money and Capital in Economic Development*, Washington, D.C.: The Brookings Institution, 1973.

Scitovsky, Tibor, "Economic Development in Taiwan and South Korea: 1965–81," *Food Research Institute Studies*, *19*, March 1985, 215–64.
Spence, A. M., "Entry, Capacity, Investment and Oligopolistic Pricing," *Bell Journal of Economics*, *8*, Autumn 1977, 534–44.

B. Fiscal Management

Although in the absence of well-organized money markets, the government relied heavily on fiscal measures to mobilize domestic resources, according to K. Choi and T. W. Kwack (in the first chapter of this section), one of the salient features of Korea's fiscal policy is that long before supply-side economics gained popularity, it was already in practice in Korea. To effect this, the share of tax and government expenditures was kept low; there was a heavy reliance on indirect consumption tax, extensive incentives for savings and investment, and less emphasis on welfare spending.

Of no less importance is the role of tax incentives in Korea's industrialization policy: numerous tax incentives were used to induce the private sector to engage in economic activities desirable for industrial development and export growth. Many enterprises (especially the large enterprises) have benefited from these tax incentives—incentives for export promotion and incentives for industries.

Choi and Kwack also examine the effects of Korea's tax policy on resources allocation. The benefits of tax incentives are measured in terms of tax concessions per unit of tax revenue collected, benefit per dollar invested, effective tax rate, and cost of capital.

Taking a rather analytical approach, J. S. Lee, in the second chapter, starts with a theoretical formulation of a growth model linking economic growth with patterns of government expenditure. The model was then tested empirically. The results show that public investment spending has a positive effect on growth. On the other hand the growth of government spending as a ratio of GNP tends to have a negative effect on the growth, possibly reflecting the crowd-out and/or disincentive effect of government expenditures.

An international comparison of government spending by Lee also reveals that in Korea the relative size of government is still small, government spending is more investment oriented, and government involvement in direct income transfers has been relatively small.

In an alternative approach to the estimation of the effect of fiscal policies on output, Paul Evans tests to see if the Ricardian equivalence holds for Korea. According to Ricardian equivalence, if economic agents follow rational expectations, government deficits may not raise real interest rates regardless of whether they are financed with bond sales (debt) or tax increases. If the government uses debt to finance its expenditures, current saving will go up in anticipation of future taxes. The result is that neither deficits nor tax cuts will affect interest rates if Ricardian equivalence holds.

Evans formulates a simple neoclassical model of an economy and applies it to the Korean data, and finds that Ricardian equivalence in fact holds true for Korea: the Korean tax system is highly distorting, and government purchases are highly productive. He notes further that the increased tax rates appreciably depress output, and that budget deficits do not much affect output.

14

Tax Policy and Resource Allocation in Korea

Kwang Choi and Taewon Kwack

INTRODUCTION

The most important aspect of Korea's tax policy in connection with her rapid industrialization has been the tax incentive system. The Korean government has applied various tax incentives, such as a preferential depreciation allowance and tax reductions and exemptions, to induce the private sector to engage in certain economic activities that seemed desirable for industrial development and export growth. Only in a few cases were they employed as countercyclical policy measures.

The purpose of this study is to examine the effects of Korea's tax policy on resource allocation. After reviewing the evolution of the tax incentive system in Korea, an effort is made to summarize some statistical data and available empirical studies in the following sections.

MAJOR TAX INCENTIVES AND THE EVOLUTION

Korea's complicated tax incentive system includes: (1) incentives for export promotion; (2) incentives for key industries; (3) incentives for small- and medium-sized firms; (4) incentives for technical innovations; (5) incentives for local industrial development; (6) incentives for foreign investment; (7) countercyclical investment incentives; (8) incentives for energy conservation and environmental protection; (9) incentives for resources development; (10) incentives for business reorganization; and (11) incentives for social welfare.[1]

Since the first 3 types of incentives among the 11 are the most important in terms of size and structural implications, they will be summarized in detail.

Tax Incentives for Export Promotion

A fully-fledged tax incentive system for export promotion was not introduced until 1960. A 30 percent corporate tax exemption was allowed on income from export business, and a 20 percent exemption was given to income from the sale of goods and services to foreign military forces based in Korea and from foreign currency income from tourism. In the following year, this system was reinforced by raising the exemption rate to a uniform 50 percent for all foreign-exchange-earnings activities.

The system was replaced in 1973 by two tax-free reserve systems: reserves for losses in the export business and reserves for overseas market development. Under the overseas market development reserves system, 1 percent of the value of total exports can be deducted from taxable income for tax-free reserves, and after a two-year grace period, the amount is evenly spread over the following three years and added to taxable income. The export loss reserve system worked on a similar basis except for the method of calculating the maximum reserve amount. Under this system, the reserve amount could not exceed the lesser of either 1 percent of the total export value or 50 percent of the profit from export business.

In 1977, another tax-free reserve system—reserves for price fluctuation—was added to the list of tax incentives for export promotion. The maximum amount that can be reserved for taxable income deduction is 5 percent of the inventory asset value at the end of the accounting period. The reserved amount is added to the taxable income after a one-year grace period.

Finally, export incentives have been provided in the form of a special depreciation system. Although the special depreciation system first became effective in 1962, export industries began to receive special benefits from this system in 1963. Machinery and equipment directly employed for foreign-exchange-earnings activities could be depreciated at rates 30 percent higher than the corresponding statutory depreciation rates. In 1967, two different special depreciation rates were applied to the export share of total sales. If the share was greater than or equal to 50 percent, a 30 percent special depreciation was allowed, whereas if the share was less than 50 percent, the applicable rate was 15 percent. In 1971, the special depreciation rate for firms whose export shares were less than 50 percent was calculated by applying the formula, 30 percent × export share × 2.

Beginning in the early 1970s, however, the government tried to reduce the scope of export incentives. The above-mentioned replacement of the 50 percent corporate tax exemption by two tax-free reserves in 1973 was the most significant change in this direction. In 1975, the system of prior tariff exemptions on imported inputs used in export production was changed to a drawback system.

Tax Incentives for Key Industries

Since the creation of the modern corporate tax system in 1949 and onward, a generous tax holiday was provided for the industries deemed "important" to national economic development. Such important industries were mostly heavy industries such as shipbuilding, machinery, basic metal, petrochemicals, and chemical fertilizers. The major tax reforms of 1967 replaced the tax-holiday incentive with an investment tax credit system, while generally maintaining the list of the privileged sectors. From the early 1970s, incentives for heavy industrialization were reinforced. In 1972, to cope with the serious economic recession, an extensive set of investment incentives was introduced. It was not, however, a pure counter-cyclical measure; instead, it reflected the strong commitment of the policymakers to heavy industrialization. In 1974, there was a major tax reform, under which all major incentives to promote key industries were unified and rearranged under the title of "special tax treatment for key industries" in the Tax Exemption and Reduction Control Law (TERCL). The special treatment provided three optional sets of incentives—tax holidays, investment tax credit, and special depreciation—to qualified firms in the selected heavy industries. Another major tax reform was implemented in 1981, which abolished the tax-holiday option altogether and limited eligibility for the investment tax credit option to the machinery and electronic industries. Hence, the special depreciation system became the most important source of incentive measures for key industries.

Tax Holiday

A very generous tax-holiday system was introduced with the enactment of the Corporation Tax Law in 1949. Under this system, selected industries were classified into one of two groups, and two different tax-holiday schedules were applied. To the first group, which included oil refining, steel, shipbuilding, iron and steel making, copper refining, cement manufacturing, and chemical manufacturing industries, a five-year corporate tax exemption of 100 percent was provided. The second group, to which a three-year corporate tax exemption of 100 percent was given, included most of the mining industries and plate-glass manufacturing.

Since then the tax-holiday system underwent several changes. The levels of benefit were substantially reduced in 1954, and later, in the early 1960s, the mix of the two industrial groups was rearranged. In 1963 the benefit to the first group was reinforced by lengthening the 100 percent exemption period to four years. This was later followed by the extensive revision of the Corporate Tax Law in 1967, which completely abolished the tax holidays for the key industries.

However, a few exceptions were still allowed from time to time, by providing tax holidays to such industries as the livestock-breeding industry in 1969 and the naphtha cracking plants in 1970.

Investment Tax Credit

The investment tax credit system became effective in 1968 as part of the tax reform package of 1967. A 6 percent investment tax credit was given to qualified firms operating in selected industries. The eligible industries were shipbuilding, steel and iron, chemical fertilizer, synthetic fiber, automobile, machinery, straw pulp, food processing, petrochemicals, electronic equipment, electrical machinery and equipment, construction, and some mining industries. The introduction of this system was to replace the tax holiday provided under the old tax law. Since tax holidays generally do not influence the level of investment in the replacement or expansion of production facilities, they may have some distortionary effects on the behavior of firms. In this sense, the introduction of investment tax credits was an improvement, but the actual benefit level was substantially reduced.

In 1970, the TERCL provided a 6 to 10 percent investment tax credit for machinery and equipment investment to the iron and steel manufacturing industries, with the higher rate being applied to larger firms. With the tax reform of 1974, which went into effect in the following year, the 6 percent investment tax credit provided by the Corporation Tax Law and the 6 to 10 percent investment tax credit provided by the TERCL were both replaced by "special tax treatment for key industries," as discussed in detail below.

Tax Incentives under the Presidential Emergency Decree of 1972

For the first time in Korea's modern history of taxation, tax incentives were employed as the centerpiece of the countercyclical investment promotion policy as mandated by the Presidential Emergency Decree for the Stabilization and Growth of the Economy of 1972.

A 10 percent temporary investment tax credit was granted for investments using domestic capital goods manufactured before the end of 1974. At the same time, a special depreciation in the range of 40 percent to 80 percent was allowed for fixed assets directly employed by firms in the key industries. The incentives provided by the Presidential Emergency Decree were absorbed by the "special tax treatment for key industries" clause in the TERCL, and the special depreciation system was provided by the enforcement decree of the corporation tax law of 1975.

Special Tax Treatment for Key Industries

The special tax treatment for key industries, first introduced by an article in the TERCL at the end of 1974, replaced most of the major industry-specific incentives provided by the corporation tax law, by the Presidential Emergency Decree of 1972, and by the old TERCL.

Under the new system, eligible firms were given the right to choose one of the following three sets of incentives: (1) a tax holiday of five years, 100 percent tax exemption for the first three years, and 50 percent exemption for the ensuing two years; (2) an investment tax credit of 8 percent for machinery and equipment investment (10 percent for investments using domestic capital goods); or (3) a 100 percent special depreciation. The supported key industries included petrochemicals, shipbuilding, machinery, electronics, iron and steel. Furthermore, in place of the special depreciation provided under the Presidential Emergency Decree, a uniform 60 percent special depreciation was offered to firms that did not qualify for the three optional benefits but were investing in machinery and equipment in the iron and steel, petrochemicals, shipbuilding, and other industries, that is, chemical-fiber, chemical-pulp, marine food processing, and other food processing.

Although the tax reform of 1981 retained the basic framework of the special tax treatment for key industries, it introduced substantial alterations into the system. First, some industries were deleted from the beneficiary list. Second, the method of providing incentives was changed. The investment tax credit option was no longer confined to the machinery and electronics industries. At the same time, the investment tax credit rate was reduced to 6 percent (10 percent for investments using domestic capital goods) from 8 percent. For most of the beneficiaries, therefore, the 100 percent special depreciation system became the only available option. This reform went into effect in 1982, and as a transitory measure, the 100 percent special depreciation was reinforced by a 5 percent investment reserve for that year only, as described previously. In 1983, the investment tax credit rate was halved to 3 percent (5 percent for investments using domestic capital goods), reflecting the downward adjustment of the corporate tax rate.

Special Depreciation for Manufacturing and Construction

The special depreciation system was first incorporated into Korea's corporate tax system in 1962. Machinery and equipment that were utilized directly 16 hours or more per day, on an average, qualified for a special 20 percent depreciation. At the same time, a different type of special depreciation was provided to mining, fishing, and electrical power generation industries; this provision, however, was terminated at the end of 1962. The new type of incentive reduced the asset lifetime for tax purposes to two thirds of the statutory lifetime.

In 1969, the 16-hour, 20 percent special depreciation rule was made applicable to heavy construction equipment employed by construction firms. From 1972 on, the 16-hour condition was relaxed to 12 hours. Hence, heavy construction equipment and machinery and equipment utilized directly 12 hours or more per day could enjoy a 20 percent special depreciation as stated in the enforcement decree of the corporation tax law.

In addition, beginning in 1975, a 40 to 80 percent special depreciation was given to newly installed assets using domestic machinery and materials; this provision partly replaced the special depreciation provided by the Presidential Emergency

Decree of 1972. The 80 percent special depreciation was applied to the mining, fishing, manufacturing and construction sectors, while the 40 percent version was applied to other sectors. However, this system was discontinued at the end of 1982.

Tax Incentives for Small and Medium Firms

When preferential tax treatment is not constrained by industry specification, such a tax incentive scheme is called functional tax incentive. The functional incentive scheme is closer than the industry-specific incentive scheme to the original purpose of providing tax incentives to correct market failures arising from various causes. In recent years, Korea has seen a growing dominance of the functional tax incentive scheme over the industry-specific scheme, which implies a reduction in distortion in the operation of the market. In the following, a summary is made for two functional tax incentive schemes: tax incentives for small and medium firms (SMFs), and tax incentives for research and development (R&D).

During the 1960s and 1970s, the tax incentives geared specifically to promote SMFs were nominal. In 1968, a 30 percent special depreciation was granted to SMFs operating in the mining or manufacturing sectors for their investment in machinery and equipment. The special depreciation rate was raised to 50 percent by the tax reform implemented in 1977.

In the 1981 revision of the TERCL, which went into effect in the following year, the investment reserve system was made available to SMFs. The annual reserve limit is 15 percent of the book value of fixed business assets, as evaluated at the end of the previous accounting period. This amount is deducted from taxable income and, if after a grace period of four years the actual investment expenditures exceed the reserve amount, it is evenly spread over the following three years to be added to taxable income. If actual investment expenditures are below the reserve amount, the difference is immediately added to taxable income in the fourth year.

For a market economy to function properly, it must be competitive. Competition depends on the presence of many small firms and the absence of overwhelmingly large ones. In Korea, conglomerates have been dominant forces in domestic production and employment. Switching from the previous policy of the 1960s and 1970s under which most tax incentives were targeted at large firms to capitalize on economies of scale, the government has adopted the policy of helping people with entrepreneurial inclinations and know-how to establish themselves in independent businesses. This change in policy direction has been revealed by a series of tax incentive measures taken by the government in the early 1980s.

Tax incentives for the establishment of SMFs include those for newly organized firms and those for companies investing in newly organized firms. When SMFs are newly established in the rural districts to run business in the manufacturing, mining, construction, transportation, or fishing industries, or when SMFs are organized in technology-intensive industries, the personal income tax is exempted for the first four years and reduced to 50 percent for the subsequent two years. Furthermore, the property tax on the business assets of newly organized SMFs is reduced by 50 percent for five years, and the acquisition tax and the registration tax are reduced by 50 percent for two years.

Tax incentives for companies investing in newly organized SMFs include (1) nontaxation of capital gains; (2) tax-free reserves for investment loss; and (3) separate taxation on dividend income at a 10 percent rate. With respect to capital gains accruing from the transfer of real estate for business purposes at the time of merger, the personal income tax and the special surtax on corporate income are waived.

EFFECTIVE TAX RATES AND COST OF CAPITAL

Computing the benefits of tax incentives and evaluating the extent of their effectiveness are not easy tasks. The benefits of tax incentives can be measured in terms of tax concessions per unit of tax revenue collected, benefit per dollar invested, effective tax rates, and cost of capital. Of course, since all these measurements are interrelated with each other, one can be translated into another.

Tax Expenditures and Benefits from Tax Incentives

A yearly amount of tax exemption and reduction, usually called tax expenditures under the provision of TERCL and other tax laws in Korea, is summarized in Table 14.1.[2] Although the trend is not smooth throughout the whole period covered, tax expenditures as a percentage of tax revenue collected have been declining. The share of tax exemption and reduction in the national tax revenue collected de-

Table 14.1
Estimates of Tax Exemption and Reduction (in 100 million won and percent)

	National Taxes			Local Taxes		
Years	Tax Revenue (A)	Tax Exemption and Reduction (B)	B/A	Tax Revenue (A)	Tax Exemption and Reduction (B)	B/A
1970	3.648	1.457	30.3	.332	n.a.	n.a.
1975	13.910	4.636	28.0	1.588	n.a.	n.a.
1980	58.077	7.657	14.7	7.677	1.084	14.1
1981	72.579	9.157	14.3	9.144	1.379	15.1
1982	83.964	10.470	14.3	11.192	1.240	11.1
1983	100.507	8.304	9.7	13.972	1.727	12.4
1984	108.997	7.899	8.6	15.084	1.506	10.0
1985	118.764	10.668	11.8	16.546	1.400	8.5

Sources: Ministry of Finance and Ministry of Home Affairs

Table 14.2

Net Benefit from Tax Incentives per One Dollar Invested in Machinery by Firms in Typical Key Industries (Manufacturing) for Selected Years

Year[a]	Discount[b] Rate	Tax[c] Rate	20% (80%)[d,e] Special Depreciation	Tax Holiday	Incentives for Key Industries[d,e]			Total[e,f]
					Special Depreciation	Investment Reserves	Investment	
1963	.525	.20	.008	.185	--	--	--	.186
1968	.560	.45	.017	--	--	--	.060	.077
1970	.498	.45	.018	--	--	--	.060	.078
1973	.333	.40	.056	--	--	--	.060	.116(.156)
1976	.405	.40	.017(0.55)	.367	.065	--	.080(.100)	.369(.374)
1982	.305	.38	.016(0.55)	--	.062	.034	.060(.100)	.096(.096;.153*)
1983	.258	.33	.014	--	.052	--	.030(.050)	.052(.052;.064*)

Source: Kwack (1984c).

[a]The selected years are when major tax reforms were effected.
[b]Curb market interest rate is used as a proxy for discount rate.
[c]Surtaxes to the corporation tax are not considered.
[d]Assumed asset lifetime for tax purposes is 11 years and assumed economic depreciation rate is 11%.
[e]The figures in parentheses represent the benefit of investment made with domestically produced machinery. Incentives for export promotion are not considered.
[f]Interactions and overlappings of incentives are taken into account when the figures in the Total column are calculated. The figures with asterisks are applicable to the machinery or electronic industries.

creased drastically from about 30 percent in the early 1970s to about 10 percent in the mid-1980s. There was a decrease in the absolute amount of tax expenditures in 1983 and 1984 for national taxes and in 1982, 1984, and 1985 for local taxes.[3]

Table 14.2 shows the net benefits from various tax incentives for one dollar of investment for those years during which the major tax reforms were effective. Several interesting features are observed. First, tax incentives rendered the highest benefit during the latter half of the 1970s, as shown in the last column of Table 14.2. Among the types of preferential tax treatment for key industries provided by TERCL, the tax-holiday option generated the highest support. In fact, one of the main reasons for the 1981 tax reform was to terminate this option. Third, the recent decrease in the interest rate and the statutory corporate tax rate has drastically reduced the benefits of tax incentives.

Effective Tax Rates

In order to examine the role various tax incentives have played in allocating resources among industrial sectors, it is necessary to calculate the effective tax rate by sector. Using a modified version of the effective tax rate formula by D. W. Jorgenson and M. A. Sullivan (Hulten, 1981), Taewon Kwack (1984c) estimated the effective tax rate by sector, as shown in Table 14.3. According to the estimation,

Table 14.3
Effective Marginal Tax Rates by Sector (in percent)

		1973	1975	1978	1980	1981	1982	1983
Processed Food, Beverage & Tobacco		50.6	55.1	42.8	46.7	57.1	58.6	39.5
Textile, Leather, Paper & Printing		49.8	54.3	42.1	46.1	56.2	57.6	38.7
Construction Materials		50.3	54.6	42.8	46.5	56.6	58.1	39.7
Chemical Products	(General)	48.9	54.2	41.1	45.3	55.8	57.1	37.6
	(Special)	46.3	38.8	29.5	32.0	42.4	50.8	34.8
Basic Metal &	(General)	49.0	53.2	41.9	45.5	55.0	56.4	38.1
Metal Products	(Special)	46.9	38.7	31.0	32.9	42.6	50.8	35.8
Machinery, Electrical	(General)	49.3	53.7	42.0	45.8	55.6	57.0	38.4
& Electronic Equip.	(Special)	47.1	39.1	30.9	33.0	43.0	51.2	36.0
Statutory Maximum Tax Rates		40.0	40.0	40.0	40.0	40.0	38.0	33.0
Inflation Rates in Capital Goods Market (3 Year Moving Average)		17.0	33.7	8.2	19.4	24.3	21.5	9.7

Source: Kwack (1984b)

Notes:"General" rates are applicable to firms which are not qualified to get the special tax treatment and the "Special" rates are for qualified firms.

which incorporated a detailed account of Korea's complicated tax incentives over time, the relative size of the incentives provided for the key industries was substantial, particularly so during the latter half of the 1970s.

Table 14.3 also shows that a typical Korean firm has been paying corporate income taxes at an extremely high effective rate in spite of the complicated and numerous tax incentives. It should be noted that the effective tax rate is affected not only by the statutory tax rate and tax incentives but also by the discount rate and the inflation rate. The major reason for the high effective tax rate in Korea is the high inflation in the capital goods market and the tax depreciation system based on historical cost.[4]

Cost of Capital

One very common and accepted method of examining the effects of tax incentives on corporate investment behavior is to estimate the marginal cost of capital.

Table 14.4
Cost of Capital by Type of Asset and a Measure of Distortion (all industries)

	Estimated Cost of Capital				Neutral Cost of Capital[a]		Measure of Distortion[b]	
	Buildings & Construction	Machinery & Equipment	Transportation Equipment	All Assets	Machinery & Equipment	All Assets	Machinery & Equipment	All Assets
1963	.365	.426	.430	.391	.546	.507	-.120	-.116
1964	.392	.423	.448	.407	.585	.556	-.162	-.149
1965	.484	.517	.564	.502	.578	.545	-.061	-.043
1966	.529	.601	.717	.600	.597	.546	.004	.054
1967	.497	.581	.694	.578	.595	.536	-.014	.042
1968	.524	.589	.669	.582	.591	.533	-.002	.049
1969	.570	.649	.742	.657	.552	.491	.097	.166
1970	.491	.603	.665	.586	.539	.466	.064	.120
1971	.438	.541	.612	.529	.508	.440	.033	.089
1972	.297	.401	.488	.402	.422	.362	-.021	.040
1973	.223	.300	.415	.305	.330	.285	-.030	.020
1974	.265	.324	.414	.330	.362	.327	-.038	.003
1975	.314	.371	.489	.394	.349	.316	.022	.078
1976	.309	.385	.495	.392	.371	.328	.014	.064
1977	.263	.371	.496	.376	.369	.315	.002	.061
1978	.263	.416	.542	.408	.420	.351	-.004	.057
1979	.239	.429	.551	.398	.437	.345	-.008	.053
1980	.234	.414	.524	.380	.442	.353	-.028	.027
1981	.168	.318	.419	.296	.333	.261	-.015	.035
1982	.239	.375	.462	.350	.308	.240	.067	.110
1983	.176	.297	.384	.278	.277	.218	.020	.060

Source: Choi et al. (1985).
[a]Real discount rate and economic depreciation rate.
[b]Estimated cost of capital minus neutral cost of capital.

There are several different approaches to deriving a cost-of-capital formula for a given economy using a specific type of financial and tax system.

Using the Hall-Jorgenson scheme of the cost of capital, Kwack developed a cost-of-capital formula applicable to the Korean economy. Based on the assumption that the financial resources have been allocated efficiently through the perfectly competitive curb market, his model incorporates not only tax incentives such as tax holidays, tax credit, and tax-free reserves, but also other unique features of the Korean economy including the collateral loan system and export loan system.[5]

An empirical estimation of the cost of capital by Kwack is presented in Table 14.4, which shows the trends of the cost of capital by type of asset, a proxy for the neutral cost of capital and a measure of distortion due to tax incentives. The estimated results reveal several interesting features. The absolute level of the cost of capital is rather high, mainly due to the assumption that the curb market is efficient and that firms resort to the curb market for their financing of investments at the margin. Among the types of investment assets, the estimated cost of capital is highest in transportation equipment, while the lowest is in building and construction.

The degree of distortion due to the tax system can be measured by the difference between the estimated cost of capital and neutral or distortion-free cost of capital, where the latter is, by definition, the discount rate plus economic depreciation minus the expected inflation rate. One salient feature of Table 14.4 is that the tax incentive system provided substantial support for investment in machinery and equipment in the early 1960s, the 1972–74 period and the 1978–81 period, as shown by the negative figures of tax distortion. With the introduction of the 1981 tax reform, effective in 1982, tax distortion rose substantially.

Effects of Export Tax Incentives

While Korea's export takeoff started from an unusually low base, and was supported by a general expansion of world trade, it would not have been possible without decisive and innovative policies. These included a rationalized exchange regime, strong tax incentives, selective import liberalization, directed credit, and a host of finely tuned, export-promoting schemes. Any proper investigation into the effects of government policy on exports should take into account not only tax incentives but also other policy instruments.

In a recent study, Kwack evaluated the effectiveness of export incentives in promoting exports. One notable aspect of his study is that he provides a base for comparing effects of tax incentives, as explained in some detail above, with those of financial incentives. Kwack based his estimates of the effects of export incentives on the concept of cost of capital, as shown in Table 14.5. The effects of the tax and financial incentives are measured by variations in cost of capital when the incentives are individually or jointly introduced. The first four columns of Table 14.5 show the cost of capital based on alternative assumptions about the nature of

Table 14.5
Effects of Export Incentives: Cost of Capital (in percent)

Year	Reference Case [A]	All Incentives [B]	Financial Only [C]	Tax Only [D]	[A-B]	[A-C]	[A-D]
1960	40.61	22.58	20.80	38.41	18.02	19.80	2.20
1961	35.87	28.40	26.74	34.76	7.47	9.13	1.11
1962	35.78	24.95	23.63	34.83	10.38	12.15	0.95
1963	42.11	29.98	28.57	39.67	12.13	13.54	2.44
1964	42.56	32.73	29.26	38.21	9.83	13.30	4.36
1965	53.35	38.90	35.71	46.63	14.45	17.64	6.71
1966	63.44	46.89	42.29	53.58	16.55	21.15	9.87
1967	60.03	38.57	34.76	52.48	21.46	25.27	7.55
1968	62.29	37.39	31.95	51.74	24.90	30.34	10.55
1969	66.15	40.03	35.12	53.51	26.11	31.03	12.64
1970	61.85	35.08	30.35	50.74	25.77	31.51	11.11
1971	58.03	33.46	28.81	47.83	24.58	29.22	10.21
1972	42.96	29.28	25.25	37.36	13.68	17.71	5.60
1973	33.29	23.23	24.59	31.15	10.05	8.70	2.13
1974	35.28	21.97	23.23	32.88	13.31	12.05	2.40
1975	42.47	27.50	29.26	39.46	14.97	13.31	3.01
1976	44.94	30.85	32.73	41.85	14.09	12.21	3.09
1977	45.85	32.65	34.64	42.77	13.20	11.21	3.08
1978	54.03	35.88	37.92	50.45	18.15	16.11	3.57
1979	56.08	34.58	36.59	52.29	21.51	19.58	3.79
1980	52.38	32.35	34.11	48.96	20.02	18.27	3.42
1981	38.19	26.07	27.62	35.67	12.12	10.57	2.52
1982	48.09	35.10	36.84	45.48	12.99	11.25	2.60
1983	37.00	30.36	31.66	35.37	6.64	5.34	1.62
1984	35.83	29.93	31.22	34.26	5.90	4.61	1.56
1985	34.89	29.00	30.24	33.37	5.89	4.65	1.52
1986	33.84	28.40	29.62	32.37	5.44	4.22	1.47

Source: Kwack (1988).

export incentives, while the last three represent the historical effects of export incentives. The first of the last three columns shows the aggregate effects of both tax and financial incentives because it represents the difference in the cost of capital without either tax or financial incentives, and the cost of capital with both. Likewise, the second-to-last column shows the partial effects of financial incentives, and the last column shows the partial effects of tax incentives.

Several interesting features can be observed from Table 14.5. First, measured in terms of the cost-of-capital effects, the export sector has been enjoying substantial benefits from the export incentive scheme. Second, the most lavish provision of export incentives was during the 1960s and 1970s, while the effects of the export promotion scheme were notably reduced. Third, the tax incentives to promote exports have played only a minor role, while financial incentives have assumed a major role in the export-led development process, as a comparison of the last two columns shows. The relatively strong effects of the tax incentives during the early 1970s was due to the existence of tax-free reserves. Fourth, the fact that in the 1960s the effects of the financial incentives were greater than the total effect means that, in that period, the tax incentives had actually had a negative effect on export promotion.

INDIRECT TAXES AND RESOURCE ALLOCATION

Indirect taxes have an impact on the sectoral allocation of investment through differences in tax burdens and variations in relative price effects among sectors. Table 14.6 shows an estimate by Kwack (1984a) of average indirect tax rates by sectors and the effects of indirect taxes on the relative price structure, based on the input-output table.

As the first three columns of Table 14.6 show, industries with low indirect tax rates are primary, textile and related products, chemical products, construction materials, basic metals and metal products, general machinery, and other manufac-

Table 14.6
Average Indirect Tax Rates by Sector
and Their Effects on the Relative Price Structure

	Indirect Tax Rate			Relative Price Effects		
	1973	1975	1980	1973	1975	1980
1. Primary	.0047	.0045	.0042	1.0247	1.0227	1.0223
2. Processed Food	.1018	.1369	.1475	1.1486	1.1827	1.1731
3. Textile & Leather	.0126	.0245	.0180	1.0711	1.0744	1.0360
4. Chemicals (Coal & Petroleum excluded)	.0129	-.0101	.0247	1.0878	1.0410	1.0575
5. Construction Mat.	.0188	.0296	.0249	1.0798	1.0783	0.9998
6. Basic Metal & Met. Products	.0077	.0151	.0064	1.0755	1.0751	0.9953
7. General Machinery	.0063	.0189	.0268	1.0592	1.0664	1.0497
8. Electrical Equipment	.0387	.1150	.0665	1.0999	1.1799	1.0805
9. Electronic Equipment	.0400	.0714	.0397	1.0974	1.1357	1.0713
10. Transportation Equip.	.0483	.0417	.0574	1.1057	1.0896	1.0758
11. Other Manufacturing	.0113	.0256	.0232	1.0657	1.0703	1.0419
12. Coal & Petroleum Products	.1291	.1214	.0702	1.2014	1.1820	1.0905
13. Electricity & Gas	.1245	.0510	.0220	1.2250	1.1333	0.7463
14. Constructing	.0065	.0127	.0551	1.0538	1.0584	1.0624
15. S.O.C. and Other Service	.0467	.0255	.0167	1.0813	1.0538	1.0071

Source: Kwack (1984a).

turing, while the sectors with relatively high indirect tax rates are processed food, electrical equipment, and coal and petroleum products.

The estimated results of the relative price effects of Korea's indirect tax system,[6] shown in the last three columns, clearly indicate that indirect taxes in Korea have played a noticeable role in affecting the relative price structure.

In 1973 and 1975, before the value-added tax was introduced, the relative price effect did not show much variation, except for the processed food industry, the consumer durable goods sector (such as electrical and electronic equipment industries), and the energy sector (such as coal products and electricity and gas). Due mainly to the VAT refund on the purchase of capital goods, the uneven effect of indirect taxes on the relative price structure became significant. Throughout the whole period under investigation, the relative price effect of indirect taxes is most notable in the processed food sector, to which the alcoholic beverage industry belongs. The indirect tax system in Korea embodies the will of the government to curtail expenditures on sumptuous goods such as alcoholic beverages and high-priced consumer durables.

CONCLUDING REMARKS

The characteristics of Korea's fiscal policy during the industrialization period include a relatively small public sector, adherence to a balanced budget, comparatively low taxes, liberal use of tax incentives for investments, heavy reliance on indirect taxes, little significance of property taxes, increased public saving, relatively little spending for redistributive social services, and the budgeting of scarce resources for industrial development.

Long before supply-side economics gained a prominence in theoretical and policy discussions, Korea had practiced the policy implied in supply-side economics. The fact that the fiscal policy in Korea was geared to the policy line of supply-side economics is borne out by the low share of tax and expenditures in GNP, heavy reliance on indirect consumption tax, extensive tax incentives for saving and investment, and less emphasis on welfare spending.

The most important aspect of the tax policy in Korea in connection with her rapid industrialization has been the tax incentive system. The Korean government has applied various tax incentives to induce the private sector to engage in economic activities that seem desirable for industrial development and export growth. Most enterprises have engaged in heavy and chemical industries, and export industries have benefited from these tax incentives.

The question arises as to whether and in what respect the lessons of the Korean experience in tax policies can be transferred to other countries, developed or developing. Although Korea's success in industrialization cannot be attributed to tax policy alone, the Korean experiences do deserve further attention. There has been less appreciation of the role of tax policy in the development of Korean economy mainly because not much has been written in English about its role.

NOTES

1. See Choi (1988) and Choi et al. (1985) for detailed discussion of the current structure and historical development of tax incentives in Korea.

2. Since the Korean government has not adopted the tax expenditure budget officially, the figures in Table 14.1 are not necessarily exact to a theoretical extent.

3. For more details of tax expenditures in Korea, see Choi (1988).

4. It should be noted that the model on which the estimation of the cost of capital is based assumes that firms, at the margin, rely on the curb market for their investment financing. Because, in general, firms depend on multiple sources for financing their investments, the assumption that investments are financed through the curb market is somewhat vulnerable. However, in characterizing the investment and financing behavior of Korean firms in the 1960s and 1970s, the assumption made by Kwack can be reasonably justified. First of all, most firms actually relied on the curb market to finance investments even though they also used other financial means. Furthermore, the neoclassical concept of marginal cost of capital is defined on the assumption of perfect financial market. In Korea the curb market can be regarded as an efficient market, though not perfect.

5. The estimation of the cost of capital is based on a rather complicated formula, which incorporates not only the tax system but also the financial system in Korea. For details see Choi et al. (1985, pp. 71–92).

6. The relative price effect is calculated from input-output data based on the following equation:

$$P = \left\{(C^{-1} - A') + (V - I)C - (V - I)DB'(C^{-1} - A')^{-1}\right\}P*$$

where

P is the relative price vector;
C is a diagonal matrix where diagonal elements are (1 + commodity tax rate) of each sector;
A' is the transpose of the domestic I-O coefficient matrix;
V is a diagonal matrix whose diagonal elements are (1 + VAT rate) of each sector;
I is an identity matrix;
D is a diagonal matrix whose ith element is (K_i/Q_i), the marginal capital output ratio of the ith sector;
B is a capital coefficient matrix;
$P*$ is the vector of value added ratio.

The commodity tax refers to all indirect taxes other than VAT. The first term

$(C^{-1} - A')^{-1}P*$ is the relative price vector when there is no VAT. The second term $(V - I)CP*$ is the VAT effect. VAT is levied on the output price, which includes other indirect taxes. The last and most complicated term reflects the VAT return on the purchase of capital goods.

REFERENCES

Choi, Kwang, *The Tax Expenditure Budget and Fiscal Management* (in Korean), Seoul: The Korean Society of Public Finance, March 1988.
————, et al., *Public Policy, Corporate Finance and Investment: The Experiences of Japan, Korea and Taiwan*, Tokyo: Institute of Developing Economies, 1985.
Hulten, Charles R., ed., *Depreciation, Inflation and Taxation of Income from Capital*, Washington, D.C.: The Urban Institute, 1981.
Kwack, Taewon (1984a), *Industrial Restructuring Experience and Policies in Korea in the 1970s*, Working Paper 84-08, Korea Development Institute, August 1984.
———— (1984b), "Budget Policies and Investment Allocation," in K. Choi and J. W. Kim, eds., *National Budget: Goals and Priorities* (in Korean), Seoul: Korea Development Institute, 1984.
———— (1984c), "Investment Incentives in Korean Tax System and Their Economic Effects," in K. Choi, ed., *Tax Reforms in Korea: Major Issues and New Direction* (in Korean), Seoul: Korea Development Institute, 1984.
————, "Public Finance, Trade and Economic Development: The Role of Fiscal Incentives in Korea's Export-led Economic Growth," Paper presented at the 44th Congress of the International Institute of Public Finance, Istanbul, August 1988.
Ministry of Finance, *History of Korean Tax System* (in Korean), Seoul, 1979.

15

Government Spending and Economic Growth

Jisoon Lee

INTRODUCTION

The Korean economy has undergone a rapid growth process in the last 40 years, especially since the early sixties. The fact that the per capita income, which was $67 in 1953, has grown to $3,098 by 1987 clearly attests to this phenomenon.[1] During the same period the importance of the economic activities performed by the government sector has also rapidly increased. One indication of this is the growth of the share of government spending in GNP. It was less than 11 percent in 1953, but it had risen to the 20 percent level by 1986.

Faced with the above observations one might ask whether there exists any meaningful relationship between economic growth and government spending. This study is an attempt to get answers to that question. First, the basic "facts" concerning government spending activities in Korea since 1953 will be summarized. This is to clearly lay out the basic patterns of government spending to be explained.

With the basic facts thus summarized, this study will then investigate the relationship between economic growth on one hand and the relative size and composition of government spending on the other hand. The investigation is carried out by setting up a simple endogenous growth model and testing its implications.

The model adopted in this study is an extension of the neoclassical growth model of Solow. The extension made here is to include government spending as arguments in utility and production functions of the agents. Government spending is divided into public consumption and public investment. The former enters into the utility function and the latter enters into the production function. The model, thus, is an extension of the models of Bailey (1971) and Barro (1981). It is also related to the recent works by Romer (1986) and Lucas (1988) in that all three models consider the case of increasing returns to scale as a mechanism to generate endogenous

persistent growth. In this study there exist increasing returns to scale because of
the public good aspects of government investment spending.[2] The model predicts
that growth rate in per capita income is negatively correlated with the share of
government spending in GNP when it is in some well-defined sense "too" large
and it is positively correlated with the share of government spending going to public
investment.

The study finds that government spending in Korea has the following patterns.
First, the importance of the government sector in the national economy has grown
rapidly during the period. This is true both absolutely and relatively. The average
annual growth rate of real government spending during the period has been
9.0 percent. The average annual growth rate in real GNP, on the other hand, has
been 7.6 percent. As a result the share of government spending in GNP, which is
one measure of the relative importance of the government, has also grown from
10.9 percent in 1953 to 20.2 percent in 1986.

Second, as shares of GNP, both consumption and investment components of
government spending have substantially risen in this period. However, there has
been a shift from investment-oriented government spending toward consumption-
oriented spending from about 1970. That is, the share of consumption components
in total government spending has been rising since 1970.

Third, the functional classification of government spending shows that defense,
education, and economic services have been the three largest spending items. Their
relative shares have more or less remained unchanged during this period. The share
for general administration, however, has been declining in recent years, while the
share of welfare spending has been growing.

Fourth, the division of government spending into central and local governments'
spending shows that the central government in Korea spends more than four times
as much as the combined local governments do. This division has remained
unchanged throughout the period and does not show any trend movement.

Fifth, an international comparison of government spending patterns reveals that
in Korea, (1) the relative size of government is still very small, (2) government
spending is more investment oriented, (3) government activities involving direct
income transfers have been weak, (4) the government has been actively engaged
in providing various economic services to the private sector, and (5) government
spending is very much centralized.

The empirical investigations performed in this study indicate that economic
growth rates are indeed negatively correlated with the share of government spending in GNP and positively correlated with the share of public investment in GNP
(or in total government spending). The negative correlation between the share of
government spending and growth rates appears to be a long-run phenomenon.
There is also an indication that the relative size of government spending affects the
growth performance, but not vice versa.

The organization of the study is as follows. First, the basic patterns of government spending in Korea since 1953 are summarized. A brief international comparison of spending patterns is also made in that section. Next, a simple growth model in which government spending is an essential element determining the dynamic growth path of the economy is proposed. The next section contains the empirical results of the study, and the final section concludes the study.

PATTERNS OF SPENDING

The Overall Size of the Government

There could be many different ways of measuring the size of a government. This study used the absolute amounts of government spending and their relative shares in GNP as alternative measures for the size of a government. Here the size of a government is an indicator of how important the government sector is in the overall economy.

Table 15.1 and Figure 15.1 summarize the time series patterns of the variable "government spending/GNP" based on National Income and Product Accounts. They reveal that there exist both trend and cyclical movements in the series. The long-run trend is clearly a rising one. In 1953 the share of government spending in the GNP was 10.9 percent, whereas in 1986 it rose to 20.2 percent. This rising share indicates that government spending on the average has been growing much more rapidly than have other components of the GNP.

The rise in the share of government spending in GNP, however, has not been monotone. Instead, there have been three long cycles in the series. As can be seen from Figure 15.1, the relative size of the government rose very rapidly after the Korean War: it rose from 10.9 percent in 1953 to 22.4 percent in 1961. This rapid rise seems to reflect the fact that government spending rose substantially throughout the 1950s despite the slow growth in the overall economy. It appears that this increase was largely due to the rapid expansion of the basic apparatus of government. Since 1961, however, the share declined rapidly to 13.6 percent in 1964. This decline was due to a decline in the absolute amount of real government spending during 1963 and 1964. It is an indication that the government at that time was more concerned with stabilizing the economy.

The second cycle, measured from one trough to the next one, runs from 1964 to 1973. Its peak level was 19.6 percent recorded in 1968, and it was 12.9 percent at the trough of 1973. During this period government spending grew initially much more rapidly than the other components of GNP as a result of rapid increases in public investment spending. However, from 1972 to 1973 the absolute amount of real government spending fell as public investment spending activities became moderate. This, coupled with the robust expansion of the overall economy during the period, has contributed to a reduction in the share of government spending.

The third cycle runs from 1973, and there are indications that the cycle was still

Figure 15.1
Share of Government Spending in GNP

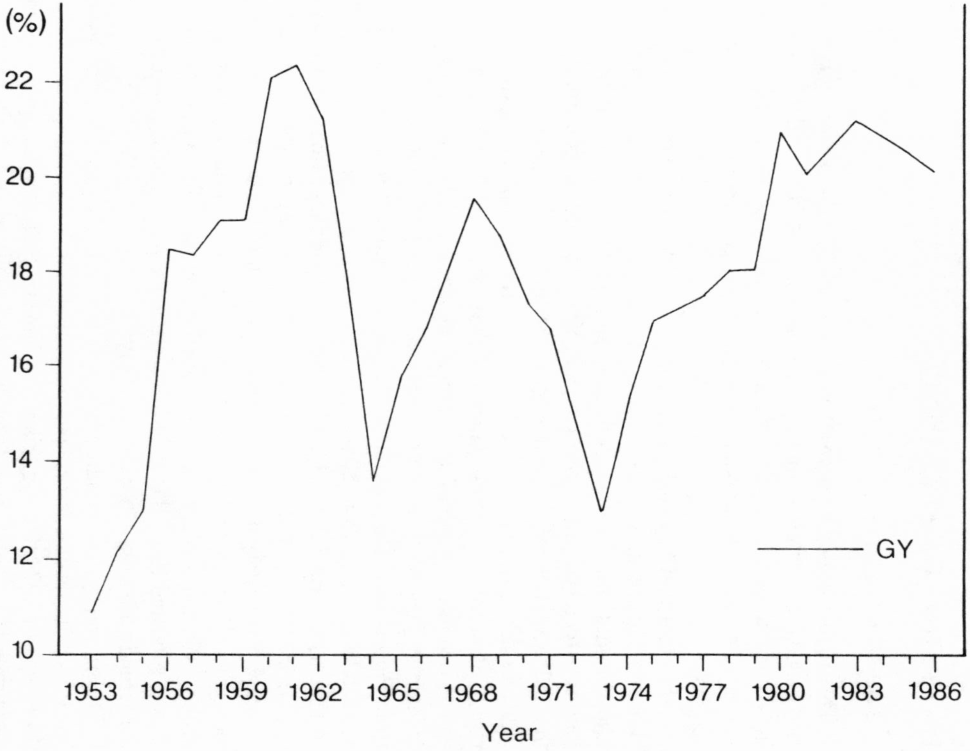

Table 15.1
Share of Government Spending in GNP (in percent)

Year	GCY	SBY	SUBY	TRY	CY	GIY	TRCY	IY	NLY	GY
1953	7.89	0.46	0.04	0.00	8.40	0.77	0.15	0.92	1.55	10.86
1954	10.24	0.57	0.08	0.00	10.89	1.72	0.41	2.13	-0.91	12.11
1955	8.82	0.46	0.68	0.13	10.10	2.00	0.35	2.35	0.54	12.99
1956	9.16	0.43	0.88	0.06	10.53	2.09	0.36	2.45	0.55	18.50
1957	10.83	0.73	0.75	0.07	12.37	4.08	0.59	4.68	1.30	18.36
1958	12.77	0.77	0.15	0.08	13.77	3.56	1.10	4.66	0.67	19.09
1959	14.18	0.56	0.04	0.11	14.90	3.76	0.89	4.64	-0.43	19.11
1960	14.51	0.98	0.11	0.17	15.76	3.35	0.67	4.01	0.23	22.11
1961	13.62	1.35	0.71	0.12	15.80	3.74	0.76	4.50	0.21	22.38
1962	13.95	1.14	0.63	0.05	15.76	4.32	0.40	4.72	0.76	21.25
1963	13.88	1.13	0.17	0.04	12.21	3.71	0.28	3.99	1.45	17.69
1964	8.52	0.78	0.15	0.03	9.48	2.52	0.13	2.65	1.47	13.60
1965	9.29	0.81	0.00	0.05	10.15	3.20	0.18	3.38	2.15	15.68
1966	9.97	0.92	0.04	0.05	10.99	4.44	0.53	4.97	0.74	16.70
1967	10.16	1.01	0.62	0.04	11.27	4.70	0.49	5.20	1.69	18.16
1968	10.44	1.08	0.13	0.04	11.69	6.16	0.50	6.66	1.28	19.63
1969	10.24	1.12	0.16	0.03	11.56	7.62	0.50	8.12	-0.91	18.77
1970	9.53	0.95	0.27	0.02	10.77	5.35	0.54	5.89	0.76	17.42
1971	9.84	1.06	0.36	0.01	11.27	5.21	0.53	5.74	-0.25	16.76
1972	9.87	1.21	0.41	0.01	11.51	4.58	0.69	5.27	-1.99	14.79
1973	8.37	1.21	0.42	0.00	10.00	3.54	0.58	4.12	-1.20	12.92
1974	9.09	1.51	2.02	0.00	12.63	3.57	1.20	4.78	-2.08	15.33
1975	11.14	0.74	1.64	0.19	13.71	3.36	0.48	3.84	-0.58	16.97
1976	11.01	0.65	1.42	0.18	13.26	3.11	0.46	3.57	0.43	17.26
1977	10.83	0.81	1.45	0.20	13.28	3.51	0.66	4.18	0.44	17.51
1978	10.45	0.79	1.37	0.21	12.83	3.85	0.64	4.49	0.74	18.05
1979	9.95	1.06	1.29	0.29	12.60	4.30	1.12	5.43	0.05	18.08
1980	11.64	1.31	1.07	0.27	14.28	4.53	0.92	5.44	1.29	21.01
1981	11.93	1.34	0.92	0.31	14.50	4.26	1.00	5.26	0.34	20.10
1982	12.05	1.55	0.83	0.33	14.75	4.59	0.96	5.55	0.36	20.66
1983	11.45	1.51	0.85	0.30	14.11	4.66	0.99	5.65	1.46	21.23
1984	10.66	1.56	0.92	0.34	13.47	4.79	0.89	5.68	1.73	20.87
1985	10.84	1.64	0.72	0.35	13.54	4.70	1.05	5.76	1.25	20.54
1986	10.89	1.48	0.69	0.38	13.45	3.97	0.88	4.85	1.87	20.17

Source: Bank of Korea, *National Income Accounts*, various issues.

Note: Shares in GNP. GC = Final Consumption of Gov't; SB = Social Security Payments; SUB = Current Subsidies; TR = Current Transfers; C = Total Gov't Consumption; GI = Fixed Capital Formation by Gov't; TRC = Capital Transfers by Gov't; I = Total Gov't Investment; NL = Net Lending; G = Total Gov't Spending.

in progress as of 1986. One remarkable fact about the third cycle is that it depicts a steady growth in the importance of the government sector. This growth is mainly due to the persistent increases in consumption spending made by the government during this period.

The trend and cycle movements of the relative size of the government indicate that governmental activities grew much more rapidly in the 1950s than did the

Figure 15.2
Share of Spending Components in GNP

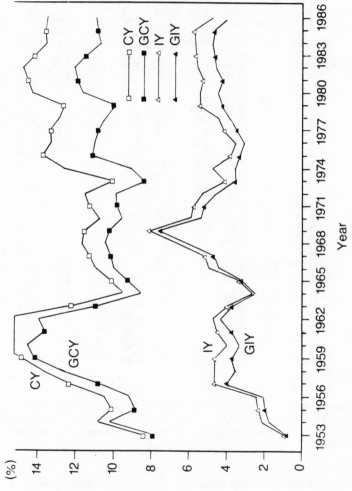

general economy. During the 1960s the government had grown in tandem with the growth in the general economy. Since the early 1970s, however, the government sector has persistently outgrown other sectors of the general economy.

Economic Classifications

This is a classification of government spending according to whether it belongs to consumption activities or investment activities. We are interested in the economic classification because consumption and investment activities have different economic implications. Consumption affects the welfare of the agent directly, whereas investment does so indirectly by altering outputs available in future periods.

Tables 15.1 and 15.2 depict economic classifications of government spending. The numbers in Table 15.1 are shares in GNP, while the numbers in Table 15.2 are shares of each spending component in total government spending. Figures 15.2 and 15.3 respectively represent the same in graphs.

Table 15.1 and Figure 15.2 indicate that the consumption components of the government spending as shares of GNP possess a clear upward trend. If we treat as exceptions the numbers for 1960–62, during which government consumption spending unexpectedly increased rapidly, it is easy to see that government consumption spending has steadily grown in its importance throughout the whole period. It is hard to say the same for the investment components. In fact there is an indication that the share for the investment components had peaked by 1970 and since then its importance has more or less remained unchanged at a slightly lower 6 percent level than the peak level of 8.1 percent recorded in 1969. These numbers suggest that both the consumption and investment components of government spending have steadily grown in their importance until the early 1970s. Since then, the importance of the consumption components continued to grow, while that of the investment components remained unchanged.

Table 15.2 and Figure 15.3, which contain information on the composition of government spending, show a somewhat different picture. As shares of total spending, government's final consumption has clearly become less important during the period. Thus its share has fallen from the high 80 percent level in the early 1950s to slightly more than 50 percent in 1986. Shares for transfers and subsidies, on the other hand, have been definitely rising throughout the period. Their combined share was 4.6 percent in 1953, whereas in 1986 it was 13 percent. As a result, even though the relative importance of final consumption activities has become weaker, the combined shares for the government's consumption activities have become more important since the late 1960s.

As shares of total spending, investment spending by the government grew very rapidly until 1969, but it has since declined slightly from the peak level. Thus the share that was 7.1 percent in 1953 rose persistently to 40.8 percent in 1969. By

Figure 15.3
Share of Each Component in Total Spending

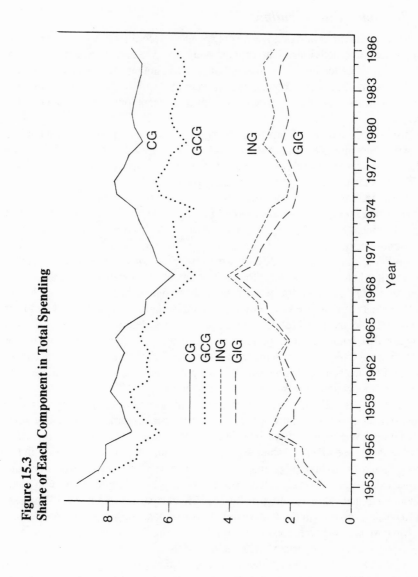

Table 15.2
Government Consumption and Investment (shares in total: in percent)

Year	GCG	CG	GIG	ING
1953	84.75	90.13	8.29	9.87
1954	78.65	83.64	13.22	16.36
1955	70.87	81.12	16.07	18.88
1956	70.60	81.13	16.12	18.87
1957	63.52	72.57	23.95	27.43
1958	69.35	74.73	19.31	25.27
1959	72.59	76.24	19.22	23.76
1960	73.37	79.71	16.93	20.29
1961	67.10	77.84	18.43	22.16
1962	68.12	76.95	21.11	23.05
1963	67.12	75.36	22.89	24.64
1964	70.26	78.15	20.77	21.85
1965	68.64	75.03	23.65	24.97
1966	62.48	68.85	27.82	31.15
1967	61.72	68.46	28.56	31.54
1968	56.90	63.69	33.59	36.31
1969	52.03	58.73	38.74	41.27
1970	57.21	64.64	32.13	35.36
1971	57.81	66.26	30.61	33.74
1972	58.85	68.59	27.31	31.41
1973	59.27	70.81	25.09	29.19
1974	52.26	72.56	20.52	27.44
1975	63.45	78.12	19.14	21.88
1976	65.39	78.76	18.48	21.24
1977	61.99	76.07	20.12	23.93
1978	60.35	74.07	22.23	25.92
1979	55.21	69.89	23.87	30.11
1980	59.00	72.39	22.95	27.61
1981	60.39	73.39	21.56	26.61
1982	59.33	72.67	22.62	27.33
1983	57.92	71.41	23.56	28.59
1984	55.67	70.35	25.01	29.65
1985	56.14	70.17	24.37	29.83
1986	59.55	73.49	21.71	26.51

Note: Shares in Total Government Spending. GCG = Final Consumption; CG = GCG + Subsidies and Transfers; GIG = Government Investment; ING = GIG + Capital Transfers.

1986, however, the share has fallen back to 23.2 percent of total spending. Shares for capital transfers show a similar picture. As a result, the combined shares for investment and capital transfers, which measure the extent to which the government is involved in public capital formations, show an inverse U-shaped pattern.

Functional Classifications

Government spending can also be classified according to its purposes. This is the functional classification of government spending. This classification shows the types of activities in which the government is engaged. The activities are broadly classified as general administration, defense, education, health, welfare, housing, community developments, economic services, and others.

Table 15.3 shows a functional classification of government spending for the general government.[3] It is evident from the table that economic services, defense, and education have been the three most important items of spending. Spending for health care and community development, however, has been rather small.

The share for general administration, which was at the 14 percent level in 1987, possesses a downward trend: it has decreased from the 18 percent level in 1971. This persistent decrease seems to be an indication that the government in Korea is becoming more efficient. The share for law enforcement and maintenance of social order, which is a part of the general administration, however, has not decreased at all.

The share for defense spending, which is about 23 percent of total government spending, does not show any trend movement. During the three-year period from 1976 to 1979, though, military spending had temporarily surged to more than 26 percent of total government spending before falling back to the 22 percent level

Table 15.3

Functional Classification of Spending: General Government (in percent)

| Year | Administration | | | Def | Edu | Health | Wel | House | Econ | Others |
	Sum	Gen	Law							
1971	17.7	12.8	4.7	22.5	17.7	2.6	4.0	6.7	26.4	2.4
1972	17.7	12.2	4.7	23.1	17.6	2.2	3.7	6.5	27.3	2.7
1973	18.9	14.6	4.2	23.6	18.3	2.3	3.5	7.5	23.0	2.9
1974	15.4	11.3	4.0	22.7	14.6	1.8	3.4	6.7	23.1	5.4
1975	16.6	12.6	3.7	22.9	13.6	1.7	4.9	5.8	32.4	2.1
1976	13.1	9.2	3.8	26.4	14.6	1.6	4.1	5.8	31.1	3.3
1977	13.7	9.5	3.9	25.9	14.6	2.0	4.1	5.7	29.5	4.5
1978	13.7	9.6	3.8	27.1	14.1	2.4	3.9	6.0	29.0	3.9
1979	12.8	8.6	3.4	22.2	14.2	2.0	4.8	6.3	33.9	3.8
1980	12.9	8.3	4.1	25.4	14.8	2.0	5.5	6.4	28.8	4.3
1981	13.6	8.6	4.2	23.4	14.9	1.9	4.6	9.4	27.9	4.3
1982	14.0	8.8	4.4	22.9	16.5	2.7	7.5	6.0	26.1	4.7
1983	15.4	9.9	4.7	22.9	17.6	2.5	4.2	7.5	25.4	4.6
1984	14.3	9.2	4.5	21.8	16.8	2.2	4.6	9.7	22.6	5.2
1985	14.6	9.3	4.5	21.6	16.3	2.3	4.5	8.5	26.7	5.4
1986	14.9	9.2	4.7	22.5	16.7	2.4	5.5	8.9	23.4	5.8
1987	14.0	9.8	4.1	22.7	15.8	3.4	5.8	7.2	24.9	6.3

Source: Bank of Korea, *Economic Statistics Yearbook*, 1988.

Note: Gen = General Administration, Law = Law Enforcement, Def = Defense, Educ = Education, Wel = Welfare, House = Housing and Community Development, Econ = Economic Services.

in 1979. This pattern in defense spending does not seem to indicate any fundamental change in government policies toward national defense. Rather, it seems to reflect the efforts taken by the Park regime to garner support from the military sector for its increasingly totalitarian rule by raising military spending, before it collapsed in 1979.

Spending for education, which includes spending for public education and subsidies for private schools, shows a U-shaped pattern. Its average share was about 18 percent in the early 1970s. It fell to about the 15 percent level in 1974 and remained at that level until 1981. It has since risen back to the 16.5 percent level by the middle of the 1980s.

Spending for health care, welfare, and housing and community development, which can be broadly grouped as social welfare spending, is a relatively small portion of total government spending. There exists, however, a weak but definite upward trend in the series. This upward trend, which is especially noticeable for the period after 1979, is an indication that the government in Korea has begun to take a larger role in providing the social safety net.

Finally, note that the item "economic services" is the most important component of the government spending. According to Table 15.3, the government spends on an average more than a quarter of its total budget for the provision of economic services. These include government spending to build up infrastructure such as highways, dams, railways, communication systems, and public utility systems. They also include government spending to build large scale industrial complexes, to improve agricultural lands, and to foster research and development. The importance in total government spending of the item "economic services," though, has been reduced in recent years. This may indicate that the government has begun to switch away from the practice of relatively direct economic management toward more indirect management.

Extent of Centralization

It is of some interest to find out to what extent the governmental functions are centralized in Korea. One measure to gauge this is the relative spending share of the central government versus the combined local governments. According to this measure, governmental functions in Korea are very much centralized. For example, in 1986 the central government spent approximately 20 percent of GNP, whereas the local governments spent about 10 percent of GNP.[4] Thus it appears that about two thirds of the total government spending is made by the central government. Further, this division of governmental functions between the central and local governments does not show any trend.

In fact, the central government spends more than two thirds of the total budget, because more than one quarter of the central government spending is transfers to local governments. This implies, then, that the relative size of the net spending made by the local governments is about 5 percent of GNP. Thus the central government is approximately four times as big as the local governments. If we take into account the fact that none of the local government officials are popularly elected, the degree of centralization may in fact be greater than what the above numbers suggest.

An International Comparison

Table 15.4 tells how important government sectors are in some of the selected countries.[5] It shows that the relative size of the government in Korea is smaller than those in most of the other countries. One exception is Japan; the size of the government in Japan is about 18 percent of her GNP. In contrast to this, the average share of government spending for the industrial countries, which is 44.2 percent, is almost twice as big as it is for Korea. The comparison with the Hungarian or Romanian economy is even more dramatic. Note finally that in this regard Taiwan is very similar to Korea.

Table 15.4 also contains information on the functional classification of government spending for each country. It shows that the share for defense spending in Korea is larger than the average level, while spending on health care and welfare is much smaller than the average level. Spending on education, on the other hand, is at about the same level as the average for other countries.

Table 15.5 shows another way of classifying government spending according to its functions. It depicts shares in total spending of each spending category. According to the table, in Korea the share for defense spending is much higher, the share

Table 15.4
Relative Size of Government: World (in percent)

	Total	Defense	Education	Health	Welfare
Industrial Countries	44.2	4.3	5.0	5.3	14.1
U.S.	36.5	6.1	5.0	4.1	9.6
W. Germany	48.7	2.8	4.2	8.1	21.7
U.K.	45.0	5.2	5.4	4.6	14.2
Singapore	26.5	5.5	5.6	1.7	1.8
Japan	18.2	n.a	n.a	n.a	n.a
Taiwan	23.0	5.5	3.7	0.5	0.8
Argentina	36.1	1.8	3.4	1.4	8.7
Chile	33.3	3.6	5.0	1.9	13.7
Hungary	59.4	2.3	3.1	4.0	15.9
Korea	24.8	5.4	4.2	0.6	3.5

Source: IMF, *Government Statistics Yearbook*, various issues.

Note: Figures in Table 15.4, Table 15.5, and Table 15.6 are averages of 1980–85.

Table 15.5
Functional Classification: World Central Government (in percent)

	GA	DF	ED	HL	WL	HS	EC	OT
U.S.	5.2	24.9	1.8	11.3	29.1	2.5	8.3	16.7
		[16.5]	[13.8]	[11.3]	[	26.4		]
Germany	4.1	9.2	0.7	18.7	50.2	0.3	7.1	9.6
		[5.8]	[8.6]	[16.7]	[	44.4		]
Singapore	11.1	20.1	20.2	6.2	0.9	5.6	15.0	18.9
Taiwan	11.3	23.9	19.0	2.9	4.7	8.1	17.0	14.1
Argentina	9.9	8.8	9.5	1.8	37.8	0.5	20.3	8.6
		[5.1]	[9.5]	[3.8]	[	24.1		]
Chile	11.3	11.5	13.2	6.1	39.0	4.8	7.1	6.4
		[10.9]	[16.6]	[5.8]	[	41.0		]
Hungary	15.7	6.9	1.6	3.6	21.0	1.7	38.8	12.2
		[3.9]	[5.2]	[6.8]	[	26.7		]
Korea	9.4	26.6	16.6	1.3	5.2	4.8	21.9	13.2
	[14.6]	[21.6]	[16.3]	[2.3]	[4.6]	[7.3]	[26.7]	[5.4]

Note: GA = General Administration; DF = Defense; ED = Education; HL = Health; WL = Welfare; HS = Housing; EC = Economic Services; OT = Others. Numbers in [ ] are for the General Government. For Singapore there is no distinction between the General and the Central Government.

for education is somewhat higher, the share for public health care is lower, and the share for welfare spending is much lower than the average level of the countries compared. It is also the case that in Korea the share for economic services in total government spending is much higher than the average level of all the countries. In sum, it appears that, aside from providing defense and educational services, providing various economic services has been the most important economic activity taken by the Korean government.

Table 15.6 depicts an economic classification of the "central" government spending for each country. It shows that the share for current spending is below average for Korea. For Korea it is about 78 percent of total spending, whereas for most of the other countries it is 90 percent or higher. Among current spending, the purchase of final goods and services is as important as the transfer payments in Korea. For most of the other countries, however, transfers are much more important. Note that most of the transfers in Korea are transfers to local governments, whereas in other countries they are mainly to households. Japan, which is similar to Korea in this respect, is an exception.

The share of capital spending in total central government spending is higher in Korea than the average level of the other countries. It is about 12 percent of total

Table 15.6
Economic Classification: World Central Government (in percent)

	Total	Current Spending GC	IN	TR	(Local)	Capital Spending	Lending
U.S.	92.8	29.5	15.5	47.9	7.4	4.6	2.6
Germany	93.1	33.7	5.2	54.2	4.2	5.5	1.5
U.K.	94.7	30.7	9.9	54.2	15.0	4.5	0.8
Singapore	77.6	53.8	18.8	4.9		25.7	-4.2
Japan	83.3	13.2	19.0	51.1	40.8	14.9	1.8
Taiwan	65.9		1.1			34.1	n.a.
Argentina	76.7	24.1	11.5	41.1	4.0	7.7	15.6
Chile	89.3	32.1	6.3	51.0	2.8	9.9	0.8
Hungary	89.6	18.7	2.0	68.8	9.2	10.6	-0.1
Korea	77.5	36.5	6.7	34.4	22.7	12.2	10.3
	[70.0]	[50.7]	[6.7]	[12.6]		[22.9]	[7.1]

Note: GC = Goods and Services (current); IN = Interests; TR = Transfers; Local = Transfers to Local Governments. Numbers in [ ] for Korea are for the General Government.

spending, which is 2.5 times as large as those for industrial countries. Japan, Chile, Argentina, and Hungary are similar to Korea in this respect. For Singapore, however, the share is about twice as large as that for Korea.[6]

A Summary

The analyses made in the above section indicate that government spending activities in Korea in the period from 1953 to 1986 have the following patterns.

Both the absolute and relative sizes of government have rapidly grown in this period. Real government spending, which is a measure of the absolute size of the government, has grown on an average of 9 percent per year during the period. The share of government spending in GNP, which is a measure of the relative size of the government, has also grown from 10.9 percent in 1963 to 20.2 percent in 1986. The share of government spending, however, is still smaller than that for most of the other countries. That is, despite the rapid growth in governmental activities, the government sector in Korea is still relatively small.

An economic classification of government spending shows that the share for current spending, though still smaller than the high level experienced in the earlier periods, has been increasing since the end of the 1960s. This increase has been mainly due to a persistent increase in transfers. The share for capital spending, on the other hand, rose very rapidly from the initial low level of less than 1 percent of GNP to about 8 percent by the end of the 1960s. Since then it has remained around the 5 percent level without showing any trend.

Even though there is a clear indication that the share of current spending, that is, consumption spending, has been increasing since 1970, it is still the case that the share of investment spending in total government spending is judged to be very large by the international standard. That is, government spending in Korea has been more investment oriented than that of other countries.

This last point is made clearer with the functional classification of government spending. According to this, more than 27 percent of total government spending is used to provide various economic services. For industrial countries this share is less than 10 percent.

Another noticeable pattern of spending in Korea is the low share of transfer payments in terms of the economic classification, and the low share of spending for health care and welfare in terms of functional classification. This reflects the fact that in the past the Korean government has not actively pursued income redistribution policy measures. Rather, the main policy goal has always been to promote economic growth and it shows up in the relatively large share of investment spending.

Finally, government spending in Korea is quite centralized. About 80 percent of total government spending is made by the central government. The remaining 20 percent spent by the local governments is also heavily influenced by the policy directives of the central government.

GOVERNMENT SPENDING AND ECONOMIC GROWTH: THEORY

The Model

In this section a simple model of economic growth is developed.[7] Consider an economy populated with a large number of homogenous agents who have the following utility function:

$$\int_0^\infty e^{-\rho t} \frac{[c^\alpha GC^{1-\alpha}]^{1-\sigma} - 1}{(1-\sigma)} \, dt \tag{1}$$

where c = per capita consumption of private goods, GC = consumption of public goods = government spending on consumption goods, and parameters ρ, α, and σ respectively represent the time discount rate, the relative importance of private versus public consumption, and the degree of risk aversion. Thus, the welfare of the typical agent in the economy depends on his lifetime consumption of private and public goods. The public goods are truly public and not individually appropriable.

The typical agent has the following production technology:

$$y(t) = F(k(t), GK(t)) = k(t)^{\eta}GK(t)^{\varepsilon},\tag{2}$$

where k = per capita private capital stock, and GK = public capital stock. Parameters η and ε represent respectively the productivity of private and public capital.

The government in this economy collects income taxes at the rate of τ from the agents and provides public goods GC and GI, where GI is the public investment made by the government. Each agent in the economy, then, after paying taxes to the government, uses its after-tax income for consumption and private investment. Thus:

$$c + \dot{k} = (1 - \tau)y = (1 - \tau)F(k, GK),\tag{3}$$
$$G = GC + GI = \tau y,\tag{4}$$

where in the last equation, the population size N is assumed to be equal to 1. Also, for simplicity of the analysis, assume GK to be equal to GI.[8] Then GK in the above equation can be replaced by GI. Finally, let $GI = iG$. That is, a fraction i of total government spending G is assumed to be used for public investment.

Since $G = GC + GI$ represents public goods and services, each individual agent would regard the time path of $\{GC(t), GI(t)\}_0^{\infty}$ as given. Therefore, the economic problem faced by the typical agent is given by the following:

$$\max \{c, \dot{k}\} \int_0^{\infty} e^{-\rho t} \frac{[c^{\alpha}GC^{1-\alpha}]^{1-\sigma} - 1}{(1 - \sigma)}\, dt\tag{5}$$

subject to: $c + \dot{k} = (1 - \tau)k^{\eta}GI^{\varepsilon}\tag{6}$

The solution to this problem is determined by the following pair of state-costate equations together with the boundary conditions.

$$\dot{q}/q = \rho - \eta B k^{\eta/(1-\varepsilon)-1}\tag{7}$$

$$\dot{k} = Bk^{\eta/(1-\varepsilon)} - D(1/q)^{1/(1-\alpha(1-\sigma))}(k^{\eta/(1-\varepsilon)})^{(1-\alpha)(1-\sigma)/(1-\alpha(1-\sigma))}.\tag{8}$$

where $B = (1 - \tau)(i\tau)^{\varepsilon/(1-\varepsilon)}$ and $D = [\alpha(1 - i)\tau(i\tau)^{\varepsilon/(1-\varepsilon)}]^{(1-\alpha)(1-\sigma)}$. The boundary conditions are given by the initial condition $k(t) = k_0$ and the transversality condition:

$$\lim_{t\to\infty} e^{-\rho t}q(t)k(t) = 0\tag{9}$$

The solution would have different economic implications depending on whether $\eta + \varepsilon$ is less than, equal to, or greater than 1. Note that when the value of the government investment GI is substituted into the production function, it becomes

$$y = Ak^{\eta/(1-\varepsilon)}$$

Therefore, when $\eta + \varepsilon < 1$, there exists an overall decreasing return to scale; when $\eta + \varepsilon = 1$, an overall constant return to scale; and when $\eta + \varepsilon > 1$, an overall increasing return to scale. In the first case, there would not be any persistent growth in the economy. Instead the economy would converge to the steady state. In the second case, the economy would exhibit a constant and persistent growth path. Finally, in the third case, the economy might not have any stable growth path.[9] In this study only the second case is considered.

When $\eta + \varepsilon = 1$, it is clear from equation (7) that the rate of change in the shadow price $q(t)$ is constant. Thus, $\dot{q}/q = \rho - A\eta$. Typically this is a negative number and the shadow price declines over time at the constant rate $\rho - A\eta$. Let $g = A\eta - \rho$. Then, $q(t) = q_0 e^{-gt}$. Now from equation (8) given above, when $\eta + \varepsilon = 1$, the following expression is obtained:

$$\dot{k}/k = B - D[q^{-1}k^{-\sigma}]^{1/[1-\alpha(1-\sigma)]} \tag{10}$$

A solution to equation (10) will be sought by assuming that $k(t)$ grows at a constant rate and by verifying that such a solution satisfies the boundary conditions. Now $\dot{k}/k = \text{constant}$ implies from equation (10) that qk^{σ} must also be constant. If $qk^{\sigma} = \text{constant}$, this in turn implies that $\dot{k}/k = -(1/\sigma)(\dot{q}/q)$.

Therefore,

$$\dot{k}/k = g/\sigma = (A\eta - \rho)/\sigma \tag{11}$$

Now we want to verify that when k grows at the rate given by equation (11), it should satisfy both equation (10) and the transversality condition. Let the constant qk^{σ} be equal to z. Then from equations (10) and (11), z must be such that

$$z = [D\sigma/(B\sigma - B\eta + \rho)]^{1-\alpha(1-\sigma)} \tag{12}$$

where B and D are as given above. Then from $qk^{\sigma} = z$, we must have

$$q_0 = [D\sigma/(B\sigma - B\eta + \rho)]^{1-\alpha(1-\sigma)}k^{-\sigma} \tag{13}$$

Since q_0 must be nonnegative, equation (13) requires that $B\sigma - B\eta + \rho \geq 0$. Finally, the transversality condition will be satisfied if and only if $B\sigma\eta - B\eta + \rho \geq 0$. Since when $B\sigma\eta - B\eta + \rho \geq 0$, then $B\sigma - B\eta + \rho \geq 0$, too, the necessary condition for the conjecture to be the solution is $B\sigma\eta - B\eta + \rho \geq 0$.

Therefore, under the assumption that $B\sigma\eta - B\eta + \rho \geq 0$, the growth rate of k is given by

$$\dot{k}/k = (\eta(1-\tau)(i\tau)^{\varepsilon/(1-\varepsilon)} - \rho)/\sigma \tag{14}$$

Of course, output per person y also grows at the same rate since $y = (i\tau)^{\varepsilon/(1-\varepsilon)}k$ when $\eta + \varepsilon = 1$.

Implications

The growth rate given by equation (14) has several important implications. Of these, those concerned with the relationship between the growth rates and the preference and technology parameters of the model are as follows:

a.   The growth rate is a decreasing function of the discount rate ρ. That is, an economy populated with more time-impatient agents would have lower growth rates than the economy whose agents are more time patient. The high ρ economy cares more for current than future consumption and saves less for capital accumulation.

b.   The growth rate is a decreasing function of the degree of relative risk aversion parameter σ. When agents are more risk averse, they value the relatively certain current consumption more highly than future consumption. Hence less capital accumulation and lower growth rates.

c.   The growth rate is an increasing function of the productivity parameters η and ε. That is, when either the private capital stock or the public capital stock becomes more productive, then growth rates would increase. This implies that the more productive the economy is, the faster the growth rates would be.

Now what does the theory say about the relationship between economic growth and government spending? There are two predictions of the theory relevant to the question. First, the model predicts that the growth rate of the economy as a function of the relative size of the government spending in GNP depicts an inverse U-shaped pattern. Thus it starts to rise from the level $-\rho/\sigma$ when the relative size of the government spending τ is equal to 0, reaches its maximum value when $\tau = \varepsilon$, and then declines continuously to the level $-\rho/\sigma$ again as τ grows to 1. This implies that growth rates and the relative size of government spending have a positive correlation when the size of the government is not "too" big, but the relationship turns into a negative correlation when the size of the government grows beyond a certain critical level. It is interesting to note that the critical level of the relative size of the government is determined by the productivity parameter ε of the public capital in the production function. See Figure 15.4.

The second prediction of the model is that the growth rate of the economy is a monotone increasing function of the parameter i. Recall that parameter i measures the share of government spending that goes into public investments. Thus the growth rate of the economy would be higher, the larger the share of the government spending used for public capital formation. Theoretically, the growth rate would be at its maximum when $i = 1$, that is, when all of the government spending is used solely for investment purposes. However, this would not be the welfare maximizing strategy. If the government spends all of its tax revenues solely for investment purposes, then there would not be any resource left for public consumption GC. Without public consumption, though, citizens would be extremely unhappy, since GC constitutes an argument for its utility function. See Figure 15.5.

GOVERNMENT SPENDING AND ECONOMIC GROWTH: EVIDENCE

This section reports the estimation results of the model suggested in the preceding section. The goal here is to empirically find out the relationship between the growth rate of the economy, the relative size of government spending, and the share for public investments in total government spending. Annual data for each of these series from 1953 to 1986 are used in the estimation. Three-year and five-year moving average data as well as the actual numbers have been used.

Scatter diagrams of the data suggest that the relationships we are interested in are more pronounced in the long run. For example, the relationship between the shares of government spending in GNP and the growth rates in GNP does not show up when actual annual data are used in the scatter diagram. However, the negative relationship between them becomes very distinct when long-run average data are used. This observation applies equally well to the relationship between the investment ratio and growth rates. The scatter diagram of the pair of the data, economic growth rates and investment ratio, also reveals that the functional relationship between them is a concave one. Recall that this concave relationship is an indication that the parameter ε is smaller than the parameter η. See Figure 15.5.

The first set of estimations investigates the possible existence of linear relationships between growth rates on one hand and the shares of total government spending in GNP and the shares of public investment spending in GNP (or in total government spending) on the other hand.

Table 15.7 contains the estimation results. Several alternative specifications were used in the estimation. In each case, the dependent variable is the growth rates, and the independent variables are the relative size of the government and the shares for the public investment. The estimation results indicate that there exists a strong negative relationship between the relative size of the government and the growth

Figure 15.4
Economic Growth and Government Spending

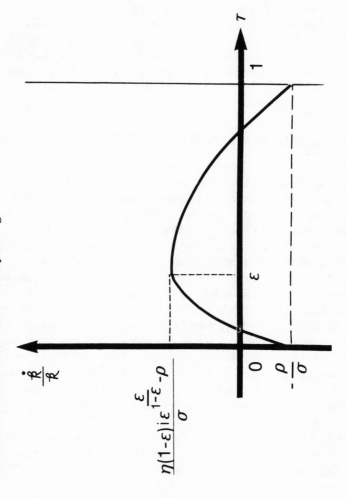

282

Figure 15.5
Economic Growth and Public Investment

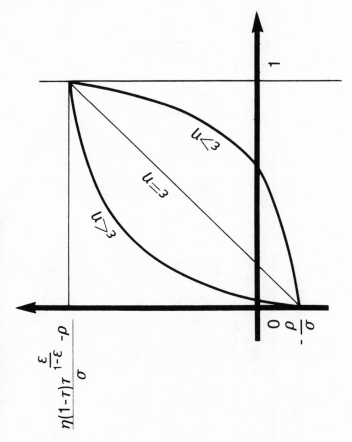

Table 15.7
Economic Growth and Government Spending

dep. var	dy	dy	dy	dy	mdy	mdy	mdy	mdy	m5dy	m5dy	m5dy	m5dy
constant	0.14 (3.01)	0.07 (1.30)	0.15 (2.74)	0.09 (1.52)	0.10 (2.94)	0.04 (1.00)	0.13 (2.64)	0.078 (1.59)	0.17 (5.47)	0.11 (2.83)	0.21 (4.58)	0.12 (2.26)
gy(0)	-0.81 (-2.80)	-0.51 (-2.02)	-1.54 (-3.55)	-1.24 (-3.01)	-0.58 (-2.77)	-0.32 (-1.83)	-1.19 (-2.83)	-0.89 (-2.45)	-0.94 (-5.71)	-0.64 (-3.89)	-1.61 (-2.08)	-0.88 (-1.31)
gy(-1)			1.24 (2.09)	0.99 (1.72)			1.01 (1.65)	0.71 (1.36)			1.19 (0.88)	0.55 (0.50)
gy(-2)			-0.41 (-0.89)	-0.23 (-0.56)			-0.49 (-1.23)	-0.33 (-1.01)			-0.62 (-0.83)	-0.42 (-0.67)
iy(0)	1.77 (2.84)		1.71 (1.80)		1.66 (3.27)		3.44 (2.23)		1.56 (4.41)		3.32 (2.24)	
iy(-1)			-1.29 (-1.16)				-4.51 (-1.75)				-3.74 (-1.42)	
iy(-2)			0.84 (1.02)				2.6 (1.71)				1.69 (1.11)	
ing(0)		0.36 (2.89)	0.54 (2.34)			0.34 (3.67)		1.11 (3.61)		0.30 (4.26)		1.09 (3.15)

ing(-1)				-0.56 (-1.81)				-1.58 (-3.06)				-1.59 (-2.55)
ing(-2)				0.29 (1.53)				0.82 (2.81)				0.83 (2.33)
obs	33	33	32	32	31	31	29	29	29	29	27	27
R**2	.27	.22	.27	.33	.26	.31	.35	.49	.60	.58	.63	.69

Note: Numbers in ( ) are t-ratios. R**2 is the RBAR-square. dy = Growth Rates in GNP; mdy = Three-Year Moving Averages of dy; m5dy = Five-Year Moving Averages of dy, and similarly for gy, iy, and ing; gy = Shares of Government Spending in GNP; iy = Shares of Public Investment in GNP; ing = Shares of Public Investment in Total Government Spending.

rates of the economy. The results also indicate that there exists an equally significant positive relationship between the public investment shares and the growth
rates. These relationships remain unchanged when lagged variables are also included in the regression. In fact none of the coefficient estimates for the lagged
regressors are statistically significant. When long-run average data are used in the
estimation, however, the results are somewhat different. First, not only the current
but also the lagged investment share variables appear to be significant. Hence there
exists some evidence that the investment share variable has a persistent long-run
effect on economic growth. Second, the statistical significance of the model
improves markedly when more long-run data are used. The following is the
representative result:

$$m5dy = .11 - .64\,m5gy + .30\,m5ing$$
$$\quad\;\;\;(2.83)\;\;(-3.89)\quad\;\;(4.26)$$

t-ratios in ( ). R**2 = .58

where m5dy, m5gy, and m5ing are respectively five-year averages of the growth
rates, the shares of the government spending in GNP, and the budgetary shares of
the investment spending.

So far the estimation has been made under the maintained hypothesis that the
relative size of government spending affects the growth performance of the
economy, but not vice versa. Even though this maintained assumption seems to be
a sensible one to make, there is nothing in reality that precludes the reverse
relationship. In order to investigate this possibility, a second set of estimations is
performed. This time, the relative size of the government spending variable is used
as the dependent variable and the growth rates as the independent variable. The
results are contained in Table 15.8. It is clear from the results that the negative
relationship between these two variables indeed runs from the relative size variable
to the growth rate variable. In each case, the right-hand size variable turns out to
be either statistically and/or numerically insignificant. One exception is when m5gy
is regressed against m5dy.

Let us now turn to an explicit estimation of the growth rate—equation (14).
Equation (14) suggests a nonlinear relationship among the growth rates, the investment shares, and the relative sizes. Table 15.9 reports the results of the estimation
of these nonlinear relationships. As they are estimated, the parameter ε is the only
one that is explicitly identifiable. Its estimates suggest that the value lies between
0.086 and 0.114. If we accept the assumption of the model that $\eta + \varepsilon = 1$, then these
estimates suggest implied values of η lying between 0.886 and 0.915. Note finally
that the parameter eta* given in Table 15.9 corresponds to η/σ. Thus, from the
estimates of η, the implied values of the parameter σ can be calculated. It turns out
to be that σ lies between 0.592 and 0.673.

Table 15.8
Government Spending and Economic Growth

dep. var.	gy	gy	mgy	mgy	m5gy	m5gy
constant	0.19 (20.64)	0.21 (19.58)	0.19 (15.73)	0.22 (18.62)	0.21 (23.41)	0.23 (24.97)
dy(0)	-0.16 (-1.43)	-0.178 (-1.90)	-0.18 (-1.17)	- 0.21 (-0.98)	- 0.44 (-3.75)	- 0.43 (-1.48)
dy(-1)		-0.142 (-1.49)		-0.097 (-0.33)		-0.02 (-0.06)
dy(-2)		-0.53 (-0.55)		-0.20 (-0.94)		-0.16 (-0.57)
obs	33	33	31	31	29	29
R**2	.03	.15	.01	.24	.32	.50

Note: Numbers in ( ) are t-ratios.

Table 15.9
Parameter Estimation

	actual	MA3	MA5
eta*	1.53 (3.39)	1.32 (4.08)	1.48 (6.57)
epsilon	0.095 (4.31)	0.114 (5.33)	0.086 (5.14)
rho*	0.833 (2.96)	0.655 (3.33)	0.839 (5.79)
R**2	0.23	0.35	0.60
eta	0.905	0.886	0.915
sigma	0.592	0.673	0.617

Note: Numbers in ( ) are t-ratios.

The estimation results support the implications of the model. The model predicts that when the relative size of government spending is larger than the value of the productivity parameter of public investment, an increase in the size of government spending lowers the growth rates. The regression results show that (1) the value of ε is about .10 for the Korean economy, (2) there exists a significant negative relationship between the growth rates and the relative size of the government, and (3) this relationship is running from the relative size variable to growth rates. Since throughout the sample period the share of government spending has consistently been larger than 10 percent of GNP, these findings support the model.

The model also predicts that the growth rates of the economy would be higher, the larger the share of public investment in total spending. This prediction is also confirmed by the estimation results. There exists a significant positive relationship between the growth rates and the share of public investment spending in GNP or in total government spending.

What are the combined effects on the economic growth rates of a change in government spending? The answer to this question depends on how the increased spending is used. Suppose that m5gy = .20 and m5ing = .30. That is, 20 percent of GNP is used by the government and 30 percent of it goes to public investment. The model predicts that in this case the growth rate is 7.16 percent. Suppose now that the share of government spending is increased by one percentage point to 21 percent of GNP. If the increased spending is entirely used for additional public consumption, then the growth rate would decrease to 6.13 percent. If, on the other hand, the increased spending is used entirely for additional public investment, then the growth rate would increase to 7.56 percent. Finally, if the increased spending is divided between consumption and investment components according to their current shares, then the growth rate would decrease to 6.56 percent. Note that in each case considered, the elasticity is respectively -1.13, 0.40, and -0.60.

The finding that ε and η are respectively equal to 0.09 and 0.91 suggests that during the sample period the private capital has been about ten times as productive as the public capital. Therefore, even though there exists evidence that the public capital has been productive and has helped the economy to grow, it still appears to be the case that the accumulation of the private capital has been mainly responsible for the rapid economic growth. The finding that $\varepsilon = 0.09$ also suggests that the relative size of the public capital stock in Korea is about 9 percent of the total capital stock.

CONCLUDING REMARKS

Three tasks have been performed in this study: the basic patterns of government spending in Korea since 1953 have been summarized, a theoretical model explaining the relationship between economic growth and patterns of government spending has been formulated, and the predictions of the model have been tested.

The share of government spending in GNP has grown rapidly in Korea. This growth, which was more due to the rapid growth in public investment spending in the earlier period, has in recent years been more due to the persistent increase in transfer payments. Nevertheless, the relative size of government spending in Korea is still much smaller than those for most of the industrial, Latin American, and East European countries. Japan, Singapore, and Taiwan are exceptions in this regard: their governments' spending shares are comparable to that of Korea. It is interesting to note that in these four countries government spending has been much more investment oriented than that of most of the other countries.

The empirical results confirm the predictions of the theoretical model. They suggest that while the overall growth of the relative size of government spending has been unfavorable to economic growth, public investment spending has been an important factor in explaining the economic growth in Korea. There is also evidence that about 10 percent of the economic growth can be attributed to the accumulation of public capital.

The importance in the overall economy of government spending in Korea does not show any indication of a downward movement. If any, there are indications that the importance would grow further in coming years. There exists a strong pressure stemming from the various interest groups that the government should more actively engage in income redistribution measures. At the same time it would be difficult for the government to reduce other government spending items. In fact, the demand for public services seems to have an income elasticity greater than one. Therefore, unless the spending shares for national defense are drastically reduced as a result of, say, a better relationship between North and South Korea, it is most likely that government spending would continue to grow at a faster rate than other components of GNP. According to the empirical results obtained in this study, this further growth in the relative size of the government spending will be unfavorable to the future growth of the overall economy.

NOTES

1. The Korean economy had also experienced relatively rapid growth in the seventeenth and eighteenth centuries. See Yi (1985).

2. Barro (1988) has a model similar to the one suggested in this chapter.

3. The general government, which excludes government enterprises from the public sector spending, is a sum of central and local governments' spending.

4. The combined share of 30 percent is clearly "too" large, but this is due to a double counting.

5. The selection of the countries is somewhat arbitrary. They are respectively representatives for industrial countries, Asian developing countries, Latin American countries, or East European countries.

6. The figure for the general government, however, is comparable to that for Singapore. It is 23 percent for Korea.

7. Barro (1988) has a model similar to the one given here. The expositions given here, however, are much more formal.

8. Of course, *GK* must be the sum of current and past net public investment.

9. Even in this case, with suitable restrictions on the production function, a stable growth path may exist.

REFERENCES

The Bank of Korea, *National Income Accounts*, Seoul: various years.

———, *National Accounts*, Seoul: 1987.

———, *Economic Statistics Yearbook*, Seoul: 1988.

Bailey, Martin J., *National Income and the Price Level*, New York: McGraw-Hill, 1971.

Barro, Robert J., "Output Effects of Government Purchases," *Journal of Political Economy*, *89*, December 1981, 1086–121.

———, "Government Spending in a Simple Model of Endogenous Growth," NBER Working Paper Series, 1988.

IMF, *Government Finance Statistics Yearbook*, Washington, D.C.: 1988.

Lucas, Robert E. Jr., "Mechanics of Economic Development," *Journal of Monetary Economics*, *22*, August 1988, 3–42.

Romer, Paul M., "Increasing Returns and Long-run Growth," *Journal of Political Economy*, *94*, December 1986, 1002–37.

Yi, Kibaek, *A New History of Korea*, Cambridge: Harvard University Press, 1984.

16

The Output Effects of Fiscal Policy in Korea

Paul Evans

INTRODUCTION

Following Robert Barro (1981), this study formulates a simple neoclassical model of the Korean economy and fits it to data. The resulting estimates suggest that government purchases in Korea are highly productive, that increased tax rates appreciably depress output, and that budget deficits do not much affect output.

The rest of the study is organized as follows. The first section lays out the neoclassical model and then formulates a regression equation consistent with it. The regression equation relates output to government purchases, to the effective marginal tax rate on income, and to the budget deficit. The second section reports the results from fitting the regression equations and discusses the results. The third section draws some conclusions.

A NEOCLASSICAL MODEL

Government purchases of goods and services total G and are composed of a permanent and a transitory component:

$$G \equiv GP + GT \tag{1}$$

where

$$GP \equiv \overline{R} \int_0^\infty G(t) \exp\left[-\int_0^t R(s)\,ds\right] dt \tag{2}$$

$$\bar{R} \equiv 1 \Big/ \int_0^\infty \exp\left[-\int_0^t R(s)\,ds\right] dt \tag{3}$$

and t and s are indices of time. In addition to purchasing goods, the government makes transfer payments, pays interest on the government debt, and finances its spending by levying distorting taxes and selling debt.[1] Hence the government faces the budget constraint

$$\dot{D} \equiv G + R{\cdot}D - T \tag{4}$$

where D is the real government debt, R is the real after-tax interest rate, and T is taxes net of noninterest transfer payments. For simplicity, all debt is assumed to have a one-period term to maturity. If the present value of the government debt infinitely far in the future is zero, the differential equation (4) has the following solution for D:

$$\bar{R}{\cdot}D = TP - GP \tag{5}$$

where

$$TP \equiv \bar{R} \int_0^\infty T(t) \exp\left[-\int_0^t R(s)\,ds\right] dt$$

Each moment households receive a full factor income of the form[2]

$$F = F(G) \tag{6}$$

with $F_1 > 0$. Full factor income is increasing in G because government purchases provide the private sector with productive inputs and with a flow of consumption services. Households allocate their total full income to current consumption of market goods, to current consumption of nonmarket goods such as leisure, and to saving. The consumption of market goods and the consumption of nonmarket goods, both measured in units of market goods, are given by

$$C = C(FP + \bar{R}D - TP, \tau, R, R*) \tag{7}$$

and

$$L = L(FP + \bar{R}D - TP, \tau, R, R*) \tag{8}$$

where FP is permanent full factor income, τ is a measure of how distorting taxes are,[3] and $R*$ summarizes the future path of R. It is assumed that $0 < C_1 < 1$, $C_2 = -L_2 < 0$, $C_3 < 0$, $0 < L_1 < 1$, and $L_3 < 0$. Market consumption is decreasing in the tax distortion τ, and nonmarket consumption is increasing, because only the former is taxed. Both types of consumption fall as the real after-tax interest rate R rises, thereby improving the trade-off between present consumption and future consumption. $\overline{RD} - TP$ is the contribution of the government to permanent full income. Market consumption and nonmarket consumption are increasing in permanent full income because both are normal goods.

I assume that net investment is generated according to the neoclassical investment model; that is, net investment is increasing in the gaps between the desired and actual capital stocks. I further assume that governmentally provided inputs into production are neither substitutes for nor complements with private capital. The investment function therefore takes the form

$$I = I(\tau, R, R*) \tag{9}$$

with $I_1 < 0$ and $I_2 < 0$. Net investment is decreasing in τ and R because future desired stocks of capital decrease as the tax distortion τ or the current real after-tax interest rate R rises. Future real interest rates may also affect desired future capital stocks and hence current net investment.

Equilibrium in the goods markets requires that

$$C(FP + \overline{RD} - TP, \tau, R, R*) + L(FP + \overline{RD} - TP, \tau, R, R*) + I(\tau, R, R*) + G = F(G) \tag{10}$$

The current real interest rate R changes in order to equate the demand for goods in the right-hand member to the supply of goods in the left-hand member. Note that net investment is defined to include the trade balance (sometimes referred to as net foreign investment).

To characterize the equilibrium real interest rate, I first assume that households think that

$$\overline{RD} - TP = -GP + \lambda \dot{D} \tag{11}$$

If households are aware that equation (4) holds, then $\lambda = 0$. In other words, Ricardian equivalence holds so that households treat government budget deficits as equivalent to current taxes. If instead households lack foresight, they may think that an increased government budget deficit resulting from decreased current taxes or increased current transfer payments implies decreased permanent taxes. In that case, λ is positive. Alternatively, households may suffer from the opposite illusion so that λ is negative.

I then assume that households calculate permanent full factor income according to

$$FP = \varphi(GP, R, R*) \tag{12}$$

with $\varphi_1 > 0$ and $\varphi_2 < 0$. Permanent full factor income is increasing in GP because increasing private capital or permanent government factor inputs will raise factor income now and in the future. Because R and $R*$ summarize the real after-tax interest rates at which households discount the future, FP must depend on R and $R*$ as well. The higher R is, the more future full factor incomes are discounted and hence the smaller FP is.

If households have homothetic utility functions and the economy experiences neither population growth nor technological progress, the marginal propensity to consume from permanent full income is one.[4] Consequently,

$$C + L = FP + \bar{R}D - TP + c(R, R*) \tag{13}$$

with $c_1 < 0$.

Equations (10)–(13) imply that

$$\varphi(GP, R, R*) - GP + \lambda\dot{D} + c(R, R*) + I(\tau, R, R*) + GP + GT = F(GP + GT) \tag{14}$$

If households understand how output is generated, $\varphi_1 = F_1$. One can therefore rewrite equation (14) as

$$c(R, R*) + I(\tau, R, R*) + GT + \lambda\dot{D} = f(GT, R, R*) \tag{15}$$

with $f_1 = F_1 > 0$ and $f_2 = -\varphi_2 > 0$.

It is straightforward to solve equation (15) for the equilibrium real interest rate. The result takes the form

$$R = R(GT, \lambda\dot{D}, \tau, R*) \tag{16}$$

with $R_3 < 0$. R_1 is positive, zero, or negative as F_1 is less than, equal to, or greater than one. Increasing the marginal tax rate depresses net investment and hence bids the real interest rate down. Increasing the budget deficit raises, lowers, or leaves the real interest rate unchanged as λ is positive, negative, or zero.

The reduced form for market output is

$$Y \equiv F - L$$

$$= F(GP + GT) - L\left\{\varphi[GP,R(GT,\lambda\dot{D},\tau,R*),R*] - GP + \lambda\dot{D},\tau,R(GT,\lambda\dot{D},\tau,R*),R*\right\}$$

or

$$Y = Y(GP, GT, \lambda\dot{D}, \tau, R*) \tag{17}$$

with $0 < Y_1 < F_1, Y_3 > 0, Y_4 < 0$, and $Y_2 \gtreqless F_1$ as $F_1 \gtreqless 1$. Output should be an increasing function of the permanent and transitory components of government purchases and a decreasing function of the marginal tax rate. The marginal product of government purchases should be greater than the derivative of output with respect to permanent government purchases. It should also be less than the derivative of output with respect to transitory government purchases if the marginal product of government purchases exceeds one but less than that derivative if the marginal product of government purchases is less than one. Finally, a budget deficit should raise, lower, or leave output unchanged according to whether λ is positive, negative, or zero.

Although the neoclassical model analyzed above does not fully describe how economies of industrial and especially less-developed countries actually operate, it may provide a useful framework for empirical analysis. Therefore, in the next section, I use time-series methods to estimate an equation of the form

$$\Delta Y_t = \alpha + \beta\Delta\tau_t + \gamma_P\Delta GP_t + \gamma_T\Delta GT_t + \delta\Delta DEF_t + U_t \tag{18}$$

Δ is the difference operator, *DEF* is a measure of the budget deficit, and U is an error term that incorporates the effects of $R*$ and all variables from which I abstract in the model. I estimate equation (18) in differences on the assumption that at least some of the variables abstracted from are difference-stationary variables. By estimating equation (18), one can put lower and sometimes upper bounds on MPG, the marginal product of government purchases, since

$$\gamma_P < \text{MPG} \tag{19}$$

and either

$$\text{MPG} < \gamma_T \tag{20}$$

if MPG < 1 or

$$\gamma_T < \text{MPG} \tag{21}$$

if MPG > 1. In addition, one can learn how distorting the Korean tax system is and whether Ricardian equivalence holds.

THE EMPIRICAL ANALYSIS

In this section, I estimate equation (18) for the Korean economy. I choose the Republic of Korea for this analysis because it has been a less-developed country for most of the sample period, because fairly good data are available for it, and because its fiscal variables have varied considerably.

Because Korea has undergone rapid growth over the sample period, it is advisable to transform Y, G, and DEF in order that the error term U have a constant variance. I have therefore divided real gross domestic product,[5] real government purchases, and the real government budget deficit by the exponential time trend that best fits the real gross domestic product series.[6] The resulting series appear to be homogeneous.[7] I use the same symbols and names to refer to these scaled variables in the rest of the chapter that I used in the theoretical section to refer to the analogous unscaled variables.

The first step in the empirical analysis is to decompose government purchases G into its permanent and transitory components. One could do so by fitting a forecasting equation to G, forecasting the future path of this variable from each starting date, and applying the discrete-time analogue of equation (2) to these forecasts. That procedure, however, is generally difficult to apply and probably does not yield results appreciably different from those obtained by using the procedure suggested by Beveridge and Nelson (1981).

In their approach, G is assumed to be generated by the stochastic process

$$\Delta G_t = \sum_{i=0}^{\infty} \varphi_i V_{t-i} \tag{22}$$

where φ_0, φ_1, φ_2, ... are parameters with $\varphi_0 = 1$ and V_t is an independently and identically distributed error term with a zero mean and a finite variance. They then equate the permanent component of G to the limiting conditional mean

$$GP_t = \lim_{k \to \infty} E(G_{t+k} \mid G_t, G_{t-1}, G_{t-2}, \ldots) \tag{23}$$

In other words, they equate GP to the expected steady-state value of G. Beveridge and Nelson show that GP follows the random walk

$$GP_t = GP_{t-1} + \left[\sum_{i=0}^{\infty} \varphi_i \right] V_t \tag{24}$$

Therefore, one can generate the series $\{GP_t\}$ by fitting a univariate process of the form (22) to the series $\{G_t\}$, assuming a value for GP_0 and plugging the fitted values for $\varphi_1, \varphi_2, \varphi_3, \ldots$ and $\{V_t\}$ into equation (24). The transitory component of G is then just $G - GP$. The choice of GP_0 is not crucial because it affects only the sample means of GP and GT. It is convenient to choose GP_0 so that the sample mean of GT is zero.

I applied the methodology of Box and Jenkins (1976) to identify the univariate process generating the annual series for G over the sample period 1953–83. The series G appears to be nonstationary in its levels. The first four sample autocorrelations of ΔG are –.06, –.14, .08, and –.06. Under the null hypothesis that ΔG is serially uncorrelated, the standard error of these sample autocorrelations is approximately .18. Consequently, G is empirically indistinguishable from a random walk with $\varphi_1 = \varphi_2 = \varphi_3 = \cdots = 0$ so that $GP = G$ and $GT = 0$. It follows that γ_T is not identified and cannot be estimated. I therefore estimate the equation

$$\Delta Y_t = \alpha + \beta \Delta \tau_t + \gamma \Delta G_t + \delta \Delta DEF_t + U_t \tag{25}$$

and make use only of the restriction

$$MPG > \gamma \tag{26}$$

As my measure of *DEF*, I use the ratio of the official budget deficit to the GDP deflator times trend output. This variable is no doubt contaminated by the influence of output on tax collections and transfer payments. Because, however, it is difficult to construct a measure of *DEF* purged of this influence, I have ignored any biases that the endogeneity of *DEF* may produce.

In order to measure the extent of tax distortions in the Korean economy, I use the ratio of nominal government receipts to nominal gross domestic product. This measure has obvious weaknesses, but no easily calculable quantity seems better. It may exhibit some endogeneity if the Korean tax system is on balance either progressive or regressive. The lack of any apparent trend in the series since 1960, however, suggests that endogeneity may not be a serious problem.

I have fitted equation (25) to these data, using ordinary least squares. The result is

$$\Delta \hat{Y}_t = -0.56 - 1.19\Delta \tau_t + 1.07\Delta G_t - 0.16\Delta DEF_t \tag{27}$$
$$\quad\;\; (0.81) \quad (0.55) \quad\;\; (0.70) \quad\;\;\; (0.53)$$

$$R^2 = .167, \quad \text{S.E.E.} = 4.32, \quad \text{D.W.} = 1.62, \quad Q(15) = 10.5$$

where the figures in parentheses are standard errors. The error term is well characterized as white noise, and the coefficient on *DEF* does not differ significantly from zero at any conventional significance level. Therefore, one cannot reject the null hypothesis that Ricardian equivalence holds in Korea.

Because δ does not differ significantly from zero, I have reestimated equation (25), restricting δ to be zero. The result is

$$\Delta \hat{Y}_t = -0.59 - 1.13\Delta\tau_t + 0.94\Delta G_t \tag{28}$$
$$\phantom{\Delta \hat{Y}_t = } (0.79) \quad (0.49) \quad (0.55)$$

$$R^2 = .166, \text{S.E.E.} = 4.25, \text{D.W.} = 1.56, Q(15) = 11.4.$$

Again, the error term is well characterized as white noise. The estimated coefficients on ΔG_t and $\Delta\tau_t$ are significantly positive and negative, respectively, at the 5 percent significance level. The neoclassical theory developed above is therefore supported.

Equation (28) has interesting implications for public policy in Korea. It is likely that the marginal product of government purchases in Korea is greater than one since γ, which is a lower bound on MPG, is estimated to be 0.94.[8] If so, a distortion-free transfer of resources from the private sector to the public sector improves welfare in Korea. If the transfer takes place through the tax system, however, output is estimated to fall by $1.13 - 0.94$, or 0.19, units. In this case, an improvement in welfare is much less likely to take place. Transferring one unit of resources from taxpayers to the recipients of transfer payments reduces output by 1.13 units, an amount larger than the transfer. Taxes in Korea therefore appear to be highly distorting. If so, reforming the tax structure or reducing transfer payments could appreciably improve the efficiency of the Korean economy.

CONCLUSIONS

The neoclassical model laid out above implies a framework for empirical analysis, which I have applied to data from the Republic of Korea. The estimates obtained suggest that the marginal product of government purchases exceeds one, that the Korean tax system is highly distorting, and that Ricardian equivalence holds. These findings can be used to justify tax reform and perhaps increased government purchases and decreased transfer payments in Korea.

NOTES

1. I assume in the model below that capital markets are perfect. In such a world, it does not matter whether the national debt is owned by domestic residents or by foreign residents.

2. I am abstracting here from changes in the relative prices of goods. It is helpful to think of F(·) as a production function.

3. If a flat income tax raised all the revenue, τ would be the income tax rate. I assume that τ will remain at its current level forever.

4. The assumption that the economy is static is not crucial for the results below. If there is exogenous growth in population or exogenous disembodied Harrod-neutral technological progress, the same results obtain where consumption, investment, output, and so on, are scaled by population or effective population units and the real interest rate is net of the growth rate. Permanent changes are then changes in the level of a growing series, keeping the shape of the series constant.

5. In the theoretical analysis, I have focused on net output. In the empirical analysis, I use the gross series because it is more readily available. The implications of the theoretical analysis should also apply to the gross series.

6. Each of the ratios used in the empirical analysis is measured in percentage points. The series Y, G, τ, and *DEF* are published in Evans (1988).

7. If the Korean economy has experienced population growth and disembodied Harrod-neutral technological progress over the postwar period, these variables would also be the appropriate proxies for the variables used in the theoretical analysis. See note 5.

8. Obviously, it is possible that MPG < 1 since the 95 percent confidence interval for γ is (.01, 1.87). All other statements below must also be qualified because the coefficients are estimated with error.

REFERENCES

Barro, Robert J., "The Output Effects of Government Purchases," *Journal of Political Economy, 89,* December 1981, 1086–121.

Beveridge, Stephen, and Nelson, Charles R., "A New Approach to Decomposition of Economic Time Series into Permanent and Transistory Components with Particular Attention to Measurement of the 'Business Cycle,'" *Journal of Monetary Economics, 7,* April 1981, 151–74.

Box, George E. P., and Jenkins, G. M., *Time Series Analysis, Forecasting and Control.* San Francisco: Holden-Day, 1976.

Evans, Paul, "The Effects of Fiscal Policy in Korea." *International Economic Journal, 2,* Summer 1988, 1–14.

C. Labor Market

In the macroeconomic analysis of the developing economies, the labor market is often neglected due to the existence of a chronic excess supply of labor and underemployment. This is no longer the case in Korea after the mid-1970s when the policy emphasis shifted to the development of heavy/chemical industries. Since then much attention has been paid to the importance of the labor market. The study by Choongsoo Kim estimates supply and demand functions for labor as well as the wage function. Kim observes from the Korean data that contrary to the Harris and Todaro model, real wage growth rates and urban-rural wage differentials were higher during the 1974–80 period than the earlier period while the unemployment rates were lower. In other words, in Korea, employment expansion and real wage growth occurred simultaneously. This, in part, explains why the labor share of Korea has increased much faster than that of Japan and other countries, especially during the 1970s and 1980s. Kim's analysis of the labor share also leads to a rejection of the "low wage" hypothesis for Korea.

17

Labor Market Developments
in Macroeconomic Perspective

Choongsoo Kim

INTRODUCTION

For effective management of macroeconomic policies, it is essential to understand the interrelationships among the commodity, money, and labor markets. In under-developed economies, however, the emphasis of economic management is generally placed on bringing equilibrium to only the commodity and money markets. The main reason for the neglect of labor market conditions is that due to a chronic excess supply of labor and the existence of underemployment, macroeconomic policies targeting the labor market, for example a wage policy to maintain balance between the supply and demand for labor, are considered to be of limited importance.

For the case of Korea, until the mid-1970s, labor-intensive light industries not requiring many highly skilled technicians led economic growth, and labor market factors hindering economic growth did not appear. On the other hand, as the heavy and chemical industries began emerging as the leading sector of economic growth, a disequilibrium in the market for skilled technicians and engineers occurred, which subsequently caused considerable wage increases and price inflation as well as widening wage differentials among occupations. Since then, much public attention has been paid to the importance of labor market policy, which began playing a major role in bringing about macroeconomic equilibrium.

If we look at the future circumstantial changes in the Korean labor market by distinguishing the demand and supply sides, we find that a disequilibrium will persist in the labor market. That is, supply side pressures in the labor market will increase continuously at least during the next five to ten years. This is primarily because the largest age cohort of the baby-boom generation is entering the labor market in the late 1980s. Moreover, due to a doubled enrollment quota of colleges market in the late 1980s. Moreover, due to a doubled enrollment quota of colleges in the early 1980s, the supply of college graduates has been increasing sharply in recent years. Also, the female labor force participation rate will continue to rise due to a declining total fertility rate and greater educational attainment.

On the other hand, the demand for labor is likely to grow much more slowly in the future than before. In order to improve the international competitiveness of the economy, the main emphasis of economic and industrial policies will be on the development of technologies. Under these circumstances, it is generally expected that the labor-absorptive capacity corresponding to growth of the economy is going to decrease. The recent surge of wage increases originating from labor strikes and disputes has induced firms to accelerate the adoption of automative processes, which will contribute further to the declining labor-absorptive capacity of economic growth.

In this study, we examine the changing patterns of the Korean labor market and also investigate the determinants of the supply and demand for labor with a special focus on the relationship between the wage rate change and labor market conditions. The study unfolds as follows. In the next section, statistics of the Korean labor market and underlying policy issues are described. Empirical findings of the estimated results using quarterly time-series data are presented and analyzed in the next two sections. Finally, policy implications are discussed in the last section.

STATISTICAL DESCRIPTION OF THE LABOR MARKET

One common characteristic of growing economies is that the size of the labor force grows faster than that of the population. As shown in Table 17.1, we find a similar phenomenon for Korea. During 1964-73, the average population growth rate was 2.3 percent per annum, while the labor force grew by one more percentage point, 3.4 percent per year. The gap between the two rates widened in the mid to late 1970s when the Korean economy recorded very high growth rates. The two main sources for labor force growth are population increases and migration from rural to urban areas. Due to a decline in total fertility rate that can be attributed to effective birth control policies, the rate of population growth began diminishing rapidly beginning in the early 1970s. However, continuous industrialization policies induced migration of rural people to urban areas, which contributed to total labor force increases. One important point to note is that while the labor force increased the unemployment rate fell during the same period, implying a faster expansion of employment opportunities. For example, the average nonfarm unemployment rate fell from 9.7 percent during 1964–73 to 6.2 percent during 1974–80 to 5.2 percent during 1981–87.

Perhaps the most unique feature of the Korean labor market development path is that while unemployment rates have fallen, real wage growth rates have remained at a high level. The determination of wages and employment (and unemployment)

Table 17.1
Labor Force and Wage Growth Rates (in percent)

Year	Population	Labor Force	Unemployment Rate		Real Wage (A)[b]	(B)[c]
1964	2.65	1.27	7.7	(14.4)[a]	- 5.7	-11.4
1965	2.58	4.85	7.4	(13.5)	4.3	10.3
1966	2.55	2.39	7.1	(12.8)	6.0	4.0
1967	2.36	2.47	6.2	(11.1)	10.5	17.9
1968	2.35	3.79	5.1	(9.0)	14.6	18.2
1969	2.29	2.50	4.8	(7.8)	19.4	23.6
1970	2.21	3.15	4.5	(7.4)	9.2	22.3
1971	1.99	3.36	4.5	(7.4)	2.3	10.7
1972	1.89	4.85	4.5	(7.5)	2.2	- 0.2
1973	1.78	4.95	4.0	(6.8)	14.3	5.4
1974	1.73	4.14	4.1	(6.8)	8.7	7.3
1975	1.70	2.15	4.1	(6.6)	1.5	5.5
1976	1.61	5.84	3.9	(6.3)	16.8	15.8
1977	1.57	2.91	3.8	(5.8)	21.5	20.8
1978	1.53	3.66	3.2	(4.7)	17.4	18.7
1979	1.53	1.97	3.8	(5.6)	8.8	7.9
1980	1.57	1.75	5.2	(7.5)	-4.6	-3.2
1981	1.57	1.77	4.5	(6.5)	-1.0	5.6
1982	1.56	2.52	4.4	(6.0)	7.0	9.2
1983	1.53	0.32	4.1	(5.4)	8.5	9.2
1984	1.46	-0.95	3.8	(4.9)	5.7	7.3
1985	1.34	3.80	4.0	(4.9)	7.3	7.3
1986	1.25	3.38	3.8	(4.7)	9.1	5.1
1987	1.23	4.70	3.1	(3.8)	8.3	6.4
1988	1.21	2.26[d]	2.6[d]	(3.1)[d]	8.1[e]	--
Average						
1964-73	2.27	3.36	5.6	(9.8)	7.7	10.1
1974-80	1.61	3.20	4.0	(6.2)	10.0	10.4
1981-87	1.42	2.22	4.0	(5.2)	6.4	7.2

Sources: Economic Planning Board (EPB), *Monthly Statistics of Korea*, November 1988; EPB, *Annual Report on the Economically Active Population Survey*, various issues.

[a]Unemployment rate in nonfarm household.
[b]Nominal wage in manufacturing sector deflated by the consumer price index.
[c]Nominal wage deflated by GNP deflator, manufacturing sector.
[d]Average during January through September of 1988.
[e]Average during January through June of 1988.

levels for labor-surplus developing economies are generally analyzed using the theoretical framework developed by Harris and Todaro (1970). According to the Harris-Todaro model, as wage differentials between urban and rural sectors widen, the unemployment rates in urban sectors rise due to migration. A market clearing equilibrium wage rate is finally reached with a reduced employment probability.

This model does not explain the changing patterns of unemployment and wage growth in the Korean labor market. Contrary to the model, in Korea, real wage growth rates and urban-rural wage differentials were higher during 1974–80 than during 1964–73, while the unemployment rates were lower. Indeed, a unique feature of the Korean labor market development is that the employment expansion and the real wage growth occurred simultaneously. In this respect, the hypothesis that the success of the Korean economy is mainly attributable to maintenance of a low wage policy may not have an empirical foundation. It is true that due to a strong stabilization policy in the 1980s and relatively slower economic growth, the real wage growth in the 1980s was lower than in earlier years.

The industrialization and the corresponding changes in employment structures are depicted in Table 17.2. A dramatic reduction in agricultural employment characterizes the changing patterns of industrial employment composition. During the past 25 years, the proportion of agricultural employment fell from over 60 percent in the early 1960s to about 20 percent in the late 1980s. A comment is in order. The employment expansion of secondary industry has been very rapid until the mid 1970s, but has slowed down since then. The average employment share of the mining and manufacturing industry was 12.6 percent in 1963–73, 21.5 percent in 1974–80, and 24.2 percent in 1981–87. This phenomenon represents the effects of changing industrial policies during the mid 1970s when huge investments were made in the heavy and chemical industries. These policies, indeed, lowered the labor-absorptive capacity of industrial production. The relative slowdown of employment expansion in these industries, together with a sharp increase in real wages during the same period as shown in Table 17.1 are frequently cited as supporting evidence for the turning point hypothesis (Bai, 1982). This hypothesis argues that until the mid 1970s, economic growth was mainly led by the labor-intensive light industries, the supply of unskilled labor being almost unlimited. However, following the shift in industrial policy toward the fostering of capital-intensive heavy industries, the demand for skilled and educated manpower increased. The lack of skilled manpower, however, resulted in substantial wage increases. In this regard, the mid 1970s serves as a benchmark period in that the labor surplus argument no longer appears relevant thereafter.

On the other hand, relative employment expansion of the tertiary sector increased quite rapidly beginning in the mid 1970s, playing a key role in absorbing the persistent migration from agricultural to industrial sectors.

One of the more frequently cited characteristics of the Korean labor market is the long working hours. As presented in Table 17.3, average weekly working hours in Korea are considerably longer than in Japan and Taiwan. A comparison of working hours in the manufacturing industries of Korea and Taiwan reveals that while average weekly working hours were about the same until the mid 1970s, they began increasing in Korea and declining in Taiwan. To a certain extent, the rising working hours in the Korean manufacturing industry also reflects the effects of

Table 17.2
Industrial Composition of GNP and Employment (in percent)

Year	GNP (in constant prices)			Employment		
	Agri-culture	Mining & Manu-facturing	SOC & Others	Agri-culture	Mining & Manu-facturing	SOC & Others
1963	41.1	9.7	49.2	63.1	8.7	28.2
1964	43.5	9.8	46.7	61.9	8.8	29.3
1965	40.7	11.0	48.3	58.6	10.4	31.0
1966	40.3	11.2	48.5	57.9	10.8	31.3
1967	35.4	12.7	51.9	55.2	12.8	32.0
1968	32.3	14.0	53.7	52.4	14.0	33.6
1969	31.3	14.7	54.0	51.3	14.3	34.4
1970	28.7	16.4	54.9	50.4	14.3	35.3
1971	27.2	17.5	55.3	48.4	14.2	37.4
1972	26.5	18.7	54.8	50.6	14.2	35.2
1973	24.7	21.0	54.3	50.0	16.3	33.7
1974	24.6	22.4	53.0	48.2	17.8	34.0
1975	24.2	23.5	52.3	45.9	19.1	35.0
1976	23.2	25.1	51.7	44.6	21.8	33.6
1977	21.1	25.8	53.1	41.8	22.4	35.8
1978	17.4	28.3	54.3	38.4	23.2	38.4
1979	17.5	29.0	53.5	35.8	23.7	40.5
1980	15.1	32.0	52.9	34.0	22.6	43.4
1981	17.4	32.4	50.2	34.2	21.3	44.5
1982	16.9	32.0	51.1	32.1	21.9	46.0
1983	16.1	32.1	51.8	29.7	23.3	47.0
1984	14.9	33.8	51.3	27.1	24.2	48.7
1985	14.8	33.3	51.9	24.9	24.5	50.6
1986	13.8	34.6	51.6	23.6	25.9	50.5
1987	12.2	37.0	50.8	21.9	28.1	50.0
Average						
1963-73	31.9	15.5	52.6	53.8	12.9	33.3
1974-80	19.9	27.1	53.0	39.7	20.7	40.1
1981-87	16.0	36.5	47.5	27.5	24.2	48.3

Sources: Bank of Korea, *National Accounts*, 1988; EPB, *Annual Report on the Economically Active Population Survey*, various issues; EPB, *Monthly Statistics of Korea*, November 1988.

changing industrial policies. As stated earlier, due to a sudden shift toward promoting heavy and chemical industries, a lack of skilled technicians and engineers became apparent, resulting in longer working hours at the time of rapid economic expansion. The increase in working hours has also been attributed to a rise in wage rates.

Industrial (or international) competitiveness is generally measured by unit labor costs defined as nominal wage increases minus labor productivity gains (and foreign exchange fluctuations considered). Table 17.4 shows components of unit

Table 17.3
Weekly Hours of Work

	KOREA					JAPAN	TAIWAN
	All Industry	Manu- facturing	Wholesale & Retail	Transpor- tations	Social & Per- sonal Services	Manufac- turing	Manufac- turing
1970	51.6	53.4	48.6	53.9	50.2	43.2	--
1971	50.6	52.0	50.7	55.6	49.9	42.4	--
1972	50.9	51.7	50.5	51.7	51.5	42.2	--
1973	50.7	51.4	52.4	51.5	46.3	41.9	52.3
1974	49.6	49.9	50.7	51.9	47.0	39.9	50.0
1975	50.0	50.5	49.3	51.0	48.2	38.6	50.7
1976	50.7	52.5	49.1	50.5	46.7	40.0	51.3
1977	51.4	52.9	50.9	49.5	46.2	40.2	51.3
1978	51.3	53.0	50.8	49.4	46.4	40.4	50.9
1979	50.5	52.0	49.4	49.5	45.9	41.0	50.7
1980	51.6	53.1	50.5	50.4	47.2	41.0	50.9
1981	51.9	53.7	50.4	50.9	47.0	40.8	48.4
1982	52.2	53.8	51.0	51.9	47.4	40.8	48.1
1983	52.5	54.4	50.9	52.4	47.3	41.0	48.1
1984	52.4	54.3	49.9	53.4	46.8	41.6	48.6
1985	51.9	53.8	50.0	53.2	46.6	41.4	47.4
1986	52.5	54.7	49.7	52.8	46.2	41.0	48.1
1987	51.9	54.0	49.5	51.9	46.1	41.2	48.1
1988[a]	50.6	52.2	49.1	51.2	46.0	41.4	--

Sources: Ministry of Labor, *Report on Monthly Labour Survey*, ROK, various issues; *Monthly Statistics of Japan*, various issues; *Statistical Yearbook of the Republic of China*, 1987.

[a]Average during January through June.

labor costs by industry. Assuming that the manufacturing industry represents the tradable goods-producing sector and the social overhead capital (SOC) and services industry represents the nontradable goods-producing sector, the general expectation is that growth rates in wages and labor productivity are both higher in the manufacturing industry than in other industries. However, we find no significant differences in wage growth rates between the two sectors, although labor productivity growth in the manufacturing industry has been generally higher than in the tertiary industry. It is interesting to observe that during the period before 1980 when labor productivity of the tertiary sector was substantially lower than that of the manufacturing industry, the wage growth rate was, contrary to expectations, even slightly higher in the tertiary sector than in the manufacturing sector. Interestingly enough, the gaps in wage rates and labor productivity between the secondary and tertiary sectors have been maintained during the 1980s. Before 1980, industrial competitiveness always favored the manufacturing industry as compared to the SOC and services industry, which partly explains the rapid relative expansion of the manufacturing industry as shown in Table 17.2 earlier. If this pattern continues in the future, the growth rate of the manufacturing sector will slow down, a

Table 17.4
Unit Labor Costs by Industry (in percentage changes)

Year	Nominal Wage		Labor Productivity		Unit Labor Costs	
	Mining & Manu-facturing	SOC & Others	Mining & Manu-facturing	SOC & Others	Mining & Manu-facturing	SOC & Others
1971	16.0	15.9	13.8	-0.2	2.2	16.1
1972	13.5	21.6	7.5	6.2	6.0	15.5
1973	17.6	10.6	5.9	12.0	11.7	-1.4
1974	35.6	24.4	1.3	0.1	34.3	24.3
1975	26.8	33.6	2.1	0.5	24.7	33.1
1976	33.2	42.3	0.7	10.9	32.5	31.4
1977	33.2	31.9	9.4	5.5	23.8	26.4
1978	34.0	35.5	11.7	-0.1	22.3	35.6
1979	28.5	24.6	5.4	-1.7	23.1	26.4
1980	22.9	23.6	7.7	-13.9	15.2	37.5
1981	20.2	21.2	11.6	-3.5	8.6	24.7
1982	14.6	16.1	-1.3	0.7	15.9	15.4
1983	11.9	8.5	4.6	10.6	7.3	-2.1
1984	7.7	6.9	10.9	4.2	-3.2	2.7
1985	10.2	7.8	-1.0	-0.9	11.2	8.7
1986	9.2	7.5	6.9	8.1	2.3	-0.6
1987	11.3	9.3	0.9	8.3	10.4	1.0
Average						
1971-73	15.7	16.0	9.1	6.0	6.6	10.1
1974-80	30.6	30.8	5.5	0.2	25.1	30.7
1981-87	12.2	11.0	4.7	3.9	7.5	7.1

Sources: Ministry of Labor, *Report on Monthly Labor Survey*, June 1988; Bank of Korea, *National Accounts*, 1988.

phenomenon that has already begun to appear since the early 1980s. The low productivity in the SOC and services industry in earlier years largely reflects employment expansion policies at the time.

An inappropriate real wage may significantly distort a country's patterns of trade (Krueger, 1983). The basic implication of the Heckscher-Ohlin-Samuelson model is that for a country like Korea where labor is abundant, the wage-rental ratio must be lower; otherwise, it would be more profitable to produce more capital-intensive goods. In fact, this point is directly related to the low wage hypothesis stated earlier, which has been a prevailing view, particularly among advocates of trade protectionism abroad and those most concerned with labor rights issues. One way to inspect this argument is to see whether or not workers have been appropriately compensated for their contributions to economic growth. In order to determine the welfare implications of real wage changes, we examine the changing patterns of labor shares out of GNP by decomposing GNP growth rates into shares of real wage

Table 17.5
Decompositions of Labor Share: All Industries (in percent and ratio)

Year	GNP Growth Rate $(\dot{g})$	Labor Share[a]	Real Wage Changes[b] $(\dot{w})$	Employment Changes $(e\dot{m}p)$	$\dfrac{\dot{w}}{\dot{g}-e\dot{m}p}$	Changes in Capital/ Labor Ratio[c]
1971	9.1	40.6	2.2	3.3	0.38	10.99
1972	5.3	40.1	1.0	4.9	2.50	6.04
1973	14.0	40.6	-0.6	5.5	-0.07	6.62
1974	8.5	39.1	1.1	4.0	0.24	9.00
1975	6.8	40.8	3.9	2.1	0.83	10.73
1976	13.4	41.9	12.0	6.1	1.64	6.13
1977	10.7	44.1	14.0	3.0	1.82	11.11
1978	11.0	46.8	11.1	4.3	1.66	13.27
1979	7.0	49.1	6.9	1.3	1.21	16.73
1980	-4.8	52.4	-1.5	0.1	--	13.35
1981	6.6	52.1	4.6	2.5	1.12	7.55
1982	5.4	53.9	8.5	2.5	2.93	6.78
1983	11.9	55.5	6.9	0.9	0.63	9.51
1984	8.4	54.9	4.7	-0.5	0.53	11.53
1985	5.4	54.8	5.0	3.7	2.94	6.26
1986	12.5	54.5	5.8	3.6	0.65	6.58
1987	12.0	54.2	6.4	5.5	0.98	5.11
Average						
1971-73	9.5	40.4	0.9	4.6	0.94	7.88
1974-80	7.5	44.9	6.8	3.0	1.23	11.47
1981-87	8.9	54.3	6.0	2.6	1.39	7.61

Sources: Bank of Korea, *National Accounts*, 1988; EPB, *Annual Report on the Economically Active Population Survey*, various issues; EPB, *Monthly Statistics of Korea*, November 1988.

[a]Ratio of Compensations of employees to national income in current prices.
[b]Nominal wage changes subtracted by the changes in GNP deflator.
[c]Capital stock data were obtained from the data base of KDI quarterly econometric model.

increases and employment changes. In Table 17.5, we find that labor shares, defined as the ratio of employee compensation to national income (in current prices), increased dramatically from 40.6 percent in 1971 to 54.2 percent in 1987. We can easily see how high this rate was by comparing it with statistics for Japan and West Germany.[1] For Japan, it took about 25 years for the labor share to increase by 18 percentage points, that is from 50.3 percent in 1961 to 68.9 percent in 1985. For West Germany, the labor share increased by only 5 percentage points over the past two decades, that is, from 49 percent in 1963 to 54 percent in 1985. In Korea, the labor share increased particularly significantly during the 1970s, jumping by more than 11 percentage points, from 40.6 percent in 1971 to 52.4 percent in 1980.

To elaborate further, we now decompose the GNP growth rate into wage and employment growth rates based upon the relationship $GNP = wL + rK$. By differentiating the above equation with respect to time, we find that the labor share remains constant if and only if the sum of the increasing rates of real wage ($\dot{w}$) and employment ($\dot{emp}$) is equal to the GNP growth rate ($\dot{g}$).[2] Thus, we construct an index, $\dot{w}/(\dot{g} - \dot{emp})$, that measures the relative wage growth after controlling for the effects of employment growth. If the value of the index exceeds one, we can safely conclude that the welfare of workers has improved from a social welfare perspective.[3] Since the index values vary widely from year to year, we compare average index values. We find that not only has the average value exceeded one since the mid 1970s, but also the index values show an increasing trend; that is, the average value increased from 0.94 during 1971–73, to 1.23 during 1974-80, and to 1.39 during 1981–87. This finding negates the low wage hypothesis mentioned earlier. One interesting point to note is that during the period when real wages increased both in absolute and relative ($\dot{w}/(\dot{g} - \dot{emp})$) terms, the capital-labor ratio also increased. This result is an expected economic relationship as long as the relative increase in real wages (or a relative decrease in the costs of capital) has affected investment behavior positively.

LABOR SUPPLY AND DEMAND EQUATIONS

Specifications of Model and Explanation of Variables

In this section, we investigate the determinants of supply and demand for labor equations. The age- and sex-specific labor supply equations and industry-specific labor demand equations are estimated using quarterly time-series data from the first quarter of 1970 to the second quarter of 1988.[4]

The labor supply equations are empirically specified as follows.[5]

$$LFER_{ij} = f(SER_{ij}, RP_y, UPM, W, W/W*, LFPR_{ij}(-1))$$

where SER is the school enrollment rate, RP_y is the ratio of the population aged 15–24 to the population 15 years and over, W is the real wage, $W*$ is $\sum_{i=1}^{4} \alpha_i W_{t-i}/4$ and UPM is the unemployment rate of prime age males (25–59 years old). Subscripts i and j represent sex and age groups. SER is used only for age groups under 24 years old and for the case of females an age-specific TFR_j (total fertility rate) variable is added. The arguments for each explanatory variable are as follows.

The UPM variable is expected to capture the effects of short-run cyclical variations on the labor supply, and the unemployment rate of prime age males instead of the total unemployment rate was used because the variation of this rate basically depends upon the cyclical conditions of the economy. The W variable was used to incorporate the labor-leisure choice issue discussed in the permanent income model and the $W/W*$ variable was used as a proxy for the relative standard of living discussed in the relative income model. Although schooling and labor activities are not incompatible theoretically, the labor supply behavior of students may be different from those of nonstudents; thus SER was introduced mainly as a control variable.

A comment is in order with regard to the RP_y variable.[6] Under the assumption that the workers of different age groups are not perfectly substitutable, the variable was used to capture the overcrowding effects of the entrance to the labor market of a certain large age cohort. That is, if a baby-boom generation enters the labor market, the relative skill structure of the labor force will change toward a heavy concentration of unskilled labor. This will enhance competition within the group, which will affect the labor force participation behavior of the group.

The empirical specification of the industry-specific labor demand equation takes the following form.[7]

$$E_i = f(GNP_i, W_i, RUM, t, E_i(-1))$$

where RUM is the interest rate of the unregulated money market representing the capital cost and t is a time trend variable that captures the effects of technological development on employment demand.

Labor Supply Equations for Males

Two notable observations from the labor force participation rates are the following. First, for age groups under age 25, the labor force participation rates declined over time, particularly for the younger age groups. This is basically attributable to the sharply rising school enrollment rate during the past two decades. Specifically, between 1970 and 1987, the enrollment rate for the age group 15–19 rose from 43 percent to 79 percent and for the age group 20–24 from 14 percent to 46 percent. Second, the participation rate for the old age group 60 and over, shows an increasing trend, partly reflecting a longer life expectancy.

In Table 17.6, the estimated results of the labor force participation rate equations for males are presented. D1, D2, and D3 are seasonal dummies. Since all variables take logarithmic transformations, the estimated coefficients represent constant elasticities. In order to examine the serial correlation of estimations when the lagged dependent variables are included, Durbin's h statistic is calculated.[8] The results show that generally the serial correlation problem does not appear to be serious for most age groups. Estimated results are summarized below by explanatory variables.

Table 17.6
Labor Force Participation Rate Equations: Males

VAR/Age	15-19	20-24	25-49	50-59	60+
Constant	0.8808 (2.16)	-0.3890 (-1.36)	-0.2074 (-3.71)	-0.2583 (-2.00)	-0.9533 (-3.63)
ln SER	-0.1557 (-1.58)	-0.1425 (-3.40)	--	--	--
ln RP_y	0.1324 (2.03)	0.0092 (0.29)	0.0844 (5.78)	0.0390 (1.84)	0.0065 (0.17)
ln UPM	0.0830 (1.83)	0.0242 (1.06)	-0.0072 (-1.06)	-0.0047 (-0.27)	-0.0118 (-0.37)
ln W	--	0.0589 (1.84)	0.0244 (3.76)	0.0078 (0.61)	0.0108 (0.46)
D1	0.3726 (11.27)	0.1268 (7.40)	0.0290 (4.24)	0.0723 (3.88)	0.3833 (7.64)
D2	0.2085 (6.62)	0.1121 (6.81)	0.0363 (7.18)	0.1278 (9.94)	0.5502 (17.88)
D3	0.0478 (1.58)	0.0827 (5.41)	0.0320 (7.41)	0.1081 (9.50)	0.3768 (17.87)
ln DEP (-1)	0.8954 (16.62)	0.5350 (5.04)	0.0711 (0.68)	0.0430 (0.36)	0.4242 (3.81)
R^2	0.9749	0.9156	0.8044	0.7760	0.9300
SEE	0.0780	0.0363	0.0115	0.0300	0.0538
Durbin's h	-0.6983	-0.9500	1.8776	--	-0.8293

Note: Figures in parentheses are t-statistics.

First, the SER variable produced, as expected, negative coefficients for both young age groups, although the coefficient is marginally significant for the younger age group. The estimated elasticity turns out to be about the same for both groups, about 0.15. Second, the RP_y variable yielded positive coefficients for all groups, reflecting the social phenomenon that the overcrowding of a certain group increases the labor force participation activities of all groups. An interesting point to note is that the statistical significance of the coefficient for the younger age group is stronger than those for others, indicating the relatively severe competition within the group, which is consistent with our earlier theoretical expectations.

Table 17.7
Employment Demand Equations by Industry

VAR	All Industry		Mining & Manufacturing		SOC & Services	
	Eq. 1	Eq. 2	Eq. 1	Eq. 2	Eq. 1	Eq. 2
Constant	4.4907	3.8051	2.1051	-0.6187	3.3843	3.7497
	(4.58)	(3.67)	(3.17)	(-0.52)	(3.25)	(2.71)
ln GNP	-0.1549	-0.1904	0.7087	0.3643	-0.0169	0.2278
	(-1.98)	(2.62)	(5.66)	(2.09)	(-0.18)	(1.85)
ln W	0.2018	0.3329	-0.3411	0.0950	-0.0474	-0.2259
	(3.45)	(5.23)	(-3.53)	(0.51)	(-1.05)	(-2.90)
ln RUM	-0.0109	-0.011	0.0291	0.0305	0.0103	0.0162
	(-0.69)	(-0.07)	(1.57)	(1.65)	(0.74)	(1.15)
t	0.0034	0.0544	-0.0063	0.0908	0.0056	0.0018
	(2.55)	(3.48)	(-3.38)	(2.51)	(2.57)	(0.07)
ln GNP × t	--	0.0060	--	0.0084	0.0056	-0.0029
		(3.90		(2.69)		(-2.58)
ln W × t	--	-0.0088	--	-0.0137	--	0.0022
		(-3.92)		(-2.73)		(0.82)
D1	0.1209	0.1795	-0.0385	-0.0591	-0.0210	0.0075
	(3.48)	(4.96)	(-2.12)	(-3.08)	(-1.19)	(0.35)
D2	0.2147	0.2554	-0.1037	-0.1168	-0.0130	0.0194
	(8.37)	(9.92)	(-6.32)	(-7.11)	(-0.77)	(0.81)
D3	0.1232	0.1764	0.0080	0.0043	0.0189	0.0432
	(3.95)	(5.64)	(0.55)	(0.34)	(1.23)	(1.94)
ln DEP(-1)	0.3982	0.3325	0.5637	0.5939	0.6647	0.6463
	(2.89)	(2.42)	(6.07)	(6.62)	(7.61)	(6.73)
R^2	0.96238	0.9797	0.9872	0.9886	0.9892	0.9906
SEE	0.0353	0.0318	0.0417	0.0400	0.0322	0.0305
Durbin's h	--	--	-1.1915	-0.7188	0.5227	-0.5196

Note: Figures in parentheses are t-statistics.

Third, the theoretically expected signs of the coefficient on UPM are negative if the discouraged worker hypothesis is to be empirically supported. While the sign of the coefficients for age groups 50–59 and 60 and over turn out to be negative, the coefficient is statistically insignificant for both groups. On the contrary, the coefficient for the group aged 15–19 is positive and statistically significant. the conjecture for this outcome is that as economic conditions worsen, the secondary labor force is likely to participate more in the labor market to maintain their aspired living standard, which is in fact the implication of the additional worker hypothesis.[9]

Employment Demand Equations

The estimated results of the demand equation are reported in Table 17.7. For each industry, we present two equations. The first is a basic equation and the second includes two additional variables: ln GNP × t and ln W × t. The rationale for the inclusion of the two interaction variables is the following. As stated earlier, the labor absorptive capacity of economic growth has been declining due to technological development and a deepening of the industrial structure. Obviously, as the proportion of capital- and technology-intensive industries increases, given the economic growth, the employment demand requirement for a unit production is likely to decline. In order to investigate this phenomenon, the interaction variables were introduced. To elaborate, the coefficient on GNP, b_1 for example, is assumed to change over time rather than remain constant. Therefore, by including both variables, GNP and GNP × t, the actual coefficient of GNP will be $b_1 + b_2 t$, where b_2 is an estimated coefficient on the GNP × t variable. Thus, if we find a positive value of b_1 and a negative value of b_2, then we would infer that the labor absorptive capacity of economic growth declines over time. The same logic can be applied to the wage variable. With low substitutability between capital and labor or the existence of excess supply of labor as was the case in Korea in earlier years, the wage rate changes could not have responded adequately to the changing environment of the labor market. However, as the industrial structure advances and the labor factor becomes costly due to substantial wage rises, then the substitutability of capital and technology for labor will increase. This pattern is expected to be captured by the addition of the interaction variable, W × t.

The estimated results are summarized below. First, looking at the all industry equation, the coefficients of GNP and W in the basic equation were negative and positive respectively, which is contrary to our theoretical expectations. However, we find that the signs of the coefficients on the interaction variables were the same as expected. To explain more specifically, the coefficient of GNP is, in fact, -0.1904 + 0.0060 × t, which indicates that from the thirty-second quarter of the sample period (that is, if t > 31.7, then the value will be positive), the value of the coefficient of GNP will turn out to be positive as expected. On the other hand, the coefficient of W will be negative as expected from the thirty-eighth quarter.

Based on the above results, we can safely conclude that the expected effect of GNP growth and wage changes on employment demand has been maintained from the late 1970s. However, the hypothesis that the labor absorptive capacity of economic growth would show a decreasing trend was not supported statistically. According to the above estimated results, the employment elasticity with respect

316

C. Kim

to GNP would increase rather than decrease, by 0.0060 per period, contrary to our expectations. On the other hand, the estimated result of the wage variables turned out to support our conjecture that the employment demand becomes more sensitive with respect to wage changes over time. From the above findings, we can draw the following conclusions. The declining labor absorptive capacity phenomenon hypothesis generally neglects the impact of wage changes on employment demand, by regressing employment changes only against GNP changes. In this context, we find that in Korea the declining labor absorption phenomenon is still not apparent, while the negative impact of wage increases on employment demand contraction has already appeared and the magnitude of impacts is increasing.

A similar pattern is also observed in the mining and manufacturing industry. One interesting finding is that the estimated elasticities of employment demand with respect to GNP and wage rates are both higher than those of other industries, which are rather expected results. That is, for the case of SOC or service industries, employment may be affected by government social policies, for example, the public employment policies during economic recessions to boost the economy. However, for the case of the manufacturing industry, the employment demand is related more to changes in relative factor prices.

The estimated results of the SOC and service industries reveal a slightly different pattern of employment demand from that of the mining and manufacturing industry. That is, the employment demand elasticity with respect to GNP growth has been declining, while the wage elasticity has remained constant over time. One caveat is in order. About 40 percent of those employed in the tertiary industry are self-employed and unpaid family workers whose employment status is not directly related to employee wage changes. Further, government employees constitute a significant portion of the employed persons in the industry whose wage changes reflect government policy changes rather than market conditions. As stated above, the employment in this industry may thus be determined largely by government employment policies.

WAGE EQUATIONS

In this section, we examine the determinants of wage rate changes, focusing especially on the impact of labor market tightness on wage changes.

Theoretical Considerations

Perhaps the most widely used specification for wage equations is the expectations-augmented Phillips curve. That is,

$$w_t = \alpha_0 + \sum_{i=0}^{k} \beta_i U_{t-i} + \sum_{i=1}^{m} \gamma_i p_{t-i} + \varepsilon_1$$

where *w* and *p* are increasing rates of wages and prices, respectively, *U* is an unemployment rate, and ε_1 is a disturbance term. The distributed lag structure was introduced for *U* and *p* because it generally takes time for firms to make necessary adjustments corresponding to changes in labor market conditions. In the traditional Phillips curve analysis, the distributed lag structure is generally used for p, but not for *U*. But practically all wage negotiations between firms and labor unions cover a certain time period. Thus if a distributed lag structure is not introduced, it imposes unnecessary restrictions on the estimations. The direct effect of *U* on *w* is captured by the sum of βi's, but there is, in fact, an indirect impact that is transmitted from the price equation. Generally, the price equation may be specified as follows:

$$p_t = \delta_0 + \delta_1 m + \delta_2(w - q) + \delta_3 D + \varepsilon_2$$

where *m* represents the increasing rate of factor costs except wages, *q* is productivity growth, and *D* denotes aggregate demand. If we insert the price equation into the wage equation, we find that the lag structure of *p* simply represents an infinite lag structure of *U*, which indeed captures the indirect effect of *U* on *w*. Following Hamada and Kurosaka (1986), we use consumer price index (CPI) changes for *p*.

The analysis focuses mainly on the following. The *U* variable is replaced by the UGAP variable defined below, and the coefficient on UGAP is assumed to be a function of time, that is, $\beta(t)$ rather than a fixed β. This is based upon the same logic applied in the analysis of the employment demand equations.[10] The UGAP variable is defined as *U - Un*, where *Un* represents a full employment unemployment rate or a nonaccelerating inflation rate of unemployment. The *Un* variable was constructed by removing the impact of the short-run cyclical component of unemployment, while the effect of secular swings due to demographic changes is incorporated. Specifically, from $\ln Ui = \alpha_0 + \alpha_1 \ln UPM + \alpha_2 \ln RPy$, *UPM* = 2.5 percent was inserted instead of actual values to calculate *Un*. The selection of 2.5 percent as a benchmark value of *UPM* was made given the consideration that historically wage rates have accelerated when *UPM* has been below 2.5 percent. The value was therefore chosen as a minimum level that does not accelerate wage inflation.

Empirical Findings

The estimated equations are reported in Table 17.8. Considering that the dependent variable is a rate of change, rather than an absolute level, the explanatory power of the equations is regarded as fairly strong. The serial correlation problem does not appear to be serious. The first equation is a basic one. It indicates that as prices rise by 1 percent, wages increase by about 0.53 percent the next period. There is a trade-off between unemployment and inflation in that a 1 percentage

Table 17.8
Wage Equations

VAR	Eq. 1	Eq. 2	Eq. 3
Constant	5.6679	5.8795	5.5646
	(6.11)	(6.82)	(5.13)
UGAP	-1.3024	--	--
	(-2.25)		
(UGAP × t)$_t$		-0.0366	-0.0155
		(-3.47)	(-1.35)
t-1			-0.0117
			(-2.72)
t-2			-0.0084
			(-2.34)
t-3			-0.0055
			(-0.94)
t-4			-0.0032
			(-0.51)
t-5			-0.0014
			(-0.31)
			Σ-0.0456
			(-3.240)
p_{t-1}	0.5317	0.4980	0.2069
	(3.65)	(3.60)	(1.63)
t-2			0.1583
			(2.71)
t-3			0.1153
			(2.75)
t-4			0.0780
			(1.35)
t-5			0.0463
			(0.77)
t-6			0.0203
			(0.49)
			Σ0.6250
			(3.19)
D1	-7.2207	-7.1734	-7.9713
	(-6.52)	(-6.95)	(-7.48)
D2	-0.9069	-0.8390	0.3043
	(-0.83)	(-0.83)	(0.31)
D3	1.8427	1.9364	2.5068
	(1.70)	(1.90)	(2.51)
R^2	0.7173	0.7447	0.7572
SEE	2.9982	2.8490	2.8257
D.W.	2.0238	2.0539	2.1237

Note: Figures in parentheses are t-statistics.

point increase in the unemployment rate causes a reduction in the wage inflation rate by 1.3 percent.

By substituting UGAP × t for UGAP, we find that the magnitude of the coefficient on p becomes a little smaller, while the coefficient on the UGAP × t variable becomes more significant and the explanatory power of the equation increases. One possible explanation of this finding is that the Phillips curve might have shifted upward over time. For example, during stagflation periods, we frequently observe that both U and w increase over time, refuting the theoretically expected inverse relationship between the two variables. Furthermore, the implicit contract in labor negotiations would make the slope of U in the wage equation steeper. The estimated result indicates that the impact of a 1 percentage point additional increase in the unemployment rate on the reduction in wage inflation is increasing by about 0.15 percent per year.

SUMMARY AND CONCLUSIONS

In this chapter, we examined the development path of the Korean labor market during the past two and a half decades, investigated the determinants of age- and sex-specific labor force participation rates and industry-specific employment demands, and inspected the relationships among wage inflation, labor market tightness and price inflation. Some important findings are summarized below.

First, perhaps the most unique feature of the Korean labor market is the simultaneous occurrence of employment expansion and real wage growth, a phenomenon not readily explained by conventional labor market theories for developing economies. Consequentially, we observed that the labor share of Korea has increased much faster than those in other nations including Japan and West Germany. These observations negate all alleged hypotheses that the strong performance of the Korean economy is mainly attributable to maintenance of a low wage policy.

Second, the estimated results for age- and sex-specific labor force participation behavior reveals that the discouraged worker effect has not been apparent for most groups except for females aged 20–24. For prime age workers, changes in real wage rates that capture the labor-leisure choice behavior turn out to be an important determinant. For younger age groups of both sexes, demographic compositional changes that reflect an overcrowded labor market appear to have a strong influence on the labor force participation decision.

Third, analysis of employment demand determination does not produce supporting evidence for the hypothesis of a declining labor-absorptive capacity of economic growth. On the other hand, the empirical results indicate that the negative impact of real wage increases on employment demand has become stronger over time. These findings imply that the seemingly apparent phenomenon of declining labor-absorptive capacity of economic growth has not been caused simply by continuous development of labor-saving technology, but has also resulted from increasing factor substitution of capital and technology for labor due to the relatively rapidly increasing factor costs of labor. In other words, as long as relative factor prices remain stable, employment is likely to continue to expand as the economy grows.

Fourth, we find a significant inverse relationship between wage inflation and the unemployment rate after controlling for the effect of changes in the nonaccelerating inflation rate of unemployment on wage inflation. Also, we observe that the impact of labor market tightness on wage inflation has increased over time, reflecting upward shifts of the Phillips curve.

NOTES

1. *Yearbook of Labor Statistics*, ILO, 1986.

2. Needless to say, the statistics that strictly satisfy the definitional relationship are unobtainable. In practice, the above relationship is used rather to compute the imputed values of wages for non-wage earners such as self-employed and unpaid family workers or rental prices of capital. Thus, the absolute magnitude of each variable of the relationship may not be accurately calculated. In this study, however, we are comparing percentage changes of each term of the relationship, which holds under the assumption that the unobservable component of each term moves consistently with the observable component over time.

3. The term social welfare is loosely defined here. As long as labor share increases, it is meant here that workers' welfare improved.

4. Industry-specific wage data were collected beginning in 1970.

5. The empirical specification is based on Wachter (1972). For discussions on the labor supply equations, see Mincer (1962), Tellar (1964), and Perry (1977).

6. For a detailed discussion, see Wachter and Kim (1982).

7. The specification follows Ball and St. Cyr (1966).

8. See Johnston (1984).

9. To economize space the findings from the estimation of labor supply equations for females will be summarized in the last section.

10. Perloff and Wachter (1978) used the UGAP variable in testing Okun's law for the U.S. economy.

REFERENCES

Bai, Moo Ki, "The Turning Point in the Korean Economy," *The Developing Economies*, June 1982, 117–40.

Ball, R. J., and St. Cyr, E.B.A., "Short Term Employment Functions in the British Manufacturing Industry," *Review of Economic Studies*, *33*, July 1966, 179–207.

Hamada, K., and Kurosaka, Y., "Trends in Unemployment, Wages and Productivity: The Case of Japan," *Economica*, *53*, supplement 1986, S275–S296.

Harris, J. R., and Todaro, M. P., "Migration, Unemployment, and Development," *American Economic Review, 60*, March 1970, 126–42.

Johnston, J., *Econometric Methods*, third edition, New York: McGraw-Hill, 1984.

Krueger, A. O., *Trade and Employment in Developing Economies: Synthesis and Conclusions*, Vol. III, Chicago: University of Chicago Press, 1983.

Mincer, J., "Labor Force Participation of Married Women," in H. G. Lewis, ed., *Aspects of Labor Economics*, Princeton: Princeton University Press, 1962.

Perloff, J. M., and Wachter, M. L., "A Production Function Nonaccelerating Inflation Approach to Potential Output: Is Measured Output Too High?" Discussion paper 20a, University of Pennsylvania, April 1978.

Perry, G. L., "Potential Output and Productivity," *Brookings Papers on Economic Activity I*, 1977, 11–47.

Tellar, A., "The Relation of Labor Force to Employment," *Industrial and Labor Relations Review, 17*, April 1964, 454–51.

Wachter, M. L., "A Labor Supply Model for Secondary Workers," *Review of Economics and Statistics, 54*, May 1972, 141–51.

Wachter, M. L., and Kim, Choongsoo, "Time Series Changes in Youth Joblessness," in R. B. Freeman and D. Wise, eds., *Youth Labor Market Problem: Its Nature, Causes, and Consequences*, Chicago: University of Chicago Press, 1982, 155–98.

Part Five

THE BIG BUSINESSES (*JAEBULS*)
AND MANAGEMENT STYLES

One of the unique characteristics of Korean economy is the rise of big business groups—*jaebuls*—and business concentration. The rise of *jaebuls* can be traced back to the government-business nexus whereby big business, serving as a loco-motive for economic growth, was entrusted with the execution of the government's policies. In the early days of rapid economic growth, the growth of large-scale firms meant taking advantage of economies of scale, new capital intensive technology, and organizational and marketing superiority, especially in the international arena.

In the first chapter of this section, Y. K. Lee gives a succinct overview of the causes and consequences of Korea's big business giants, and the role of government policies affecting *jaebuls'* growth. He draws attention to the peculiarity of Korea's *jaebuls* by showing that as of 1985, five *jaebuls* accounted for 23.0 percent of the total sales in the manufacturing sector, and the top ten *jaebuls* accounted for 30.2 percent of the total sales. Eleven Korean conglomerates made the 1987 *Fortune* 500 list of largest non-U.S. industrials. Lee gives a mixed evaluation of the role of big business groups in Korea's economic development, and warns that business concentration is inimical to economic democracy and that the highly leveraged expansion of firms makes Korea's economy vulnerable to economic shocks and could undermine economic efficiency.

In the second chapter, E. H. Kim focuses on the unusually high degree of financial leverage in Korea's corporate sector. His study dispels the common perception that the Japanese corporate sector has an equally high degree of financial

Korean firms. The average equity to total value (equity plus debt) ratios were calculated and compared with those for Japanese and U.S. corporations. In order to avoid the bias in book value-based measures, Kim used equity ratios based on market value of equity. The uniqueness of financial structure among Korean corporations is that the largest firms have the highest financial leverage. For example, during the 1984-86 period, more than one third of the largest 10 percent of the listed firms had equity ratios of less than 5 percent. Kim cites the income tax system and government's frequent bailouts of ailing large firms as key factors contributing to the extreme financial leverage among Korean firms.

In the last chapter, Alice Amsden examines, in an interesting way, the management profile in the large Korean firms in conjunction with the subcontracting practice in the automobile industry as an example.

Korea's modern industrial firms are typically under the ownership and control of the original founder or his son. But the top managers are unrelated familially to the chairman and are recruited from diverse sources. A *jaebul's* structure is multidivisional, but its general office tends to be relatively small. A small or nonexistent general office is indicative of how decision making is distributed between owners and salaried managers—who are entrusted with decisions about product, R&D, and marketing.

Subcontracting is viewed as an ideal vehicle by which the progressive practices of modern industrial enterprise spread to the remainder of the economy. The production system of subcontractors is an extension of the prime contractors, and salaried managers themselves are often transferred to the subcontracting firms, thereby raising the education level of the subcontractors. In this respect, subcontracting has tended to generalize the practices of salaried managers. At the same time the efficiency of salaried management has become one of Korea's competitive strengths.

18

Conglomeration and Business Concentration in Korea

Young Ki Lee

INTRODUCTION

The rise of big business groups is a striking feature of Korea's economic development. Most Korean conglomerates, commonly known as *jaebuls*, were founded less than a generation ago as small businesses by entrepreneurs who still exercise strong control over them. From these humble beginnings, big business groups expanded by diversifying into a wide range of business areas. Many now produce and export a variety of products from toys and textiles to automobiles and tankers.

In terms of structure, contemporary Korean *jaebuls* resemble the *zaibatsu* of the Meiji era in Japan. Korean *jaebuls* are usually organized around a few flagship companies that control and own stock in other companies. The controlling power of a group is concentrated in the hands of the owner-founder, generally called "chairman."

There is, however, an important difference between Korean *jaebuls* and Japanese *zaibatsu*. Prewar *zaibatsu* controlled their own banks. *Jaebuls*, on the other hand, must rely on government-controlled credit institutions. This is central to government-business relations in Korea and has an important bearing on the extent of private economic power.

There have been mixed evaluations of the growth of big business groups in Korea. Some say that big *jaebuls* have been instrumental in the rapid growth of the Korean economy. The emergence and existence of *jaebul* groups were necessary for the big push in the takeoff stage of Korea's economic development. Only through the organizational and entrepreneurial superiority of business groups could Korea participate in the world markets for shipbuilding, automobiles, steel, high-tech semiconductors, and so forth.

However, many also criticize the *jaebuls*, accusing them of borrowing excessively to finance expansion, buying or squeezing out small- and medium-sized companies, and charging high prices made possible by their monopolistic market power. Concentration of economic power and wealth in the hands of a few individuals is being strongly criticized by those who argue that it was the government's generous allocation of subsidized loans to businesses expanding into strategic industries that propelled the rapid growth of the *jaebuls* in the 1960s and 1970s.[1]

The Korean government seems to be rethinking its past favoritism toward large firms. Though the government inevitably relied upon big business groups for large-scale development projects and export promotion, it has been trying to curb their unlimited expansion and to prevent them from exercising their market power over small- and medium-sized firms. In addition, the government is stressing financial and managerial assistance to small- and medium-sized firms.

In the next section, this study reviews the status of big business groups in the Korean economy in terms of aggregate size. The following sections briefly discuss the causes and consequences of business concentration. The next section describes government policies affecting *jaebuls*, and the final section concludes the study.

THE RELATIVE SIZE OF BIG BUSINESS GROUPS IN KOREA

Share of Economic Activity

The formation and growth of conglomerate business groups has had a strong effect on Korea's economy and on business activity in Korea. Table 18.1 shows the continuous growth in the *jaebuls'* share of manufacturing sector activity. For the top five *jaebuls*, the share of manufacturing sales increased from 15.7 percent in 1978 to 23.0 percent in 1985.[2]

This is a remarkable rate of relative increase given the extremely rapid growth of Korea's overall economy. Not only did *jaebuls* grow faster than the economy as a whole, but the largest groups grew even more rapidly than the smaller groups. The employment share of *jaebuls*, however, decreased during the early 1980s, reflecting the *jaebuls'* moving into more capital-intensive industries.

The public is concerned at how quickly the concentration of economic power in Korea has increased in only thirty years from a negligible level in the early 1950s.

International Comparison of the Size of Korean Business Groups

Eleven Korean conglomerates were listed in 1987 among the *Fortune* 500 largest industrials outside the United States (Table 18.2). Four of them were ranked in the top one hundred. Korean conglomerates have made big jumps in the rankings in

Table 18.1
***Jaebul* Share in Manufacturing Sector (in percent)**

Groups	Sales			Employment			Value Added	
	1978	1982	1985	1978	1982	1985	1982	1985
Top								
5	15.7	22.6	23.0	9.5	8.4	9.7	17.4	18.7
10	21.2	30.2	30.2	13.9	12.2	11.4	23.1	24.2
20	29.3	36.6	36.4	18.2	16.0	15.5	29.4	34.4
30	34.1	40.7	40.2	22.2	18.6	17.6	33.2	39.6

Source: Updated from K. U. Lee (1985).

recent years. The Samsung Group, for example, ranked 38th out of 500 in 1984, and 20th in 1987, with a sales volume of US $21 billion. The group also ranked 32nd on the list of the world's 50 biggest industrial corporations. The Lucky-Goldstar Group has also gained in the rankings from 43rd in 1984 to 32nd in 1987.

The *Fortune* rankings, however, exaggerate the size of Korean corporations to a certain degree, since the sales volume of Korean groups are aggregated for all affiliated companies. Although the aggregate size of Korean big business groups is large, they pale in comparison with major overseas companies. Table 18.3

Table 18.2
The Size of Korean Conglomerates: International Comparison

Group Name	Rank in Fortune 500		Total Sales (1987)
	1984	1987	(million US$)
Samsung	38	20	21,054
Hyundai	39	--	--
Lucky-Goldstar	43	32	14,422
Daewoo	48	35	13,438
Sunkyung	62	90	6,782
Ssangyong	--	153	4,583
Korea Explosives	185	181	3,564
Pohang Iron & Steel	209	186	3,533
Hyundai Motor Co.[a]	--	191	3,437
Hyosung	216	206	3,258
Hyundai Heavy Ind.[a]	--	225	2,965
Doosan	413	430	1,478

Sources: Fortune, August 1, 1988; Updated from Jones, 1984.

[a]Affiliates of Hyundai Group. Although Hyundai Group as a whole is not listed in 1987 in the *Fortune* 500, the group is one of the top five conglomerates in Korea. It was ranked in 1984 as the 39th largest non-U.S. industrial, immediately following the Samsung Group.

Table 18.3
Relative Size of Korea's Large Enterprises, 1987 (in US $ million)

Industry	Company Name	Country	Sales
Automobiles	Hyundai Motor Co.	Korea	3,437
	Daewoo Motor Co.	Korea	1,164
	G.M.	U.S.A.	101,782
	Toyota Motor Co.	Japan	41,455
Electric & Electronics	Samsung Elec. Co.	Korea	2,883
	Goldstar Co.	Korea	2,458
	Westinghouse Elec.	U.S.A.	10,679
	Hitachi Ltd.	Japan	30,332

Sources: Korea Investment Trust Co., 1988, *Major Companies in Korea*; and *Fortune*, August 1, 1988.

compares the relative size of Korea's leading companies with major American and Japanese companies in the same lines of business. Hyundai Motor Company, the largest automobile maker in Korea, is only about one-thirtieth the size of GM in terms of sales volume, and Samsung Electric Company is less than one-tenth the size of Hitachi of Japan.

While each group is gigantic in size, individual companies within a group are still small by international standards. These statistics clearly indicate that Korean conglomerates are highly diversified with a large number of affiliated companies.

Characteristics of Korean Business Groups

Significant characteristics of major business groups in Korea include the following:

a. The leading four Korean conglomerates[3] are substantially larger than the next largest groups. In 1987, the sales volume of Daewoo, the fourth largest group, was almost twice that of the next largest group, Sunkyung.

b. Most groups have general trading companies (GTCs) and construction companies as their major business lines. This often results in severe and sometimes cut-throat competition among big groups in export and overseas construction markets. The tendency of *jaebuls* to expand their business lines over a wide range of products often has led to overinvestment and excessive production capacity. When the government decided, for example, to promote heavy electrical and machinery industries, many *jaebuls* jumped competitively into these lines of business with huge capital investments, consequently resulting in overcapacity in the aggregate.

c. On the average, the top few leading companies in each conglomerate group contribute dominantly to the group's aggregate sales volume. The remaining companies in each group thus share only a small portion of the group's total sales. For the Hyundai Group in 1984, 31 affiliate companies accounted for only 28.5 percent of the group's aggregate sales. These statistics reflect a common feature of big business groups: they are highly diversified conglomerates engaged in a wide range of business activities.

d. Industrial groups in Korea are prohibited from owning and controlling banks. Although a few *jaebuls* have financial affiliates such as insurance companies, securities houses, and provincial banks, big business groups are prohibited from owning more than 8 percent of outstanding equity shares of major commercial banks in order to prevent the banks from being controlled by a few *jaebul* groups. This is one significant difference between Korean *jaebul* groups and Japanese big business groups, which include banks that serve as the groups' financial centers. Since Korean *jaebuls* must rely heavily on government-controlled credit allocations, *jaebul* growth is dependent upon government credit supply policy. This is central to government-business relations in Korea and has an important bearing on the extent of private economic power.

e. Group companies are linked by interlocking directorates and crossholding of stocks, both of which strengthen the controlling power of the owner or founder, who usually owns about 10–20 percent of the total outstanding shares of the group's companies as a whole.

BACKGROUND OF THE RAPID EXPANSION OF BIG BUSINESS GROUPS

Most of Korea's big business groups began as small shops or factories after the Korean War in the early 1950s. Several factors explain the rapid expansion of *jaebuls*, including the government's confidence in their experience and organizational superiority, distorted factor markets (especially for credit), the opportunity to gain profits from inflation, and strong entrepreneurial ambition to build corporate empires.

Economic Development and Government-Business Interaction: A Principal-Agent Relationship

During the period of rapid economic development, the Korean government explicitly and implicitly favored big business groups. One theory on the increasing concentration of economic power in a rapidly growing economy is that "economic concentration is a natural result of economic growth. Economic modernity means taking advantage of economies of scale in technology, organization, and marketing. It requires placing resources in the hands of those entrepreneurs who have shown themselves most capable of survival in the international arena. The rapid rise in business concentration is thus merely one inescapable facet of the transformation of a growing economy from a primitive economic structure to one which is modern and internationally competitive."[4]

In this respect, it seems that the increased economic concentration or rise of big business groups may in part be a requirement for rapid economic growth. X-efficiency in terms of organizational and entrepreneurial advantages possessed by *jaebuls* may have been particularly important in their moving into new, large-scale, capital-intensive areas requiring modern technology, such as heavy and chemical industries.

This theory may provide grounds for the government's tendency to rely on big business groups to achieve efficiency through economies of scale, especially in the heavy and chemical industries, and to promote exports by setting up general trading companies.

In this respect, the interaction between the government and large private enterprises can be thought of as a principal-agent relationship. One may view the government as playing the role of a principal body in designing economic development programs. It achieves growth targets by using the private sector as its agent for investment, production, and export. For the successful implementation of industrial programs, the government has exerted considerable influence over business activities by providing various incentives and subsidies to private industries complying with government plans.

The most powerful tool in directing the private sector was the allocation of scarce financial resources such as bank credit and foreign exchange. Underpriced credit was channeled predominantly into target industries and thus into the hands of a relatively small number of business groups. This behavior may be attributable not only to political favoritism toward *jaebuls* but also to the government's belief in the *jaebuls*' proven record of performance and efficient use of resources.

The government often rescued troubled firms, mostly large ones, in order to avoid massive unemployment and the consequent collapse of the financial system due to bankruptcies. The government bailout practices substantially reduced the downside risk of business ventures and thus encouraged entrepreneurs to launch high-risk, high-return, large-scale projects, which contributed greatly to the emergence of big business conglomerates in Korea.

GTCs and Conglomeration

In 1975, the government introduced the "general trading company (GTC)" system to promote exports. The GTCs were designed to play the role of "window" or "representative" of small- and medium-sized export enterprises by taking care of all aspects of their export trade. In other words, a functional division of labor between export traders and producers was to be promoted.

It was the government's intention to encourage scale expansion of GTCs by appointing trading subsidiaries of large business groups to be GTCs. The government originally imposed requirements for companies to be designated as GTCs, such as minimum export volume and minimum number of export products. This policy led to excessive competition not only among GTCs but also between GTCs and export producers.[5]

Theoretically, trading companies can, as commissioned merchants, act as intermediaries in export trade transactions even if they have no equity interests in the concerned manufacturing activities. Alternatively, GTCs themselves can take the initiative of setting up their own manufacturing ventures to create and exclusively capture business opportunities. Korean GTCs have adopted the latter strategy in order to maximize economies of scope. This has resulted in the establishment of manufacturing firms by GTCs, or in mergers and takeovers of export producers, thus increasing the concentration of economic and market power in large business groups.

The Distorted Credit Market

The credit market has been the most distorted and imperfect market in the Korean economy. Capital generally has been underpriced throughout the rapid growth period. Inflation-adjusted real rates of interest on official loans have been negative or near zero during most of the 1960s and 1970s.[6]

Under such conditions, the size and power of big business groups can be used to special advantage in exploiting quasi-rents accompanying loan market disequilibria. Quantitative access to low-priced capital is a critical factor in determining the speed of enterprise growth. Privileged access of big groups to credit enables them to enjoy advantages in product markets when competing with non-*jaebul* groups, including small- and medium-sized firms.

Entrepreneurial Ambition to Build Corporate Empires

Businessmen have a variety of ambitions. Some entrepreneurs seem to be primarily interested in the profitability and growth of their firms as organizations for the production and distribution of goods and services. Their energy is directed toward improving the quality of their products, reducing costs, and developing technologies.

Another type of entrepreneur is driven by the desire to create a powerful industrial empire extending over a wide range of businesses. Successful empire-building entrepreneurs must have initiative and be aggressive. They are primarily interested in extending the scope of their activities through the establishment of new firms and through the acquisition or elimination of competitors. This unusual penchant for expanding operations can be loosely characterized as empire-building behavior.[7]

Many Korean conglomerates seem to have followed "growth first" or "revenue maximization" strategies during the period of their rapid emergence in the nation's economy. In this regard, many Korean entrepreneurs seem to have aggressively sought to build business empires. Aggressiveness was necessary in undertaking risky projects such as the construction of world-class shipyards, or the development of large-scale automobile factories. However, the desire to build corporate empires has also resulted in the excessive expansion of business groups to the detriment of sound social and economic development.

CONSEQUENCES OF BUSINESS CONCENTRATION

The fast growth of giant enterprises or business groups has been a major part of Korea's industrialization and economic development. Their rapid expansion, however, has also created unwanted consequences and potential problems.

Diminished Resilience of the Economy

When individual firms or groups of firms grow to excessively large dimensions the resilience of an economy to changing circumstances is diminished. This was the case for the Korean economy in deep recession in the mid-1980s when it was forced to undergo major industrial restructuring, including the scaling down of some established industries, especially large ones suffering from overcapacity. Large firms could cut down operations and prolong the agony of painful adjustment, but this did not obviate the necessity of change. Smaller firms, however, could adjust much more easily and with less pain to the new environment by changing the pattern and scale of manufacturing.

Business Concentration and Economic Democracy

The case against unlimited expansion through conglomeration and concentration of economic power is not confined to economic considerations only. There is a potential danger that high economic concentration of wealth and power will dominate other interests and thus hinder the development of economic democracy.

Growth through conglomeration has no known size limitations. Unlike internal expansion—a response to an increase in demand for an individual firm's products—expansion through conglomeration originates as a managerial decision. Conglomerate expansion is largely an intentional act rather than a natural or inevitable consequence of market forces. Horizontal mergers are limited by the demand for a particular product; vertical mergers are bounded by a particular production and distribution system; both of these types of integration are also more directly constrained by existing fair trade laws.

Growth through conglomeration may come at the expense of more productive uses of investment capital. Conglomerate expansion probably confers no benefits on the economy as a whole and may well impose substantial long-term social and political costs. It undermines independent decision making as economic and political power is absorbed by acquiring firms. This seriously hinders political and social progress.[8]

Private Efficiency vs. Social Efficiency

Too much emphasis placed on the efficiency of economies of scope has resulted in the conglomeration of big business groups. Although the internal efficiency of big business groups might have been increased by vertical and horizontal integration of production and marketing activities, such expansion does not necessarily enhance overall efficiency from a social standpoint. Dominance of big business groups inevitably reduces fair economic opportunities for smaller firms and undermines a competitive market environment. When private efficiency is achieved at the cost of reduced social welfare or increased social inequity, it is a pseudo-efficiency not desirable for the society.

Increased Aggregate Risk Due to Excessive Leverage

Korean firms in general are highly leveraged. The debt-equity ratio of the average manufacturing firm is around 4 to 1. The bigger a firm's size, the higher this ratio, due to credit-financed expansion. A higher debt-equity ratio increases financial risk, amplifying the impact of business fluctuations. The excessive size of business firms, in combination with their weak financial structure, increases the overall risk to the Korean economy and reduces the allocational efficiency of financial resources.[9]

If a large Korean enterprise gets into trouble, the whole group, which is so large that it cannot be allowed to fail, is endangered. Therefore, the existence of large groups forces the government to implicitly or explicitly guarantee group credit. On many occasions, the government has bailed out troubled firms by providing them with special loans and/or tax concessions. This inevitably reduces the amount of funds available to other more productive firms or industries, and thus reduces the overall efficiency of resource allocation.

Product Market Distortions

One of the most undesirable consequences of the concentration of economic power, or the growth of *jaebuls*, involves potential product market distortions. Typical market distortions caused by big business groups are horizontal and vertical predations.

The potential for horizontal predation is large since the most common market structure (for big business groups) is a single *jaebul* and many non-*jaebul* compet-

itors in a single market. Group affiliation allows *jaebul* enterprises to behave in a
noncompetitive fashion. Rents accruing to *jaebuls* in one market can be used to
cross-subsidize noncompetitive behavior in other markets. Such horizontal predation by *jaebuls* reduces competitiveness in product markets and endangers the
existence of small- and medium-sized competitors.

Capital Inflation through Cross-holding of Shares

Cross-holding of shares among member companies of a group is one common
means of interlocking member companies, thus reinforcing the controlling power
of the owner. In the mid-1980s, the share of equity shares exchanged among
affiliated companies within a group was, on the average, close to 50 percent of the
total outstanding shares of the group. Share cross-holding inflates the capital base
of the companies involved without any corresponding increase in actual investment. Since book-value-based debt-equity ratios of borrowing firms are an important lending criterion used by banks, an inflated equity capital base will increase
the borrowing limit of each company when lenders do not take into account the
fact that a simple exchange of stock ownership does not increase the debt capacity
of the companies.

Share cross-holding between affiliated companies strengthens the controlling
power of large shareholders or owners of industrial groups without requiring
additional equity contributions. This hurts the interests of general-public shareholders who hold a smaller share of stocks outstanding after the two companies
exchange stocks. Although holding companies are not permitted in Korea, share
cross-holding among affiliated group companies results in a pyramid of share
ownership, which facilitates control of the economy's physical assets by a few
individuals.[10]

Capital inflation from share cross-holding can also result in excessive corporate
profits or product prices for consumers. Since the government often allowed firms
to earn only a fair rate of return on invested capital to control prices during periods
of high inflation, inflated capital bases made it possible for firms to charge higher
prices and thus earn excess profits at the consumers' expense.

When capital inflation through share cross-holding occurs among all affiliated
companies in a group, the implications for the control power, the creation of
additional fictitious borrowing capacity, and price distortion can be enormous.

PUBLIC POLICIES ON THE CONCENTRATION
OF ECONOMIC POWER

Beginning in the mid-1970s, the government began to pay attention to the *jaebul*
issue and the concentration of economic power. In an attempt to restrain the rapid
expansion of conglomerate groups and to promote fair trade practices, the govern-

ment introduced various measures and regulations. These included special presidential directives, a bank credit control system, and the Fair Trade Act.[11]

Special Presidential Directives of 1974

Facing ever-increasing criticism of government favoritism toward big business groups and their increasingly dominant position in the nation's economy, the government issued a set of special presidential directives aimed at opening up privately held firms to public ownership and control, reducing reliance on debt to improve companies' capital structures, and prohibiting illicit wealth accumulation through socially undesirable practices.

The directives signified a turning point in the government's attitude toward *jaebuls*. Their ultimate goals were to prevent the accumulation of business assets by a few individuals, to induce privately held firms to go public in order to expand their managerial and financial capabilities, and ultimately to promote the international competitiveness of Korean business enterprises through modernization of family-oriented management styles.

For these purposes, the government provided financial and tax incentives for companies to go public.[12] At the same time, heavily indebted firms were directed to improve their financial structures by increasing the share of equity in financing new projects. In an effort to enhance the public credibility of corporate reporting, an external auditing system, disclosure requirements, and a tax surveillance system were also enforced.

Introduction of the Bank Credit Control System

One of the most significant steps in curbing the excessive expansion of conglomerates and in reducing their heavy reliance on bank borrowing was the introduction of a monitoring and control system for bank credit allocation, especially for a designated group of top *jaebul* firms.

Since, as discussed earlier, privileged access of *jaebuls* to subsidized bank loans was considered a major factor in the rapid expansion of Korean conglomerates, the "prime bank system" was introduced in 1974, which assigned banks to monitor specific heavily indebted companies for effective credit control.

Under this system, business groups with outstanding bank credit above a certain amount and with high debt-equity ratios were ordered to improve their financial structures and were prohibited from establishing or acquiring additional businesses, receiving loan guarantees, purchasing stocks of other companies, or acquiring nonoperating real estate.

The prime bank system has been modified and strengthened since its introduction. In 1984, for example, the government temporarily froze the aggregate amount of bank loans and guarantees extended to the top five *jaebul* groups. According to the new scheme, the so-called basket system, *jaebul* groups as a whole became subject to credit limits. This reflected government determination to curb the highly leveraged expansion of *jaebuls*, and the scheme proved effective in curbing the share of bank loans to top conglomerates groups.[13]

Introduction of the Fair Trade Act

In order to promote fair trade practices in the marketplace, the "Monopoly Regulation and Fair Trade Act" was promulgated by law in December 1980. Its goal was to encourage fair and free competition by prohibiting market-dominating power by entrepreneurs and excessive concentration of economic power.

The act prohibits any business combinations that may substantially restrict market competition. When it seems likely that market competition may be compromised in a particular field of trade, companies are prohibited from acquiring stocks of or interlocking directorates with other companies unless they are granted permission by the minister of the Economic Planning Board.

This provision seems to have significantly reduced horizontal and vertical integration of firms. However, since mixed- or conglomerate-type integration of firms engaged in unrelated business lines is not explicitly restricted by law, there have been substantially more mixed combinations than vertical or horizontal integrations.

In this way success in moderating market concentration in individual markets may perversely result in a net increase in business or economic concentration in the economy as a whole. That is, less market concentration in each of a set of industries may be accompanied by increased aggregate concentration.

Other Measures

There are several other measures directly or indirectly preventing increases in business concentration and reducing the unfavorable consequences of such concentration. For example, programs to open up Korea's domestic market to foreign firms should force domestic manufacturers, including *jaebuls*, to increase efficiency and lower prices at home in order to cope with foreign competition.

Commercial banks are required to lend at least 35 percent of their total loans to small-and medium-sized firms. Although this is part of the government program to promote small-and medium-sized industries, it implies a significant change in government policy since more loans to these firms inevitably reduces credit available for big groups.

Through direct or indirect measures, the government also encourages big *jaebuls* to spin off affiliated companies whose business lines fall in areas specially designated as small-and medium-sized industries. In addition to selling off these companies, big *jaebuls* are encouraged to reduce their excessively wide range of business lines and to specialize more in their major business activities.

CONCLUDING REMARKS

The purpose of this chapter is to provide a brief overview of the causes and consequences of Korea's big business giants that have shown remarkable growth throughout the industrialization of the Korean economy.

There are somewhat mixed evaluations of the role of big business groups in economic development. On one hand, they have provided economies of scale and managerial X-efficiency. Aggressive, risk-taking entrepreneurship was crucial in enabling the Korean economy to transform itself from an underdeveloped and primitive industrial economy to a modern, capital-intensive, and high-technology oriented one. The government has relied on and favored big business groups to secure their active participation in large-scale development projects and export promotion.

On the other hand, many are deeply concerned about the Korean *jaebuls'* increasingly dominant position in the Korean economy. Criticism is directed against their excessive borrowing, expansion of business lines even into areas normally dominated by small- and medium-sized firms, and their exploitation of opportunities to make windfall profits from imperfect markets.

Since subsidized bank credit was believed to be one of the most important factors in the rapid expansion of *jaebuls*, the government has placed special emphasis on the bank credit control system, which has had mixed success in slowing down the growth of *jaebuls*. The Monopoly Regulation and Fair Trade Act also aims at decreasing unfair market practices and business combinations.

The government is also trying to promote small- and medium-sized industries, and has placed restrictions on *jaebuls'* expansion into these areas.

During the 1960s and 1970s, economic policy put more emphasis on efficiency, which was believed to be enhanced by placing scarce resources in the hands of a small group of entrepreneurs who were thought to have had special abilities in using resources productively. This policy resulted in the concentration of economic power and problems of social equity.

The government has begun, through a number of measures, to stress harmonized development of business enterprises of all sizes so as to realize the advantages of "bigness" while promoting the flexibility of "smallness."

NOTES

1. The early studies on the issue of economic concentration in Korea were by SaKong (1980) and Jones and SaKong (1980).

2. The share of *jaebuls* in 1985 is comparable with 1982, after a period of sharp

increases during 1978–82. This may be partly attributable to government policy measures aimed at curbing excessive growth of *jaebul* groups.

3. Although the Hyundai Group did not appear in the *Fortune* 500 list in 1987, it is one of the four largest conglomerate groups in Korea.

4. See Jones and SaKong (1980).

5. See D. Cho (1983) and S. Cho (1985) for detailed discussions on the role of GTCs in Korea.

6. See Cole and Park (1983) for a review of Korea's financial system and policies. Korea's repressed financial market is now undergoing major liberalization aimed at enhancing the efficiency of the market.

7. See Penrose (1980) and Keenan and White (1982).

8. Especially with the political democratization since 1987, calls for equity in income and wealth distribution have become more insistent. Concentration of economic power in the hands of a few individuals or business groups has become a major target of public criticism. See Spruill (1981) and Keenan and White (1982) for discussions on conglomerates in the capitalist economies.

9. Friedman (1981) discusses the externalities of corporate financial structure increasing the aggregate risk of a nation's economy due to excessive debt financing.

10. See Bonbright and Means (1969).

11. See Jones and SaKong (1980) for details of the various government measures.

12. Due to strong government encouragement, more than 100 firms went public in 1988. There are now over 500 companies listed on the Korea Stock Exchange with a total market capitalization of over US $100 billion as of April 1989.

13. The *jaebuls'* share of bank loans has been decreasing substantially since the early 1980s.

REFERENCES

Bonbright, J. C. and Means, G. C., *The Holding Company: Its Public Significance and Its Regulations*, New York: Augustus M. Kelly Publishers, 1969.

Cho, Dong Sung, *General Trading Companies in Korea* (in Korean), Seoul: Pan Moon Sa, 1983.

Cho, Sung-Hwan, *Government Promotion Measures for General Trading Companies*, Hawaii: East-West Population Center, 1985.

Cole, David and Park, Y. C., *Financial Development in Korea*, Cambridge: Harvard University Press, 1983.

Friedman, Benjamin M., "Financing Capital Formation in the 1980s: Issues for Public Policy," National Bureau of Economic Research, Working Paper No. 745, Cambridge, Mass., Sept. 1981.

Jones, L. P., "Notes on Government Policy Towards Jaebul: An Update," Unpublished manuscript, Korea Development Institute, Seoul, 1984.

————, and SaKong, Il, *Government, Business and Entrepreneurship in Economic Development: The Korean Case*, Cambridge: Harvard University Press, 1980.

Keenan, M. and White, L. J., *Mergers and Acquisitions*, Lexington: Lexington Books, 1982.

Lee, Kyu Uck, *Business Combinations and Economic Concentration* (in Korean), Seoul: KDI Press, 1985.

Penrose, E. T., *The Theory of the Growth of the Firm*, Oxford: Basil Blackwell, 1980.

SaKong, Il, *Economic Growth and Business Concentration of Economic Power* (in Korean), Seoul: KDI Press, 1980.

Spruill, C. R., *Conglomerates and the Evolution of Capitalism*, Carbondale: Southern Illinois University Press, 1981.

19

Financing Korean Corporations: Evidence and Theory

E. Han Kim

INTRODUCTION

One of the issues of great concern to economists, policymakers, and members of Korea's business community has been the unusually high degree of financial leverage in Korea's corporate sector. There seems to be a general consensus that corporate financial leverage is excessive and that it has a harmful effect on the stability of the economy. However, there are those who point out that Japan's corporate sector has an equally high degree of financial leverage and that it has provided Japanese corporations with a competitive edge in the world marketplace by lowering their cost of capital.

In this study I document the average equity to total value (equity plus debt) ratios for all nonfinancial corporations listed on the Korean Stock Exchange during the period 1977 through 1986. These ratios are compared with those of Japanese and U.S. corporations. The results show that when equity ratios are based on book values, U.S. firms have the highest equity ratios, followed by Japanese and then by Korean firms. However, intercountry comparisons based on book values are misleading. In Japan a substantial portion of corporate assets have not been revalued since World War II; in Korea, there have been frequent revaluations of corporate assets. Furthermore, the revaluations in Korea have been done primarily by firms whose real values exceeded book values. There has not been an offsetting revaluation of firms whose real values were below book values. Thus, there is a selection bias that makes comparison of book value-based equity ratios between Korea and Japan meaningless.

To avoid the bias in book value-based measures, I measure equity ratios based on market value of equity. The market value-based measures show that Korean corporations have much lower equity ratios than Japanese corporations, while Japanese corporations' equity ratios are roughly equivalent to those of American corporations. The ten-year average equity ratio for Korean corporations during the period 1977 through 1986 is 16 percent, while those of Japanese and American corporations have fluctuated within a 40 to 50 percent range.

The data on Korean corporations also reveal a highly significant inverse relation between equity ratio and firm size. The largest firms have the weakest financial structure throughout the sample period. During the latter part of the sample period, a substantial fraction of the largest listed firms have very little equity in their capital structures.

In the third section I identify the main causes for the high financial leverage in Korea: (1) ceilings on bank interest rates and loan guarantee fees; (2) low interest loans for targeted industries; (3) frequent government bailouts of large corporations; and (4) favorable tax treatment of debt relative to equity at both the corporate and personal levels. The first three factors have kept the before-tax cost of debt artificially low, especially for large corporations. The favorable tax treatment of debt has made the after-tax cost of debt even lower relative to equity.

In the fourth section I examine the potential impacts of recently suggested financial reforms, which would remove some of the above causes, on corporate investments. The final section contains a summary and some concluding remarks.

EMPIRICAL RESULTS

To investigate the degree of financial leverage in the Korean corporate sector, the equity to total value (equity plus debt) ratio is computed for all nonfinancial firms listed on the Korean Stock Exchange during the period 1977 through 1986. Due to new listings, delistings, mergers, bankruptcies, and incomplete information, the sample size varies from a low of 274 in 1977 to a high of 296 in 1986.

In computing the equity ratios, two measures for the value of equity are used. One is based on the book value and the other on the market value. The market value of equity is defined as the total number of shares outstanding at year end multiplied by the average market price per share during the year.

Table 19.1 reports value-weighted average equity ratios for Korea. Also presented are average equity ratios for Japan and the United States, compiled by Michel and Shaked (1985) for the period 1977 through 1981. Michel and Shaked's average ratios are equally weighted and are based on 130 American manufacturing firms and 130 industry-matched Japanese firms.

The first three columns in Table 19.1 present book value-based average equity ratios. They suggest that in 1977 the average equity ratios for Korea and Japan were about equal, with Korea becoming more highly leveraged than Japan over time. The data also show that Japan was much more highly leveraged than the United States.

Table 19.1
Mean Equity to Total Value (Equity plus Debt) Ratios for Korea, Japan, and the United States (in percent)

	Book-Value-Based			Market-Value-Based		
	Korea[a]	Japan[b]	U.S.[b]	Korea[a]	Japan[b]	U.S.[b]
1977	29.7	27.6	48.1	27.7	40.6	43.1
1978	22.3	28.5	46.3	28.2	47.1	42.4
1979	21.6	29.1	46.6	17.4	44.1	44.9
1980	17.3	30.1	46.5	11.0	45.4	49.4
1981	18.1	31.7	47.1	11.3	43.8	46.6
1982	19.2	N/A	N/A	10.2	N/A	N/A
1983	19.8	N/A	N/A	11.2	N/A	N/A
1984	19.9	N/A	N/A	12.4	N/A	N/A
1985	20.6	N/A	N/A	12.8	N/A	N/A
1986	25.3	N/A	N/A	20.6	N/A	N/A
Average	21.4	29.4	46.9	16.3	44.2	45.3

[a]Value-weighted average for all nonfinancial firms listed on the Korean Stock Exchange for which complete data are available. The sample size varies from a low of 274 in 1977 to a high of 296 in 1986.
[b]Equally weighted average for 130 American manufacturing firms and 130 industry-matched Japanese firms, compiled by Michel and Shaked (1985).

These book value-based equity ratios, however, are misleading. They reflect historical costs, not the firm's real value. In Japan, book values tend to greatly understate real values because a large portion of corporate assets have not been revalued since the Second World War; consequently, equity ratios based on book value underestimate real equity ratios.

Korean corporations, on the other hand, have had frequent revaluations of corporate assets. The revaluation process has created a unique selection bias. The government's credit allocation procedure has been closely tied to book value-based measures of financial leverage; greater bank loans are granted to firms with high equity ratios. In the presence of artificially low bank interest rates, this allocation procedure has induced Korean firms to maximize book value. Thus, firms with real values greater than book values have revalued their assets, while firms with real values less than book values have not. As a consequence, the average book value of Korean firms during the sample period overestimates the average real value.

To obtain a better proxy for the real equity value, I use stock market price data. The stock market is forward-looking; that is, stock prices reflect the market's expectation of firms' future earnings. To the extent that the market's expectation is unbiased, equity ratios based on market prices of stocks provide unbiased estimates of the real equity ratios. The last three columns in Table 19.1 show average equity ratios based on the market value of equity. These results contrast

Table 19.2
Market Value-Based Mean Equity to Total Value (Equity plus Debt) Ratios for Korea and the United States (in percent)

		Value-Weighted			Equally Weighted	
	N[a]	Korea	N[b]	U.S.	Korea	U.S.
1977	274	27.65	1,674	48.62	30.13	46.45
1978	275	28.17	1,700	44.76	29.56	44.74
1979	290	17.41	1,728	43.73	20.57	45.91
1980	293	10.98	1,755	45.73	14.00	48.49
1981	281	11.34	1,796	45.04	14.25	48.82
1982	281	10.23	1,856	44.79	14.03	49.27
1983	275	11.24	1,874	48.15	15.02	51.90
1984	284	12.40	1,820	48.37	17.82	51.54
1985	282	12.82	N/A	N/A	18.43	N/A
1986	296	20.60	N/A	N/A	23.01	N/A
Average	283	16.28	1,775	46.15	19.69	48.39

[a]All nonfinancial firms listed on the Korean Stock Exchange for which complete data are available.
[b]All nonfinancial firms included in the Annual COMPUSTAT file for which complete data are available.

sharply with those using book values. When measured using market value, Japan's average equity ratio increases so much that the difference between Japan and the United States disappears completely. This finding clearly contradicts the common belief that Japanese firms are more highly leveraged than U.S. firms.

In contrast, Korea's average equity ratio decreases substantially when the market value of equity is used. Table 19.1 reveals that the Korean financial structure deteriorated sharply in 1979 and 1980; the average equity ratio dropped from 28 percent in the 1977–78 period to11.5 percent in the 1980–85 period. There was little improvement in financial structure until 1986, when the real GNP grew at a phenomenal rate of 12.3 percent—versus 5.4 percent in 1985—and the equity ratio increased to 20.6 percent.

One possible explanation for the sudden drop in equity ratios during the 1979–80 period is the 1979 oil shock and the low corporate earnings during the subsequent recession in 1980. Korea suffered a negative real GNP growth rate during this period. The same oil shock also hit the United States, however, and had a severe adverse effect on its economy. The real GNP growth rate in the United States was also negative in 1980. (Japan managed to survive the oil shock without suffering a noticeable drop in the real GNP growth rate.) Thus, if the oil shock and the subsequent recession are to explain the sharp drop in the equity ratio for Korea, a similar drop in equity ratio should also be observed for the United States. The last column in Table 19.1 shows no such drop for U.S. firms in 1979 or 1980.

Table 19.3

Equally Weighted Average Equity Ratios for Deciles by Size for All Listed Nonfinancial Korean Corporations, 1977–86 (in percent)

Decile	1977	1978	1979	1980	1981	1982	1983	1984	1985	1986	Total
(smallest)											
1	43.89	36.08	32.16	22.81	21.60	23.25	26.06	25.81	27.54	33.11	29.23
2	33.39	32.44	26.08	17.65	17.92	19.41	18.32	23.37	25.59	26.93	24.11
3	29.21	29.51	22.03	16.63	19.29	16.93	16.24	18.74	22.79	24.85	21.62
4	28.34	27.02	22.13	15.21	13.87	12.06	16.78	21.34	17.30	20.63	19.47
5	29.56	26.14	24.14	15.82	11.87	12.86	13.86	18.12	19.48	21.71	19.36
6	34.68	35.38	13.37	9.07	13.46	13.84	13.70	18.11	20.28	23.52	19.54
7	27.59	29.17	17.78	13.74	11.71	11.08	12.06	15.93	15.30	20.08	17.44
8	28.45	28.10	17.16	9.74	12.65	13.68	15.02	17.43	15.08	23.48	18.08
9	22.45	21.65	13.51	10.29	9.30	7.83	8.44	10.08	10.57	19.12	13.32
10	23.97	29.95	17.37	9.15	10.62	9.03	9.76	9.40	9.96	16.67	14.59
(largest)											
Total	30.13	29.56	20.57	14.00	14.25	14.03	15.02	17.82	18.43	23.01	19.69

To provide more complete data for U.S. firms, I compute both value-weighted and equally weighted equity ratios for all nonfinancial U.S. firms included in the annual COMPUSTAT file from 1977 through 1984.[1] These firms are much more representative of U.S. firms than those reported in Table 19.1. The sample size varies from a low of 1,674 in 1977 to a high of 1,874 in 1983. The fifth column in Table 19.2 presents value-weighted average equity ratios for the United States. Apparently, the 1979 oil shock and the subsequent recession had no noticeable impact on equity ratios of U.S. corporations. This comparison between Korean and U.S. data suggests that there are factors unique to the Korean economy that affect corporate financing behavior differently than in the United States.

The last two columns in Table 19.2 show equally weighted average equity ratios for Korea and the United States. Comparison of these ratios with the value-weighted ratios reveals an interesting fact about the cross-sectional variation in financial leverage. In Korea, the equally weighted averages are consistently higher than the value-weighted averages for every year in the sample period. Since large firms are weighted more heavily in a value-weighted average than in an equally weighted average, the difference suggests that larger firms in Korea are more highly leveraged.

To investigate this issue more closely, the sample of Korean firms is divided into deciles by size. Table 19.3 shows equally weighted average equity ratios for each decile from 1977 through 1986. In each year the larger decile firms have smaller average equity ratios than the smaller decile firms.

Table 19.4

Percentage of Firms with Equity Ratios Less than 5 Percent Among the Top Decile (by Size) Firms and Among the Rest of the Firms Listed on the Korean Stock Exchange

Year	All Firms		Largest Ten Percent of Firms	Remaining Firms
	N[a]	Percentage		
1977	274	1.46	0	1.69
1978	275	2.18	0	2.43
1979	290	2.07	10.34	1.15
1980	293	11.95	30.00	9.89
1981	281	14.23	25.00	13.04
1982	281	15.30	21.43	14.62
1983	275	10.91	17.86	10.12
1984	284	13.03	37.93	10.20
1985	282	9.57	41.38	5.93
1986	296	6.86	31.82	4.71

[a]The sample includes only nonfinancial firms listed on the Korean Stock Exchange for which complete data are available.

To document the extent of the disparity in financial structure between the largest firms and the others, Table 19.4 tabulates the fraction of firms that had equity ratios below 5 percent among the top decile firms and among the remaining firms. The results are rather striking. During the period 1984 through 1986, 37 percent of the top decile firms had equity ratios below 5 percent, whereas only 7 percent of the remaining firms had such low equity ratios.

CAUSES OF THE HIGH FINANCIAL LEVERAGE

The evidence presented in the preceding section suggests that the financial structure of Korean firms is unique and that the high financial leverage has been caused by factors that are country specific. The fundamental causes for the high financial leverage stem from the Korean financial and income tax systems. The financial system makes the before-tax cost of debt artificially low, and the income tax system makes the after-tax cost of debt even lower relative to equity.

Financial System

Low Interest Loans for Targeted Industries

These loans have been used extensively by the government as a means of promoting certain industries that it deems important for the development of the Korean economy. The interest rates on these loans are substantially lower than the market rate, which provides an incentive for eligible firms to borrow more than they would otherwise. These loans also create arbitrage profit opportunities and may not have been very effective in stimulating facility investments. I will return to this issue in the next section.

Ceilings on Interest Rates and Loan Guarantee Fees

Until 1988, there were explicit ceilings on interest rates and on loan guarantee fees that banks could charge. In Korea credits have often been allocated via nonprice rationing. Thus the existence of the ceilings has often forced banks to extend (guarantee) loans to high risk borrowers at contractual rates (fees) below the market clearing risk-adjusted rates (fees). This means that high-risk firms have been able to obtain loans at rates below their opportunity cost of capital, which again provides an arbitrage profit opportunity and the incentive to maximize borrowing.

Bailouts of Large Corporations

During the sample period the government bailed out many large corporations that were financially insolvent. These bailouts were so frequent that the public almost came to expect a government bailout whenever a large corporation got into financial trouble. The stated intentions of the bailouts were to protect workers from unemployment and/or to protect the international reputation of Korean corporations overseas. These bailouts often prolonged the lives of firms that were not economically viable and hence had low equity values.

More importantly, the expectation that big firms would be bailed out whenever they became insolvent lowered the perceived default risk of large corporations and enabled them to borrow funds at below their opportunity cost of capital. Consequently, big firms had an even greater incentive to maximize their borrowing and to increase their size—via borrowing—in order to become eligible for the benefits associated with being a large corporation.

The Corporate and Personal Income Tax System

During the sample period the income tax system was as much responsible for the high financial leverage as was the financial system. The corporate tax system encouraged firms to borrow and the personal tax system had made investors prefer debt securities to common stocks. Thus, the tax system reduced both the supply of and the demand for common stocks, thereby stifling the growth of the stock market. Without a well-functioning stock market that is necessary for an efficient allocation of equity capital, the cost of equity was prohibitively high, on both before- and after-tax bases.[2]

Tax Deductibility of Corporate Interest Payments

Corporate interest payments are tax deductible, whereas returns to stockholders are not. This tax deductibility of interest payments reduces the after-tax cost of debt relative to equity. The tax advantage of debt exists in both Korea and the United States, and hence there is no real difference between the two countries at the corporate level. What distinguished the two countries' tax system during the sample period was at the personal level.

Personal Taxes on Interest Income versus Income from Stocks

In the United States, about one third of the average rate of returns from holding stocks comes in the form of dividends, and the rest in the form of capital gains.[3] The U.S. Tax Code specifies that both interest and dividends be taxed at the ordinary rate, whereas, until the Tax Reform Act of 1986, capital gains were taxed at only 40 percent of the ordinary rate. Since capital gains were (are) not taxable until realization, the present value of the capital gains tax rate was even lower than 40 percent of the ordinary rate. Furthermore, if an investor does not sell stocks until death or donates them to tax-exempt institutions, the effective rate becomes zero. Thus, until 1987 the personal tax rate on income from stocks, the average of dividend tax and capital gains tax, was substantially smaller than the tax rate on interest income. This made holding debt securities disadvantageous relative to holding stocks.

The personal tax disadvantage of debt reduces the demand for corporate debt, which leads to a lower equilibrium price for debt. A lower price for debt means a higher yield and hence a higher before-tax cost of debt. Miller (1977) analyzes this issue while assuming that all debt is riskless and that income from stocks is not taxed. With these assumptions, he concludes that the higher cost of debt negates the entire tax benefit of corporate borrowing. In subsequent extensions of the Miller model, DeAngelo and Masulis (1980), Kim (1982) and (1989), and Ross (1985) show that under-utilization of tax shields in low earnings states and the various leverage-related deadweight costs (for example, bankruptcy costs, the moral hazard problems associated with risky debt, and various contracting and recontracting costs associated with financial distress) reduce the supply of corporate debt (relative to equity). The smaller supply means a higher price for debt and a lower before-tax cost of borrowing than those in Miller's equilibrium. Thus, these more refined theories show that there is still a positive tax advantage of debt; however, after netting out the personal tax disadvantages of debt, the magnitude of the tax advantage of corporate borrowing is greatly reduced.

In Korea, there was no such offsetting effect at the personal level during the sample period. During the period 1976 through 1985 stocks listed on the Korean Stock Exchange provided an average annual dividend yield of 10.4 percent and an average annual capital appreciation of 6.0 percent. Although capital gains have never been taxed in Korea, dividends could (can) be taxed at as high a rate as 70 percent (including the defense and residence taxes). Thus, the high dividend yields on Korean stocks during the sample period meant that the average tax rate on income from stocks for a wealthy investor could be considerably higher than the effective tax rate on interest income. For example, in January 1985 the effective maximum tax rate on interest income (including final withholding tax, defense tax, and residence tax) was only about 13 percent, whereas the weighted average tax rate on income from stocks for the highest tax bracket investor was 44 percent ($70\% \times 10.4/(10.4 + 6.0)$). Thus, in contrast to the United States, there was a substantial personal tax advantage of holding debt securities relative to equity, especially for the wealthy investors who controlled Korean corporations and made corporate financing decisions.

To contrast the differential impacts of the Korean and American tax systems on corporate financial structure, consider an investor in Korea and another in the United States, each of whose marginal corporate and personal income tax rates were the maximum rates in their country as of January 1985. Also assume that the fraction of the Korean and the American investors' income that came in the form of dividends and capital gains were the same as the average stock in each country during the sample period. Based on these assumptions, Table 19.5 shows calculations of how much of one dollar of operating earnings would remain with the

Table 19.5

Comparison of the Net Tax Advantage of Corporate Borrowing after Personal Taxes, Assuming Maximum Marginal Income Tax Rates as of January 1985

	Korea	U.S.
Corporate Tax Rate: t_c	.40	.46
Tax Rate on Interest: t_i	.13	.50
Tax Rate on Dividends: t_d	.70	.50
Present Value of Future Capital Gains Taxes: tg	0	.10[a]
Proportion of Income from Stocks as Dividends: X_d	.63	.33
Average Tax Rate on Income from Stocks: $t_{ps} = t_d \cdot X_d + t_g(1 - X_d)$	.44	.23
After-Corporate-and-Personal-Tax Return of $1 of Operating Earnings to a Stockholder: $(1 - t_c)(1 - t_{ps})$	.34	.42
After-Corporate-and-Personal-Tax Return of $1 of Operating Earnings paid out as Interest: $(1 - t_i)$	.87	.50
Net Tax Advantage of Debt Relative to Equity[b] $[(1 - t_i) - (1 - t_c)(1 - t_{ps})]/(1 - t_i)$	.61	.16

[a]Assuming that the present value of future capital gains tax is worth one-half of the capital gains tax rate, 50% $(.4)/2 = 10\%$.

[b]See Miller (1977) or Kim (1982) for a formal derivation of this expression.

investor in each country after all corporate and personal taxes were paid. In Korea, if the operating earnings were paid out as a return on equity, only 34 cents was left after taxes, whereas if the earnings were paid out as interest, as much as 87 cents was left. Hence, the tax disadvantage of equity relative to debt was $(.34 - .87)/.87 = -.61$. In other words, the investor in Korea could have increased his after-tax return by 61 percent by converting his claim in the firm from equity to debt.

Table 19.5 also shows that in the United States, 42 cents would be left if the earnings were paid out as a return on equity; if the earnings were paid out as interest, 50 cents would be left. Hence, the relative tax disadvantage of equity was $(.42 - .50)/.50 = -.16$; that is, the investor's after-tax returns would increase by 16 percent if his claim took the form of debt rather than equity. According to the theory of optimal capital structure, this tax advantage of debt should be weighed against the costs of financial distress when firms decide on their financial structure. In other words, firms would borrow until the marginal tax advantage of debt equals the marginal costs of financial distress.[4]

In Korea, the marginal tax advantage of debt was almost four times (.61/.16) the tax advantage in the United States. Consequently, the optimal financial structure was obtained at a much higher level of debt. For large firms, this tax incentive to borrow was further exacerbated by the frequent government bailouts and the expectations thereof. Since a high probability of bail-outs means a low probability of default, the ex ante costs of financial distress did not increase with increased leverage as fast as they would otherwise. In other words, the bailouts (and expectations thereof) have significantly reduced the default risk premium component of contractual interest rates that big firms had to pay. Without the deterrent effect of high interest costs, there was no counterbalancing force that would prevent large firms from going for all debt financing.[5]

POTENTIAL IMPACTS OF FINANCIAL REFORMS ON CORPORATE INVESTMENT

In the preceding section I have identified several factors in the Korean financial system that have kept the before-tax cost of debt artificially low. Recently, there have been several suggestions for financial reform to achieve more efficient allocation of financial resources. These suggestions include deregulation of interest rates and elimination of government bailouts of financially troubled large corporations. Indeed, the government moved one step closer to financial liberalization in 1988 when it announced its intention to eliminate the ceilings on bank interest rates and loan guarantee fees. Opponents of financial reforms, however, argue that these reforms may have an adverse impact on corporate investments and that government intervention in financial markets is necessary for stable, long-term growth of the economy. In this section, I examine the validity of these arguments.

Elimination of Bailouts

This financial reform will eliminate expectations of future bailouts and will give the proper incentive for large corporations to improve their financial structure. Opponents of this reform, however, argue that bailouts of large corporations are necessary to prevent large scale unemployment.

The notion that a big firm's bankruptcy will create massive unemployment is more apparent than real. If a firm can be liquidated in an orderly fashion, the profitable units will be taken over by other management teams and the workers will remain employed. The unprofitable units will be closed, which will lead to a more efficient allocation of corporate resources. In the long run, this will increase total employment in the economy. In Kim and Schatzberg (1987) we find that voluntary corporate liquidations in the United States lead to an average 34 percent positive revaluation of the firm. The gains from liquidations arise from redeployment of liquidating firms' resources into more efficient allocations.

Elimination of Interest Subsidies
and Deregulation of Interest Rates

The artificially low-interest loans for targeted industries give eligible firms explicit interest subsidies, while the ceilings on bank interest rates and loan guarantee fees give implicit interest subsidies to risky firms. Proponents of these interest subsidies argue that they increase facility investments by lowering firms' cost of capital and thereby increase the total employment in the private sector.

To examine the validity of this argument, note that any profit-maximizing firm will follow the Net Present Value rule in making investment decisions: accept projects with yields greater than the cost of capital and reject projects with yields less than the cost of capital. This investment rule will not be affected by whether or not the firm receives interest subsidies. Thus, interest subsidies will generate additional investments if and only if the subsidies can induce (force) the firm to undertake projects with returns less than the cost of capital. I argue that this does not happen in general; instead, the eligible firm is likely to invest the low cost funds in speculative assets (like financial securities and real estate) rather than in facilities with low returns. Corporate investments in speculative assets generate little additional employment.

To illustrate my argument, consider Figure 19.1 which describes the process of a typical firm's investment decision. The figure depicts the marginal cost of capital (MCC) line and the marginal rate of return (MRR) curve. The marginal cost of

Figure 19.1

The Impact of Subsidized Loan B_1 at MCC – k on Corporate Investments in Productive Assets: $B_1 < I^*$

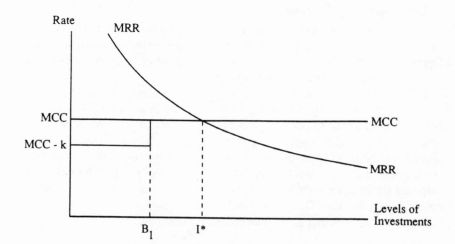

capital should be a constant in a competitive capital market, and the firm is facing a decreasing marginal rate of return from facility investments. Without interest subsidies, the firm will invest up to I* where the marginal cost of capital is equal to the marginal rate of return.

Suppose that the firm is given an opportunity to obtain a subsidized loan in the amount of B_1 at the rate of MCC minus k. The firm's cost of capital will be lower by k up to B_1. If B_1 is less than the original level of investment I*, it does not affect the marginal cost of capital at I* and hence will not increase the investment level. The subsidized loan will only enrich the owners of the firm by kB_1 without achieving its goal of increased corporate investments in facilities.

Figure 19.2 depicts the case in which the subsidized loan, B_2, is greater than I*. Even in this case, it is unlikely that the firm will increase its investment in facilities. Note that the cost of capital is the opportunity cost that the owners of the firm forgo by not investing elsewhere. In other words, the marginal cost of capital line also represents the investment opportunity set available to the owners of the firm via speculative assets such as financial assets and real estate. Consequently, their optimal investment decision requires investment in facilities only up to the original I* and the rest in speculative assets. This investment path is traced by the thicker line in Figure 19.2. Again, the subsidized loan will only enrich the owners of the firm without increasing facility investments.

The objective of increasing the level of corporate investment beyond I* to I' in Figure 19.2, can be achieved only if the government can devise a perfectly enforceable rule that prohibits firms from investing the subsidized loans in anything

Figure 19.2
The Impact of Subsidized Loan B_2 at MCC – k on Corporate Investments in Productive Assets: $B_2 > I^*$

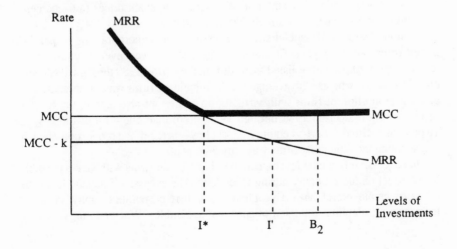

but the facility that yields rates of return below the firm's opportunity cost of capital. Thus, the policy of increasing facility investments via interest subsidies will be effective only if both of the following conditions are met: (1) the loan is tied to a specific facility that has a rate of return below the firm's cost of capital and (2) the process of the investment is verifiable at every stage of its completion. The first condition provides an incentive for the firm to cheat; that is, to under-invest in the facility and use the subsidized loans to earn arbitrage profits by investing in speculative assets. The second condition is either impossible or prohibitively expensive to satisfy because of limitations in information technology. Further, both conditions give a strong economic incentive for collusion between the firm and the supervising agent. In short, interest subsidies will rarely succeed in increasing facility investments.

SUMMARY AND CONCLUSION

This study provides evidence on the degree of financial leverage in Korea's corporate sector and explanations for the extreme leverage. I also examine the possible impacts of some of the recently suggested financial reforms on corporate investments.

When financial leverage is properly measured for Korean corporations, the results show that the average equity ratio for all nonfinancial firms listed on the Korean Stock Exchange was 16 percent during the period 1977 through 1986. This is in sharp contrast to the average equity ratios for Japan and the United States, both of which have been fluctuating within a 40 to 50 percent range.

The high financial leverage among Korean firms can be traced to the 1979 oil shock and the subsequent recession in 1980. The average equity ratio dropped from 28 percent in the 1977–78 period to 11 percent in 1980 and stayed within the 10 to 13 percent range until 1985. In 1986, the ratio increased to 21 percent due to a vigorous economic recovery and a drastic increase in stock prices (a 67 percent increase in the Korean Composite Stock Price Index).

A unique feature of financial structure among Korean corporations is that the largest firms have the highest financial leverage. The six-year average equity ratio for the largest 20 percent of listed firms during the period 1980 through 1986 was only 14 percent, whereas the average for the remaining firms was 21 percent. The greatest proportion of firms with virtually no equity are also among the largest firms. During the period 1984 through 1986, more than one third of the largest 10 percent of listed firms had equity ratios below 5 percent; the proportion of such firms among the remaining firms was only 7 percent.

This excessive financial leverage among big Korean firms will have a destabilizing effect on the economy during recessions. The excessive financial leverage can also create moral hazard problems such that corporations may sacrifice long-term profitability in pursuit of speculative gambles. When earnings are low and a firm is in financial distress, the excessive financial leverage creates a perverse incentive for the firm to accept an unprofitable project that is risky and to reject a profitable project that is safe.[6] Such an investment strategy leads to low expected profits and further financial deterioration. Thus, low earnings during a recession can trap a highly levered firm into a vicious circle that will eventually lead to bankruptcy.

In this study I identify several key factors that have caused the extreme financial leverage among Korean firms. First, the income tax system gave a strong incentive for firms to borrow. In addition to the tax deductibility of interest payments, major stockholders' effective tax rate on interest income was substantially less than that on income from stocks during the sample period. This personal tax system was exactly the opposite of the U.S. system, which taxed interest income much more heavily than income from stocks. Based on tax rates as of January 1985, my estimates show that the marginal net tax advantage of debt in Korea was almost four times that in the United States. In the presence of such a tremendous difference in the tax incentive, it is hardly surprising that Korean corporations relied on debt so much more than did U.S. corporations.

Second, the government's frequent bailouts of large corporations have prolonged the lives of many corporations that were not economically viable and hence had weak financial structures. More importantly, frequent bailouts have raised expectation of future bailouts, which allowed large corporations to borrow funds at below their opportunity cost of capital. This not only has induced the firms to maximize borrowing but also provided the incentive to increase their size (by borrowing) to become eligible for the benefits associated with being a large "indispensable" firm.

The notion that a large corporation's bankruptcy will create massive unemployment is more apparent than real. If a firm can be liquidated in an orderly fashion, the profitable units will be taken over by other management teams and the workers will remain employed. The unprofitable units will be closed, which will lead to a more efficient allocation of corporate resources. In the long run, this will increase total employment for the economy. In a study (1987) I conducted with John Schatzberg we find that voluntary corporate liquidations in the United States lead to an average 34 percent positive revaluation. The gains from liquidation arise from redeployment of liquidating firms' resources into more efficient allocations.

Third, the often-used low-interest loans for facility investments in targeted industries give explicit interest subsidies, while the ceilings on bank interest rates and loan guarantee fees give implicit interest subsidies to risky firms. These subsidies have provided a strong incentive for eligible firms to increase their financial leverage.

There is a common belief that these interest subsidies increase facility investments and hence increase the total employment in the private sector. By examining the process of corporate investment decisions in a standard theoretical corporate finance framework, I show that the interest subsidies will rarely succeed in increasing facility investments. Instead, they will only enrich the owners of eligible firms and encourage corporations to speculate in financial securities and real estate by providing arbitrage profit opportunities.

NOTES

This chapter is partially based on a paper I presented at the plenary session of the 1986 Korean Economic Association International Convention held in Seoul, Korea, and on my technical report to the Korea Development Institute in 1987. I am indebted to Dr. Young Ki Lee of KDI for numerous discussions that have helped to shape my thinking about the financial structure of Korean corporations and to Professor Stanley Kon of the University of Michigan for helpful suggestions. My research assistants Myeoung-Kyun Kim, Sang Beum Kim, David Sauer, and Sarabjeet Seth provided excellent assistance in data collection and computer programming. The views expressed herein are solely my own.

1. Some real estate-related firms such as REITs (Real Estate Investment Trusts) are similar to financial institutions and hence are excluded from the sample. The sample period ends in 1984 because that is the last year for which the COMPUSTAT file had data available at the time of this study.

In computing the equity ratios, preferred stocks are excluded from both the numerator and the denominator because they are hybrid securities that have characteristics of both debt and equity. To check whether exclusion of preferred stock had a material effect on the results, the average ratios were recomputed, treating preferred stocks first as stocks and then as debt. In each case the equity ratios changed by about 1 percent with no qualitatively distinguishable results.

2. For a more in-depth discussion on the cost of issuing equity in Korea, see Kim and Lee (1989).

3. For the historical rate of returns on common stocks and bonds from 1926 to 1984, see *Stocks, Bonds, Bills, and Inflation: 1985 Yearbook.*

4. I have derived the precise definition of the optimality condition in Kim (1978) and (1982) and generalized it further in Kim (1989). See Bradley, Jarrell, and Kim (1984) and Buser and Hess (1986) for the latest empirical evidence in support of this version of the theory of optimal financial structure.

5. Another bias in the Korean personal tax system that favored debt over equity was the tax on retained earnings of unlisted firms. This tax provision treated retained earnings of unlisted firms as if they were paid out as dividends, which reduced the incentive to retain earnings. The tax on retained earnings was abolished in 1985.

6. See Jensen and Meckling (1976), Myers (1977), and Chen and Kim (1979) for further discussion on moral hazard problems associated with risky debt.

REFERENCES

Bradley, Michael, Jarrell, Gregory, and Kim, E. Han, "On the Existence of an Optimal Capital Structure: Theory and Evidence," *Journal of Finance, 39,* July 1984, 857–78.

Buser, Stephen A. and Hess, Patrick J., "Empirical Determinants of the Relative Yields on Taxable and Tax-Exempt Securities," *Journal of Financial Economics, 17,* December 1986, 335–56.

Chen, Andrew H. and Kim, E. Han, "Theories of Corporate Debt Policy: A Synthesis," *Journal of Finance, 34,* May 1979, 371–84.

DeAngelo, Harry and Masulis, Ronald, "Optimal Capital Structure under Corporate and Personal Taxation," *Journal of Financial Economics, 8,* March 1980, 3–30.

Jensen, Michael G. and Meckling, William H., "Theory of the Firm: Managerial Behavior, Agency Costs and Ownership Structure," *Journal of Financial Economics, 3,* May 1976, 305–60.

Kim, E. Han, "A Mean-Variance Theory of Optimal Capital Structure and Corporate Debt Capacity," *Journal of Finance, 33,* March 1978, 45–64.

———, "Miller's Equilibrium, Shareholder Leverage Clienteles and Optimal Capital Structure," *Journal of Finance, 37,* May 1982, 301–18.

———, "Corporate Financial Structure in Korea: Theory, Evidence, and the Need for Reform," Proceedings of the Plenary Session of the Second International Convention of Korean Economists, Seoul, August 1986.

———, "Optimal Capital Structure in Miller's Equilibrium," in Sudipto Bhattacharaya and George M. Constantinides, eds., *Frontiers of Modern Financial Theory,* Totowa, NJ: Rowman and Littlefield, 1989, 36–48.

———, and Lee, Young K., "Issuing Stocks in Korea," forthcoming in S. Ghon Rhee and Rosita P. Chang, eds., *Research on Pacific-Basin Capital Markets,* New York: Elsevier Science Publishers, 1989.

———, and Schatzberg, John D., "Voluntary Corporate Liquidations," *Journal of Financial Economics, 19,* December 1987, 311–28.

Michel, A. and Shaked, I., "Japanese Leverage: Myth or Reality," *Financial Analysts Journal, 41,* July/August 1985, 61–67.

Miller, Merton, "Debt and Taxes," *Journal of Finance, 32,* May 1977, 261–75.

Myers, Stewart, "Determinants of Corporate Borrowing," *Journal of Financial Economics, 5,* November 1977, 147–75.

Ross, Steven A., "Debt and Taxes and Uncertainty," *Journal of Finance, 40,* July 1985, 637–56.

Stocks, Bonds, Bills, and Inflation: 1985 Yearbook, Chicago: Ibbotson Associates, 1985.

20

The Rise of Salaried Management

Alice H. Amsden

THE MANAGEMENT SYSTEM
OF "LATE" INDUSTRIALIZATION

Since the late nineteenth century, industrialization has been executed by the salaried manager, the soul of the modern industrial enterprise. As Alfred Chandler writes, "Large industrial enterprises with their teams of managers . . . appeared suddenly and simultaneously in the United States and Europe in the last decades of the nineteenth century [and a little later in Japan, only because Japan was later to industrialize]" (1987, pp. 2–3). The modern industrial enterprise evolved into an institution that comprises large-scale operating units, is multidivisional—producing many related products—and is hierarchical—key decisions are made by salaried managers who occupy various consecutive layers of authority and gradually supersede owner-managers as chief executives.

There are, however, notable differences within this general framework, as Chandler reminds us. The structure of the modern industrial enterprise and the specificities of managerial capitalism vary by century, country, and even company. An identifiable management system associated with "late" industrialization, however, does appear to exist in broad outline. I will be concerned below with its general characteristics and why it has worked especially well in Korea.

By industrializing "late" I mean a growth process based on learning or borrowing foreign technology, rather than generating new technology, which was the hallmark of leading firms in the eighteenth century in Britain and the nineteenth century in the United States and Germany (the First and Second Industrial Revolutions respectively). The fact that even leading firms in countries ranging from Japan, Korea, and Taiwan to Brazil, India, and Turkey have had to expand without the advantage of proprietary technology has created common characteristics regarding both the state's role in stimulating investment and the modern industrial enterprise's role as agent of industrial diversification. Japan, Korea, Taiwan, and the slower-growing late-industrializing countries have all conformed to the same basic patterns regarding state intervention and management. Yet there are significant variations within these patterns that help to explain why growth rates have differed.

In what follows I will say little about state policy and will concentrate on the modern industrial enterprise (the reader is referred to Amsden [1989a] for a fuller treatment of both subjects). Suffice it to say here that late industrialization may be understood as a process wherein the state intervenes with subsidies to get relative prices "wrong" because dominant firms do not have novel technology with which to compete, and even in labor-intensive industries like cotton textiles they find low wages an insufficient weapon to wield against more productive firms from higher wage countries. The states in Japan, Korea, and Taiwan, far from relying on the free market mechanism, have gotten relative prices deliberately "wrong" by allowing targeted firms in targeted industries to borrow at artificially low interest rates and to export from a protected home market. The "wrong" prices have been right in Korea, Japan, and Taiwan not because they were closer to free market equilibria but because the state had sufficient power over big business to allocate subsidies based on performance standards, according to the principle of reciprocity rather than giveaway. The disciplinary power of the state over big business has driven up productivity, and high growth rates of productivity and quality are ultimately the basis on which firms from Japan, Korea, and Taiwan have competed internationally. Discipline of big business by the state should be taken as background to the analysis of the modern industrial enterprise that follows.

Regarding the modern industrial enterprise, its analysis in late-industrializing countries must start with two facts. First, the modern industrial enterprise takes the form of the diversified business group. The proceedings of the International Conference on Business History attest to the ubiquity of *zaibatsu*-like structures: "In developing countries such as South Korea, Taiwan, the Philippines, Thailand, India, Brazil and Argentina . . . industrial groups which resemble Japan's former zaibatsu have sprung up since the Second World War" (as cited in Amsden, 1989a, p. 115). Why the diversified business group is omnipresent in late-industrializing countries warrants careful study, and whether it is the optimal agent of industrial change requires even more careful study still. For now we take this form of doing business in late-industrializing countries as a fact, and merely note that one needn't reinvent the wheel to understand its origins. One may take as a starting point for understanding it Alfred Chandler's observation that since the late nineteenth century, industrialization has been spearheaded by firms that are quite large and diversified, not by a great number of small firms that are highly specialized. Even in Taiwan, big business in the form of state enterprise and multinational firms appears to have been the progenitor of small- and medium-size operations (Amsden, 1989b).

What is noteworthy about the modern industrial enterprise of late industrialization is that it tends to be relatively widely diversified into unrelated products yet relatively centrally coordinated, and one may speculate that these two characteristics are related to industrializing late. One advantage of industrializing in the second half of the twentieth century is that firms with political backing can diversify very quickly and very widely under the centralizing control of a single family by borrowing technology and capital from overseas. They need not specialize in a single field bounded by their own technological expertise, or finance their expansion by diluting their equity.

Second, whereas the firm that grows by innovating new products and processes tends to have the R&D lab and marketing office as its strategic focus, the best firms in all late-industrializing countries have the shopfloor as their strategic focus, because it is here that borrowed technology must be operationalized and improved. Whether in Korea (Amsden, 1989a), India (Lall, 1987), or Latin America (Katz, 1987), well-managed firms that increase their market share do so by investing resources to realize incremental improvements in quality and productivity. Whereas the hero of the First Industrial Revolution was the entrepreneur, and that of the Second Industrial Revolution, the general manager, the protagonist of late industrialization is, in Veblenesque fashion, the production engineer. The production engineer alone has a technical understanding of how borrowed technology works.

We may now put two and two together and suggest that in a wide range of late-industrializing countries, the flourishing of the diversified business group and its strategic focus on the shopfloor reflect the fulfillment of the defining need of industrializing late; namely, the need to learn how to borrow technology and improve upon it. If we go one step further, we may ask, what does it take to excel at such a process? The answer to this question can help us understand the superiority of the management practices of Korea, Japan, and Taiwan. Presumably, in some small or large part, leading firms in these countries have grown especially fast by managing the learning experience especially well.

What does a corporation have to do well to manage learning? First, it must have access to a large supply of learners, at all levels of the employment hierarchy, including engineers who, in late industrialization, do not come through the ranks of manual workers but are recruited direct from the universities. The plain fact of the matter is that Korea, Japan, and Taiwan have industrialized rapidly in part because they have invested relatively heavily in education, including technical education at the university level.

Second, managing industrialization well means motivating the work force, not least of all educated engineers from the most prestigious universities who are the gatekeepers of foreign technology transfer. Once established with government patronage, the *jaebul* or Korean business groups prospered by attracting the best engineers. They did so by offering them high pay, opportunities for promotion that were otherwise blocked in smaller family-dominated firms, the prospect of interesting work, and the chance to enhance their skills through company training. At present, many of the best university graduates in Korea are considering employment with some of the smaller groups, say, KIA Motors rather than Hyundai Motors in the automobile industry, because the smaller groups are regarded as having less bureaucracy and better opportunities for advancement. In the preceding 25 years, however, the biggest business groups were considered to be the premier employers.

Third, a good management system from the viewpoint of the country concerned means one that diffuses the engineering and management skills of the best-run firms to sequentially newer industries and smaller establishments. In Korea the top *jaebuls* did this in several ways.

Good management was spread within the group to effect a transition to more complex industries. Effectively borrowing new technology to enter a new industry requires project execution capability, and *jaebuls* like Hyundai, Samsung, Lucky-Goldstar, and other widely diversified groups enhanced their project execution capability by entering new industries with a task force composed of personnel already within their group possessing prior experience in establishing greenfield plants. In effect, the *jaebuls* developed an economy of scope in diversification (see Amsden, 1989a, ch. 5). They diversified widely and they became good at diversification, thereby reducing its social costs.

There has also been a tendency among some *jaebuls* to recruit managers at the group level, train them, and then allocate them across industry-level subsidiaries. This practice has helped to distribute competent managers to the less glamorous industries.

Finally, good management has diffused outward from the big groups by means of subcontracting. In the Korean automobile industry, for example, many subcontractors are owned or managed by former employees of Hyundai or Daewoo Motors (Amsden, 1989a, ch. 7).

In sum, the management system of late industrialization has the shopfloor as its strategic focus within the context of the diversified business group. The system appears to have worked especially well in Korea because a large supply of well-trained engineers has been employed in the diversified business groups. These groups have grown in conjunction with government subsidization and discipline. Even if one dislikes them from the viewpoint of equity, these groups have had to be well managed and their management standards have been diffused—outward to other firms through subcontracting, and inward from industry to industry through the circulation of personnel within the group.

Obviously all these points cannot be substantiated below and the reader is referred to Amsden (1989a) for an analysis of the automobile, textiles, steel, shipbuilding, and cement industries. The discussion below limits its attention to two issues. In the next section, aggregate data are presented to suggest that even as managerial capitalism has spread in Korea, a strategic focus on the shopfloor and a preference of firms to hire engineers over general managers have prevented overhead costs from going through the roof. The final section presents a brief case study of a subsidiary of the Samsung group in a pedestrian industry, papermaking. The point is to show that even in an unglamorous industry that is protected from foreign competition, with little chance of large financial gains in export markets, the big groups manage carefully and well, as evidenced by incremental improvements in productivity and quality. I undertook this case study with Professor Linsu Kim, and the reader is referred to Amsden and Kim (1985) for a fuller discussion.

SHOPFLOOR FOCUS AND OVERHEAD

The *jaebul*'s structure is multidivisional, but its general office tends to be relatively small (like those of American conglomerates). In fact, some large Korean firms do not have any general office, secretariat, or staff to serve the president and his retinue. Among 218 large firms surveyed by the College of Business Administration, Seoul National University, as many as 30 percent had none (SNU, 1985).[1] Among the 200 or so firms (large and small) that did have general offices, the functions that they undertook on a regular basis were limited. Most functions were undertaken centrally only when the need arose, in which case managers operating at the group or company level were pulled together to form a temporary task force. Such task forces, for example, executed decisions about entering new industries.

A small or nonexistent general office is a key characteristic of the Korean modern industrial enterprise and is indicative of how decision-making power is distributed between owners and salaried managers. Decisions at the top tend to be made by owners autocratically, rather than bureaucratically. Most decisions, however, are not made at the top. According to SNU's survey, salaried managers made decisions about production, R&D, and marketing, and these managers were assigned where their skills were needed most: to the shopfloor, the plant, or the company level.[2] Firms concentrated over half their efforts on production and R&D (which in the mid-1980s typically concerned the absorption of foreign technology), with marketing taking up much of the remainder of their time.

This picture of the distribution of power—which shows strategic and financial decisions in the hands of a single individual or family, and decentralized decision-making in other areas—is lent support by statistics on the growth and composition of Korean management. Table 20.1 provides data on manufacturing employment in the period 1960 through 1980, broken down into six categories: engineers, managers, sales, service, clerical and production workers. The data show that between 1960 and 1980, there was an increase in the absolute number of engineers, managers, sales, and service employees (call them white-collar workers, excluding for the moment the clerical category). Nevertheless, the ratio of white-collar to blue-collar, or production, workers *declined* from 0.13 in 1960 to 0.10 in 1980. This is a rather stunning fact. It suggests that even as Korean firms learned,

Table 20.1
Managerial Resources in the Manufacturing Sector, 1960–80

Employment Category	1960	1970	1980	Increase 1980/1960
Engineers	4,425	16,252	44,999	10.2
Managers	31,350	47,166	69,585	2.2
Sales	5,025	27,778	68,716	13.7
Service	13,660	22,740	49,522	3.6
Clerical	17,330	143,849	356,362	20.6
Production	404,735	1,188,406	2,206,851	5.4
Total	479,975	1,447,520	2,797,030	5.8
Administrative/ Production (ratio)[a]	0.13	0.10	0.10	--
Administrative and Clerical/Production (ratio)	0.18	0.22	0.27	--

Source: Korea Institute for Educational Development, 1983.

Note: Includes transportation and communication workers in the manufacturing sector.
[a]Administrative includes engineers, managers, sales and service workers.

diversified, and evolved into modern industrial enterprises, complete with managerial hierarchies, they tended to keep their overhead expenses in check. To use the terminology of the classical economists and Marx, they maintained a more or less stable or even declining ratio of "unproductive" to "productive" workers.

By contrast, Melman (1951) points out that "the businessmen [sic] charged with administering the manufacturing firms of the United States have devoted increasing resources to administration functions of their firms since the turn of the twentieth century" (1951, p. 89). Melman's observation applies equally well to many European countries. In the period 1978–85, there was an "alarming increase" in the number of white-collar workers in the United States, coupled with a decrease in the blue-collar category— +21 percent and -6 percent respectively (Amsden, 1989a).

If one includes clerical staff among white-collar workers in the Korean data, then between 1960 and 1980 the ratio of white- to blue-collar workers also rose, from 0.18 to 0.27. Nevertheless, the fact that the increase in the white- to blue-collar ratio in Korea was accounted for by a rise in clerical workers has acted to contain manufacturing costs, not to inflate them. Most clerical workers in Korea are women, with vocational or secondary high school degrees. They handle a wide variety of bookkeeping functions that in higher-wage countries now tend to be computerized. Discrimination against women workers in Korea is so severe that not only are they paid far less than men (about 45 percent as much on average), they are also pressured to leave paid employment when they marry, although this custom may be changing. Thus, clerical workers represent a variable cost that does not rise with seniority.

Furthermore, although both the number of general managers and the number of engineers in Korea rose absolutely between 1960 and 1980, the latter increase was far greater than the former. The number of engineers increased tenfold, that of general managers by a factor of only 2.2 (see Table 20.1). The ratio of general managers to engineers fell from 7.0 in 1960 to 1.5 in 1980. This suggests an orientation toward production in Korean manufacturing firms rather than toward sales or finance, although in certain industries, sales include technical people who are tied closely to production. Insofar as Korea competes in world markets on the basis of its manufacturing capabilities, it invests its money where its competitive advantage lies.

The number of levels in the managerial hierarchies of larger firms has also been kept in check. Larger firms have a greater number of departments and sections than do smaller firms. Their management is more extensive. They also tend to have a larger number of subordinates per section chief. Nevertheless, they have only marginally more managerial layers. In fact, in the case of firms with 200–300 workers and those with over 5,000, the smaller firms have more levels of hierarchy than the larger (SNU, 1985). The compactness of the hierarchical structure suggests that engineers who have entered the manufacturing sector in increasing numbers in Korea since 1960 have kept in close touch with the ranks.

It is now time to descend to the micro level and to examine how an actual company has managed the learning process.

THE STANDARD OPERATING PROCEDURES OF A WELL-MANAGED *JAEBUL* SUBSIDIARY

The Chonju Papermaking Co., a subsidiary of the Samsung group, represents the professionally managed firm in Korea *par excellence*. In the mid 1980s it employed roughly 700 people and had annual sales of about $100 million. It is the Samsung group's third manufacturing facility and operates in an industry that has little chance in Korea of dynamic growth.

The Korean paper industry has existed behind trade barriers with prices administered by the government. By international standards, domestic prices are high and quality is low due to the input mix of waste paper materials. Facilities have not been modernized much and consequently, capacity utilization has been low. The papermaking industry in the advanced countries tends to employ more engineers per 1,000 people employed than the textile industry but fewer engineers per 1,000 employed than the cement, steel, chemicals, and petrochemicals sectors. Accordingly, the degree to which the Korean paper industry has relied on foreign technical assistance has been greater than in textiles but less than in the continuous processes, with the exception of cement.

The Korea Papermakers Association maintains that most of its members continue to rely on turnkey transfers for their capacity expansions. Turnkey transfers among all industries were most prevalent in papermaking as late as 1983 (Federation of Korean Industries, 1984). Papermakers have not worked closely with local capital goods suppliers to develop capability in papermaking machinery. A local content law enacted by the government in 1977 to stimulate the domestic papermaking machinery industry has either been rendered irrelevant by the paucity of capacity expansions or has been circumvented, as in the case of Chonju, by the self-fulfilling prophesy that the capability of local equipment manufacturers is inadequate to supply the calibre of papermaking machinery required.

Learning in the Korean papermaking industry has tended to be relatively sluggish because many firms have been slow to invest in new equipment embodying new technology. I estimated three learning curves for the papermaking industry, one for the period 1958 to 1982 and one for each of two subperiods, 1958 to 1970 and 1970 to 1982. By comparison with several other industries in Korea, the learning rate turns out to be low, 83 percent, and changes only marginally between the two subperiods, suggesting a constancy rather than acceleration in the learning rate.

The Korean papermaking industry, however, appears to be dualistic in nature, with 60 percent of output accounted for by 15 or so firms (out of a total of 140). Chonju is the largest among them (although only 175th as large as International Paper, the world's leading paper supplier). Despite heavy protection of papermaking in Korea and little export activity, learning in Chonju, and in the papermaking subsidiary of another big business group, the Ssangyong *jaebul*, appears to have reached a rather high standard because it conforms with groupwide norms.

Chonju is part of a vertically integrated chain in the Samsung group. Chonju supplies a key input to another Samsung subsidiary that publishes a daily newspaper (*The Joong-ang Daily News*). Chonju is fed by a Samsung plant that manufactures bleached ground pulp and by a joint venture that produces pulp in New Zealand. To fit into this network, learning in Chonju is institutionalized. Decisions are made by a team of professional managers in accordance with specified rules, and operations are procedurized—production practices are standardized and documented, and technology is codified where possible.

The Samsung group's influence is felt in two regards. First, Chonju is covered by group-level policies concerning training, appointments, and promotions. Training of newly recruited managers in Samsung occurs at the group level. One purpose of such training is to build personal groupwide ties. After training, managers in the same class are dispatched to different subsidiaries, with two intended effects. Communications between subsidiaries are strengthened. Talent is dispersed, at least in the case of young managers, across subsidiaries. This helps to ensure that undesirable outposts, such as Chonju (located near a small town in central Korea), receive their quota of quality personnel with up-to-date knowledge of standard operating procedures and the outside world. In the mid-1980s about one quarter of Chonju's managers had been with the company for less than two years. Rotation of managers further increases the need for procedurization.

Second, Chonju's pattern of acquiring technological capability has been influenced by what appears to be group-level policy to seek third-party advice when buying proprietary technical assistance for new ventures. Of the three Samsung subsidiaries that Professor Linsu Kim and I studied—Chonju, Cheil Wool, and Samsung Heavy Industries—all sought third-party advice at major growth points. Third-party advice was sought in order to avoid getting scalped and to gain greater technical and economic knowledge about a newly penetrated industry.

Chonju sought third-party advice at the time of its establishment from Ishikawajima Harima Industries of Japan to assess the economic feasibility of entering papermaking; to choose the most appropriate technology; and to procure the best available make within the chosen range. This constituted Chonju's starting point to acquire technological knowledge about the core of its production equipment. Then, after buying German papermaking machinery, Chonju unpackaged its technology still further by hiring private consultants (from Europe and Japan) for particular functions: machinery assembly, electrical systems and motors, initial plant operation, quality control, and general engineering problems.

Chonju continues to rely heavily on machinery suppliers for capacity expansions, but it has nonetheless internalized a sequentially larger number of elements of project execution capability. In a $75 million investment project for a 400 tons/day papermaking line in 1985, Chonju evaluated the feasibility of the project on its own; made its own choice of machinery supplier, Mitsubishi Heavy Industries (which builds papermaking machinery under license from a U.S. firm); undertook startup jointly with Mitsubishi; and had enough know-how to require Mitsubishi to modify its designs to suit Chonju's specific requirements. Enough knowledge has been stored in the form of bids from machinery suppliers and documents about alternative technologies to learn from earlier capacity expansions, even with changes in personnel.

Chonju deliberately worked from the ground up in getting to know its process equipment. It introduced computerized process monitoring control systems only in 1978, ten years after production commenced. Before that, the process was monitored manually. Such monitoring, in conjunction with quality control circles, has underscored Chonju's attempts to raise productivity and quality incrementally. Table 20.2 provides evidence of Chonju's success. In the case of Papermaking Line 3, for example, between 1978 and 1980 the speed of the line was raised, down days were reduced, the defect ratio was lowered by a factor of 3, and production per day was increased by 25 percent.

Chonju has provided its work force with both on-the-job and formal training. In

Table 20.2
Process Improvements in the Chonju Paper Co., 1971–80

| | Line 1 | | | Line 2 | | | Line 3 | |
	1971	1974	1983	1971	1974	1983	1978	1980
Weight (g/m^2)	53.3	54.6	65.0	53.1	54.9	65.0	54.0	54.0
Width (m/m)	3456	3573	3572	2364	2364	2364	4728	4728
Speed (m/min)	460	440	440	338	360	350	620	750
Down days	24.3	20.6	17.0	16.2	15.2	17.0	40.0	17.0
Defects ratio (%)	7.0	6.5	7.0	11.6	5.8	11.0	17.0	5.0
Closed days	12.1	3.73	1.0	11.9	2.8	1.0	----	1.0
Production per day (MT/D)	94	121	121	50	63	63	200	250

Source: Amsden and Kim (1985)

1979 Chonju also established a central R&D laboratory with technical assistance from the Oji Paper Company of Japan. The lab employs 40 workers, including 14 with engineering degrees. The annual budget for R&D as a percentage of total sales has amounted to about 0.6 percent, which compares favorably with 0.9 percent in Oji. Most R&D provides support for operations and for the importation of foreign technical assistance for capacity expansions.

The Chonju Papermaking Company may not be the most brilliant learner in Korea, but it has pursued its studies competently and redounds to the credit of its parents.

FOREIGN INFLUENCE ON THE MANAGEMENT SYSTEM OF LATE INDUSTRIALIZATION

It is hard to know the degree to which, if at all, manufacturing systems matter in explaining differences in growth rates across countries. But there is much to suggest that they matter a great deal. They are likely to influence both allocative (strategic) efficiency and technical (functional) efficiency. Excluding state enterprises, private managements ultimately decide which market signals or government initiatives to follow in establishing new industries or expanding existing capacity. Once they make allocative decisions, they are the principle factor determining how efficiently new investments function.

All late-industrializing countries, however, appear to have roughly similar management systems, which, in dominant firms, feature a strategic focus on the shopfloor in the context of the diversified business group. Therefore, if one believes that management systems explain significant differences in growth rates across late-industrializing countries, then one must specify their finer distinctions.

By way of conclusion, one of the finer distinctions in management systems of late-industrializing countries that may help to explain Korea's outstanding performance relates to foreign influence. Foreign influence impinges on the managerial capitalism of late industrialization through technical assistance and direct (equity) investment.

The preponderance of foreign technical assistance flowing into Korea has come from Japan, which may have given Korea an edge over other late-industrializing countries that were culturally and geographically further afield than Korea from Japan. Japan may not have been as close to the world technological frontier as the United States, or as generous in transferring its proprietary know-how, but it emerged as the world's premier producer, and communicated to Korea the most efficient production techniques, seriousness about the manufacturing function, and respect for scanning world markets for new technology.

On the other hand, direct foreign investment in Korea outside its export platforms has been negligible. The American and European multinationals are largely absent and the "commanding heights" are controlled by Korean firms. Little direct foreign investment outside the most labor-intensive industries may have benefited Korea if the following were true: First, it turned out that the diversified business groups were a better institution for transferring good management practices across industries and firms than the multinationals. Second, it turned out that diversified business groups were more attentive to achieving incremental productivity and quality improvements and better at infusing new technology than the multinationals.

Both these possibilities are worthy of testing because it can no longer be assumed that multinational management is better than what in late-industrializing countries has now become big business groups with experienced salaried managers attuned to the learning exigencies of their own environment. In comparing foreign and indigenous management outside the labor-intensive sectors, one would, of course, have to compare apples and apples: say, Hyundai Motors and Daewoo Motors (a joint venture that includes General Motors), or Daewoo Motors under GM management and Daewoo Motors under Daewoo management. If the management systems of indigenous firms are more structured to the needs of learning than the management systems of firms that evolved overseas as innovators, the former may be more effective than the latter.

NOTES

1. Furthermore, roughly 80 percent of a sample of 280 small firms had none. The survey of Seoul National University was conducted in 1984. It covered approximately 500 firms, depending on the survey question. The definition of small- and medium-size firm varies by question but usually refers to firms employing 500 workers or less. See SNU (1985).

2. It is assumed for simplicity that middle and top managers differentiate themselves by their assignment either to the company or to the group level, respectively.

REFERENCES

Amsden, A. H. (1989a), *Asia's Next Giant: South Korea and Late Industrialization*, New York and Oxford: Oxford University Press, 1989.

———— (1989b), "Big Business and Urban Congestion in Taiwan: The Origins of Small and Medium Size Enterprise and Regionally Decentralized Industry." Mimeo, Massachusetts Institute of Technology, 1989.

————, and Kim, Linsu, "The Acquisition of Technological Capability in South Korea." Mimeo, Development Research Department, Productivity Division, World Bank, Washington, D.C., 1985.

Chandler, A. D. Jr., *Scale, Scope, and Organizational Capability*, Mimeo, Harvard Business School, Boston, 1987.

Federation of Korean Industries, *Industrial Technology Development Survey* (in Korean), Seoul, 1984.

Katz, J. M. (ed.), *Technology Generation in Latin American Manufacturing Industries*, New York: St. Martins, 1987.

KIED [Korea Institute for Educational Development], "Study on the Demand and Supply of Science and Engineering Manpower at Master's and Ph.D. Levels" (in Korean), Mimeo, Seoul, 1983.

Lall, S., *Learning to Industrialize: The Acquisition of Technological Capability in India*, London, Macmillan, 1987.

Melman, S., "The Rise of Administrative Overhead in the Manufacturing Industries in the United States 1899–1947," *Oxford Economic Papers*, *3*, February 1951, 62–112.

Seoul National University [SNU], *Current Situation and Task to Be Done by Korean Firms* (in Korean), College of Business Administration, Seoul, 1985.

Part Six

INCOME DISTRIBUTION
AND COLLECTIVE BARGAINING

The most elusive dream for development planners is to combine economic growth with more equitable distribution of income. For many, trying to bring about economic growth itself is a dream, but to achieve both growth and equity is almost an impossible task; only a select few have been successful in achieving both. In every society income distribution is not only an economic issue but also a political issue. This issue often manifests itself in the labor movement and, in an extreme case, leads to a violent labor unrest. In Korea, during its "growth first" period (1960s and 1970s) there was a benign neglect of income distribution and the welfare of labor. However, in the recent period, especially after 1987 as government allowed more democracy, the violent labor unrest has become a pervasive phenomenon that threatens the future progress of the economic system. Therefore, it is appropriate that we introduce two chapters that address the nature of income distribution and labor issues in Korea.

The first chapter by J. G. Yoo is a comprehensive review of income distribution based on much of his own investigation and that of others. Yoo first examines the time trend of income and welfare inequalities based on the empirical results of Choo and Yoon (1984), Kim and Ahn (1987), and Yoo and Kwon (1987). The findings show that although the income and welfare inequality of Korea declined temporarily during the 1969–71 (or –74) period, on the whole, it increased. This leads to the conclusion that, in general, Korea has not harmonized equality with growth. Casual observations point to three major factors that may have been responsible for the pattern of income and welfare inequalities of Korea; namely, the government interest rate policy and the trend of urbanization as well as business concentration.

One of the ironies in Korean economic development, as was the case with other industrialized economies in their early stages of development, is that the absence of effective labor unionization is cited as one of the reasons why Korea was able to grow fast, or, that the rapid economic growth has occurred at the expense of basic workers' welfare and rights.

In the second chapter of this section, written by S. I. Park, the author points out that effective industrial relations were not permitted to develop in Korea because of the government's authoritarian paternalism. Under this system, the powers of rule making and decision making in the management of industrial disputes and grievances was vested in the hands of the government authority. As we have observed repeatedly throughout this book, during its "growth first" period government favored business, especially large businesses. What has not been mentioned is that the government's favor of business also included government's protection of business from labor disputes. Without this protection, business would not have functioned as effectively and also the economy would not have grown as fast.

One of the conclusions put forth by Park is that government's long-standing authoritarian paternalism has deprived both the management and workers of opportunities to learn the benefits of free collective bargaining. What Korea needs is a modern industrial relations system that can institutionalize and internalize labor disputes.

21

Income Distribution in Korea

Jong Goo Yoo

INTRODUCTION

During the last two decades, 1965–85, following the "static and dynamic asset redistribution phase of 1945–63" as labeled by Adelman and Robinson (1978), Korea achieved one of the highest rates of economic growth in the world. Its annual growth rate of GNP was 13.2 percent during that period. A number of studies on income distribution in Korea emerged during this period (for example, by Oshima, 1970; Mizoguchi et al., 1976; Adelman and Robinson, 1978; Rao, 1978; and Choo and Kim, 1978), and they have yielded two common conclusions (with the possible exception of Choo and Kim). First, the household income distribution of Korea is among the most equal in the developing world. Second, during the high growth period of the 1960s and 1970s, Korea did not experience the typical decline in equality of household income distribution implied by Kuznets' U-curve. For example, in World Bank publications and in other international forums, Korea has been hailed as a prime example of how growth can be achieved with equity. According to the data presented in these forums, Korea is among only a handful of less-developed nations that have achieved a level of equality comparable to that of the advanced world economies.

However, the validity of these conclusions about income distribution in Korea is somewhat questionable due to inadequate attention given to the household income data. A survey of the entire household population is almost necessary for an assessment of the nature of household income distribution. However, in Korea, a national survey of income or expenditure does not exist. This problem would not be critical if the surveys are managed to cover the entire population.

Recently, a number of studies on income distribution in Korea (for example, by Choo and Kim, 1978; Choo and Yoon, 1984; Kim and Ahn, 1987; Yoo and Kwon,

1987; and Yoo, 1988) have appeared, and they have made great efforts either to include the excluded incomes or to estimate inequality using more reliable household expenditure data than the household income data.

The main objectives of this study are as follows: first, to review the time trend of income and/or welfare inequality of Korea reported by several recent studies on income distribution in Korea; and second, to examine the factors of inequality.

On the basis of these recent studies on income distribution in Korea, we could conclude that: (a) although the income and welfare inequality of Korea declined during the 1969–74 period relative to that of the 1964–68 period, it increased during the 1975–85 period; (b) the inequality of Korea is mostly affected by the distribution of property incomes; (c) the incomes of farm households in Korea is distributed more equally than that of nonfarm households, thus suggesting that the inequality of household income and welfare distribution in Korea is largely determined by the inequality of nonfarm household groups. On the basis of our empirical results (Yoo and Kwon, 1987, and Yoo, 1988), it is not possible to conclude that Korea avoided the typical decline in equality of household income distribution implied by Kuznets' U-curve during its high growth period.

In the next section, we describe the availabilities and problems associated with existing Korean household income data. The empirical results and their implications are summarized in the third section. The sources of income and welfare inequalities in Korea are analyzed in the fourth section. A summary and conclusions are given in the final section.

KOREAN INCOME DISTRIBUTION DATA

Time series data for household income and expenditure in Korea are available only from two sources: *City Household Income and Expenditure Survey* (CHIES) and *Farm Household Economic Survey* (FHES). The two surveys have been conducted continuously since 1963. As in most developing countries, Korea, too, has data problems such as coverage exclusions, definitional inconsistencies and ambiguities, and probable response biases.

In Korea, the problem of coverage exclusion is very serious. The two surveys, CHIES and FHES, exclude a significant portion of the household population (see Table 21.1).

According to the CHIES reports, all non-city households (i.e., households in villages [*Myeons*] and towns [*Eubs*]) are excluded. The households engaged in agriculture and fisheries, and the households whose income and expenditures are difficult to calculate, are also excluded in the CHIES. Until 1977, there were two additional exclusions in the CHIES: first, all the households on public assistance and classified as a low income class by law; and second, all the households whose incomes are above the income ceiling set by the CHIES criterion in every year. However, in 1978, the income ceiling set by the CHIES criterion was abolished.

Table 21.1
Uncovered Households in Both CHIES and FHES Surveys (Based on Housing and Population Census, 1980)

	Number of Households (1,000 Households)	Share of the Households to All Households (%)
Urban self-employed households	1,628	20.4
Non-farm households in rural area	1,307	16.4
Wage and salary earning households	835	10.5
Self-employed households	472	5.9
Fishery households	157	2.0
Small farm households and wage earning households in rural area	42	0.5
	———	———
Total	3,134	39.3

Source: Choo and Yoon, 1984, p. 4.

As a result, the CHIES now includes the incomes of the highest income class households, and the CHIES also tries to include the low income class households (that is, the households on public assistance). The FHES also excludes all the non-farm households in rural areas and farm households in cities. The nonfarm households in cities are covered by the CHIES, but the nonfarm households in noncities are not covered by either survey.[1] Furthermore, in the CHIES reports, the income figures of self-employed households (that is, medical doctors, lawyers, private businessmen, and so on) are not reported, but only expenditure figures of the self-employed households are reported.

According to Table 21.1, at the minimum, approximately 39.3 percent of Korea's total household population is excluded. The fact that this exclusion is large and that the exclusion contains sensitive groups of population, namely, the very rich (for example, medical doctors) and the very poor (for example, small farm households), means that the derived degree of income inequality based on these data sources may not be reliable.[2]

Choo and Yoon (1984) and Kim and Ahn (1987) made great efforts to include the excluded incomes in both CHIES and FHES reports. They, first, assumed that the consumption pattern (that is, average propensity to consume) of the self-employed household group is the same as that of the salary and wage earners' household group. Under this assumption, and with the reported expenditure data in the CHIES reports, they estimated the income of the self-employed households in cities by income classes. Second, they assumed that the income of nonfarm households in rural areas is proportionally less than that of urban households in each income and occupational class. They also assumed that the incomes of fishery households are proportionally less than those of farm households.

However, their assumptions are still somewhat questionable. First of all, the high income classes such as medical doctors and lawyers have, in general, a tendency to under-report their incomes. Furthermore, in their studies Choo and Yoon (1984) and Kim and Ahn (1987) have failed to include the "imputed income" from housing in city households. The imputed income from housing is one of the major components of the property income of a city household in Korea (see Table 21.5). Consequently, their results of income inequality may have biased toward equality. Recently, Yoo and Kwon (1987) included the imputed income from housing into household income, and by using the expenditure figures, they estimated the welfare inequality among urban households in Korea based on an "income-consumption-welfare" nexus in which an individual's income affects his consumption opportunities and his economic welfare.[3]

However, these studies on income and/or welfare inequality in Korea by Choo and Yoon (1984), Kim and Ahn (1987), and Yoo and Kwon (1987), are all based on reported income and expenditure figures in both CHIES and FHES reports. As in other statistical reports, individual family figures are not available from the two surveys. Instead, only the mean income and/or expenditure figures of each income and/or expenditure brackets are reported, so that, regarding the above three studies, one has to assume that the mean income and expenditure of each income and expenditure bracket is the representative of each income and expenditure class. This assumption is also likely to bias the actual estimation of the inequality in Korea toward equality.

THE TIME TREND OF INEQUALITY IN KOREA

The time trend of inequality in Korea during the 1965–85 period is given in Table 21.2 and Figure 21.1. The results by Choo and Yoon (1984) and Kim and Ahn (1987) are the estimations of Gini indices, whereas the inequality results by Yoo and Kwon (1987) are the translog indices of relative inequality[4] based on the model presented by Jorgenson and Slesnick (1984). The time periods of these three empirical results are longer than any other empirical results presented in the international forums, and the three results are based on more reliable household income and expenditure data than any other studies on income and welfare distributions in Korea. Therefore, the inequality trends presented in this paper should give a more comprehensive and reliable time trend of income and welfare inequalities in Korea.

Table 21.2
The Indices of Inequality in Korea

Year	All Households Choo-Yoon	All Households Kim-Ahn	Non-Farm Households Choo-Yoon	Non-Farm Households Kim-Ahn	Farm Households Choo-Yoon	Farm Households Kim-Ahn	Relative Welfare Inequality Index (Yoo and Kwon) $\rho=-1$	Relative Welfare Inequality Index (Yoo and Kwon) $\rho=-2$
1965	.3439	.3652	.4167	.4935	.2825	.2062	.06806	.17590
1966		.3542		.4386		.2079	.06955	.17660
1967		.3687		.4255		.1935	.07339	.19784
1968		.3608		.4044		.1924	.07455	.20358
1969		.3457		.4075		.1957	.05485	.15395
1970	.3322	.3457	.3455	.3861	.2945	.1941	.05455	.12509
1971		.3377		.3835		.2141	.05802	.13624
1972		.3570		.4130		.2195	.06454	.16507
1973		.3920		.4563		.2145	.05571	.14288
1974		.3944		.4675		.2170	.05615	.14281
1975		.3905		.4708		.1940	.06540	.19917
1976	.3908	.4048	.4118	.4813	.3273	.2171	.06589	.22878
1977		.3964		.4713		.2079	.09028	.32612
1978		.3828		.4490		.1783	.07819	.27618
1979		.3919		.4460		.1586	.06222	.20815
1980		.3860		.4437		.1455	.07503	.24150
1981		.3734		.4293		.1438	.07329	.24074
1982	.3574	.4056	.3705	.4688	.3061	.1522	.07213	.24431
1983		.4005		.4613		.1300	.06778	.21290
1984		.3937		.4348		.1275		
1985		.4105		.4676		.1211		

Sources: Choo and Yoon, 1984; Kim and Ahn, 1987; and Yoo and Kwon, 1987.

Yoo and Kwon's experiment was made, as in Jorgenson and Slesnick's (1984) model, with alternative values of ρ, where $\rho = -1$ and $\rho = -2$. The $\rho = -1$ means that the marginal social contribution of an individual's welfare is independent of the welfare of others. This implies that the iso-welfare curves are straight lines or, in short, that people are indifferent to the distribution of welfare as in the Gini social welfare function. On the other hand, the $\rho = -2$ means that the marginal social valuation of an individual's welfare depends crucially on the welfare levels of others.[5] Therefore, it would be more desirable to choose the value of ρ not equal to $\rho = -1$ but $\rho < -1$.

The three sets of empirical results in Table 21.2 and Figure 21.1 suggest the following:

First, in Korea, the incomes of the farm household group are distributed more equally than the incomes of the nonfarm household group, and the income inequality of the nonfarm household group dominates the income inequality of Korea.

Second, the results by Kim and Ahn (1987) show that farm household income distribution deteriorated during the 1971–76 period compared with that of the

Figure 21.1
Time Trend of Inequalities

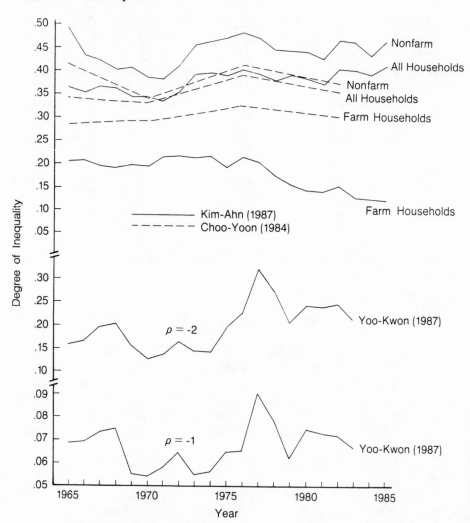

1965–70 period, but has displayed a rapidly improving trend in recent years. On the whole, their results show a gradually improving trend in the income distribution of the farm household group. On the other hand, the results of Choo and Yoon (1984) suggest that the degrees of income inequality of the farm household group in Korea are greater than those of Kim and Ahn (1987), and that the time trend of income inequality of the farm household group does not show an improving trend.

One of the reasons of these discrepancies between the two independent estimations is the difference in data sampling. That is, Choo and Yoon (1984) divided the classes of the farm household group according to the level of household income, whereas Kim and Ahn (1987) divided the classes by the acreage of arable land of each farm household. The difference of the arable land of farm households would, in general, not clearly reflect the difference of household incomes. From this it appears that the results of Choo and Yoon (1984) may be more reliable than the results of Kim and Ahn (1987)[6] and hence, we may conclude that, although the farm household income distribution in Korea shows an improving time trend in recent years, the farm household income distribution during 1970-85 has deteriorated relative to that of the last half of the 1960s.

Third, both results show that the income distribution of the nonfarm household group in Korea improved during the 1965–71 period, but rapidly deteriorated during the 1972–78 period, and, from 1979, although the income inequality seems to have slightly improved, the degree of inequality is still higher than that of the early 1970s.

Fourth, as mentioned earlier, since the income inequality of Korea as a whole is significantly affected by the income distribution of the nonfarm household group, the trend of income inequality of all household groups is almost the same as that of the nonfarm household group. The correlation coefficient between the two inequalities is +.78. Also, the income distribution of all household groups in Korea improved during the 1965–71 period, but deteriorated during the 1972–76 period, and, after 1976, it remained about the same.

Finally, the results of Yoo and Kwon (1987) with $\rho = -2$ also show almost the same time trend of inequality among urban households as those of nonfarm household groups reported by the other two studies. As shown in Table 21.3, the number of urban households (that is, urbanization ratio) in Korea has continuously increased from 34.6 percent in 1965 to 50.1 percent in 1975, and to 66.2 percent in 1985. This means that the importance of the income distribution of urban households upon the income and/or welfare inequality in Korea as a whole is becoming greater.

As discussed earlier, in the estimation of the income inequality by Choo and Yoon (1984) and Kim and Ahn (1987), the imputed income from the owner-occupied or yearly rent-deposit housing (that is, income from properties) was not included in each household's global income figure. It is well established in the literature that the incomes from properties are distributed more unequally than the

Table 21.3
Household Distribution in Korea (in 1,000 households; percent)

Year	Total (A)	All Area Non-farm	Farm	Total (B)	Urban Area Non-farm	Farm	Rural Area Total	Non-farm	Farm	Urbanization Rate (%); (B)/(A)
1965	5,022	2,350	2,672	1,738	1,591	147	3,284	759	2,525	34.6
1966	5,133	2,406	2,727	1,859	1,706	153	3,274	701	2,573	36.2
1967	5,244	2,471	2,773	1,983	1,827	156	3,261	644	2,617	37.8
1968	5,355	2,650	2,705	2,111	1,959	152	3,244	691	2,553	39.4
1969	5,465	2,803	2,662	2,242	2,092	150	3,223	712	2,511	41.0
1970	5,576	3,016	2,560	2,377	2,234	143	3,199	782	2,417	42.6
1971	5,791	3,244	2,547	2,555	2,411	144	3,235	834	2,402	44.1
1972	6,005	3,490	2,515	2,740	2,595	145	3,265	895	2,370	45.6
1973	6,219	3,713	2,506	2,930	2,786	144	3,289	927	2,362	47.1
1974	6,433	4,031	2,402	3,128	2,988	140	3,306	1,044	2,262	48.6
1975	6,648	4,235	2,413	3,331	3,190	141	3,317	1,045	2,272	50.1
1976	6,912	4,555	2,357	3,581	3,441	140	3,331	1,114	2,217	51.8
1977	7,176	4,859	2,317	3,840	3,700	140	3,337	1,158	2,179	53.5
1978	7,441	5,175	2,266	4,108	3,970	138	3,333	1,205	2,128	55.2
1979	7,705	5,502	2,203	4,384	4,249	135	3,321	1,253	2,068	56.9
1980	7,969	5,708	2,261	4,670	4,529	141	3,299	1,179	2,120	58.6
1981	8,290	6,162	2,128	4,983	4,849	134	3,307	1,313	1,994	60.1
1982	8,612	6,529	2,083	5,307	5,173	134	3,305	1,355	1,950	61.6
1983	8,933	6,857	2,076	5,639	5,505	134	3,294	1,352	1,942	63.1
1984	9,254	7,204	2,050	5,982	5,848	134	3,272	1,356	1,916	64.6
1985	9,575	7,568	2,007	6,334	6,201	133	3,241	1,367	1,874	66.2

Sources: Kim and Ahn 1987, which is based on *Population and Housing Census* conducted by EPB, *Agriculture Census, Agriculture and Fisheries Statistical Yearbook, Fisheries Statistical Yearbook, Fishery Industry Survey Report* conducted by the Ministry of Agriculture, Forestry, and Fisheries.

incomes from labor.[7] This means that, if the imputed income of each household is included in its global income, then the income inequality of Korea might be greater than the ones reported by them. Another point worth mentioning is that the distributions estimated by Choo and Yoon (1984) and Kim and Ahn (1987) are household income distributions, whereas the distribution by Yoo and Kwon (1987) is per capita term household expenditure distribution. There is no doubt that households differ in size, age composition, educational level, and other character-istics that explain the different expenditure patterns among households. Hence, the modeling of the effects of the household characteristics (that is, household equiv-alence scales)[8] is useful in both aggregate economic analysis and microeconomic analysis in order for the model to be plausible. And the incomes are, in general, under-reported, so that expenditure figures are more reliable than income figures. From this standpoint, it is possible that Yoo and Kwon (1987) may have provided a more reliable estimate of inequality in Korea.

All in all, the results reported by these three studies are fairly consistent with one another. In fact, the results by Choo and Yoon and Kim and Ahn are even more consistent with the study by Yoo and Kwon when $\rho = -2$ is assumed. Even though the results presented in various international forums suggest that the income distribution in Korea is one of the best in the developing world, the conclusion that emerges from the study by Yoo and Kwon (a welfare distribution approach with $\rho = -2$) and those by Choo and Yoon and Kim and Ahn (income distribution approaches) is that the income and/or welfare distribution in Korea is not as egalitarian as popularly believed.

THE SOURCES OF INEQUALITY

The income of a household can be divided into two sources: labor income and property income. As discussed earlier, it is argued that the labor incomes are distributed more equally than the incomes from properties. It is also well estab-lished in the literature that income inequality is affected by the rate of return from the different forms of wealth.

Based on above arguments, Yoo and Kwon (1987) recently suggested three major factors that may have been responsible for the inequality in income and welfare in Korea: namely, the real interest rate, the trend of urbanization, and business concentration.

In Korea, monetary authority, through its interest rate policy, exerts a direct and significant influence on the values of real estate properties. At the same time, in the controlled environment of low interest rate policy, which tends to discourage private saving in the official banking institutions, the real estate market has emerged as the only popular medium for private saving and investment. Given the inverse relationship between the values of real estate properties and interest rates,

Table 21.4

Within Group Inequality Indices among Urban Households in Korea, 1984

	Relative Welfare Inequality Indexes ($\rho=-1$)	Gini Indexes			
		Income (I)	Expenditure (I)	Income (II)	Expenditure (II)
All households	.05268	.29344	.26755	.26402	.22898
Occupation of household head					
Wage Earners	.03671	.17783	.16604	.15419	.15408
Salary Earners	.04132	.16893	.18188	.18290	.18618
Self-employed	.05821	.32136	.28904	.29464	.24852
Age of household head					
24 or less	.05332	.20270	.22591	.22511	.21812
25-29	.03808	.16745	.17143	.19621	.17432
30-34	.05539	.31521	.32578	.29793	.26425
35-39	.04941	.26584	.20121	.26700	.22188
40-44	.05145	.26795	.26301	.27456	.24034
45-49	.04967	.30311	.22674	.28640	.19821
50-54	.03769	.27124	.25440	.19900	.17313
55 or more	.06884	.33186	.31311	.29893	.27033

Source: Yoo, 1988, p. 128

Notes: 1. As discussed earlier, the social welfare function with $\rho=-1$ means the Gini social welfare function: people are indifferent to the distribution of welfare. It is very unrealistic. But, for the purpose of comparison with the Gini indices, the relative welfare inequality index when $\rho=-1$ is assumed.

2. The Gini indices of income I and expenditure I are based on the distributions of household incomes (Y_k) and expenditures (M_k), respectively, whereas the Gini indices of income II and expenditure II are the inequality results based on per capita term household income ($Y_k/m_o(A_k)$) and expenditure ($M_k/m_o(A_k)$) distributions. As discussed earlier, the modeling of the effects of the household characteristics, $m_o(A_k)$, is useful in both aggregate economic analysis and micro-economic analysis in order for the model to be plausible. Therefore, the inequality results based on the per capita term household income and expenditure distributions would give more reliable information.

a decrease in interest rate can benefit the upper income group more than it does the lower income group, thereby widening the income gap between the two groups.

Industrialization in Korea during the last two and one-half decades went hand in hand with urbanization (see Table 21.3). The urbanization in Korea has brought about a shift in economic activity from the rural sector, where the incomes are relatively and evenly distributed, to the urban sector, where income inequalities are much more pronounced.[9] And the rapid growth of urban population, along with the rapid growth of urban income, has created a pent-up demand for urban housing constitutes the major component of Korean urban households' assets (see Table 21.5). According to the *Population and Housing Census* conducted by EPB, the housing supply ratios (that is, number of houses/number of households) in all cities in each census year were 84.8 percent in 1960, 63.1 percent in 1966, 58.2 percent in 1970, 56.3 percent in 1975, 59.2 percent in 1980, and 57.7 percent in 1985. This means that, over the last two decades, especially during the mid 1970s, Korea has enjoyed the biggest boom in real estate markets.

A casual observation by Yoo and Kwon (1987) indicates that, during the high interest rate policy period (1965–71), the degree of welfare inequality seemed to decline, while the converse was the case during the 1972–77 (the low interest rate policy) period. Again, during the recent high interest rate period (1978–81), the degree of welfare inequality seemed to decline slightly. Also, their simple regression analysis shows a negative relationship between the welfare inequality index with $\rho = -2$ and the real interest rate. This and above facts imply that the low interest rate policy benefited the rich more than it did the poor, thereby further deteriorating the degree of equality among urban households in Korea.

In Korea, the official nominal interest rate in the organized money market is annually set by government. Therefore, the height of the real interest rate depends crucially on the inflation rate. That is, a high inflation rate had brought a great capital gain to the haves, thereby widening the income gap between the haves and have-nots in Korea.

Recently, Yoo (1988) also shows the importance of the capital gain (or the imputed income) from housing to the income and welfare distributions of urban households in Korea using one year (1984) cross-section data from the CHIES. The empirical inequality results of Yoo (1988) are given in Table 21.4.

As shown in Table 21.5, the major components of the property income of an urban household in Korea are (1) imputed income from housing, (2) interest and dividends, (3) rent received, and (4) gifts and assistance.[10] The imputed income from housing is the monthly rental value, at a going, unorganized money-market interest rate, of owner-occupied and/or yearly rent-deposit housing. The imputed income from housing is the largest component in the household property incomes (that is, the share of imputed income in the household property income is 61.8 percent).

The degree of inequality of the self-employed household group is greater than those of the wage earning and salary earning household groups. The fact that the share of property income of the self-employed household group is larger than those of other occupational groups implies that the inequality of urban households in Korea is significantly affected by the distribution of income from properties, especially by the distribution of the income from housing, and that an increase in the number of self-employed households (due to rapid urbanization along with industrialization) deteriorates the equality of urban households and hence, the overall equality.

Table 21.5
The Share of Various Incomes of Urban Households in Korea, 1984 (in percent)

	Total	Labor Income	Income from Subsidiary Jobs	Property Income				Gifts and Assistances	Others
				Sub-total	Imputed Income	Interest and Dividends	Rent Received		
All households	100.0	50.2	23.0	23.3	14.4	1.0	1.9	5.9	3.5
Occupation of household head									
Wage Earners	100.0	77.9	2.5	16.0	12.0	.8	1.1	2.1	3.6
Salary Earners	100.0	76.4	1.3	18.7	14.4	1.2	1.4	1.7	3.6
Self-Employed	100.0	5.2	58.5	33.1	16.4	1.0	3.0	12.7	3.3
Age of household head									
24 or less	100.0	53.6	4.1	36.7	14.0	2.0	2.8	17.8	5.6
25-29	100.0	62.1	13.3	20.1	12.8	.6	.5	6.1	4.5
30-34	100.0	54.7	19.9	22.0	14.4	.9	1.0	5.7	3.5
35-39	100.0	48.9	27.4	21.0	14.0	1.0	1.1	4.8	2.7
40-44	100.0	46.9	27.8	23.3	15.2	.9	1.9	5.3	2.1
45-49	100.0	49.6	26.9	20.9	14.5	.7	2.6	3.0	2.6
50-54	100.0	45.6	28.9	20.6	14.3	1.4	2.6	2.4	4.9
55 or more	100.0	28.4	28.8	38.1	17.6	1.5	6.6	12.3	4.7

Source: Yoo, 1988.

The difference of the shares of property income between the wage earning household group and the salary earning household group is relatively insignificant compared with the difference of the shares of property income between the self-employed household group and the other two groups. This means that the difference of the inequalities between two groups, the wage earning household group and the salary earning household group, largely comes from the distribution of labor income. In Korea, the wage difference by schooling and by occupations in the wage earning household group is relatively small compared with the salary difference by schooling and by occupations in the salary earning household group. This means that, as argued by Choo and Yoon (1984), the inequality in the distribution of labor incomes is largely affected by the salary difference by schooling and by occupations in Korea.

The incomes from "subsidiary jobs" might be either labor income or property income or both. But, in the CHIES, the incomes from subsidiary jobs are not clearly divided into labor income and property income. If we assume, albeit highly speculatively, the incomes from subsidiary jobs as labor income, then, from the comparison of the within-group inequality indices (Table 21.4) and the shares of labor income and property income (Table 21.5), we can easily find a positive relationship between the degree of inequality and the share of property income, and a negative relationship between the degree of inequality and the share of labor income.[11] From these we can conclude that an economic policy that affects the property incomes has a significant influence upon the income and welfare distributions of urban households and hence, the overall inequality in Korea.[12]

Korea's industrialization, especially in the heavy and chemical sectors during the mid 1970s, brought a high inflation (that is, the consumer price index for all cities increased 24.3% in 1974, 15.3% in 1976, and 18.3% in 1979), which, in turn, brought a great capital gain to the rich, thereby further deteriorating income equality in Korea. And the heavy and chemical industrialization policy, along with export-oriented policy, has also brought business concentration, which may very well have contributed to the growing income and welfare inequality in Korea. As shown in Table 21.6, the share of total value-added by the ten largest business conglomerates increased from 13.9 percent in 1973 to 23.4 percent in 1978 and to 28.9 percent in 1985.

The existence of a large underground economy in Korea has also distorted the actual degrees of income and welfare inequalities in Korea. The size of the Korean underground economy was more than half of its GNP during the recent 1978–85 period.[13] The incomes generated from this underground economy are usually not reported and not taxed by the government and not included in household income; therefore, the existence of the large underground economy in Korea is one of the factors that not only distorted the actual indices of income inequality, but also diminished the credibility of the indices of income inequality published by either the Korean government or the international organizations.

Table 21.6
***Jaebul* Groups' Contribution to Total Shipment in the Manufacturing Sector (in percent)**

	1977	1981	1985
10 Largest	21.2	28.4	30.2
20 Largest	29.3	35.3	36.4
30 Largest	34.1	39.7	40.2

Source: Economic Planning Board (EPB), Seoul, Korea

Rapid changes in family size during the last high-growth period of 1965–85 has also, by and large, affected the distribution of household incomes in Korea. The proportion of small and nuclear families for all areas in Korea has rapidly increased from 76.8 percent in 1970 to 83.4 percent in 1985 (see Table 21.7), thereby causing a decrease in the average number of persons per family from 5.2 in 1970 to 4.1 in 1985. This rapid change in family composition would also be, as suggested by Kuznets (1976), one of the factors affecting the distribution of household incomes in Korea. The decrease in family size means an increase in the number of households, which might induce the increasing demand for housing, and it, in turn, might have affected the distribution of household property incomes.

In the classification of family head by age in Table 21.4, the degree of within-group inequality of the last group (age of family head more than 55 years) is the highest, and the degree of within-group inequality of the first group (age of family head less than 24 years) is much greater than that of the second group. The first group households are, in general, newly married couple households, whereas the last group households are, in general, old aged couple households. The incomes of the two groups, the first and the last, very much depends on the "gifts and assistance" (see Table 21.5) from parents and from children. This means that, since social security programs are not yet popular in Korea, the distribution of inheritances is also one of the factors affecting the income and welfare inequalities of Korea.

Other factors such as "off-farm income" and wage and salary differences by schooling and by occupations seem also to affect the household income distribution in Korea. The increase of the proportion of "off-farm income" in the farm households (see Table 21.8) seems to improve the income equality of the farm household group in Korea. The reduction of wage and salary differences by schooling and by occupations in recent years (see also Table 21.8) seems to improve the distribution of labor incomes of the nonfarm household group in Korea.

Table 21.7
Household Composition by Size of Family (in percent)

	Year	Small and Atomic Family[a]	Large Family[b]	Others[c]	Average Person in a Family
All Areas	1970	76.8	23.2	--	5.2
	1975	79.8	20.1	--	5.1
	1980	81.6	17.0	1.5	4.5
	1985	83.4	14.9	1.7	4.1
Urban Areas	1970	84.6	15.4	--	4.9
	1975	85.6	14.4	--	4.9
	1980	85.1	13.0	1.9	4.4
	1985	86.0	12.0	2.0	4.0
Rural Areas	1970	71.0	29.0	--	5.5
	1975	74.0	26.0	--	5.4
	1980	76.4	22.7	.9	4.7
	1985	78.5	20.4	1.1	4.2

Source: EPB, *Housing and Population Census*, various issues.

[a]The small and atomic families means the family with one person, one generation, or two generations.
[b]The large family means the families with three or more generations.
[c]Others means the families composed of various family lines.

Table 21.8
Wage and Salary Differences and Off-Farm Income (in percent)

	1970	1976	1980	1985
Wage and salary difference by schooling (College graduates/ middle-school graduates)	302.1	388.6	332.2	303.4
Wage and salary difference by occupations (Administrative and managerial workers/average)	270.9	343.6	298.3	256.0
The ratio of off-farm income of a small farm household cultivating less than 1.5 hectare	49.2	43.5	65.7	67.6

Sources: Choo and Yoon 1984; EPB, *Major Statistics of Korean Economy*, various issues.

CONCLUSION

In this study we first examine the time trend of income and welfare inequalities in Korea based on the empirical results reported by Choo and Yoon (1984), Kim and Ahn (1987), Yoo and Kwon (1987), and Yoo (1988). The findings show that although the income and welfare inequality of Korea declined temporarily during the 1969–71 (or –74) period, on the whole, it deteriorated. This leads to the conclusion that, in general, Korea has not harmonized equity with growth; on the contrary, equity has deteriorated with growth. Even with the Gini indices, it is not possible to conclude that Korea has avoided the typical decline in equality in household income distribution implied by Kuznets' U-curve, during its high growth period. The findings also suggest that the inequality among urban households predominantly contributes to the inequality of Korea, whereas the income distribution of the farm household group exerts a positive effect.

A casual observation by Yoo and Kwon (1987) points to three major factors that may have been responsible for the pattern of income and welfare inequalities in Korea: namely, the government interest rate policy (or inflation rate) and the trend of urbanization as well as business concentration. The real interest rate (or inflation rate) seems to explain, at least in part, the cyclical fluctuations in income and welfare inequalities, whereas urbanization and business concentration explain the time trends of income and welfare inequalities.

In Korea, where the real estate market serves as the only popular outlet for household savings and investment, the interest rate policy can exert a direct impact on the values and returns on the properties, thus benefiting the rich more than it does the poor. The official nominal interest rate in Korea is annually set by government. Therefore, the real interest rate in Korea crucially depends on the inflation rate. That is, a high inflation rate had brought a great capital gain to the haves, thereby widening the income gap between the haves and have-nots. Urbanization can also affect the income and welfare inequalities in Korea because it entails a shift in economic activity from the rural sector, where incomes are relatively evenly distributed, to the urban sector, where income inequalities are much more pronounced. Business concentration and the concentration of wealth (and income) also seem to go hand in hand.

The salary differences by schooling and by occupation, by and large, seem to affect the distribution of labor incomes in the nonfarm household group. The distribution of inheritances from parents also seems to be one of the factors affecting the income and welfare inequalities. Furthermore, the existence of a large underground economy in Korea has not only distorted the income and welfare inequalities toward equality, but also has made the people distrust the indices of income inequality published either by the Korean government or by international organizations.

It is also likely that the actual degree of welfare inequality of urban households in Korea would be much greater than the results reported by Yoo and Kwon (1987): the exclusion of the sensitive groups of population, the very rich and the very poor, from the CHIES is likely to have biased the results toward equality.

NOTES

1. For further discussion of Korean data problems, see Choo (1979), pp. 83–92, and Choo (1982), pp. 401–18.

2. Bhalla (1979) also arrived at the same conclusions.

3. See Bentzel (1970), and Jorgenson and Slesnick (1984).

4. For further discussion of the indices and model, see Jorgenson and Slesnick (1984) and Yoo and Kwon (1987).

5. The value of ρ ranges from $\rho = -1$ to $\rho = -\infty$. The latter means that society has infinite aversion to inequality of welfare. Where the ρ lies between these extremes depends on the importance attached to the redistribution of welfare toward the bottom groups. See also Atkinson (1970) for the effects of the different values of the degree of aversion to inequality.

6. Kim and Ahn (1987) also arrived at the same conclusion. See Kim and Ahn (1987) for further discussion of the data sampling problems.

7. See Kravis (1960, 1973).

8. For the empirical estimation of household equivalence scales of urban households in Korea, see Yoo and Choo (1987).

9. From the simulation of growth with equity using a macroeconomic model of Korea, Hasan and Rao (1979, pp. 85–94) found an upward trend in the Gini coefficient during the 1976–90 period (from 0.383 in 1976 to 0.456 in 1990, assuming 7.9 percent growth path of GNP). Also, they cite urbanization as a possible cause for the upward trend in the Gini coefficient.

10. There are many controversies as to whether the "gifts and assistance" are property incomes or not. In Korea where social security programs are not yet popular, the gifts and assistance are largely given by parents' income, which might be generated from the wealth of parents. The wealth of parents in Korea is generally inherited by their children. Therefore, we assume, for the convenience of analysis, the "gifts and assistance" as property income.

11. See also the simple regression of Yoo (1988) for these relationships.

12. Kim and Ahn (1987) also suggest macroeconomic factors that affect the distribution of household incomes in Korea that are, by and large, the same as the factors suggested by Choo and Yoon (1984).

13. For further discussion and estimation of Korea's underground economy, see Choi (1987). According to Choi, based on Tanzi's method, the sizes of the

underground economy in the United States and Japan relative to GNP are about 8 percent and 4–5 percent, respectively.

REFERENCES

Adelman, I. and Robinson, S., *Income Distribution Policy in Developing Countries: A Case Study of Korea*, Stanford: Stanford University Press, 1978.

Atkinson, A. B., "On the Measurement of Inequality," *Journal of Economic Theory*, 2, September 1970, 244–63.

Bentzel, R., "The Social Significance of Income Distribution Statistics," *Review of Income and Wealth, 16*, September 1970, 253–64.

Bhalla, S. S., *The Distribution of Income in Korea: A Critique and a Reassessment*, Unpublished manuscript, The World Bank, 1979.

Choi, Kwang, *A Study of the Underground Economy in Korea* (in Korean), Seoul: Korea Economic Research Institute, April 1987.

Choo, H., *Income Distribution and Its Determinants in Korea*, vol. I (in Korean), Seoul: Korea Development Institute, 1979.

———, *Income Distribution and Its Determinants in Korea*, vol. II (in Korean), Seoul: Korea Development Institute, 1982.

———, and Kim, D., *Probable Size Distribution of Income in Korea: Over Time and by Sector* (in Korean), Seoul: Korea Development Institute, 1978.

———, and Yoon, J., "Size Distribution of Income in Korea, 1982: Its Estimation and Sources of Change" (in Korean), *Korea Development Review, 6*, Seoul: KDI, March 1984, 2–18.

Economic Planning Board, *City Household Income and Expenditure Survey*, Bureau of Statistics, Seoul, 1965–85.

Hasan, P., and Rao, D. C., *Development Issues in the 1980s, Korea: Policy Issues for Long-Term Development*, Baltimore: Johns Hopkins University Press, 1979.

Jorgenson, D. W., and Slesnick, D. T., "Aggregate Consumer Behavior and the Measurement of Inequality," *Review of Economic Studies, 51*, July 1984, 369–92.

Kim, D., and Ahn, K. S., *Korea's Income Distribution, Its Determinants, and People's Consciousness about Distribution Problem* (in Korean), Seoul: Jung Ang University Press, 1987.

Kravis, I. B., "International Difference in the Distribution of Income," *Review of Economics and Statistics, 42*, September 1960, 408–16.

———, "A World of Unequal Incomes," in Income Inequality, *The Annals of American Academy of Political and Social Science, 409*, September 1973, 61–80.

Kuznets, Simon, "Demographic Aspects of the Size Distribution of Income: An

Exploratory Essay," *Economic Development and Cultural Change*, *25*, October 1976, 1–94.

Ministry of Agriculture and Fisheries, *Farm Household Economic Survey*, Agriculture and Fisheries Statistics Bureau, Seoul, 1965–85.

Mizoguchi, R., Kim, D. H., and Chung, Y. I., "Overtime Changes of the Size Distribution of Household Income in Korea, 1963–71," *The Developing Economies*, *14*, 1976, 261–79.

Oshima, H.T., "Income Inequality and Economic Growth: The Post-War Experience of Asian Countries," *Malaysian Economic Review*, *15*, 1970, 373–91.

Rao, D. C., "Economic Growth and Equity in the Republic of Korea," *World Development*, *6*, March 1978, 383–96.

Yoo, J. G., "An Analysis of the Degree of Income and Welfare Inequality among Urban Households in Korea in 1984" (in Korean), *Korea Development Review*, Seoul: KDI, Summer 1988, 117–40.

————, and Choo, H., "A Cross-Sectional Analysis of the Household Equivalence Scale in Korea" (in Korean), *Korea Development Review*, Seoul: KDI, Summer 1987, 71–85.

————, and Kwon, J. K., "Welfare Inequality Among Urban Households in South Korea: 1965–1983," *Applied Economics*, *4*, April 1987, 497–510.

22

Industrial Relations Policy in Korea: Its Features and Problems

Se-Il Park

INTRODUCTION

In theory, there are three agents in shaping the industrial relations system in a country: labor unions, industrialists, and the government. During the early stages of industrialization, however, labor unions tend to play only a passive and less significant role in formulating industrial relations, mainly because the abundant supply of labor greatly reduces the unions' strength. Managers are also lacking in modern labor management skills and in fact do not feel any necessity to gain them; their businesses can prosper through quantitative expansion of exploiting yet-un-explored resources (mainly unskilled labor) rather than through qualitative improvement in utilizing already-employed resources.

Therefore, the most active as well as responsible agent in shaping an industrial relations system in a developing country is inevitably the government—that is, the development planners. The development strategy, the philosophy and character of the industrializing elites, and the ruling planner—the top bureaucrats of the government—in fact determine the major features of the industrial relations system as well as the paths for its further development. This is especially true in a country such as Korea, where industrialization and economic development plans have been initiated, implemented, and tightly monitored by government bureaucrats.

A brief historical sketch of the Korean labor movement and of the development of the industrial relations system will help in understanding the dominant role of the government in the Korean context.

In Korea, trade unionism did not appear on the scene as a movement in its own right until 1945.[1] After World War II, in November 1945, the General Council of the Korean Trade Unions (Chun Pyong), the first national trade union organization, was formed mainly by communists and left-wing elements. It soon became apparent that Chun Pyong was more inclined to political activities and imbued with political ideals than it was interested in the betterment of the workers' economic position. To restore discipline and order at workplaces, the right-wing politicians, supported by employers, encouraged the workers to set up anticommunist workers' organizations at individual firms. Thus, in March 1946, the Federation of Korean Trade Unions (Daehan Nochong) was established to support the conservative policies of the government and to eliminate communist elements from industrial society.

A fierce competition between the two national trade union centers continued until the end of the Korean War, and it was only after 1953 that the Daehan Nochong committed itself to institutionalize genuine collective bargaining. In spite of legal prohibitions, however, the leadership of the Daehan Nochong continued its close connection with business interests. In 1955, at the request of the president of the Republic, Dr. Rhee, the Daehan Nochong became formally affiliated with the ruling party chaired by Dr. Rhee, even without the consent of the Daehan Nochong's executive members. Efforts were nevertheless continued to create union autonomy both within and outside of the Daehan Nochong.

Following the coup in May 1961, General Park placed a ban on trade unions. The ban was lifted shortly thereafter under close government supervision, and a new Federation of Korean Trade Unions, the Hankook Nochong, was established. Korea's unions were restructured into 16 industrywide, national union organizations, each affiliated with the new FKTU, patterned after the German Trade Union Center (DGB).

During the 1960s, Korean trade unions were relatively free to function as genuine collective bargaining agents, although some raised questions about the degree of real union autonomy during that period. Nevertheless, in comparison with other periods, the constitutional and statutory rights of workers to organize, bargain, and strike were relatively respected during the 1960s.

In December 1971, all of this suddenly changed with the enactment of the Special Law on National Security (Yushin regime). The requirements of this law and the associated regulations were as follows: (1) Unions were required to secure government approval prior to engaging in collective negotiation. (2) When disputes arose, government intervention would be automatic and its subsequent decision would be both final and binding. (3) All strikes or lockouts were prohibited.

This special law lasted for a decade before ultimately being lifted in December 1981. Meanwhile, however, existing labor legislation (Labor Union Law, Labor Disputes Adjustment Law, and so on) was substantially amended in December 1980. Under new laws, collective-bargaining units were decentralized from the industrial level to the individual enterprise level, following the pattern of the U.S. or Japanese industrial relations system, union shop clauses became illegal, and the minimum number of workers necessary for the establishment of a legal trade union was raised. The laws also required that labor management councils, which deal only with mutually beneficial issues such as productivity and industrial safety, be set up in each establishment.

The labor relations policy of the 1970s made collective negotiations difficult and completely banned workers' collective action. Nevertheless, the government did not restrict organizing unions in any general sense. In addition, until union shop clauses became illegal in 1981, Korean unions had been successful in negotiating "union shop" clauses that required employees to join the union as a condition of employment. This success and the government's benign neglect of union organizing activities no doubt contributed greatly to the relatively high growth rate of union membership during the 1960s and 1970s, which is shown in Table 22.1. Amendments to the labor union laws in 1981, however, not only prohibited union shop clauses but also made organizing activities somewhat difficult; probably as a result, union membership in fact dropped between 1983 and 1985. Union penetration dropped from 24.7 percent of workers in 1980 to 20.7 percent in 1985.

In sum, collective bargaining has not been permitted to mature during the past 25 years in Korea, but unions have been allowed to grow, which has produced a unique feature of the Korean industrial relations system—"Unionism without Collective Bargaining." Since workers will not cling forever to ineffective unions in representing their interests, Korean unionism will be under increasing pressure to normalize its function of effective collective bargaining in the coming years.

Table 22.1
Union Membership Growth in Korea, 1963–85

Year	Industrial Union	Branch Union	Chapter Union	Union Members	Regular Employees (thousand)	Penetration Rate (%)
1963	16	313	1820	224,420	779	28.9
1965	16	362	2255	301,523	891	33.8
1970	17	419	3063	473,259	1959	24.2
1975	17	488	3585	750,235	2340	32.1
1980	16	2618		948,134	3833	24.7
1983	16	2238		1,009,881	4545	22.2
1985	16	2534		1,004,398	4860	20.7

Source: Ministry of Labor, *An Abstract of Labor Statistics*, 1986.

Note: Regular Employees = Total employment − (self-employed + family workers + temporary employees + day employees).

A MAJOR FEATURE: THE GOVERNMENT'S AUTHORITARIAN PATERNALISM

From the above brief overview of past experience, the single most important feature of Korea's industrial relations policy has been the government's authoritarian paternalism. Industrial relations policy has been *authoritarian* in the sense that the powers of rule making and final decision making in the management of industrial disputes and grievances have been vested in the hands of the highest government authority. This means that the rules and regulations concerning industrial relations and labor disputes are drafted, implemented, and, if necessary, changed by the top government officials, with little consensus building among those concerned, that is, employers and employees. And it also means that labor disputes are frequently subject to the government's compulsory arbitration if the government deems the disputes to be against public interest.[2]

The industrial relations policy also has been *paternalistic* in the sense that the government has tried to supervise working conditions directly with little or no help from the unions and has frequently issued administrative orders, when necessary, to employers in order to improve the working conditions of employees.

Since the bargaining power of unions tends to be relatively weak in the early stage of industrialization, one way to improve working conditions and to guarantee a civilized work environment is for the government to help union strength to grow through protective labor legislation and to use the union's countervailing power to check and balance employers' strength and arbitrariness. In this respect, however, little government effort has been exercised in Korea; direct government intervention and supervision have been more common, bypassing unions' self-help efforts, in determining working conditions and in handling various labor disputes.

In summation, the government's industrial relations policy in Korea has been characterized by benign neglect of the unions' bargaining function, if not active discrimination against union activities, and by the government's direct authoritarian and paternalistic approach toward labor and labor relations issues.[3] One observer correctly described the recent situation in Korean industrial relations as follows:

> Whenever today's negotiators are unable to resolve their differences either over future terms or grievances they immediately seek a government imposed "quick fix" solution because of their decade old addiction to such a remedy. This practice consequently and unnecessarily has the effect of elevating every labor dispute to a "crisis" status and it gives each issue the appearance of being a matter of "national significance" which demands governmental intervention.[4]

Therefore, in Korea the behavior of the government agency responsible for industrial relations policy is frequently described as "firefighting." The decade-old practice of government authoritarian paternalism has inevitably discouraged the employers' and employees' initiative in negotiation and hence brought about "unionism without effective collective bargaining" in Korea. At the same time, however, the resultant malfunctioning of collective bargaining, in turn, has invited continued government intervention, thereby enforcing authoritarian paternalism in Korean industrial relations.

Why, then, has authoritarian paternalism become the dominant feature of Korean industrial relations? There have been three sets of factors—political, economic, and cultural—contributing to the emergence and development of an authoritarian paternalistic approach in Korean industrial relations.

First, as already shown, in its early years the Korean labor movement, at least up to the early 1960s, was dominated by political and ideological elements, with little or no emphasis on its economic function. Chun Pyong was influenced heavily by left-wing ideology, and Daehan Nochong was established and supported by conservative businessmen and government officials purely as a political weapon to use against Chun Pyong. None of them tried seriously to achieve the institutionalization of genuine collective bargaining.

This unfortunate historical experience has planted a deep-rooted tendency among the power elites (government and business groups) to consider every industrial dispute and workplace grievance as a political challenge, rather than as a demand for economic interests. Labor disputes have been frequently viewed as something undesirable and even a threat to the status quo, and thus as something to be suppressed as quickly as possible. There has been no room in Korean political culture to view labor disputes as a "functional" part of industrial society that is necessary for balancing and maintaining the status quo. Therefore, few efforts have been exerted to institutionalize conflicts and channel them toward self-regulation.

In addition, the division of South and North Korea since 1945 and the continuing confrontation on the peninsula has strengthened the political bias against industrial conflicts in particular and the labor union movement in general. It has been frequently argued that because of the military tension from across the 38th parallel, industrial conflicts are "luxury goods" in Korea. Especially when the tensions have been reported by the government to be mounting, this argument seems to have been accepted rather widely and easily by the majority of the Korean people. Whether the reported tension was real or imaginary had no bearing on the efficacy of the argument. Therefore, genuine efforts for institutionalizing industrial conflicts and an unbiased view of trade unionism as an essential mechanism for social progress and social stability have been extremely difficult to establish in the Korean context.

Second, it should be pointed out that the government's decade-old authoritarian paternalism has been closely related to the overall economic development strategy of Korea. As is well known, Korea has adhered to an export-led, outward-looking development strategy over the past 25 years. The development efforts have been geared toward taking advantage of the abundant supply of labor by specializing in labor-intensive manufacturing export industries, thereby generating employment opportunities rather rapidly, well beyond the constraints of the domestic market. Particularly when a country adopts an export-oriented developmental policy, rather than an import substitution-dominant one, the primary policy issue is how to make the economy and its products competitive in the world market; each country's response to this issue is often called its "competition strategy."

Strategies of competition can be broadly classified into two types: "cost-reduction strategies" and "productivity and flexibility improvement strategies." "Cost-reduction strategies" are characterized by various attempts to lower production costs and prices. One prominent way is to reduce the cost of factor inputs, like capital and labor. Policies promoting low wages, low interest rates, low grain prices, subsidization of exports and repressive industrial relations are typical examples.

"Productivity and flexibility improvement strategies," on the other hand, are geared more toward improved utilization of already-employed capital and labor. Competition through productivity and flexibility usually involves superior workmanship, better work organization, full utilization of capital, manufacturing of unique products, on-time delivery, and most importantly, good industrial and labor relations. Especially when foreign demand fluctuates and changes rather rapidly and unexpectedly, it becomes important to improve the flexibility or versatility of an economy. To respond effectively to these changes in competitive environments, the economy should improve its ability to adjust quickly to new demand situations and, when necessary, to switch quickly to new kinds of products or services. In this process, a well-functioning industrial relations system and the active and cooperative participation of workers in the adjustment process play a role of vital importance.

As a competition strategy, the Korean government has adhered to the "cost-reduction strategy" for the past quarter of a century. The productivity and flexibility improvement strategy has been adopted at times, but as an exception rather than the rule. When the economy faces an unlimited supply of labor in the early stage of industrialization, it is a rather natural and correct policy choice to adopt a cost-reduction strategy not only to improve the international competitiveness of the economy, but also to maximize the creation of employment opportunities. But once the economy has passed the so-called Lewis-type of "turning point"[5] and confronts a limited or semi-limited supply of labor, its competitive advantage should be explored in other areas, such as better utilization of inputs, human capital investment, R&D, and superior industrial relations—that is, exploiting the strategy of productivity and flexibility improvement.

Korea correctly adopted the former strategy in the 1960s, but did not shift to the latter strategy, even after the Korean economy passed the "turning point" some time in the early or mid-1970s. Adhering to a cost-reduction strategy, even when socioeconomic conditions have changed, inevitably brought about the government's authoritarian control over union activities in Korea. This control was most vividly illustrated in the 1971 enactment of the Special Law on National Security, which banned unions' collective activities. As already mentioned, the Special Law remained in force for ten years, up to 1981.

One additional point that deserves attention is that, in general, the cost-reduction strategy frequently favors large-scale operations, but the productivity and flexibility improvement strategy encourages small-scale operations with high skill intensity and high technology, in such fields as specialized machine tools, sophisticated electrical and electronic products, and high-fashion consumer goods.

Therefore, as the economy moves from the low-wage, low-productivity, low-price (standardized consumer goods) stage toward the high-wage, high-productivity, high-quality (differentiated goods) stage, small and medium industry, under the productivity and flexibility improvement strategy, play an increasingly important role in economic development. The heavy subsidies for large-scale corporations (for example, favorable credit terms) and continuing adherence to the cost-reduction strategy (for example, authoritarian industrial relations policy) in Korea retard the smooth transition of the economy to a more advanced stage. In addition, these practices reduce the employment generation capacity of the economy.

Third, the last factor contributing to the emergence of authoritarian paternalism is the influence of traditional Confucian culture on Korea society.[6] Confucianism, as is widely known, idealizes a hierarchically ordered, harmonious, patriarchal society. It features great respect for the educated, encourages collectivism, and discourages individualism. Confucianism also encourages vertical, segmental loyalties and discourages horizontal associations coinciding with the individual's functional interest. Moreover, it praises bureaucratic values; bureaucrats, as guarantors of public interest, supposedly play the most important role in the society. These elements of the Confucian culture can be summarized as: "to learn to be a son through filial piety to his father, to learn to be a subject through loyalty to the king, and to learn to be a friend through trust in friends." Under this Confucian culture, authoritarianism at the levels of both labor-management relations and labor-state relations easily finds its way into organizational and relational settings.

In addition, Confucianism is a philosophy of peace, encouraging harmony and nonviolent, informal resolution of disputes through understanding, sympathy, and empathy. Harmony is considered as a basic social virtue or norm, and conflict and personal confrontation are seen as social evils. Even when conflicts do happen, the parties involved do not rely on logic or on objective arguments, but instead appeal to the emotions and sentiments. Thus the paternalistic approach is easily combined with the authoritarian element in Confucian culture. The high respect for hierarchical and bureaucratic order and high value for peace and harmony found in Confucian tradition clearly help to explain the relative ease with which the Korean government instituted authoritarian paternalism in the Korean industrial relations system.

LABOR'S REACTION TO GOVERNMENT POLICY

The next issue to be discussed is the reaction of labor and the unions toward authoritarian paternalism. The government's authoritarian paternalism has brought about at least three major consequences. The first is the persisting high labor turnover rate in the Korean labor market. When organized reaction to the constraining industrial relations system becomes impossible due to tight control by the government, small-group or individual responses tend to take place; the prominent forms of protest or reaction to the status quo are absenteeism, high turnover rate, withdrawal of work effort on the job, and a lack of attention, cooperation, and work morale. It sometimes takes more violent expressions in fighting, spontaneous flareups, and work stoppages by small groups. Excessive alcoholism, poor discipline, shoddy workmanship, and theft are also common results of the workers' frustration and dissatisfaction.

The general conclusion from the history of the Western industrialized countries is that worker protest in the course of industrialization tends to peak relatively early and to decline in intensity thereafter. As time passes, formal organizations of workers emerge and the forms of overt protest become more disciplined and less spontaneous. Sporadic riots, violence, and explosive outbursts are replaced by an industrial relations system for establishing and administering the rules of the workplace.[7]

This general rule cannot be applied in Korea, however, because industrialization has not been accompanied by simultaneous development of collective bargaining, grievance procedures, labor courts, and other dispute-settlement machinery. Under the condition of "unionism without collective bargaining" combined with the government's "authoritarian paternalism," the dissatisfied workers can only resort to individual reactions. The only alternative left to workers who want an improvement in working conditions is to quit their current job and move to another, since the effective collective negotiations and organized action through which they could expect an improvement of working conditions are not available.

Therefore, the persisting high labor turnover rate in Korea, shown in Table 22.2, can be said to be a consequence of the government's decade-old authoritarian approach to labor relations.[8] Table 22.2 reveals that the average monthly separation rate of manufacturing workers has, since 1971, been highest in Korea. The rate has averaged about 5.15 percent in Korea during the 1980s, while the corresponding figures have been 1.35 percent in Japan and 3.65 percent in Taiwan. Interestingly enough, separation rates in Korea not only show remarkable stability over the years, regardless of the ups and downs of economic activities captured by fluctuations in GNP growth rates, but also show a slight upward trend, comparing the average figures of the 1970s and 1980s. On the other hand, turnover rates show a continuing decline in Japan. Ignoring those job movers who hop around to new jobs more than once a year, the average monthly separation rate of 5.15 percent in Korea implies

Table 22.2

Monthly Average Separation Rates in the Manufacturing Sector in Selected Countries, 1971–85 (in percent)

Year	Korea	Japan	Taiwan	GNP Growth Rate (Korea)
1971	5.4	2.2	---	9.1
1972	4.5	1.9	---	5.3
1973	4.5	2.0	3.7	14.0
1974	5.1	1.9	3.9	8.5
1975	4.4	1.7	3.3	6.8
1976	4.4	1.5	3.6	13.4
1977	5.1	1.5	3.2	10.7
1978	5.9	1.4	3.5	11.0
1979	6.3	1.4	3.9	7.0
1980	5.6	1.4	3.4	-4.8
1981	5.4	1.4	3.9	6.6
1982	5.0	1.3	3.7	5.4
1983	5.0	1.3	---	11.9
1984	5.4	---	---	8.4
1985	4.5	---	---	5.4

Sources: Ministry of Labor (Korea), *Report on Monthly Labor Survey*, November 1986; Japan Institute of Labor (Japan), *Labor White Paper*, 1984; Council for Economic Planning and Development (Taiwan), *Manpower Indicator*, 1983.

that more than 60 percent total employment in the manufacturing sector is replaced once a year.

The second consequence of authoritarian paternalism is the increase in illegal activities and the growth of the nonunion labor organization movement. Among various nonunion labor organization movements, church-sponsored groups have been the most important in Korea, especially during the 1970s. Originally, UIM (Urban Industrial Mission: Protestant) and JOC (Catholic) activities were not antagonistic toward official labor unions until the Special Law on National Security was enacted by the Yushin regime in 1971. Until 1971, the national union leaders and UIM and JOC activists were seated side by side at the education programs offered by the Federation of Korean Trade Unions (FKTU) and others.

After the Special Law, however, the church-sponsored groups began to criticize the official unions as well as the emergency regime. Of course, the authorities organized various anti-church-group campaigns to expel them from the labor scene. In fact, the prohibition of third-party intervention in labor union activities, which was introduced for the first time in labor laws in 1980, was originally designed as a countereffort by the authorities against the church-sponsored labor movement. The authorities' effort has not been very successful, however, because workers frustrated by the formal labor union activities have turned to UIM and JOC.

A new trend has been added since 1980 after the Chun regime took power: a steady increase in nonunion organization activities, not directly sponsored by church groups, but initiated by secular elements, of which the majority are students expelled from the university for antigovernment activities. Currently, there are about six secular groups actively involved in various labor activities. Though their membership is not large, it is increasingly militant and radical both in its slogans and its actions. Not only students, but also workers who have been fired from their companies for active involvement in the union movement, tend to join these nonunion organizational activities. It is said that out of 265 illegal collective work actions that took place in 1985, about 60 (22.6 percent) were initiated by these nonunion groups, either Christian or secular, in the form of demonstrations, hunger strikes, and sit-ins at public office buildings.[9]

The last but the most important consequence of authoritarian paternalism has been the continuing decline in the autonomous and independent conflict-solving capacities of both parties, employers and employees. Accustomed to the quick-fix solutions frequently imposed by the government, neither party makes sincere efforts to reach independent bilateral solutions. It has become the exception rather than the rule to observe labor and management sitting down to exchange views and information sincerely and making concessions in order to reach a mutually satisfactory joint agreement. Instead both parties tend to adopt "take it or leave it" positions, striving primarily for favorable leverage in the political bargaining with the government, neglecting good faith efforts with their real bargaining counterparts. These practices, therefore, have enormously increased the government's job as a compulsory arbitrator in all industrial disputes, a task that is frequently well beyond the government's manpower capacity.

The overburdening or overcommitment of the government inevitably results in inadequate or badly prepared intervention—that is, a decline in quality of intervention, which, in turn, tends to destabilize current industrial relations. The government labor agencies frequently enforce labor laws in an uneven and inconsistent manner, which tends to demean the integrity of the laws in the eyes of employers and employees. Thus the parties concerned are less inclined to play according to the legal rules of the game and they tend to try to gain the government's favor through illegal means. Moreover, the authoritarian paternalism (extensive government control over labor disputes and sometimes over internal union affairs) has deprived both parties of the very important opportunities to learn the benefits of free collective bargaining. In the absence of frequent government intervention, both employers and employees would have to learn step by step to appreciate the advantages of dealing and negotiating with each other. Once the practices of free collective bargaining are established and given the chance to develop, this will ultimately lead to more peaceful and orderly conduct of collective negotiations, because both parties, through experience, will learn not only their respective strengths but also their mutual interdependence.

CONCLUSION

Developing a workable and sustainable industrial relations system should be an important area of the government's labor policy in the process of industrialization. Korea's rapid economic development and remarkable success in export expansion have been well documented and well publicized. But the rapid economic growth was achieved to some extent at the expense of other areas of development, such as protection of basic worker rights and involvement of the workers' organization in the decision-making process. The government's decade-old authoritarian paternalism in the field of industrial relations has deprived both parties, employers and employees, of the very important opportunities to learn the benefits of free autonomous collective bargaining. As a result, the independent conflict-solving capacity of both parties has not improved. Korea has not established a modern industrial relations system that can institutionalize and internalize labor disputes and grievances and at the same time generate a fair income distribution acceptable to the majority of people.

There are several reasons to believe that if industrial and labor relations are not modernized, long-term economic development may be retarded in the coming decade. First, the post-Korean War generation will comprise about 75.5 percent of the total labor force within the next ten years, up from about 48.2 percent in 1980. Approximately 20 percent of the labor force will be made up of college graduates by the year 2000, and more than 55 percent of the labor force will be either high school or college graduates.[10] This postwar generation, more highly educated than its predecessors, exposed to Western-style liberalism and individualism, will harbor much higher expectations. Demands for economic equity, political participation, and social welfare will accelerate in the future, severely challenging the current authoritarian system of industrial relations. Second, according to the recent projection, the Korean economy is expected to sustain growth at an average annual rate of about 7 percent until 2000.[11] This means that Korea's per capita GNP will reach US$7,000 in 1984 prices within the next ten years or so. As per capita income rises, traditional values, culture, and human relations will change, and in such a changing environment, one cannot expect labor-management relations to continue to function paternalistically. Third, the ratio of wage and salary earners is projected to increase from about half of the total labor force in the mid-1980s to two-thirds by the year 2000. Since the labor-management issue affects wage and salary earners, their rising proportion of the labor force will inevitably increase the importance of the issue in Korean society.

Moreover, as the Korean economy becomes more advanced, workers' voluntary cooperation will play a more important role in productivity enhancement, and conversely, workers' indifference or uncooperative "go-slow" attitudes could cause serious damage to Korea's international competitiveness. Therefore, the social costs of industrial unrest—and conversely the social benefits of industrial

peace—will rise substantially as the industrial structure becomes more sophisticated and capital intensive in the future.

The discussion above leads to the conclusion that a modernization of industrial
and labor relations should be pursued seriously in Korea in the coming decade. In
this regard, a recognition of the autonomy of unions and a guarantee of free
collective bargaining should be the first steps. The role of the government in this
process should be dual: a willingness to undertake a prompt and strong intervention
in the case of "rights" disputes (for example, concerning unfair labor practices),
but a neutral, non-interventionist position in the case of "interest disputes" (for
example, wage negotiations). When the government reorients its authoritarian and
paternalistic approach toward one of setting rules and strictly monitoring their
observance, employers and employees will gradually learn to appreciate the
advantages of free collective bargaining and the importance of mutual interdependence in industrial society. More importantly, in this process, employers and
employees will develop autonomously their own style of negotiating ("true"
Korean-style industrial relations), which will reflect the cultural characteristics and
traditional values of Korean society. In conclusion, the success of future economic
development and modernization in Korea will to a great extent depend on whether
government and industry will succeed in making the union and workers a reliable
and responsible social partner in the socioeconomic and political development of
Korean society in the future.

FOLLOW-UP POSTSCRIPT

After this chapter was completed, a series of violent labor uprisings swept over
the country during July–October 1987. Until 1986, the average number of labor
strikes in Korea was about 200 a year; however, during just the three months in
question the number shot up to almost 2,800. Furthermore, not only has the
incidence of labor strife increased, but the militancy of the conflicts has increased
as well.

The cause of this surge in unrest was the government's declaration of June 29
calling for democratic reforms and the resultant relative relaxation of its tight,
year-round clampdown on labor union activities. The government's announcement
of its intention to foster democratic reforms, including the adoption of presidential
election by direct popular vote, was itself spurred by a series of antigovernment
street demonstrations initiated by students in May and June of the same year, and
quickly followed and supported by many middle-class urban dwellers.

Three factors seem to characterize the recent labor demonstrations. First, labor's
demands were far ranging, calling not only for wage increases but also for union
autonomy, fair labor practices, reform of current labor laws, and liberalization of
management's authoritarian style. While the demonstrations initially began in large

industries, where workers were relatively better paid, they later spread to smaller companies, implying that the problems were not simply bread-and-butter issues, but went to the heart of the authoritarian paternalism that has characterized Korea's industrial relations over the past decades.

Second, union democracy became an overwhelmingly dominant issue in the recent strikes. In most cases, two unions claimed to represent the employees, with each accusing the other of being controlled by the company. Although this was an internal union problem, the dissension frequently brought about work stoppages. The underlying reason for this confusion is the lack of adequate procedures in current labor laws to decide which union actually represents the workers. The elaborate representative election procedures devised by the National Labor Relations Board for U.S. unions might provide Korea with a valuable model in this regard.

The third common trait of the recent labor disputes was the sequence of illegal strikes followed by effective negotiation and bargaining sessions between labor and management. In most countries, strikes result from a failure to reach agreement through negotiation, but in Korea the process is reversed, so that labor disputes start with illegal strikes and are followed by negotiation and bargaining. This has come about partly because current labor laws make legal strikes almost impossible and partly because free collective bargaining has not been the norm in Korea. During the past two decades, labor disputes have generally been ended by direct government intervention, which has deprived workers and management of experience in carrying out effective negotiations. Both parties have thus become addicted to the government's quick-fix solutions.

The recent unrest also raises new issues for the economy. After the labor turmoil, the government hastened to liberalize the country's labor laws, a move that has incited much debate. While the short-run economic impact of the recent problems has not been serious, the long-run implications may be problematic, since the upward wage pressure is expected to become very real in the next few years. The key issues for the continuation of Korea's economic development will therefore be: First, how to increase productivity and upgrade the existing industrial structure toward a more advanced and sophisticated one. Second, how to develop the medium- and small-scale industries in Korea, and how to improve the rural economy in Korea in order to maximize productive job opportunities both in rural areas and in small production units—namely, how to change the decade-old unbalanced growth strategy toward a more balanced one. Third, how to institutionalize labor-management relations by introducing a legal framework to handle future labor disputes and grievances in an orderly fashion, and, more importantly, how to make both employers and employees learn the advantages of free collective bargaining and the importance of interdependence in industrial society with a minimum of work stoppages during this learning process.

NOTES

1. For a brief survey of the history of the Korean labor movement, see Y. K. Park (1979).

2. See Chapter V and VI of the Korea Labor Dispute Adjustment Law.

3. For an excellent analysis of the Korean industrial relations system, especially its evolution and major features during the 1960s and 1970s, see J. Choi (1983). For a brief overview of recent developments, see S. Kim (1986).

4. See M. F. Bognanno (1980, p. 12).

5. For a detailed analysis of when the Korean economy passed "the turning point," see M. Bai (1982). For the concept of "turning point," see A. Lewis (1954), and J. Fei and G. Ranis (1964).

6. An interesting study on the effects of Korean cultural values on business management in Korea can be found in D. K. Kim (1986). Kim also compares Korean with Japanese cultural values.

7. For details, see J. T. Dunlop (1971) and C. Kerr, J. T. Dunlop, F. Harbison, and C. A. Myers (1960), especially Chapter 8.

8. Besides the malfunctioning of collective bargaining, the low quality of employment service programs is also responsible for the high turnover rate in Korean industry. Most workers find their jobs through personal contacts, such as introductions and recommendations from friends and relatives. Thus people tend to accept whatever jobs are available with little labor market information, and then continue to search for better ones while employed. This high level of so-called on-the-job search activities is, in fact, one of the reasons that the average labor turnover rate is relatively high in Korea. For details and further discussion on other characteristics of the Korean labor market, see S. I. Park (1988).

9. The equivalent figures were 10 out of 88 in 1982, 18 out of 98 in 1983, 58 out of 113 in 1984, and 38 out of 176 in 1986.

10. See Korea Development Institute (1986).

11. See Korea Development Institute (1986).

REFERENCES

Bai, Moo-Ki, "The Turning Point in the Korean Economy," *Developing Economies*, June 1982, 117–40.

Bognanno, Mario, *Collective Bargaining in Korea: Laws, Practices, and Recommendations for Reform.* Consulting Paper Series No. 17, Seoul: Korea Development Institute, October 1980.

Choi, Jang-Jip, *Interest Conflict and Political Control in South Korea.* Unpublished Ph.D. dissertation, University of Chicago, 1983.

Dunlop, John T., *Industrial Relations System*, Carbondale: Southern Illinois University Press, 1971.

Fei, J.C.H., and Ranis, G., *Development of Labor Surplus Economy: Theory and Policy*, Homewood, Ill.: Richard Irwin, 1964.

Kerr, Clerk, Dunlop, J. T., Harbison, F., and Myers, C. A. *Industrialism and Industrial Man: The Problem of Labor and Management in Economic Growth*, Cambridge: Harvard University Press, 1960.

Kim, Dong-Ki, "Cultural Aspects of Higher Productivity," in Dong-Ki Kim, ed., *Towards Higher Productivity: Experiences of the Republic of Korea*, Tokyo: Asian Productivity Organization, 1986.

Kim, Sookon, *Labor Relations in Korea: System, Practice and Issues*. Paper presented to the International Symposium on Labor Relations and International Competitiveness, Sogang University, Seoul, May 22–23, 1986.

Korea Development Institute, *Korea Year 2000: Summary Report*, Seoul: KDI, 1986.

Lewis, Arthur W., "Economic Development with Unlimited Supplies of Labor," *Manchester School of Economics and Social Studies*, 22, May 1954, 139–91.

Park, Se-Il, "Labor Issues in Korea's Future," *World Development*, 16, January 1988, 99–119.

Park, Young-Ki, *Labor and Industrial Relations in Korea: System and Practice*, Seoul: Sogang University Press, 1979.

Part Seven

URBANIZATION
AND REGIONAL DEVELOPMENT

In a small country like Korea that is confronted by the increasing concentration of population and industrial activities in a few large metropolitan areas, implementing spatial policies of decentralizing the population and industries is truly a herculean task. In the first chapter of this section, K. H. Kim and E. Mills discuss the status and problems of urbanization and regional development in Korea. They point out that in Korea urbanization proceeded at a much faster pace than in other countries, which is characterized by the heavy concentration of economic activities around Seoul, the capital city, Busan, the second largest city, and along the Seoul-Busan corridor. Their article points out that the two most important reasons for migration into the metropolitan areas were employment and education opportunities in urban areas. Also, there is a serious urban-rural income disparity in Korea. Although the average farm income has improved significantly, still, in 1985, per capita real income of Korea's farming households was only 70 percent that of the urban households.

Another pressing problem addressed by these authors is the shortage of urban housing in Korea. During the period of rapid growth and urbanization, the number of urban households grew at a much faster rate than the stock of dwelling units, due largely to migration and the reduction of family size. As a result, the severe housing shortage gave rise to the high prices of housing. In fact, during the 1960-85 period housing prices went up at an annual rate of 21.7 percent. The government's favoring of industrial over housing construction, with its controls on urban housing and land markets, did not help the problem.

As a measure of interregional fiscal disparities, Kim and Mills compare the "self-sufficiency" rate—the share of self-raised revenues as a percentage of total revenue—among various local governments, and observe a wide variation of self-sufficiency rates among them. The rates are higher among cities than in the rural regions.

K. S. Lee and S. C. Choe's study summarizes the results of an investigation conducted jointly by the World Bank and Seoul National University to assess government policies intended to influence the location patterns of manufacturing industries in the Seoul metropolitan region. The policies implemented by the government consisted of (a) strict zoning regulations, (b) outright prohibitions of manufacturing activities, and (c) various financial incentives to relocate industries to outlying areas.

From various survey data, they observed that some large firms have moved from the center of the metropolitan area to peripheral areas whereas small firms have moved into the city center, and that even when firms moved out of the metropolitan region, they seldom moved very far away from the center.

Their study concludes that, on the whole, the government policies had only limited impact on the location choice of manufacturing firms in Seoul. For almost three quarters of the firms that have moved out of the Seoul metropolitan center, the decision was based on their internal reasons rather than the incentives given by the government. It also concludes that strict zoning regulations in a metropolitan area such as Seoul may hinder economic development and that spatial policies can result in net welfare losses for a country through reduced efficiency in resource use. The authors also note that the provision of infrastructure is a necessary but not a sufficient condition for the relocation of industries.

Both studies—that by Kim and Mills and by Lee and Choe—seem to agree on the ineffectiveness of the government policies on the decentralization of population and industrial activities.

23

Urbanization and Regional Development in Korea

Kyung-Hwan Kim and Edwin S. Mills

INTRODUCTION

During the last two and a half decades of economic growth in Korea, the primarily agricultural society was transformed into an industrialized economy. In 1965, 56.6 percent of employment was in agriculture, forestry and fishery, 12.2 percent in mining and manufacturing, and the remaining 31.2 percent in infrastructure and services. By 1987, the shares changed to 21.9 percent, 27.5 percent, and 50.6 percent, respectively.

As in many other countries, economic growth was accompanied by a transfer of human and non-human resources from rural to urban areas, but Korean urbanization proceeded at a pace much faster than almost any other country's. Regional development during the same period was characterized as unbalanced, as seen in the heavy concentration of economic activities around Seoul, the capital city, Busan, the second largest city, and along the corridor connecting the two cities, that is, along the northwest-southeast axis.

Urbanization Trends

During the 1960–87 period, urban population increased at an average annual rate of 5.4 percent and outpaced the growth rate of the nation's total population, 1.94 percent, by a margin of almost 3 to 1. As a result, the number of cities and the share of urban population (that is, the number of people living in cities with a population of 50,000 persons or more as a percentage of the total population) rose from 27 to 62 and 28.0 percent to 69.0 percent, respectively, between 1960 and 1987 (Table 23.1). The pace of urbanization has slowed down since 1970, but about

Table 23.1
Trend of Urbanization

	1960	1970	1975	1980	1986	1987
Total Pop.[a]	24,989	31,466	34,679	37,436	40,448	42,014
Urban Pop.[a,b]	6,997	12,593	16,793	21,434	26,465	29,010
(Seoul)[a]	(2,445)	(5,536)	(6,890)	(8,364)	(9,639)	(9,901)
Rural Pop.[a]	17,992	18,513	17,886	16,002	14,002	13,004
Urban as % of Total	28.0	41.2	48.4	57.3	65.4	69.0
(Seoul as % of Total)	(9.8)	(17.6)	(19.9)	(22.3)	(23.8)	(23.6)
C.V.[c] of % Urban	0.629	0.579	0.550	0.428	0.307	0.260

Source: Economic Planning Board (EPB), *Korea Statistical Yearbook*, various issues.

[a]In thousands
[b]Population in cities with 50,000 people or more
[c]Coefficient of variation

77–80 percent of the Korean population is expected to live in urban areas by the year 2000.

A large part of urban population growth is accounted for by net migration. During the 1960–85 period, the contribution of migration to the growth of urban population ranged from 40 to 77 percent. In the case of the largest city, Seoul, net migration accounted for 42 to 82 percent of population growth between 1960 and 1985. The contribution of migration peaked during the late 1960s and has declined steadily since 1970 (Kwon, 1985, p. 197), resulting in deceleration of urban population growth since then. (See Table 23.2.)

The most important reason for migration was employment opportunities in urban areas, followed by changes in family status due to marriage. Education was also an important factor (Kye S. Lee, 1987). A recent study reports that migration from rural to urban areas since the 1960s can be accounted for by income differential and the differential in the quality of education (Sung, 1988). This finding is

Table 23.2
Contribution of Migration to Urban Population Growth

	1960-66	1966-70	1970-75	1975-80	1980-85
Seoul	65	82	48	42	45
All Cities	41	77	45	40	33

Source: Kye S. Lee, 1987, p. 415; Kwon, 1985, p. 197; EPB, *Korea Statistical Yearbook*, 1982-86.

consistent with the conclusion from a related study of the transfer of employment from agricultural to nonagricultural sectors during the 1965–85 period, the conclusion being that migration took place in response to wage differentials between the two sectors (J. H. Lee, 1987), and with the finding that the number of college freshmen moving into Seoul was as large as 24 percent of that of net in-migrants to the city in 1984 (H. J. Kim, 1986).

Rapid urbanization took place most notably in the largest cities. In 1960, Seoul and Busan accommodated 9.8 percent and 4.7 percent of the nation's total population, respectively. By 1987, their shares increased to 23.6 percent and 8.7 percent, respectively. As for the size distribution of cities, the share of urban population living in cities with a population of one million or more rose from 51.6 percent to 66.3 percent between 1960 and 1980 and fell to 63.4 percent in 1987. On the other hand, the share of relatively small cities with a population of 100,000 or less fell drastically from 18.5 percent to 2.4 percent during the 1960–87 period.

The variation of the urbanization rate across provinces was reduced during the 1960–87 period (Table 23.1). However, fast growing young cities were concentrated in the Capital Region comprising Seoul, Inchon, and Kyong-gi Province (Suwon, Anyang, Bu-cheon, and Seong-nam) and in the southeastern coastal region around Busan (Pohang, Ulsan and Changwon). Every old city in the sluggish southwestern province of Cholla, other than Kwangju, saw its ranking drop from the 1960 standing. In 1960, Jeonju was ranked seventh; Mok-po, ninth; Gunsan, twelfth; and Yeosu, thirteenth. By 1987, their standing fell to eleventh, seventeenth, twenty-second and twenty-fifth, respectively.

Trends of Regional Development

Regional Distribution of Population

During the 1960–85 period, the capital region's share of population went up while those of all provinces other than Che-ju fell. In 1960, Seoul and Kyong-gi housed 20.8 percent of the total population between themselves, but the share rose to 28.6 percent by 1970, and 39.1 percent by 1985. This happened because the population growth rate in the capital region was more than twice as high as that of the total population, mainly due to net in-migration. The population growth of Kyong-gi Province accelerated at the time when the population growth of Seoul slowed down so that the growth rate of the region remained very high relative to those of other regions.

The population growth rates in all other regions fell behind that of the total population. Choong-chung Province and Kang-won Province (eastern mountain areas) registered growth rates of 0.5 percent and 0.1 percent, respectively, between 1960 and 1985. The population of Cholla Province (southwestern agricultural base) stood still during the period and the region steadily lost population since 1970. This was inevitable as the structure of the economy was transformed in favor of the industrial sector, which was heavily concentrated in the capital region and the southeastern coastal region. The Gini coefficient, which measures the degree of concentration of population, was 0.36 in 1966 and rose steadily to 0.44 in 1975 and to 0.54 by 1985, indicating an increasing imbalance in the distribution of population (Kye S. Lee, 1987, p. 419).

Regional Distribution of Employment

Employment was also concentrated heavily in the two fast-growing regions along the Seoul-Busan corridor. This is an outcome of the growth of labor-intensive manufacturing industries in the most populous regions since the 1960s and of the government policy to promote scale-economy-based heavy industries through the creation of large industrial complexes in areas with good harbor facilities. More than half of total establishments and 63 percent of new employment provided in such industrial complexes were located in the capital region and the southeastern coastal region (W. Y. Lee, 1985, p. 357).

Between 1960 and 1985, the share of manufacturing employment in the capital region and the southeastern coastal region combined increased from 57.1 percent to 87.9 percent, widening the regional discrepancy (W. Y. Lee, 1985, p. 341, and EPB, 1988, p. 247). These two regions together also accounted for 84.8 percent of the total value of production in manufacturing industries as of early 1986. As in the distribution of population the share of Seoul and Busan fell since 1970, whereas Kyung-gi Province in the capital region increased its share. This reflects relocation of plants out of Seoul to surrounding areas within the capital region during the 1970s. On the other hand, shares fell in all other regions relative to the two growing regions. For example, the share of Cholla Province (north and south combined) fell from 12.4 percent to 6.0 percent between 1960 and 1980.

A similar pattern emerges from overall employment figures. During the 1970s, the share of employment in all industries of the capital region went up from 40.9 percent to 48.9 percent and that of the Busan region went up from 19.0 percent to 20.5 percent. During the same period, the share of all other regions fell and the drop was most marked in Cholla Province.

Regional Distribution of Income

Urban-rural income differential: The farm household average income has improved significantly relative to the average income level of urban wage and salary-worker households since the late 1960s. In 1968, the average monthly income of farm households was 70.1 percent of that of urban households, but the former caught up with the latter by 1974 when the percentage reached 117.6 percent. Since then rural income stayed above urban income except in 1979 and 1980, but the gap between the two was only 3.9 percent in 1986 (EPB, 1987, p. 78).

Despite this apparently narrow gap in nominal income, real income figures

Table 23.3
Interregional Income Disparity

| Year | High/Low | Coefficient of Variation[a] | | Gini Coefficient |
		Yim (1987)	Kim-Mills[b]	Lee (1988)
1964		0.209		
1965		0.278		
1966		0.326		
1967		0.396		
1968		0.406		
1969		0.343		
1970	2.33[c]	0.314	0.309	0.1701
1971		0.258		
1972		0.260		
1973		0.354		
1974		0.312		
1975	2.43[c]	0.217	0.241	0.1599
1976		0.233		
1977		0.224		
1978		0.186		
1980	1.87[d]		0.205	0.1160
1985	1.53[c]		0.148	0.0880

[a]Direct comparison may not be made due to possible discrepancy in data.
[b]Calculated from data in Kye S. Lee (1988).
[c]High=Seoul, Low=South Cholla Province.
[d]High=Seoul, Low=North Cholla Province.

exhibit a different trend. During the 1965–85 period, per capita real income in rural areas ranged from 61 percent to 96 percent of that in urban areas, the 1985 figure being 70 percent (Chang, 1987, p. 157). In addition, the size of farm household debt has been growing in recent years.

Provincial income differential: There is a controversy over the empirical validity of the thesis that an income gap between regions widens during the early stages of economic growth and structural change and then narrows as development reaches a mature stage (Hansen, 1985, p. 71). The Korean experience seems to fit the thesis. Mera's study of 1963–74 GRP (gross regional product) data suggests that the coefficient of variation (standard deviation divided by the mean) measure of regional income disparity reached a peak in 1967 and declined steadily thereafter. In a more recent study of 1964–78 GRP data, Yim discovered a peak in 1968 and another peak in 1973 before the income differential fell steadily. He also found that Mera's estimates of the coefficient of variation were substantially underestimated mainly due to the underestimation of Seoul's GRP figures (Yim, 1987).

Our estimate of C.V. for four years since 1970 exhibited a decrease. Kye S. Lee's

(1987) estimate of the Gini coefficient fell from 0.17 to 0.09 during the 1970–85 period. The GRP ratio of the highest (Seoul or Inchon) to the lowest (North or South Cholla Province) region was 2.33 in 1970 and 1.54 in 1985 (Table 23.3). These findings suggest that inter-regional income disparity has declined since 1970. However, one should remember that the conclusion made above is contrasted with the trend of increasing disparity in the distribution of population and employment discussed earlier. Also, income figures were not adjusted for regional cost-of-living differences.

Interregional wage differential: The wage level continues to vary among regions. Data for 1986 show that the average wage rate was highest in Seoul, followed by Kang-won and South Cholla Province; Busan and Kyung-gi Province were the lowest wage-rate regions. The coefficient of variation for interregional wage distribution was 0.145 in 1976, 0.116 in 1977, 0.139 in 1980, and 0.119 in 1986, suggesting that the wage differential has declined except during the late 1970s (EPB, 1987, pp. 120-21).

However, what one should compare is the wage level controlling workers' characteristics, not the observed wages. Fun Goo Park's (1984) analysis of 1980 data reveals that Seoul was the highest wage region even after adjustments were made for the differences in years of schooling, and years of experience on current and on previous jobs, but that other rankings change as a result of such adjustments. He found no substantial variation for the female wage rate.

HOUSING AND HOUSING FINANCE

Historical Trends of Housing and Housing Finance

During the period of rapid growth and urbanization, the number of urban households grew at a much faster rate than the stock of dwelling units, due to migration and the reduction of family size. As a result, the shortage of housing worsened in urban areas. The housing supply ratio defined as the ratio of the number of dwelling units to the number of households in all urban areas fell from 64.8 percent to 57.7 percent between 1960 and 1985. On the other hand, the supply ratio in rural areas has increased from 89.7 percent to 93.7 percent during the period, due to the reduction of rural population.

The supply ratio exhibits substantial variation across urban areas depending upon the size and type of cities. Housing shortage is more severe in large cities. If the trend of the size distribution of cities changing in favor of larger cities continues in the future, the problem could become even worse (KRIHS, 1986, pp. 118–20).

Housing conditions should be evaluated in terms of both quantity and quality. For urban areas as a whole, there has been a significant improvement in both areas since 1970. Housing space per person increased by 75 percent, and the number of persons per room declined by 32 percent between 1970 and 1985. The percentage of housing units with piped-water, sewage facilities, a modern bathroom, and kitchen has substantially increased during the period. However, there is a large gap in housing quality between urban and rural areas as well as among cities (KRIHS, 1987, p. 35 and p. 169). As a whole, residents of cities in the capital region (with the exception of Seong-nam), large cities, and those in industrial areas seem to enjoy better quality compared with small and medium-sized cities (KRIHS, 1987, pp. 122–24).

Shortage of housing is accompanied by the high prices of housing. During the 1960–85 period, housing prices went up at an average annual rate of 21.7 percent despite a drastic slow-down in the early 1980s, exceeding the rate of increase of the consumer price index, 12.9 percent per annum, by a wide margin. The rapid increase in housing prices reflects a sharp rise in the price of developable urban land, which went up by 31.9 percent per year on the average. On the other hand, the average income of urban wage and salary earner households increased at an annual rate of 20.0 percent. Therefore, housing has become less affordable for urban households (see Table 23.4).

Housing shortage and the high purchase price of housing, together with inadequate housing finance, affect the distribution of housing tenure. According to a 1986 survey by KRIHS, the average purchase price of a dwelling unit is equal to 5.8 years' urban household income, but the ratio is much higher in good locations in Seoul. The formal housing finance sector, which is very small relative to the size of the whole financial system, fails to serve a majority of home buyers with decent loan-to-value ratios. Only 35 percent of home purchases during the 1970–85 period were financed, and loan-to-value ratios seldom exceeded 30 percent. The home-

Table 23.4
Prices of Housing, Land, and Urban Household Income

Year	Housing Price	Land Price	Urban Household Income	CPI
1965	100	100	100[a]	100
1970	379	676	236	178
1975	1,108	2,009	532	364
1980	3,936	10,772	1,739	805
1985	5,061	16,373	3,203	1,135
% Increase 1965-85	21.7	29.0	20.0[b]	12.9

Sources: KRIHS, 1987, p. 138; EPB, *Korea Statistical Yearbook*, various issues.

[a]1966 figure
[b]1966-85 growth rate

ownership ratio (the percentage of households that are owner-occupants) fell from
63.1 percent to 41.1 percent in urban areas between 1960 and 1985. The most
popular form of rental arrangements is "chonsei," under which the tenant deposits
a lump-sum amount equal to 30 to 70 percent of the purchase price to the landlord
in lieu of monthly rents during occupancy. The deposit is fully refunded at the end
of the contract period and the equity built in the form of deposit is often used as
the most important means of financing home purchases.

Government Policy toward Housing and Housing Finance

One of the reasons for the growing shortage of housing is that the Korean
government has long favored industrial over housing capital formation. Total
investment in housing was less than 2 percent of GNP during the 1960s, and was
no higher than 4 percent on the average during the 1970s (KRIHS, 1987, p. 16).
The share improved to 5.6 percent during the Fifth Five-Year Plan years of
1982–86, as the growing demand for social development was perceived as a major
policy issue. However, even that level may not be sufficient considering the
growing shortage of housing.

Another important factor is the enforcement of various forms of control in urban
housing and land markets. An obvious example is the greenbelts around major
cities, a device designed to contain the growth of large cities. The conversion of
land inside greenbelts to urban use is strictly controlled, thereby limiting the
availability of developable urban land and placing upward pressure on urban land
value (K. H. Kim et al., 1986). Another example is the government control over
the maximum sale price of new apartment units at a level much lower than the fair
market price. Such practice, coupled with the increase in land price and the shortage
of developable land, reduces incentives for private homebuilders.

Recently, the government announced an ambitious plan calling the private and
public sectors to construct two million new dwelling units by the end of 1992.
Critical to the success of this plan will be the provision of developable land and
active participation of the private sector. The government regulations mentioned
above seem to deserve reconsideration.

Inadequate housing finance reduces consumer welfare by distorting intertempo-
ral choice of housing and mobility decisions. It can also result in an inefficient
allocation of capital between housing and non-housing, and distort the rental price
of the dwelling unit of a given asset price (K. H. Kim, forthcoming). The current
housing finance system is being expanded in tandem with overall financial
liberalization.

Finally, there is a difficult task of providing affordable housing for low-income
households incapable of participating in the free market. This issue should be
addressed in conjunction with the other antipoverty programs.

GOVERNMENT POLICY TOWARD URBANIZATION AND REGIONAL DEVELOPMENT

Policymakers in many developing and industrialized countries have a dislike for large metropolitan areas. Some of the often cited reasons are that small towns and rural areas can preserve traditional cultural values and avoid the congestion and pollution of large cities. Various policy instruments have been employed at least to slow the growth of primate cities. Korea has been no exception in this regard.

In Korea, equally important was the existence of interregional inequity in terms of income, public services, and amenities resulting from unbalanced growth. Growing concern over the issue is reflected in the government's attempt to boost the growth of lagging regions in the southwest and to strike the balance across regions.

Review of Spatial Policies

Two major objectives of the Korean government's policy toward urbanization and regional development have been the dispersal of population and industrial establishments from Seoul and Busan, and promoting the growth of sluggish regional economies and smaller cities. The implementation of policy relied on many types of positive and negative incentives, financial and nonfinancial, and direct government intervention and control. In short, the Korean government took the "carrot and stick" approach.

Industrial Location Policies

Since the first set of spatial policy measures to control population growth in the capital region was adopted in 1964, industrial location policy became the major instrument. The bottom line was to control industrial development in the capital region through regulatory measures and to promote development in the lagging regions through incentives.

The regulatory measures included executive orders for relocation of polluting plants from Seoul. Various incentives were provided for relocating firms under the 1969 Local Industrial Development Law. They were offered five-year exemptions or reductions of taxes, accelerated depreciation rates, preferential loans to finance moving costs, and cheap factory sites serviced with basic infrastructure such as access roads, water and sewage, electric power, and communication systems. In 1978, the Industrial Distribution Law was enacted, and the law divided the capital region into three zones. In the dispersal zones, the establishment and on-site expansion of firms was strictly controlled. No explicit measures were taken for the status quo zones. Positive incentives were provided for firms relocating in the inducement zones. In 1982, the zones were adjusted to five.

Other Measures to Reduce Primacy

Greenbelts were designated around major cities in the early 1970s. Simply put, greenbelts impose a ban on urban development on land in a belt surrounding a metropolitan area. Seoul's greenbelt, the inner edge of which is, on the average, 15 kilometers from the center of Seoul, takes up about 14 percent of the land in the capital region. It has remained essentially unchanged since its establishment in 1971.

The resident tax was introduced to large cities in 1973. The expansion of high schools, colleges, and universities as well as the establishment of new educational institutions were prohibited within a ten-kilometer radius from the center of Seoul. Secondary government agencies were relocated to regional cities.

Recent Spatial Policies

The Second National Physical Land Development Plan (1982–91) announced in 1981 divided the nation into 28 integrated regional settlement areas (IRSA) and sought to develop each to serve its own function. The plan also designated 15 growth centers or growth inducement cities to absorb the potential migrants to Seoul, and 5 of them were located in the southwest region. The main idea was to promote rural-urban linkage and to deal with metropolitan problems simultaneously on a regional basis (S. Y. Park, 1985). In order to vitalize rural economy, the development of rural industrial estates was pursued through the provision of tax incentives, infrastructure investment, and preferential loans under the 1983 Rural Income Promotion Act.

Evaluation of Spatial Policies

Despite all the effort that has been made, the problem of unbalanced regional development is becoming a greater concern for the public. The concentration of economic as well as cultural activities in the capital region persists and the growth of the southwest agricultural region is sluggish (see above). It seems fair to say that government spatial policies were a very limited success, if at all.

First of all, attempts to disperse population from Seoul basically resulted in a spillover of population to cities in the surrounding Kyong-gi Province within the capital region. This pattern is consistent with the leapfrogging development over Seoul's greenbelt. Because of strong economic ties between the satellite cities in the capital region and Seoul, many residents in those cities commute to Seoul, increasing the demand for transportation.

The relocation of manufacturing establishments exhibits a similar trend. A recent study indicates that only 1,092 out of 24,000 manufacturing firms relocated between 1970 and 1980, and that only 318 of the relocated firms moved from large cities to other regions whereas all other moves were within the capital region (W. Y. Lee, 1985). This suggests that the scope for reducing inter-regional imbalance through the relocation of existing firms is very limited. Another important lesson from a study of the satellite cities is that people and firms moved in response to operations of land and other markets rather than to the government's spatial policies (Kyu S. Lee, 1985).

The government's dispersal and relocation policies may impose additional problems and costs. A survey of relocated firms from Seoul to Banwol New-town reveals that a large number of those firms incurred extra time and overhead costs due to the moves (Choe and Song, 1984). There is also a problem of inadequate housing, educational facilities and public services for the employees and their family members. This is true for dispersal of office employment as well as for industrial relocation. The point is that unless regions admitting relocating population and jobs are capable of providing decent levels of important services, permanent dispersal will not materialize (Lee and Hwang, 1985; H. J. Kim, 1986).

There is a fundamental limitation to the approach of inviting existing or new firms to target areas through the provision of infrastructure. It is true that there is a strong correlation between the expansion of road systems and regional growth, for example. However, the truth of the matter is that adequate infrastructure is a necessary but not a sufficient condition for the growth of a regional economy. A recent study reveals that inter-regional disparities in major social infrastructure have been reduced substantially during the 1970–85 period. For example, the coefficient of variation for the road pavement ratio declined from 0.80 to 0.23 during the period (J. G. Kim, 1987). However, the problem of concentration of population in fact worsened, as was discussed above. The upshot is again that relocation attempts can succeed only when there are viable alternative locations to move to. The provision of infrastructure is only a precondition for such locations.

The trade-off between efficiency and equity should be considered in planning and implementing spatial policies. In order to pursue maximum efficiency in resource allocation, agglomeration economies should be utilized and that requires a concentration of economic activities. However, reducing the interregional income differential is justified on equity grounds, and that requires dispersal of activities from large cities.

Another important point to realize is that direct controls on metropolitan growth are an inefficient way of dealing with congestion and pollution, two examples of special market failures that tend to be more important in large cities than elsewhere. These problems can best be dealt with by policies aimed directly at the specific distortions: pollution control progams and effluent fees, careful pricing and investment in transportation.

Finally, one of the locational premiums for Seoul has been easy interaction with the national government, which has had strong controls on businesses. The prospects for reduced government intervention with the private sector and the impending local autonomy are expected to have a positive marginal impact on mitigating concentration in Seoul.

LOCAL GOVERNMENT FINANCES, URBANIZATION, AND REGIONAL DEVELOPMENT

Local Governments and Their Financing

Local Government System

As of 1987 year-end, the Korean local government system was made up of the special city of Seoul, four direct jurisdiction cities (Busan, Daegu, Inchon, and Kwangju), 57 other cities, and 138 counties. Cities and counties are the basic local government units and they report to the provincial government in which they are located. The special city and direct jurisdictional cities report directly to the prime minister. There are no legal definitions regarding the division of labor between national and local governments. Local governments provide standard public services such as elementary education, water supply and waste disposal, police and fire protection, social services, and industrial and agricultural infrastructure.

Since the Local Autonomy Act was suspended in 1961, local governments and their financing have been under the control of the national government. The national government appoints high-ranking local civil officers, specifies kinds and levels of taxes and user fees, and approves details of local bond issues and major infrastructure investments. It also distributes shared taxes and subsidies to local governments. In short, local governments have served as field offices to execute the plans set by the national government and rely heavily on it for funds. The restoration of local autonomy is impending, but the details are yet to be worked out.

Trends of Local Government Finances

Local government budgets are composed of a general account (G/A) and various special accounts. The size of total local government expenditures has grown at an annual average rate of 23.7 percent during the 1971–87 period. Local government expenditure was equal to 41.7 percent of the spending by the national and local governments in 1987, and 8.9 percent of gross domestic product (Table 23.5).

On the revenue side, local taxes are the most important G/A revenue source. Between 1970 and 1985, local tax revenues accounted for 22.8 percent to 33.4 percent of the total G/A revenue, which also includes user fees and other nontax revenues and grants from the national government. Grants are given in the form of local shared taxes (13.27 percent of national tax collection) and project-tied subsidies, and their combined share decreased substantially from 61.8 percent to 44.2 percent over the 1970–85 period. Local borrowing has been very limited.

The composition of local expenditure has changed over the 1970-85 period. The shares of administrative spending and of social development outlays increased, while those for regional economic development spending fell.

Table 23.5
Trends of Local Government Expenditures

Year	National + Local(A)[a]	Local Expenditure(B)[a]	GDP (C)[a]	B/A[b]	B/C[b]
1971	620.6	289.9	3,378.6	46.7	8.6
1975	1,722.0	671.7	10,234.9	39.0	6.6
1980	8,072.9	3,206.1	37,830.3	39.7	8.5
1985	16,750.9	7,202.2	75,510.7	43.0	9.5
1987	20,785.5[c]	8,660.8[c]	97,531.7[d]	41.7	8.9

Sources: Bank of Korea, *National Income Accounts,* 1984; Bank of Korea, *Economic Statistical Yearbook,* 1981, 1988.

[a]In billion won
[b]Percent
[c]Budget figure
[d]Preliminary

Urbanization, Regional Development and Local Finances

Fiscal Disparities

Discussion of interregional fiscal disparities requires that appropriate standards of comparison be chosen. The most widely used measure in Korea is the self-sufficiency rate, defined as the share of self-raised revenues as a percentage of total revenue. There is a wide variation of self-sufficiency rate across local governments, ranging from 98.4 percent for Seoul to 31.1 percent for Chung-nam Province in 1985. The average overall rate for cities was 57.5 percent, much greater than the overall rate for county governments (28.1 percent). Across regions, the average self-sufficiency figure for cities was highest in the southeastern coastal region, followed by the capital region, and lowest in Kang-won and South Cholla Province. The average for rural county governments was highest in Kyong-gi Province and lowest in North Cholla Province. The interregional differential in self-sufficiency rates of all levels of local governments was reduced between 1970 and 1985, despite an increase during the early 1960s. Trends of differential in self-sufficiency among cities and counties within the jurisdiction of provinces do not reveal a clear picture (Table 23.6).

However, the current self-sufficiency measure of soundness of the financial status of local governments is defective in some important ways. For example, it is not related to the size of the budget (KRILA, 1988). Therefore, these figures should be considered in conjunction with other measures such as per capita

Table 23.6
Self-Sufficiency Rates of Local Finances[a]

		All Local Governments	Seoul	Provinces	Cities	Counties
1970	Mean(%)	38.5	90.2	21.6	45.3	18.5
	C.V.[b]	0.627	--	--	0.231	0.261
1975	Mean	44.2	89.5	23.5	55.9	28.1
	C.V.[b]	0.587	--	--	0.139	0.206
1980	Mean	54.3	93.9	38.6	67.4	32.8
	C.V.[b]	0.406	--	--	0.153	0.261
1985	Mean	58.3	98.5	41.8	57.5	28.1
	C.V.[b]	0.460	--	--	0.160	0.225

Source: Ministry of Home Affairs (MOHA), *Financial Yearbook of Local Governments*, 1977, 1981, 1986.

[a]Share of self-generated revenue as a percentage of total general account revenue.
[b]Variation among Seoul, Busan, and nine provinces for each category.

expenditure, per capita tax burden, the level of provision of major public services and the percentage of personnel and other essential administrative spending out of the total expenditure. In fact, many small local governments cannot cover even recurrent expenditures by locally generated revenues. A direct comparison of self-sufficiency rates between local governments is not appropriate also because, currently, Seoul and direct jurisdictional cities are authorized to levy a larger number of taxes than other cities and counties.

The per capita local tax revenue of all levels of local governments was highest in Seoul, and lowest in Kang-won and South Cholla Province. It also varies considerably across cities, with the ratio of the largest to smallest being about 4.5 in 1976 and 5.9 in 1985. The average of cities in provinces was highest for the capital region followed by the southeastern region, and lowest for Kang-Won and Cholla Province, the two slow-growing regions. Per capita local expenditure was largest in Che-ju or North Choong-chung Province and smallest in Busan. Per capita grants were the smallest in Seoul.

Disparity in per capita local spending widened although that in per capita local tax revenue narrowed. These may have contributed to reducing interregional income disparity to the extent that these conditions were caused by an increase in allocations of grants from the national governments in favor of the sluggish regions. Kye S. Lee's (1988) study of 1970–85 data reports that local finances have contributed to reducing interregional income disparity, although that positive role for local finances has been very limited and weakened during the period (see Table 23.7).

The level of provision of local services also varies among regions and across cities, although the gap has been narrowing (K. H. Kim, 1985; Chun et al., 1985). Figures for 1986 show that the portion of roads that is paved was 73.8 percent in the six largest cities, 69.6 in other cities, but only 34.1 percent in rural areas. The percentage of households receiving piped water was 95.3 percent, 84.1 percent and 20.2 percent, respectively, for large cities, smaller cities and rural areas. There were 36.8 percent and 6.9 percent of the households in large and smaller cities respectively that enjoyed sewage systems, but the service was not available at all in rural areas (EPB, 1988, p. 242). Overall, disparity in local services across small to medium-sized cities seems less severe than that between urban and rural areas.

Urbanization, Regional Development, and Public Finances

Urbanization puts local governments under pressure to provide local services at an adequate level and a decent quality. In general, Korea's local governments have coped with such pressure quite well. Local government finances will go through fundamental changes as local autonomy is restored in the near future. How it will affect interregional disparities is not clear. Surely, rapidly growing localities will be better able to plan and accommodate growth. However, in the light of a substantial gap in economic bases across regions, some form of equalizing grants from the national government seems inevitable for lagging regions. Also, the roles for local and national governments need to be clearly defined. Finally, spatial implications of nonspatial policies should be considered.

Table 23.7
Interregional Fiscal Disparity

Year	Per Capita Local Spending		Per Capita Local Tax		Per Capita Local Revenue	
	H/L[a]	C.V.	H/L[a]	C.V.	H/L[a]	C.V.
1970	1.62	0.145	8.83	0.892	1.68	0.153
1975	1.66	0.140	5.93	0.641	1.52	0.138
1980	3.01	0.307	4.04	0.444	2.90	0.302
1985	3.16	0.251	3.28	0.408	2.54	0.264

Source: Calculated from data in Kye S. Lee, 1985, pp. 170-75.

[a]H = High and L = Low.

NOTE

The authors gratefully acknowledge the research assistance of Kwang Yun Yi of Sogang University.

REFERENCES

Chang, Sang Hwan, "The Crisis in Korean Agriculture," in Cho, Soon, et al., eds., *Understanding the Korean Economy* (in Korean), Seoul: Seoul National University Press, 1987.

Choe, Sang-Chuel, and Song, Byung-Nak, "An Evaluation of Industrial Location Policies for Urban Deconcentration in Seoul Region," *Journal of Environmental Studies*, 14, 1984, 73–116.

Chun, Dong-Hoon, Kim, Kyung-Hwan, and Lee, Kyu Sik, "Fiscal Performance of Local Governments in the Seoul Region: Implications for Urban Deconcentration Policies," WUD Discussion Paper No. 88, The World Bank, 1985.

Economic Planning Board (EPB), *Social Indicators* (in Korean), Seoul: EPB, 1987.

———, *The Korean Economy* (in Korean), Seoul: EPB, 1988.

Hansen, Niles, "Infrastructure and Secondary Cities in Spatial Decentralization," *Korea Journal of Regional Science*, 1, December 1985, 71–84.

Kim, Hyung-Joon, "An Evaluation of Population Dispersal Policy from Seoul"(in Korean), *Korea Spatial Planning Review*, 6, 1986, 115–38.

Kim, Jong-Gie, "Infrastructure Investment and Balanced Regional Development," in H. C. Youn and K. S. Lee, eds., *The 1987 Budget and Policy Issues* (in Korean), Seoul: Korea Development Institute (KDI), 1987, 136–69.

Kim, Kyung-Hwan, "Municipal Finances in Korea: 1977–82," WUD Discussion Paper 64, The World Bank, 1985.

———, "An Analysis of Inefficiency Due to Inadequate Mortgage Financing: The Case of Seoul, Korea," *Journal of Urban Economics*, forthcoming.

———, and Mills, Edwin S., "Korean Development and Urbanization: Prospects and Problems," *World Development*, 16, January 1988, 157–67.

———, ———, and Song, Byung Nak, "Korean Government Policy Toward Seoul's Greenbelt," KRIHS Working Paper 86-02, Seoul, 1986.

Korea Research Institute for Human Settlements, *An Evaluation of Korean Housing Policy in the 1980s and Policy Issues* (in Korean), Seoul: KRIHS, 1987.

Korea Research Institute for Local Administration, *A Study on Measurement of Fiscal Capacity of Local Government* (in Korean), Seoul: KRILA, 1988.

Kwon, Won Yong, "Issues and Problems in Planning and Implementing Industrial Location Policies in Korea: A Planner's View," *The Korean Spatial Planning Review*, 4, 1985, 185–226.

Lee, Jung-Hwan, "An Empirical Test of the Theory of Inter-sectoral Transfer of

Labor" (in Korean), Paper presented at a Korean Economic Association Conference in 1987.

Lee, Jung Sik, and Hwang, Chang Yoon, "A Study on the Impact of Central Management Functions on Population Redistribution" (in Korean), *Korea Spatial Planning Review*, 4, 1985, 1–15.

Lee, Kye Sik, "Public Policy to Reduce Regional Concentration of Population," in H. C. Youn and K. S. Lee, eds., *The 1987 Budget and Policy Issues* (in Korean), Seoul: KDI, 1987, 410–62.

———, "Local Government Finances and Regional Distribution of Income," in T. W. Kwack and K. S. Lee, eds., *The 1988 Budget and Policy Issues* (in Korean), Seoul: KDI, 1988, 135–76.

Lee, Kyu Sik, "Decentralization Trends of Employment Location and Spatial Policies in LDC Countries," *Urban Studies*, 22, April 1985, 151–62.

Lee, Won Young, "Recommendations on Industrial Location Policies to Promote Regional Development," in K. S. Lee and T. W. Kwack, eds., *The 1985 Budget and Policy Issues* (in Korean), Seoul: KDI, 1985, 336–69.

Park, Fun Goo, "Regional Wage Structure," in F. G. Park and S. I. Park, eds., *Korean Wage Structure* (in Korean), Seoul: KDI, 1984, 351–78.

Park, Soo Young, "The Role of Secondary Cities in Regional Planning Strategy" (in Korean), *Korea Spatial Planning Review*, 4, 1985, 161–83.

Sung, Jin Keun, *A Study on Rural-Urban Migration in Korea* (in Korean), Unpublished Ph.D. dissertation, Department of Economics, Yonsei University, Seoul, 1988.

Yim, Chang-ho, "Changes in Regional Inequality over the Development Path: The Case of Korea, 1964–78" (in Korean), *Korea Spatial Planning Review*, 8, 1987, 35–54.

24

Changing Location Patterns of Industries and Urban Decentralization Policies in Korea

Kyu Sik Lee and Sang-Chuel Choe

INTRODUCTION

Confronted with the increasing concentration of population and economic activity in a few large cities, policymakers in many developing countries have sought to implement spatial policies to decentralize population and employment from the large urban centers. However, little is known about the effects of such policies and probable costs and welfare losses associated with them. The World Bank and Seoul National University jointly conducted a research project to assess the impacts of implementing decentralization policies and to evaluate quantitatively the relative efficiencies of alternative policies.

The research focused on policies intended to influence the location patterns of manufacturing industries that are major sources of spatial concentration of employment opportunities. Most decentralization policy instruments used in developing countries have aimed at influencing the location and relocation of manufacturing firms. The Seoul metropolitan region, where various policy instruments have been actively implemented during the past two decades, was selected as the study area.

In Korea as in other developing countries, spatial policies have taken various forms: strict zoning regulations, outright prohibitions of manufacturing activities by law, and various financial incentive schemes to relocate industries to outlying areas. The sources of uncertainties about the probable impact of these policy measures are (1) the lack of information on the observed trends of employment location patterns in LDC cities, (2) the lack of understanding of individual firms' location behavior in response to market forces; and (3) the lack of knowledge about the nature of distortions introduced by spatial policies and subsequent welfare

Figure 24.1
Ring System in the Seoul Region

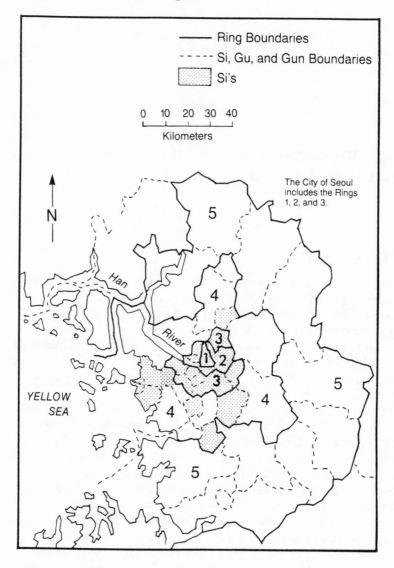

Ring Boundaries
Si, Gu, and Gun Boundaries
Si's

0 10 20 30 40
Kilometers

N

The City of Seoul
includes the Rings
1, 2, and 3.

Han

River

YELLOW
SEA

5

4

3
1
2
3

4

4

5

5

losses to the economy. The research project, which aimed at reducing these uncertainties, has produced a sufficient body of evidence to draw conclusions.

MAIN RESEARCH FINDINGS

The Korean government has used both carrot and stick to disperse industry. The 1977 Industrial Location Act prevented new factories from locating in central Seoul and empowered the government to issue relocation orders to some old establishments. Tax breaks, loan guarantees, relocation grants, and other incentives were offered to industries that moved. Large public investments were made in infrastructure and education in new industrial towns (Choe and Song, 1984).

Based on the annual Manufacturing Establishment Survey data, the trends in location patterns of employment were documented for Seoul and its surrounding regions. A set of questions on relocation included in the national industrial survey of 1982 yielded valuable data. Also, a sample survey of 500 establishments was conducted in the Seoul region. The findings can be summarized as follows (Lee, 1985):

Manufacturing Jobs Have Moved from the Center to the Periphery

Seoul and its surrounding regions were divided into five concentric rings around the central business district (see Figure 24.1). The trends were established for the period between 1973 and 1978, which was before the Industrial Location Act was implemented. The growth of jobs was fastest in the outermost ring, moderate in the intermediate rings, and negative in the central business district. Industrial employment in the outermost ring rose by 33.9 percent a year; that of the central business district fell by 7.6 percent a year (see Table 24.1).

A World Bank study of Bogota, Colombia, showed a similar pattern of industrial decentralization without any government prodding (Lee, 1989a). But the magnitude of change was four times higher in Seoul, possibly because of its faster rate of industrialization.

Small Firms Come Up in City Centers as Large Ones Move Out

Large establishments need land space at a low price for plant expansion. It is more important for them to achieve economies of scale in production than to be near city markets. Hence they tend to move out of city centers where vacant land is scarce and expensive.

But small firms tend to locate in central areas where land prices are high. They

Table 24.1
Changes in Employment and Establishments[a]
by Ring in the Seoul Region, 1973–78

| | 1973 | | 1978 | | Annual Average |
Employment	Number	%	Number	%	Growth Rate (%)
Ring 1	45,224	7.8	30,381	3.0	- 7.6
Ring 2	162,403	28.0	167,960	16.3	0.7
Ring 3	202,289	34.8	340,826	33.1	11.0
Ring 4	155,351	26.8	425,000	41.2	22.3
Ring 5	15,577	2.7	67,136	6.5	33.9
Total	580,844	100.0	1,031,328	100.0	12.2
Establishments					
Ring 1	1,567	19.0	1,144	8.8	- 6.1
Ring 2	2,786	33.7	3,091	23.8	2.1
Ring 3	1,479	17.9	3,515	27.1	18.9
Ring 4	1,829	22.1	4,248	32.7	18.4
Ring 5	608	7.4	981	7.6	10.0
Total	8,269	100.0	12,981	100.0	9.4

Source: Economic Planning Board, *Mining and Manufacturing Census,* 1973, 1978.

[a]Establishments with five or more employees.

do not need much space. More important for them is access to markets, services, and workers, which is best in city centers. Hence these areas act as incubators for small, new firms. Industrial location policies should take note of the very different needs and characteristics of firms of different sizes (Lee, 1989b).

The "incubator hypothesis" that city centers act as incubators for small, new firms was tested. City centers usually have the best services—electricity, telecommunications, banks, transport, sources of information. Major suppliers of inputs and purchasers of finished goods are located in these centers, so it is advantageous for small, new firms to start business close by. Skilled workers are available in plenty.

The 17 *gus* (subareas) of Seoul were examined to see which, if any, acted as incubators. Three criteria were used: (1) the subarea must have a substantial share of the total number of new jobs—5 percent or more; (2) the subarea's share of new jobs must be higher than its share of total jobs; (3) the average size of new firms must be small—not more than 25 or so employees. Three subareas met all three criteria. One was the central business district. Another was the oldest, largest market in the eastern part of the city. The third was the corridor linking Seoul to the fast-growing industrial city of Bucheon. This suggests that crowded central areas are good at "hatching" new industries. Hence it is bad policy to prohibit new firms from locating there. Governments still want to disperse industry from large cities. But in the absence of the facilities provided by these centers, small firms may not come up at all. Governments should not count their industries before they hatch. It will be prohibitively expensive to create incubators in new industrial towns.

Firms Don't Move Long Distances

The 1982 national survey of industries showed that 79 percent of moving establishments relocated in the same region. A quarter of them shifted from one part of Seoul to another. Of those moving out of Seoul, four fifths relocated in the outer two rings around the city. Only 7 percent of them ventured beyond the surrounding province of Gyeonggi. This strongly suggests that firms find it very costly to move long distances.

In 1978, the Korean government established a new industrial town at Banweol, less than 30 kilometers from Seoul, to draw industries away from the capital. One thousand plant sites were prepared, but the occupancy rate was low for several years. Many firms that moved to Banweol suffered excess capacity and financial losses.

These firms found that their costs were higher than anticipated. Their access to input and sales markets had worsened. They had difficulties attracting skilled workers who lived mainly in Seoul and were reluctant to commute to Banweol. Firms had difficulties obtaining business information because of poor telephone services and reduced person-to-person contacts with businessmen in Seoul. It is striking that a distance of less than 30 kilometers from Seoul was enough to thwart the development of Banweol.

Relocation Incentives Don't Have Much Impact

A survey of firms that had moved within the Seoul region showed that almost three quarters moved for internal reasons, such as the need for plant space. Only 6.5 percent were motivated by government incentives like tax breaks. Another 9.6 percent were ordered to move under new zoning laws, or because they had violated pollution regulations.

Of the many government incentives, loan guarantees were by far the most important to the relocating firms. They attached less importance to subsidized land, relocation grants, exemptions from property and capital gains tax, and investment tax credits.

In Korea as in other developing countries, there has long been a practice of credit rationing in the banking system. This is a serious policy distortion that makes it very expensive for firms outside the ambit of rationing to get credit at a reasonable rate. By offering loan guarantees to relocating firms, the government is in effect reducing this distortion. This is therefore a relatively efficient policy tool that tends to improve the allocation of resources. This helps explain why relocating firms find loan guarantees much more attractive than other incentives.

Location Policies Can Reduce Economic Efficiency

The cost of such policies can be illustrated by the outcome of penalty taxes levied on firms moving from Seoul to cities where manufacturing is discouraged. Firms moving to Bucheon, a city between Seoul and Inchon, have to pay a penalty of 500 percent of local taxes. Yet many are willing to do so, showing that the opportunity cost of moving to areas promoted by the government (such as Banweol) is even higher.

Analytical results show that the government will induce less deadweight loss (that is, the minimum social cost) by subsidizing inputs that make up a large share of the firm's costs and that are poor substitutes for other inputs, because this will result in less production distortion in terms of input mix. Similarly, the government will induce less deadweight loss by making infrastructure investments in facilities that are highly valued by the firm and are easily substituted for other inputs, because public expenditure on these facilities will enable the firm to reduce its private outlays (Murray, 1988).

Simulations of the Korean government's location subsidy schemes indicate that because of the existing distortions in the capital market resulting from credit rationing, loan guarantees (credit subsidies) to small- and medium-size firms are the most efficient subsidy. However, in the absence of overall credit rationing, credit subsidies are markedly less efficient than either land or wage subsidies. This implies that the macro credit rationing policy tends to be costly. The simulations suggest that its cost is equivalent to 4 percent of the land, labor and capital costs incurred by the Korean manufacturing sector.

In the presence of credit rationing in Korea, loan guarantees, the most widely used location subsidy, are more efficient than both land price subsidies and wage subsidies. The second most favored instrument, land price subsidies, is less efficient than wage subsidies, but the latter are seldom used in Korea. In the absence of credit rationing, wage subsidies would be the most efficient input subsidy. The policy simulation exercise clearly demonstrated that the relative efficiencies of explicit location policies depend on the nature of distortions introduced by the implicit macro development policies pursued in that country.

MAJOR POLICY CONCLUSIONS

Based on the findings of the study, several major policy conclusions may be drawn:

1. Government spatial policies have had a relatively minor impact on the location choices of manufacturing firms in Seoul. Although substantial decentralization of manufacturing employment occurred in the region in the 1970s, much of it resulted from the responses of firms to land and other market forces rather than to explicit location subsidy schemes.
2. Strict zoning regulations such as prohibiting new manufacturing activities in Seoul may hinder economic development by impeding the creation and growth of new firms and new industries. These spatial policies may result in a serious welfare loss to the economy in the long run.
3. Policy simulations show that spatial policies result in net losses for a country through reduced efficiency in resource use. The magnitude of the adverse effects varies appreciably depending on the specific types of location incentives. Also, the relative efficiencies of alternative subsidies are subject to existing macro policy distortions.
4. These findings imply that spatial policies have not been notably effective in achieving their purpose in Seoul, and they have had important adverse effects on efficiency and economic development. The adoption of public policies to influence industrial location may do more harm than good.
5. If the country has particular needs for adopting a set of spatial policies for social, political, and other non-economic reasons, analysis suggests that it is possible to choose policy instruments that are less damaging to the economy than others.

NOTE

Some part of this chapter has appeared in somewhat different form in the proceedings of two conferences (Hwang and Richardson 1987; Lim 1988).

REFERENCES

Choe, Sang Chuel, and Song, Byung-Nak, "An Evaluation of Industrial Location Policies for Urban Deconcentration in the Seoul Region," *Journal of Environmental Studies, 14*, 1984, 73–116.

Hwang, Myong-Chan, and Richardson, Harry, eds., *Urban and Regional Policy in Korea and International Experience*, Proceedings of International Workshop, Seoul: Korea Research Institute for Human Settlements, 1987.

Lee, Kyu Sik, "An Evaluation of Decentralization Policies in Light of Changing Location Patterns of Employment in the Seoul Region," Urban Development Department Discussion Paper, Report No. UDD-60, The World Bank, Washington, 1985.

——— (1989a), *The Location of Jobs in A Developing Metropolis: Patterns of*

Growth in Bogota and Cali, Colombia, London: Oxford University Press, 1989.

———— (1989b), "A Model of Intraurban Employment Location: Estimation Results from Seoul Data," *Journal of Urban Economics* (forthcoming in September 1989).

Lim, Gill-Chin, *Korea Development into the 21st Century: Economic, Political and Spatial Transportation*, Proceedings of Consortium on Development Studies, University of Illinois, Urbana, 1988.

Murray, Michael, *Subsidizing Industrial Location: A Conceptual Framework with Application to Korea*, The World Bank Occasional Paper Number 3 (New Series), Baltimore: Johns Hopkins University Press, 1988.

Name Index

Subject Index

Agriculture: and exports, 15; growth in, 12; protection of 8–9
Assassination, 4
Authoritarianism, 396–399

Bailouts, 330, 347–348; and borrowing, 355; elimination of, 351
Bank Credit Control System, 335–336
Bank of Korea, subjugation of, 186–187
Bank of Seoul: establishment of, 185; expansion of, 189
Banks: specialized, 188–189. *See also* commercial banks
Bilateral imbalances, 74
Bond market, 195
Business concentration: and capital inflation, 334; and diminished resilience of the economy, 332; and economic democracy, 332–333; and increased aggregate risk, 333; and inequality, 381; private efficiency vs. social efficiency, 333; and product market distortions,

333–334; public policies on, 334–337
Capital, cost of, 255–257
Capital allocation, 69–70
Capital deepening, differential rates of, 123–125
Capital flight, 79
Capital gains tax, 348
Capital inflation, 334
Capital intensities, increasing disparities in, 121–123
Capital market, 194–195
Capital rationing, 71–72
Chase Manhattan Bank, 189
Chemicals, 15
CHIES (*City Household Income and Expenditures Survey*), 374–376, 383–385
Chonju Papermaking Co., 365–368
Chun Pyong (General Council of the Korean Trade Unions), 393–394, 397
Clerical workers, 364–365
Collective bargaining, 395–396, 405
Colonial legacy argument, 44

About the Editor

JENE K. KWON is Professor of Economics at Northern Illinois University. He is the author of many articles in journals including *Journal of Development Economics*, *Journal of Finance*, *Kylos*, and *Applied Economics*.